**Spaces of Anticolonialism**

**GEOGRAPHIES OF JUSTICE AND SOCIAL TRANSFORMATION**

SERIES EDITORS

Mathew Coleman, *Ohio State University*
Ishan Ashutosh, *Indiana University Bloomington*

FOUNDING EDITOR

Nik Heynen, *University of Georgia*

ADVISORY BOARD

Deborah Cowen, *University of Toronto*
Zeynep Gambetti, *Boğaziçi University*
Geoff Mann, *Simon Fraser University*
James McCarthy, *Clark University*
Beverley Mullings, *Queen's University*
Harvey Neo, *Singapore University of Technology and Design*
Geraldine Pratt, *University of British Columbia*
Ananya Roy, *University of California, Los Angeles*
Michael Watts, *University of California, Berkeley*
Ruth Wilson Gilmore, *CUNY Graduate Center*
Jamie Winders, *Syracuse University*
Melissa W. Wright, *Pennsylvania State University*
Brenda S. A. Yeoh, *National University of Singapore*

# Spaces of Anticolonialism
DELHI'S ANTICOLONIAL
GOVERNMENTALITIES

**STEPHEN LEGG**

THE UNIVERSITY OF GEORGIA PRESS
*Athens*

© 2025 by the University of Georgia Press
Athens, Georgia 30602
www.ugapress.org
All rights reserved
Set in 10.5/13.5 Minion 3 by Mary McKeon

Most University of Georgia Press titles are
available from popular e-book vendors.

Printed digitally

Library of Congress Cataloging-in-Publication Data
Names: Legg, Stephen, author.
Title: Spaces of anticolonialism : Delhi's urban governmentalities / Stephen Legg.
Description: Athens : The University of Georgia Press, [2025] | Series: Geographies of justice and social transformation ; 65 | Includes bibliographical references and index.
Identifiers: LCCN 2024038399 | ISBN 9780820367842 (hardback) |ISBN 9780820367859 (paperback) | ISBN 9780820367866 (epub) | ISBN 9780820367873 (pdf)
Subjects: LCSH: Delhi (India)—Politics and government. | Delhi (India)—Historical geography. | New Delhi (India)—Politics and government. | New Delhi (India)—Historical geography. | India—Politics and government—1919-1947. | India—History—Quit India movement, 1942. | Indian National Congress. | Anti-imperialist movements—India—Delhi—History. | Civil disobedience—India—Delhi—History. | City and town life—India—Delhi—History.
Classification: LCC ds485.d3 l44 20 | DDC 954/.56—dc23/eng/20241126
LC record available at https://lccn.loc.gov/2024038399

# CONTENTS

List of Illustrations   vii

Preface   ix

**CHAPTER 1.** Anti-Imperial Delhi   1

**CHAPTER 2.** Delhi's Anticolonial Archive   37

**PART 1. DISOBEY**

**CHAPTER 3.** A Disobedient City   57

**CHAPTER 4.** The Gurdwara Sisganj: Problematizing Nonviolence   102

**CHAPTER 5.** Urban Conflict and Collaboration   135

**PART 2. QUIT**

**CHAPTER 6.** Quit Delhi: The Overground   167

**CHAPTER 7.** The Underground: Problematizing Nonviolence   205

**CHAPTER 8.** Victory?   232

**CHAPTER 9.** Conclusions   254

Notes   265

Sources and Archival Referencing   281

References   285

Index   297

## ILLUSTRATIONS

**Figures**

- 2.1. Delhi landmarks  49
- 3.1. Old Delhi and Civil Disobedience  61
- 3.2. Civil Disobedience and New Delhi  70
- 3.3. Swadeshi League Procession in Delhi  74
- 3.4. Swadeshi League Procession in Delhi  75
- 3.5. Mammoth procession on Hartal Day in Delhi  78
- 3.6. Picketing of Delhi foreign cloth shops  84
- 3.7. Boycott vs. Buy British  88
- 3.8. Phool Chand Jain and Chameli Devi in Delhi  93
- 3.9. "The Policewoman Reaches India"  94
- 3.10. Satyavati addressing a meeting in Chandni Chowk  97
- 4.1. Site plan for the Gurdwara Sis-Ganj Sahib  104
- 4.2. Gurdwara and kotwali  111
- 4.3. West outside front elevation  114
- 4.4. Plan of the Gurdwara Sis-Ganj Sahib  115
- 4.5. Some of the persons injured by firing into the gurdwara  118
- 4.6. Map from the Departmental Enquiry  132
- 6.1. Quit India and Old Delhi  181
- 6.2. Quit India and New Delhi  188
- 6.3. A 1946 protest meeting in Connaught Place  190
- 6.4. "Koi Hai?"  194
- 6.5. The Court Map of Pili Kothi  200
- 6.6. The Court Map of Pili Kothi  201
- 8.1. Women Shall Not Weep  234
- 8.2. Aruna Asaf Ali, Narayan, and Chandiwala at Delhi railway station  237
- 8.3. Nehru in Connaught Place  240

| 8.4. | "Congress Seva Dal" 242 |
| 8.5. | "This Is Not Our Victory" 250 |
| 8.6. | Gandhi, Narayan, and Aruna Asaf Ali at conference 252 |

## Tables

| 1.1. | Analytical Chapter Structure 36 |
| 2.1. | Counterinsurgency Discourses 38 |
| 6.1. | Congress Quit India Activities 169 |
| 6.2. | Phases of Quit India 170 |

## PREFACE

The origins of this book lie twenty-five years ago, when I began my doctoral research into the historical and political geographies of Delhi as the new capital of the British Raj under the supervision of Jim Duncan. In 2007 I published *Spaces of Colonialism: Delhi's Urban Governmentalities*, which explored landscapes of residential, policing, and urban infrastructure control across the new and old cities. The intention had been to turn immediately to this volume, but emerging interests in sexuality, internationalism, and constitutional change got in the way. Alongside these projects I continued to gather material on anticolonialism from archives in Delhi and elsewhere, but to also engage with bodies of scholarship that would better enable me to explore the geographies and governmentalities of the disparate forms of anticolonialism that the Indian National Congress attempted to cohere in the national capital.

My sincere thanks to the following funders, who directly supported this research: the ESRC for funding my doctorate (1999–2002) and a one-year postdoctoral fellowship (2003–4), at Fitzwilliam College and Homerton College, University of Cambridge, respectively; the British Academy for awarding me a Mid-Career Fellowship (2015–16, during which most of this text was drafted); and the Independent Social Research Foundation for making me a Mid-Career Fellow (2021–22, during which this manuscript was completed). Extra material was collected during trips to Delhi funded by the Philip Leverhulme Trust and the University of Nottingham.

Two projects, resulting in two edited collections, were particularly useful in helping me complete this book. The British Association of South Asian Studies supported a series of initiatives by Deana Heath and myself, which resulted in our 2018 collection *South Asian Governmentalities: Michel Foucault and the Question of Postcolonial Orderings*. Second, Tariq Jazeel and I developed a conference panel into our 2019 collection *Subaltern Geographies*. These collaborations have been pivotal in helping me reach the framing that supports the book that follows.

In the twenty years since completing my doctorate I have presented this work more times than I can remember, and I cannot sufficiently thank all those who have welcomed and helped me. I am indebted to conversations with Katherine Adeney, David Arnold, Sumit Baudh, Rachel Berger, Dan Clayton, Ruth Craggs, Stephen Daniels, Anindita Datta, Andrew Davies, Rohit De, Stuart Elden, David Featherstone, Federico Ferretti, Stefanos Geroulanos, Colin Gordon, Will Glover, Will Gould, Kevin Greenbank, Derek Gregory, Rob Hearn, Mike Heffernan, Greg Hollin, Mikko Joronen, Prashant Kidambi, Arun Kumar, Alan Lester, Mariana Lamego, Daniele Lorenzini, Colin McFarlane, Chris Moffat, Eleanor Newbigin, Carl Nightingale, André Reyes Novaes, Miles Ogborn, Søren Rud, Ornit Shani, Minnie Sinha, Nicola Thomas, Alex Vasudevan, and Charles Watkins. Sincere thanks to David Beckingham, Thom Davies, Jake Hodder, Susanne Seymour, and Anish Vanaik for their comments on my book proposal, and to Mick Gusinde-Duffy for his enthusiasm and support at the University of Georgia Press.

I would like to express my special thanks to my doctoral students, for their stimulation and their example; to Elaine Watts for producing the maps included here; to Ragini Jha for her exceptional translation and research assistance; to Ben Thorpe for reading the whole manuscript; and to the incredible support I have had over the years from Amar Farooqui, Sneha Krishnan, Janaki Nair, Chris Philo, and Srila Roy.

My extended family continue to be my bedrock. Thank you to Mum, Dad, Emma, Lucas, Chloe, Martin, Pat, and Richard. I dedicate this book to the innumerable people, from archivists to interviewees, academics to strangers in the street, of Delhi who have helped me navigate its two cities, and the last two decades. I hope that some of the geographies that follow can do them justice.

**Spaces of Anticolonialism**

**CHAPTER 1**
# Anti-Imperial Delhi

> It is said that Nazi fascism is cruel and rapacious and rides rough shod over the wills of innocent people while Britain, the mother of Commonwealth is always democratically progressive. If a biological survey is made of mothers that feed on their own offsprings like Britain does then only some acutely decrepit mongrel bitches who sniff around the gutters of lonely streets could be likened to this senile old mother of Democracy. To put even a semblance of faith in this bitch-mother of Democracy is either to betray the mentality of a blind little pup that is innocent of its own fate or to play a joke against history if not biology.
> —Delhi Provincial Congress Committee, 1942

On 2 January 1943 the Intelligence Bureau of the Government of India's Home Department forwarded a leaflet to R. G. Mellor, the superintendent of Delhi's Criminal Investigation Department. It had been printed by the Delhi Provincial Congress Committee, the local branch of the Indian National Congress (INC), which had launched the Quit India mass movement the previous August. The leaflet was titled "To the Communists of India" and had been placed, out of hours, in the office of a member of New Delhi's Legislative Assembly.[1] In it, Congress attacked Indian communists who had sided with the British in the "People's War" since the USSR joined the Allied forces in June 1941. These "theorising communists" of a "dialectical inspiration" were reminded that the "bastard zeal" of "bigoted imperialist" Winston Churchill had only been enhanced by the war. Their postwar fate could be glimpsed in the "interior sanctums of British democracy in India—the dark and dingy cells in the forts and prison houses all over the country where so many chosen sons and daughters of India are languishing in criminal neglect and repression." As in the chapter's epigraph, Britain was not seen as the civilizing progenitor of democracy in India but a filial cannibal, feeding on the resources and freedoms of the Indian people.

The leaflet upturns two broader misconceptions about anticolonialism in India generally and in Delhi in particular. First, it reminds us that Congress's anticolonialism was not unwaveringly committed to Gandhi's ethical project of nonviolence, peace, and all-encompassing love. During the Quit India movement especially, Congress had tolerated and encouraged experiments with violence and aggressively challenged rival forms of anticolonialism, whether political or religious, communist or communal. Second, the leaflet encourages us to reconsider the spaces of anticolonialism in the capital. When considered at all, anticolonialism in Delhi tends to be associated with processions and gatherings in the old city to the north (Singh 1972; Dhanedhar 2011). The placement of the leaflet on the desk of an unsuspecting legislative representative was a disconcerting reminder that the machinery of the Raj, administering for the British a colony of over three hundred million subjects, was staffed by Indians who were increasingly anticolonial. Viewed from the air, as on this book's cover, New and Old Delhi were dual cities of modernity/tradition, and viewed from existing literature they appear dual cities of colonialism/anticolonialism. The duality is, however, an illusion. The old city was penetrated by spaces of colonialism (Legg 2007), and the new city was periodically the target of revolutionary outrages (Lal 1999). But the city was more regularly penetrated by spaces of anticolonialism, both nonviolent and violent.

The Quit India movement found the sparse landscape and the increasingly Indianized Indian Civil Service of New Delhi to be supportive of the underground movement. The transfer of the capital to Delhi in 1911 horizontally split the city in two. The Quit India movement in 1942 vertically split the city in three, an imaginary but real underground city tyrannizing the colonial tyrants during the biggest uprising since the "mutiny" of 1857. In August 1947 the British handed over sovereignty to a partitioned subcontinent, leaving Congress to inhabit the imperial city as the first government of independent India, uniting Delhi's spaces of colonialism and anticolonialism.

This book explores anticolonial Delhi at the scale of the city, not of the nation. It begins in 1930 with the Civil Disobedience movement and continues through the Quit India movement from 1942, exploring both campaigns across New and Old Delhi and showing how both of them were problematized by the question of violence. It also explores anticolonialism in the city beyond the mass movements, showing how activism continued in the 1930s and in the frantic years between Quit India and independence. Central to the periods of both political conflict and collaboration were women's contributions, whether in private, community, or public spaces. From homemaking, picketing, and processions in the early 1930s to more radical and underground politicking in the 1940s, women emerged as unanticipated leaders in the formerly gender-conservative city of Delhi. Women's experiences in the city reflected Congress's broader grappling with the popularity of the left, which offered appealing alternatives to Gandhi's spiritual politics.

As such, the book's six main chapters are structured by comparisons of three pairings (of two mass movements, two violent problematizations, and two periods of collaboration). Running across the pairings is the picture of a city becoming more politically complex and more experimental with violence. This was in anticipation of the riots and widespread attacks that devastated the city in 1947. Partition was a result of Congress politics but also the result of the communalization of Indian society, Delhi included, that was connected to the decisions of the INC but also had its own external logic and governmentalities.

The spatial approach in this volume owes much to the work of geographers who have helped us complicate the scales and spaces through which we approach anticolonialism in relation to nationalism (Chari and Esmeir 2021; Featherstone 2012; Ferretti 2018; Kearns 2014). The work of Andrew Davies (2019), which has attended to the relational geographies of anticolonialism in twentieth-century south India, is especially pertinent. His work is relational in the sense of exploring the links and tensions between nationalists, revolutionaries, and anarchists but also in the geographic sense of exploring the maritime relations between coastal places and sea spaces. The analysis that follows complements this relational approach to moderate and more extreme politics, and to thinking about formative connective relations across space, although here the relations are across and between cities, not regions.

This book also contributes to ongoing attempts to use and test the work of Michel Foucault in South Asia (Legg and Heath 2018). It does this by approaching anticolonialism through its governmentalities. In one sense this is a narrowing of existing literature, in that it does not focus on the much broader, cultural, and elite-led project of nationalism (Chatterjee 1993; Davies 2019; Gould 2021). In approaching anticolonialism as a governmentality, however, it also exceeds formal political approaches to campaigns against empire. Instead, the approach here expansively considers the ways in which the spaces of the city were used to conduct the political conduct of its inhabitants. While valid doubts about the utility of Foucault's Eurocentric analyses remain, the case is made here that a governmentality lens can help decenter Europe from accounts of South Asian cities and politics. Analyses of colonial governmentality in India struggle to *not* be studies of Europe in the subcontinent. While attentive to the European origin of anticolonial concepts, approaches, and rationalities (Chatterjee 1986), the approach outlined here centers instead on anticolonial governmentalities.

Put simply, this involves not approaching anticolonialism as an outside. Here it is not a resistance, a problematization, or a threatening externality. Rather, Congress governmentalities are here studied as they engaged with their own outsides. As such, the colonial state is not the center of this analysis but rather a stubborn, nagging, and very violent externality—"this alien government," as it was regularly named. The Government of India problematized Congress, ranging from questioning its legitimacy to declaring the organization illegal, and constantly shaped it. Socialism and the Communist International (Comintern) were also troubling externalities that left deep impacts on Congress, including internal socialist subparties. Communalism posed more of an existential threat to Congress and likewise shaped its structure and politics. The development of communal Delhi, however, has merited study of its formation and complexity in its own right rather than as a subset of the Congress story that is the focus here (see Baul 2020; Datta 2019a; Halperin 2022; Jones 1986; Legg 2019a; Pandey 2001; Parveen 2021; Pernau 2013).

Having Congress as the focus of this book risks replacing a pro-colonial emphasis on the glories of the Raj with a pro-nationalist emphasis on the glories of one party at the expense of others. In part this acknowledges the dominant influence of Congress in the city, which was only substantially challenged in the 1940s by the rise of communal grassroots organizations in the city and the Muslim League's national campaign for an independent Pakistan. But Congress here is also only a frame for exploring much more expansive governmentalities and the spaces they produced; this book is about Congress to the extent that *Spaces of Colonialism* (Legg 2007) was about the Government of India. In that work the emphasis was on local branches of the state, the people those apparatuses encountered, and their spaces. In this bottom-up analysis the emphasis is on the Delhi Provincial Congress Committee and its community branches, the volunteers who worked in them, the people they met, and their spaces. Within these human geographies Congress's advocacy of Gandhi's projects was much disseminated, debated, adapted, and ignored.

At the center of Gandhi's politics was his commitment to truth (Gandhi [1927] 1948; Kapila 2021). While Foucault did not study anticolonial governmentalities, his last years were spent obsessing over the role of truth in self-formation and how counter- and alternative truths could be articulated and brandished (Foucault [1982–83] 2010, [1982–83] 2019, [1983–84] 2011). His work, focused on the ancient concept of parrhesia, is explored below as a means of studying anticolonial governmentalities beyond the power/resistance dichotomy. The emphasis on embodying truth in courageous speech (and performances) allows governmentalities to be studied that did not revolve around a state or a disciplinary institution. Rather, anticolonial governmentalities are here studied through the repertoire of courageous acts and preparations that built up over the interwar years and drew on and created the spaces of Delhi.

In addition to the work of geographers on anticolonialism, this book continues a dialogue with urban geographers. Though a capital city, I approach Delhi as an "ordinary city" (Robinson 2005), constituted by its everyday routines and daily conflicts, and as an exemplar of itself, not of colonial development, the dual city, or a national capital in waiting. The anticolonial governmentality approach, however, could risk subsuming the city beneath another conceptual abstraction. This is not the abstraction of a model city but of the integrated city, functioning as a whole. Colin McFarlane (2021, xii) has shown that this was a fantasy of the project of modernity that displaced and devalued the fragments of urban life. This was a fantasy that Congress shared, of a unified city, pulsing to the heartbeat of an anticolonial nationalism that it had birthed. A fragmentary analysis, by contrast, makes space for subaltern lives but also for a subaltern theorization of space which refuses totalizing urban conceptualizations (McFarlane 2019).

Used badly, Foucault's governmentality tool kit can become just such a totalizing theory (used to point at things and label them "biopower" or "conduct"). For me, governmentality works best as an analytic that provides complementary and challenging epistemological questions and answers. As explained below, the chapters of this book are structured in a way that fragments Delhi in two senses. First, six analytical fragments (episteme, visibility, techne, identities, ethos, and problematizations) that disrupt any linear or total view of the city are explored throughout. Second, the chapters move between different scales and spaces of the city, juxtaposing different but related "urban instantiations" (McFarlane 2021, 227). Some of these spaces were created by people reaching out to a broader anticolonial city; others were fragmentary projects with little interest in broader integration (80).

I return to the broader ambitions of this book in its conclusion (historical, geographical, conceptual, and substantive). In what follows I situate this approach within broader work in postcolonial and South Asian studies, before introducing Congress and Gandhi's anticolonial project. This is followed by an analysis of Foucault's work on governmentality and parrhesia and an explanation of how it structures that chapters that follow.

### Geographies of Resistance, Nationalism, and Anticolonialism

Because anticolonial struggle needed to mobilise the force of the people at large, democracy was, right from the start, the constitutive question of modernity in India. . . . In the colony, being political was prior to all else; it was the precondition to achieving not just freedom, equality and justice, but also community, sociability, intimacy, and indeed the ordinary fruits and pleasures of human life.
—**Prathama Banerjee,** *Elementary Aspects of the Political: Histories from the Global South*

Anticolonial historiography attempts to give coherence to its subject's vast scope, given that all forms of colonialism have been resisted, over time and space, in some way. The rich variety of historical trajectories are often disciplined into one triumphal arc, leading from cultural resistance, to societal overcoming, to political independence (Lee 2018).[2] The rich geographical diversity of forms of anticolonialism has also been the subject of debate. The European form of the nation-state has been presumed to be "exported" to anticolonial movements worldwide, leaving non-European imaginary communities with little left to imagine (Chatterjee [1991] 2010) but with suspicions that they might be enacting derivative versions of European originals (Chatterjee 1986). In terms of geography as a frame of anticolonial action, the consensus tends to be that space was a valuable local resource but a large-scale hindrance for anticolonial movements (Lee 2018, 438). That is, anticolonialists had to find a way to bridge and connect their local communities and causes (Guha 1983a). While internationalist "anti-imperial" campaigners might attack the empire system as a whole, "anticolonial" campaigns tended to focus on particular colonies and movements within them (Young 2015). This "primacy of the geographical element" was the great strength of anticolonial geographical counterimaginations for Said (1993, 208). But this cultural resistance was just one part of much wider geographies of anticolonialism.

Geographers have been drawn to nationalism as, in the words of John Agnew (2004), "the most territorial of political ideologies based on cultural beliefs about a shared space occupied by a kin-like, ethnic, or affinity group who face common dangers and bring to these a social bond forged through the trials and tribulations of a common history brought about by a common geography" (223). Territory is central because it grounds the nation and its shared history in something that is felt to belong exclusively to that nation (Busteed 2009). The 1980s and 1990s saw protracted debate over the nature of the nation, building on earlier scholarship regarding the technological and materialistic bases for objective and subjective senses of the modern nation (see Closs Stephens 2013, 18–28). Mirroring the emergence of postcolonial studies, more culturalist approaches debated the nation as being imagined via newly connected publics (Anderson [1983] 2006), the extent to which nationalisms were bourgeois by definition (Blaut 1987), and the scaling up of forms of supralocal attachment from the region to the nation while maintaining attachment to "the land as a historically unique and poetic landscape" (Smith 1991, 151).

Recent scholarship has reengaged these cultural interests with more diverse intellectual traditions. Bernard Yack (2001), for instance, has explored the political philosophical interconnections between nationalism and popular sovereignty, suggesting the latter explains the former more effectively than theories of modernization. Yack argues that popular sovereignty, being sovereignty granted to the government by a politically participating public, created the space for a new sense of political community ("the people") through which the modern sense of the nation arose in a newly shared communal space. Yack elsewhere focuses on the moral psychology of community, exploring how a sense of community membership comes about through liberal individualistic traditions of the people as the source of "constituent" sovereignty (Yack 2012, 7).

This is, however, an entirely Western analysis, which does not consider the social and communal differentiation of political communities, nor does it consider nonliberal forms of political community. Dipesh Chakrabarty (2007) has explored the difficulty of applying Western theories of liberalism, nationalism, and sovereignty to colonial India, because its modernity was an inherently political one. He made this case using a distinction drawn from classic Western liberal thought. "Instituted" sovereignty was constituted through the collective agreement of the people to being represented, with fear of each other precipitating obedience to a social contract. "Acquired" sovereignty, however, was obtained by force, with fear of the sovereign precipitating obedience from submission. Because the British had forcibly acquired constituted sovereignty in India, if nationalism removed the consent of the people, then what was left was domination alone. What Congress desired was popular, constituent sovereignty as a form of nationalist power in anticipation of independence (Mantena 2016). The debate over the extent to which this was achieved has been at the heart of at least forty years' worth of scholarship on Indian nationalism.

Much of this literature has grappled with the question of India's exceptionalism. In one light India was the first and most prestigious of Britain's colonial possessions to decolonize; in another it was following in the footsteps of the anticolonial revolutions in the Americas and the Caribbean in the eighteenth and nineteenth centuries and the successful demands for autonomy within the empire led by white settler colonies in the nineteenth and twentieth centuries (Young 2015, 103). For some, Gandhi's welding of nonviolent mass movements to constitutional reform and engagement was a uniquely successful hybrid; for others it marked a penetration of the masses and a targeting of their bodies, which was common in voluntary associations across interwar Europe and America (Raza and Roy 2015). By one telling, India set the template for the waves of decolonization that swept through Asia and Africa in the 1950 and 1960s; by another it was unique in terms of both its partitioning and its forcible conversion of a fragmented subcontinental empire into a federal state (Chatterji 2013).

Joya Chatterji's (2013) review of post-1857, pre-1947 Indian nationalism suggests that it had enough in common to be considered part of the European genus but had differences so stark as to demand its own forms of interpretation. India did not have a unified political consciousness, a driving state-sponsored nationalism, or a culture unified by a shared language. Like other forms of colonial-subject nationalisms, it was unified by the urge to be free, but it had to unify its demands across an unprecedentedly vast scope (in terms of space, political infrastructure, and communities). One framing for the emergence of early nationalism is to explore the opportunities for political engagement and profit offered by the structures of the colonial state, which introduced slow experiments with local self-government from the 1880s onward. This explanatory model, associated with the Cambridge School of historians, was criticized for reducing Indian nationalism to little more than a stimulus-demand response to the civilizing hand of British bureaucracy (Guha 1982). Guha (1997, 84–86) later suggested that this was effectively just British history in India, with no will of the colonized and no distinction between administrative and political history for a people whose politics was essentially imitative.

Others have explored the emergence of India as an imagined community, through its intellectual networks, social reform institutions, the political-economic construction of India as a networked space, and its journalistic and artistic outputs (Chatterji 2013, 246–48). Across these embryonic nationalist projects Partha Chatterjee (1986) traced a recurrence of colonial discourses in nationalist thought. His later work gestured more to nationalist discourses in lived worlds, where India's internal spiritual life, in which it was already thought to be sovereign, was distinguished from its external material life, in which the British continued to forcibly retain sovereignty (Chatterjee 1993). But the literary sources for the latter investigations have been criticized for failing to acknowledge the role of nationalist imagination in the material realm (Bose 2003) or to open spaces for acknowledging both the nonautonomy and creativity of subaltern spaces (Goswami 2005). Inspired by these debates, this project explores anticolonial nationalism through the scale of the urban and through reengaging subaltern scholarship, and that which it has inspired, which considers but exceeds the discursive realm (also see Chatterjee 2004).

The necessary frame for this urban study is the Indian National Congress. Founded in 1885 as a middle-class, liberal campaigning association, it attempted to bridge the spiritual and material sovereignty of India. Its annual conferences (or congresses) facilitated the need for national organization to bring together delegates and demands, laying the infrastructure for a later mass movement that could speak across regional, language, and religious divides, but could also bring their contrasts and incompatibilities into sharp relief (Chatterji 2013). For subaltern studies scholars this institutional focus marked another exclusionary elitist tradition, whereby the emphasis on bourgeois nationalist elites left the Indian people just as lacking in political originality as had neo-imperial historiography (Gould 2021).

If the Raj sought hegemony via the state, nationalist organizations sought their own hegemony via mobilizations of subaltern masses. While Congress represented India as nonviolent and unified across religious and wealth divides, violent support for communal and class-based alternative nationalisms contested this representation. Gould (2021, 50) has shown that early subalternist scholarship confounded historical and contemporary Congress claims to speak for all of India by conducting resolutely local studies, exploring "subaltern geographies" (Jazeel and Legg 2019) in all their complexity and contestation. Later work has expanded this tradition through exploring the fragmentary experiences of the national project by women, tribals, Dalits, and minority language and religious groups.

The work of the Subaltern Studies Collective has come to be read through the lens of postcolonial theory, especially after its North American relaunch in the late 1980s. This has led its emphasis on the subaltern to be interpreted as anticolonialism rather than anti-elitism, which was as much against bourgeois nationalism and authoritarian developmentalism as it was against the colonial state. As Guha (1997, x) later put it in *Dominance without Hegemony*, the primary project of the Subaltern Studies Collective had been to highlight the split in the power relations of colonial rule into the relatively autonomous spheres of the elite and subaltern. While this had consequences for how we view the colonial state (as more dependent on coercion than persuasion, supposedly unlike European states), it also altered how we approach nationalism. If the domain of politics was split, then nationalism could not just be a product of the bourgeoisie uniting civil society and the state. Rather, bourgeois nationalists would have to penetrate and mobilize the masses more effectively than the colonial state did, and produce literature and ideas that would justify this move: "A rivalry between an aspirant to power and its incumbent, this was in essence a contest for hegemony" (xiii). This left subaltern groups with the choice of whether to collaborate, resist, or ignore.

Perhaps the most brilliant subalternist reading of anticolonial nationalism is Guha's 1993 "Discipline and Mobilise" chapter from *Subaltern Studies VII* (reprinted in *Dominance without Hegemony,* Guha 1997, 100–151). Here colonial and nationalist attempts to produce hegemony were directly contrasted. Lacking the extensive resources, and legal sanction, of the colonial state, elite nationalists still claimed to speak for the interests of all subjects. They could not do this via the mechanisms of the state, which could produce only collaboration, but had to create a political sphere where they sought to mobilize the subaltern by enlisting their support, activating them in campaigns, and organizing them under elite leadership. Such mobilization would authorize the elite to act on the behalf of the subaltern. This was reported in nationalist presses and literature, in tales of enthusiastic, self-sacrificing, and united publics.

While a welcome departure from neo-imperialist historiography, for Guha this also emptied the subaltern of their politics, handing all initiative to the leadership and emptying the subaltern realm of tension, dynamism, and resistance to the hegemonic ambitions of the nationalist elite. What Guha found abundant evidence of was a common failure to adhere to Congress's attempts to discipline its followers into practicing nonviolence, and that when nationalist hegemony did not succeed by persuasion, it was sought by coercion (Guha 1997, 135). This was evidenced in the social boycott of those who failed to join in campaigns against foreign goods; the boisterousness and enthusiasm of crowds, condemned in print by Gandhi in 1920 as a "mob without a mind" (cited at 137); the murder of the twenty-three policemen burned to death at Chauri Chaura in 1922, which led to the suspension of the Non-Cooperation movement; the idolatry of Gandhi and other leaders, despite their instructions to desist; and the condemnation of communal and leftist alternatives to Congress nationalism, which were increasingly popular through the 1930s and 1940s. This amounted to a consistent elite denial of the legitimacy of subaltern, popular forms of political mobilization and a refusal to acknowledge the discipline required by subaltern carnivalesque forms of working and protesting together.

Congress responded in the 1920s by instigating two forms of subaltern control. While Guha read these forms through Gramscian categories of coercion and persuasion, we can also see these (foreshadowing the analysis below) as disciplinary and ethical prongs of a broader anticolonial governmentality. First, the "mob" was disciplined through crowd control at rallies, training Congress volunteers as "people's policemen" (Guha 1997, 145), to moderate noise, spacing, and movement during meetings. Second, Gandhi's project was an ethical one of self-formation, in which self-rule of the body (in terms of abstinence from sex, alcohol, meat, and violence) had to come before political self-rule. We will review less pessimistic readings of the Mahatma's project in the following section, but Mantena's (2022) interpretation is worth noting here. For her, Gandhi was wary of "mob" action because it relied on force and the inherent if unrealized violence of collective masses. Between Chauri Chaura and Civil Disobedience in 1930, Gandhi experimented with satyagraha so that it might enact spiritual persuasion more than collective political force. This first and foremost required constructive work and self-discipline. These two arts were learned through practice (in the city, in the village, in the home), not through the reading of texts or philosophical debate alone.

## Congress Governmentalities

### VISION AND TECHNE

Anticipating the analytical approach pursued in the rest of this book, if we are to consider Congress as the proponent of India's most widespread and influential anticolonial governmentality, we must think about the way it visualized its subjects and the rational crafts (or techne) it used in attempts to conduct their conduct. Both of these were inherently geographical, the first being the spatial vision of a party in the process of becoming a state-in-waiting, the second being a series of techniques to intervene into the spaces where people lived.

In terms of visualizing its subjects, Congress developed in the early twentieth century from an association of middle-class associations into an organization that attempted to know and represent the Indian population at large. For Banerjee (2021, 161) this saw Congress engage one of the elementary aspects of the political, "the people," and name them into being (as Yack [2012] might have it, crafting the nation out of the political community that popular sovereignty made possible). While Congress would also use the name of humanity, the crowd, and even the mob, the most common name it gave these people was "the nation." In so doing Congress attempted to surpass the visualizations of colonial governmentalities, which comprehended the people through demography (censuses and surveys), through crowds (reports on insurgencies or riots), and via society (sociologies of class, community, and caste). As an organization Congress attempted to unite these divisive visions of the Indian people into one nation. The mechanisms through which it visualized its people, however, mimicked and shadowed the visual apparatus of the colonial state.

Banerjee (2021, 167) has shown how, from its origins in the 1880s as a conference of associations, Congress developed into an organization for the people. In 1908 it produced a constitution that instituted committees at provincial, district, and taluka (or *tehsil*, a local administrative unit) levels, and in 1920 Gandhi introduced the four anna ($4/16$th of a rupee) membership, allowing mass participation and individual affiliation to the party. At the Nagpur Congress of 1920 a Congress Working Committee of fifteen members was established as the party executive, to oversee provincial committees (Arnold 2001, 115). This involved building an archive of regular reports on the activities of the people, whether in terms of numbers of members and their distribution, or their responses to calls to agitate. As such Congress sought to establish itself as the representative body for the people (as nation) and as a shadow state. It also produced, uncomfortably, a Swarajya Party that sought election in the 1920s dyarchy system, which Congress as a whole boycotted. For Chatterji (2013, 256) Congress had subordinated provincial and district committees to its central executive, which continued to be dominated by Gandhi and his supporters until and beyond independence. Though many of the territorial boundaries of provincial Congress committees were linguistic rather than colonial administrative, there was now a centralized infrastructure through which the people could be visualized, and through which attempts to direct them could be made (also see Kuracina 2010).

In terms of its techne, Congress had two compatible techniques, invoked depending on the political climate. Congress committees perpetually encouraged the sort of ethical self-fashioning and constructive improvement that would earn Indians the right to self-government (in Guha's terms, the persuasive arm of Congress, as explored through Gandhi's ethics below). In times of political agitation Congress mobilized the subaltern (using coercive discipline, as Guha has it, when central messaging was ignored). Before the turns in studies of Indian nationalism to discourse analysis, and more recently to global intellectual history, studies of the technical and applied interventions of Congress into the politics of its people (and its nation) proliferated, and some of this work has continued.

In an influential edited collection from 1977, David A. Low suggested that to so influence the people Congress had produced a parallel Raj organization, from the All-India president and working committee and annual Congresses, to Provincial Congress committees and then local city, district, taluka, ward, and village committees. Geographical variations existed across all these levels, of course, and tensions existed between central and local committees. Many of the latter were never "nationalised" (Low [1977] 2004, 26) and worked semi-independently to adapt national-level policies to local conditions. This left Congress, as Gyanendra Pandey (1977) suggested in the same volume, with patchy penetration of the countryside. In the United Provinces (UP), for instance, its base was the rural middle classes, situated between the big landlords and landless peasants.

The following year Pandey (1978) published his study of the "imperfect mobilization" of Congress in the UP (1926–34). In it he anticipated the work of the Subaltern Studies Collective, criticizing nationalist narratives of Congress's unhindered ascent, imperial narratives of Congress elites duping the masses, and Cambridge School interpretations of a nationalism responsive to constitutional stimulation (Pandey 1978, 2–6). Pandey used the geographical, economic, and social context to assess the "concrete character of nationalism" (as he reflected in the second edition [Pandey 2002, 9]). Thus, while it was important to understand urban elements of nationalism, this had to be done through a variegated sense of cities, market towns, and *qasbas* (or *kasbahs*, small market towns) and of the different groups of people who assembled there. Across these spaces Pandey insisted that the centralized structure instituted by Congress in 1920 failed to penetrate the UP until the 1930s. The principle was that each village with five Congress members would establish a collective Congress committee; each town with more than fifty thousand members would have its own committee, while some large cities would have *mohalla* (urban community) committees.

Within this infrastructure Congress used various techniques to spread its message and mobilize its people. Women could blackmail rich families by threatening to curse their weddings if they did not participate; Congress volunteers could cycle between villages distributing pamphlets; orators could give speeches in the cities; the nationalist press could spread the word; prominent leaders could engage in tours; and public demonstrations could complement standard Congress techniques of picketing the sale of liquor and foreign cloth (Pandey 2002, 63). Historically resonant dates could be used, marking

Jallianwala Bagh Day (commemorating the shootings at Amritsar in 1919) or Gandhi Day (often marking his birthday in October), as announced by *prabhat pheris* (touring groups, often of women, in neighborhoods, singing songs and making announcements [see Masselos 2007, 221–41]). Traditional forms of music and theater could also be used to draw crowds and disseminate information. Pandey was careful not to trivialize the significance of these actions. They were not mechanisms for the transmission of a mobilizing ideology. Rather, the processions, speeches, and demonstrations created the sort of militant anger that faced the Simon Commission when it arrived in 1929 (Pandey 2002, 74). Pandey's description remained of acts and techniques, however, not of the spaces in which they took place or their significance.[3] But what he did show was how these techniques increasingly alienated Muslim opinion in the 1930s through their overlaps with those of Hindu communal organizations and through the devastation of local Muslim communities in communal rioting, which Congress had been unable to stop (116).

Similar patterns of elite-subaltern interconnection have been studied across India, accounting for regional variation and innovations. Srilata Chatterjee (2002), for instance, has explored Congress politics in interwar Bengal, showing how the provincial Congress committee engaged with the "relatively spontaneous" (141) politics of the people, via district and then local committees. Interconnecting institutions included satyagraha camps where volunteers signed pledges to wear khadi (homespun cloth), face prison or torture if required, bring about *purna swaraj* (complete independence), be nonviolent, and obey Congress district committee commands. The volunteers were to spread the message of nonviolence across the province, also using Congress-run mail services linking Calcutta and the mofussil (rural districts). As with Low, however, Chatterjee emphasized the ruptures and tensions between the upper and lower scales of committees, which freed the latter to innovate as they wished. People allowed their houses to become unofficial Congress headquarters, where unions with non-Congress bodies were forged, including worker, peasant, and revolutionary organizations.

Chatterjee's emphasis was mostly on activities in Bengal Province as directed from the major cities, but the cities themselves were also intense sites of mobilization. In some senses risks were lower in the cities. Low ([1977] 2004, 27) suggested that while urban protest could lead to violence or imprisonment, rural no-rent protests could lead to eviction or loss of livelihood. But the violence that threatened cities was severe, whether from the police, bystanders, or agitated political opponents. Could these be faced, however, cities offered dense concentrations of people for recruitment and a wealth of symbolic sites for appropriation. The mechanisms of government themselves could also, rarely, be appropriated. One of the earliest studies of urban nationalism, by Rajat Ray (1979, 142), showed how the Calcutta Corporation had voted to raise the Congress flag over municipal buildings in 1930 and how corporation facilities were used to organize Civil Disobedience after Gandhi's arrest that May.[4]

The last twenty years have witnessed a resurgence of research on cities in colonial India (Beverley 2011). For Janaki Nair (2009) this work promised to take urban scholarship "beyond nationalism" and its focus on anti-colonialism, labor, and capitalism to consider colonial modernity and governance. Five years later, however, Douglas Haynes and Nikhil Rao (2013) argued that this turn had, in fact, evidenced the need to go "beyond the colonial city," suggesting that the rapid development and growth of cities in the interwar years exceeded the explanatory capacities of "colonialism." They made the case for studies that span the ruptures of 1947 and explore changes in demography, economy, migration, and city borders. Yet when they suggested the study of political change, this was via the politics of governmental and quasi-governmental organization. Another route beyond the colonial city is to explore those who contested it from within (Legg 2017; Bhattacharyya 2021).

Prashant Kidambi (2012) has shown us how we might reapproach some of the rich complexity of urban nationalism. Late nineteenth- and early twentieth-century nationalist politics, in its collaborative and liberal vein, used cities as associational spaces of civil society, where colonial elites could be petitioned and the interests of specific communities campaigned for. Douglas Haynes (1991) has reminded us of the resilience of these elitist forms of politicking, which survived each wave of Congress mass movement. Influential figures in these forms of urban politics also engaged with and influenced the newer, more radical forms of Congress agitation, however.

For Kidambi (2012) the First World War changed the nature of urban politics, facilitating the emergence of mass nationalism and a more spectacular public politics that went beyond the repertoire of the civic. Cities certainly remained places where Congress found itself rubbing up against and associating with Indian big business. These could be difficult relationships, but wealthy benefactors were often deeply influential in local Congress politics, such as Ambalal Sarabhai in Ahmedabad (Spodek 2011).

While Gandhi may have idolized the Indian village and disparaged big cities, the latter were effective campaigning grounds in which many of Congress's core campaigns could be pursued at once (Spodek 2011). The sort of techniques studied by Pandey and Chatterjee across UP and Bengal became concentrated in urban space, including hartals (total business closures), flag salutations and speeches, picketing, boycotts, and processions. From the 1970s Jim Masselos (2007) argued consistently that the city needed to be understood as a rich and dense political environment that collapsed the scale of the nation into the street, bazaar, and mohalla. Likewise, Raj Chandavarkar (1998) showed how the working classes in interwar Bombay made their mill villages and connecting streets into places of entertainment, socializing and politics: "Street life imported its momentum to leisure and politics as well; the working classes actively organized on the streets" (103).[5] These were spaces in which the urban subaltern were targeted by both traditional elites, seeking their votes, and newer nationalist elites, seeking their mobilization. As Nandini Gooptu (2001) suggested, the urban poor were both desired and feared by Congress: "the poor were either childlike, needing reform and moral and spiritual guidance, or misguided and violent, needing discipline and a strong, paternalistic, even coercive, hand of control and direction" (17).

While Gandhi may have feared the mob at times, it was also the case that he addressed the subaltern masses with deeply ethical questions, in a language they could understand (Chatterji 2013). This rhetoric sought to break down barriers between four-anna members and the Congress elite but also forge links across the city, making the moral case for city dwellers to unite against the government (Haynes 1991, 204). As Haynes noted, despite his use of metaphors from many world religions, Gandhi's ethics were infused with notions drawn from Sanskrit scriptures, including ahimsa (nonviolence); *tapas* (self-suffering or penance); *tyag* (renunciation); dharma (duty); and *satya* (religious truth) (see also Gould 2004). Yet despite enthusiasm for Non-Cooperation, the "underclass" (Haynes 1991, 245) in Surat retained a distance from the nationalist leadership, objecting to the dictatorial moral codes issues by the elite.

For Guha (1997) such techniques were the second prong in a drive for hegemony over the subaltern. For Chandavarkar (1998, 269), in his exploration of Gandhian rhetoric among the workers of colonial Bombay, the subalternist reading (of mobilization and then bourgeois suppression) was just as problematic as the Cambridge School (the fractious competition for the spoils of government) or nationalist hagiography (the mass awakening of the slumbering population). Each of these approaches saw the subaltern as a "lump" to be mobilized, emphasizing elite messages over their reception. Chandavarkar (1998, 283), in contrast, dismissed Gandhian rhetoric as bland metaphors of love and family, and focused instead on Congress's approach to industrial relationship and brokerage. Next we will move toward an approach that can recognize the role that Gandhian ethics played in Congress's anticolonial governmentality without the tactics being simply dismissed as either hegemonic tools or bland fluff.

### GANDHI'S ETHICS: EPISTEME AND IDENTITIES

The central category of politics for Gandhi was truth, rather than nonviolence or even freedom.
   —**Shruti Kapila, Violent Fraternity:** *Indian Political Thought in the Global Age*

Gandhi did not go unchallenged within Congress, nor were his dictates perfectly implemented. But there is no denying that his pragmatic philosophy and ethics of self-making were at the heart of Congress's nationalism. They can be described as nationalist in that Gandhi argued for a unity of the Indian people, transcending race, class, caste, or sex. But if the object of nationalism is the acquisition of state power, then we cannot unambiguously class Gandhi as a nationalist (Chatterji 2013, 253), given his profound skepticism about the modern state (Parel 2011). It is also impossible to delimit Gandhi's intentions to India alone. Rather, his principles were universal, with India being their origin but only their first experimental site of implementation (Devji 2012).

We can more surely position Gandhi's pragmatic politics and his ethics at the heart of Congress's anticolonial governmentality, in that the end of empire in India was a consistent demand. Anticolonialism defined the Congress episteme (the production of truth, especially regarding nonviolence) and its identities (the conception of those to be governed and the subjectivities produced). The literature on Gandhi is too vast to survey here (see Mantena 2022). What follows is a selection of interventions that have illustrated the spiritual but practical episteme of Gandhi's ethics and his ethical approach to individual identities, bodies, and politics. It was this ethical work that linked Gandhi's universalist and nationalist aspirations to the cities, streets, and homes in which urban Indians lived. Through making the universal and the national into things that could be achieved through individual, everyday action, Gandhi's ethics forged spatial and scalar links within and way beyond the city.

In terms of Gandhi's episteme, his approach to ethics and truth can be positioned within South Asian traditions, without lapsing into Orientalist stereotypes. Anand Pandian and Daud Ali (2010) acknowledge that South Asia was historically situated as the Occident's moral Other, but they insist that common trends in South Asian ethical traditions can be identified. These tend to have been less scriptural or codified, and more focused on lived experience and the embodied practice of virtuous life—that is, ethical life as the practice of freedom and the engaging of the world as filled with potential.[6] The ethical questions that arise from these traditions, therefore, include, What part of the body (mind, heart, habits, emotions) should one work on? Need this work be that of a rational, reflective mind or of an affective and multisensory self? And how do ethics lead to durable habits and techniques of the body?

Gandhi clearly fits directly into these traditions and had answers to many of these questions. But his international life and cultural cosmopolitanism (Devji 2012) also means that he must be fitted into much broader ethical traditions, beyond the Jain and Hindu foundations of his thought. Richard Sorabji (2012) has shown that in addition to Gandhi being influenced by the Gospel and the writings of Ruskin and Tolstoy, he also read and translated, in 1908, Plato's account of Socrates's defense when on trial.[7] Gandhi's praise of Socrates's commitment to truth in the face of death was published in the same year that he devised the term "satyagraha," being the relentless and forceful search for truth.[8] While Sorabji speculates on a connection between awareness of Socrates's asceticism in Plato's writings and Gandhi's commitment to brahmacharya, Veena Howard (2013) analyzes the latter roundly in the context of Indian traditions of renunciation. For Gandhi, who defined brahmacharya as the practice of celibacy, continence, and chastity, this was the key to achieving nonviolence, via the total control of the senses.

Gandhi's refusal of Western epistemes pivoted on a redefinition of civilization as a mode of conduct focused on duty and achieved via a self-discipline that could inculcate a resistant inner voice (Gandhi 1996; Mantena 2022). The Gandhian subject that resulted would ideally practice ahimsa as a protest against violence in its totality (against Harijans/untouchables/Dalits, between Hindus and Muslims, between classes) but also as a form of nonviolent protest (at specific and directed times) against monopolies of force such as the state, capitalism, or patriarchy.

In terms of the identities at the heart of Gandhi's anticolonial universalism, David Hardiman (2013) has argued for a more sympathetic reading than that of his Subaltern Studies Collective mentor Ranajit Guha. He identifies Guha's critique within a longer-standing Marxist tradition that associated Gandhi's tactics with an elite-aligned anti-revolutionism that encouraged passive resistance. The "mobocracy" comment came at the beginning of Gandhi's period of mass mobilizations, during which he made many missteps. Hardiman (2017, 60) later stressed how much Gandhi's methods changed and adapted over time, and how the academic obsession with the periods of mass agitation, 1930–32 in particular, draws attention away from ongoing constructive work that was just as much part of Gandhi's philosophy and politics. Attention to the ways in which self-rule as an individual aim was inculcated through values and self-discipline expose a swaraj based on positive commitments, not a Western sense of "independence" as the freedom to do anything (Dalton 2013). Rather than "resistance," which could be against anything, in 1907 Gandhi settled on "agraha" as an affirmative commitment to "satya" (or truth; Kapila 2021, 137). This emphasis on Gandhian principles in action also features in a recent realist interpretation of his politics, which reinforces how a spatial emphasis on the individual and the unpredictability of local interventions open up the spatial politics of Gandhi's vision. A focus on Foucault's last works, parrhesia specifically, will allow us to integrate these approaches into a spatial and more holistic study of anticolonial governmentalities.

Reconceptualizing Gandhi as a realist rather than an idealist helps shift the spaces in which we seek evidence of his impact. This case has been made by Karuna Mantena (2012) not just because of Gandhi's practice-orientation but because of a theoretical coherence between Gandhi and other realist thinkers. This entails a contextual and consequentialist approach to a world marked by inherent conflict, domination, and violence, where affect as much as reason informs politics. This is a world of unintended consequences that might inflame violence, but also a world where positive programs of ethics and social transformation can create different realities and places. Nonviolence faced unpredictable violence but also contained the latent potential for provoking an escalation into violence. Satyagraha had to be adversarial, adapting techniques such as civil disobedience, noncooperation, boycott, and strikes as necessary and as the geographical location and historical moment dictated.

This contextual approach acknowledges Gandhi's conviction that truth was both a universal, emanating from God, and an absolute that was unknowable in any final sense (Mantena 2012, 463). Making this truth manifest required the satyagrahi to put themselves at risk. Satyagrahis had to sacrifice something from which they might benefit and which put them at risk of losing something of consequence—what Foucault called parrhesia.[9] The risks varied by person and setting, and by the type of satyagraha. One type was constructive, forging bonds (for instance Hindu-Muslim unity), making space in the day for meditative contemplation (spinning cotton to make khadi and reflecting on one's relation to self and others), or political links between leaders and communities. Mantena (465) terms a second type "destructive," but we might think of it better as disruptive, being political movements of creative disruption and risk-taking parrhesia.

We can link this realist approach to broader conceptions of sovereignty using a distinction made by one of the great analysts of nonviolence. Gene

Sharp (1973, 8) argued that nonviolent movements mobilize their supporters through propagating a new approach to power relations that seek to overturn traditional conceptions regarding the source of power. The traditional "monolith theory" suggested that people depend on the goodwill of the government; that power resides at the pinnacle of society; that power is self-perpetuating and durable; and that the only way to take this power is through violence. The newer model, which Sharp named "pluralistic-dependency theory," suggested that the governmental system depends on the goodwill of the people; that power arises from society; that political power is fragile and depends on support and cooperation; and that the way to change power is nonviolent noncooperation.

In Chakrabarty's (2007) terms, the former model is that of acquired sovereignty, while the latter is instituted. The former represents the body of political theory that regards sovereignty as a matter of supreme command, the latter in terms of political authorities (Coleman 2009). But Sharp shows us that this is a broader model of power in its entirety. Coterminous with Foucault's developing theories of relational and circulatory power, Sharp was inspired as much by Gandhi as by the social and political revolts of the late 1960s. He analyzed and catalogued the arsenal of nonviolent tactics but did not focus on the ethical dimensions of Gandhian nonviolence specifically and their consequences for the broader movement of which the tactics were a part. I will suggest in the following section that Foucault's late works present us with a way of doing this.

### GEOGRAPHIES OF RESISTANCE, GOVERNMENTALITY, AND PARRHESIA

The most consistent criticism of Foucault's later work on power and genealogy was that it left no space for resistance, unveiling for us a barren landscape of docile bodies and subjectivized identities (Legg 2019b). When Foucault (1982) addressed such critiques in print, he suggested that resistance always accompanied power, or else there would just be obedience. Mark Kelly (2009) has shown that this response of Foucault's sat between two phases of his research into what we can, problematically, think of as "resistance." In the late 1970s Foucault conceived of resistance as a negative, the act of freeing oneself from limits; in the 1980s he moved toward conceiving of resistance as a positive act of self-formation. Noting the first of many similarities to the foregoing literature on Congress and Gandhi, this could also be considered the difference between Gandhi's understanding of "independence," or the freedom to do anything, and "swaraj," being the positive commitment to self-discipline. Kelly

(106) shows that for Foucault, liberation from domination (such as anticolonialism) and nuanced self-formation (or one version of nationalism) were compatible forms of resistance. In his 1980s work Foucault referred more to ethics and critique, but this came after some detailed explorations of the links between resistance and power (to which he returned in some of his last publications; see Foucault 1982).

Foucault (1979, 95) depicted power as a network between points of resistance. What, then, was the difference between power and resistance? Resistance had to be as adaptive and strategic as power (see Davidson 2011, 27). Like power, it was multiple and integrated into global strategies; this is resistance as counterpower (Kelly 2009, 111). However, while power relationships can network widely across sites, acts of resistance tend to lack these networks and infrastructures.[10] Kelly (157) hinted at the value of Foucault's last lecture courses for taking these questions further, via the connections between politics, ethics, and the government of self and others. One anticipation of these later concerns that Kelly highlighted was that of "counter-conducts."

Counter-conducts were first mentioned in the *Security, Territory, Population* lectures where Foucault ([1977–78] 2007, 191–226) introduced the concept of governmentality and the "pastoral" directing of conduct. This emphasis removed the docile subject of discipline and introduced the self-conducting and directed subject of governmentality. Resistance was here reapproached not as refusal but as the crafting of different ways of conducting conduct (Binkley and Cruikshank 2016). Counter-conducts did not thus only respond to the network of power but created their own networks of being governed otherwise.

This concept, a relatively fleeting one in Foucault's lectures, has been widely influential. Arnold Davidson (2011) suggests that counter-conduct added the ethical component that resistance, as a concept, had been lacking and opened up new ways to link conduct to politics. Daniele Lorenzini (2016) has shown, however, that while the concept allowed Foucault to study a positive form of resistance, it was dropped in later work in favor of the study of subjectivation. This took Foucault further away from the study of resistance, which remained focused on particular situations, and toward the study of how one might change one's sense of subjectivity so as to refuse to be conducted in a particular way. This would not be so as to achieve freedom but to practice freedom in order to give rise to other, rather than counter-, forms of conduct and subjectivity (Lorenzini 2016, 19; also Barrett 2020).

Foucault turned to the ancient European world to pursue the interconnections between self-other relations, politics, and ethics (McGushin 2007; Miller

2021). His lectures regularly referenced the possible connections between this research and the present day. For some, these works cohere as a grand genealogy tracing the birth of the modern subject of the Reason of State who became the liberal check on the power of the sovereign (Harcourt 2021; Lais 2019).

An alternative approach is to see Foucault's works on ethics and the ancient world as the drawing out of "contingent universals" (Koopman 2013). This period saw him extend his study of governmentality back two thousand years before when his initial definition had suggested governmentalities came into being (Foucault [1977–78] 2007, 108–9). The purpose of these writings was to give us new ways to reflect on our own subjectivization (and those of the historical subjects we study), to explore freedom as a self-transformational practice, and to highlight the insidious and subtle dangers that exist in who we are (and who our historical subjects were becoming; Koopman 2013). The last two books Foucault published directed us toward Greco-Roman guides to conducting conduct, especially regarding sexuality, the body, pleasure, and *The Care of Self* (Foucault 1986a, 1986b). But his final lectures and research brought him back to something resembling resistance. This was parrhesia, defined as frank speech, free speech, truth-telling, or the act of having the *Courage of Truth* (Foucault [1983–84] 2011, [1982–83] 2010, [1982–83] 2019).

We will return to a detailed discussion of parrhesia and/as governmentality below. But here we can note that Foucault dwelled on two forms of parrhesia in classical Greece. The first was political parrhesia in the Periclean age (c. 495–429 BCE), when the ability to speak the truth forcefully in public assemblies was protected. The second was philosophical parrhesia, in the post-Periclean period when the risks of political truth-speaking did not merit its potential benefits and political rhetoric supplanted parrhesia in public (the political/nonpolitical distinction used will be challenged later). Plato, Socrates, and the Cynics were held up as examples of truth-speaking outside formal political spheres, though in three very different modes.

First, Plato (428/7–348/7 BCE) was recounted in the court of Dionysius II, attempting to counsel the tyrannical ruler. Though this parrhesia took place in a political space, for Foucault ([1982–83] 2010, 225) it marked a site of applied philosophy, an attempt to produce a new relationship of self-to-self. Second, Plato's teacher and mentor Socrates (c. 470–c. 399 BCE) was tracked through the streets of Athens, confronting citizens with probing questions and testing their souls in the hope of provoking newer and truer relationships to themselves. Finally, Foucault explored the complex philosophy of the Cynics, from the fourth century BCE to the third century CE, especially through their most famous early practitioner. Diogenes (412/404–323 BCE), a contemporary of

Plato, embodied his truth in the street, in his body, and in his scandalous behavior. His truth was that Athenian culture and politics were hypocritical. His courageous means of showing this was to take common philosophical principles and run them to their extremes. If to be true was to be not hidden, then the Cynic would be naked; if it was to be pure, then the Cynic would be destitute; if it was to be "straight" then the Cynic would be natural and live as of nature; if living by the truth meant being unchanging, then the Cynic would be wholly incorruptible (Foucault [1983–84] 2011, 218–28). Though both parrhesiasts, Plato and Diogenes were bodies apart: Plato in the Academy, formulating the teachings of Socrates into a metaphysical philosophy; Diogenes homeless, naked, and masturbating in the street. Both lived their truths, but both also took risks to tell their truths to those who might fashion a new relationship to themselves and others.

As such, the aim of both political and philosophical parrhesia was not to outline a new model of a more just society but to create the conditions for people to question their attitudes and behaviors (Koopman 2013). While Foucault focused on politics and philosophy as sites of parrhesia, courageous truth-telling could and can occur across various realms (on artistic parrhesia, see Brigstocke 2013). What all forms of parrhesia have in common, however, is their rootedness in specific situations, geographies, and periods. Parrhesia can therefore be thought of as an embodied and performed act of problematization, intensifying difficult situations and posing them in new languages of risk and reflexivity (Barnett 2015). That is, there is inherent *spatiality* to parrhesia. Though already the subject of exhaustive commentary, these works continue to repay deep engagement and creative application (Lorenzini 2023; Walker 2022; Walters and Tazzioli 2023). But can we think of forms of parrhesia as ways into, and component parts of, broader governmentalities?

**Parrhesia and Governmentality**

Foucault was simultaneously a master of self-reinvention and of retrospectively recasting his previous works as always *really* being about his current interests (from the will to know, to power, to the production and then manifestation of truth; see Legg 2016c, 871). The production of truth-effects was certainly a constant interest through his career, but his turn to genealogical analysis in the 1970s saw a marked rupture in his approach to the subject (Dean and Zamora 2021). While his earlier, archaeological works attempted to do away with the (humanist) subject, his works on discipline and governmentality explored the constitution of the subject by apparatuses and, ultimately, by themselves. This turn was accompanied by a shift in Foucault's approach to politics and a turning away from the concept of revolution. The turn was also from the idea of a benevolent, pastoral welfare state and toward risky, daring forms of self-creation.

Mitchell Dean and Daniel Zamora (2021) have explored the interlinkages between these two developments in the late works of Foucault, relating to the subject and to politics. One exploration takes us to the controversy over Foucault's interest in, and possible support for, neoliberalism as a model for subject-politics-economy-state interactions. While, for Foucault, dominant Marxist notions of resistance in his time emphasized revolution and state-led centralization, neoliberal theory proffered micro-resistances to the state and the idea of the individual as the entrepreneur of themselves (Dean and Zamora 2021, 40, 71). Stimulated by this model of the self, if not this model of economics (Foucault [1978–79] 2008), Foucault then turned to the classical world to see how selves had been constituted in the past, whether through Greco-Roman care of self (via guided choice) or early Christian hermeneutics of the self (via obedience and, later, confession, Dean and Zamora 2021, 93).

The emphasis on subjectivity turned attention to individuals, who were constantly making decisions, who were constituted by their situated practices, and who were always surrounded by the hidden margins of freedom in every relationship (Dean and Zamora 2021, 148). Resistance, in this approach, would be against that which assigns to us a relation to ourselves, and it would promote a new relationship of the self to self and to others. Dean and Zamora conclude their stimulating review of the latter Foucault by revisiting the debates on his normativity and campaigns, rather than exploring how the parrhesia lectures rewedded subjectivity to a different form of politics or related to the previous work on the care of self.

These are the concerns of Lauri Siisiäinen's (2018) work, which explicitly sets out to craft a tool kit for rethinking resistance in Foucault's later works. While counter-conducts and radical protests might provide small-scale disruptions to broader governmentalities, Siisiäinen suggests that parrhesia and the care of self constitute counterdiscursive strategies that need to be understood through bodies that resist in affective, sensual, interpersonal modes. Rather than seeing care of self guides to conduct and well-being as regulatory impositions, she positions them alongside acts of parrhesia as interventions that sought to protect and amplify freedom (14). Both these forms of truth-seeking and truth-telling prepare subjects for struggles, making us aware of influences on us and means of alternate self-fashioning.

Postcolonial scholars have taken existing feminist works on Foucault's analyses of ethics (Butler 2009) and pushed them in new and challenging dimensions. Saba Mahmood (2012) has responded to the critical reception accorded to her 2005 Foucauldian exploration of what she termed feminist subjects within the Islamic revival in late twentieth-century Egypt. Her aim was to explore modalities of female agency that exceeded the liberatory projects of the West. Agency was instead explored as capacities (embodied, rational, technological) and conceptions of the subject that these capacities produced. Pious Muslim women were shown to actively transform their lifeworlds and environments (dress, speech, the care for the poor) in an ethical and political system that appeared deeply patriarchal to Western eyes. Jettisoning the language of resistance, Mahmood turned to Foucault's sense of ethics as practice as a way of conceiving agency beyond the subversion of popular norms. Rather than attempting any straight application of Foucault's studies of the classical world to the near-present, she used Foucault's (1986a, 26–27) fourfold approach to ethics (substance, subjectification, techniques, and telos) to explore the specific practices through which historically and geographically located moral norms were lived.

Drawing on Mahmood, Srila Roy (2018) has considered the conduct of conduct and counter-conducts via technologies of feminist ethical self-formation in contemporary India as a means of exploring plays of resistance and freedom within neoliberalism. Rather than a narrative of patriarchal domination of misogyny, Roy examines how feminists conduct other women's conduct not to find a way "out" of neoliberalism but to find ways of governing themselves differently. This takes Foucault's injunction to explore the play of power through free subjects seriously, for instance, through encouraging women to loiter and enjoy public space freely as means and ways of creative self-transformation (Roy 2018, 214–15).

These moments constitute the affective, sensual, and interpersonal modes that Siisiäinen suggested mark new ways into thinking about resistance and biopolitics. But rather than just counterlives or conducts, Siisiäinen (2018, 129) emphasized the possibility of affirmative political forms of both discourse and being. In Foucault's work the best example she found of this "affirmative biopolitics" was that of the Cynics. These philosopher activists' affective, bodily performances and capacities against dominant forms of biopolitics inverted relationships between truth, politics, and the self, while also caring for others. This marked the articulation of a "political spirituality" in opposition to Greek philosophy and modes of life. We will turn now to the notion of political spirituality before addressing parrhesia so as to explore what sort of cohesive governmentality analysis this could lead us to.

Even Foucault's most loyal followers would admit that his journalistic foray into Middle Eastern politics was not a success (Afary and Anderson 2010, 7). From late 1978 to early 1979, contemporaneous with his lectures on neoliberalism (Foucault [1978–79] 2008), Foucault visited and wrote about the Iranian "revolution" that resulted in the overthrowing of the Western-aligned Pahlavi dynasty and the establishment of an Islamic republic. His sense of having found a "collective revolution" has been criticized for its latent Orientalism (Afary and Anderson 2010, 18), for failing to acknowledge the divisions between Islamists and secularists, nationalists and Marxists, feminists and fundamentalists, and for failing to anticipate the emergence of a new moral order disciplined by an authoritarian police state (Dean and Zamora 2021, 123).

What was it, however, that Foucault felt he had found, and how might it have influenced his turn from revolution to the ethics of subjectivity and the transformational potential of desubjectivization? If what was happening in Iran was a revolution, for Foucault it was based on both collective and individual self-transformation via the shared ordeal of political transformation. If this was "resistance," it was resistance as being able to differ from oneself—to become something new (Dean and Zamora 2021, 131). This was not via the discipline of armed struggle but a perceived collective self-sacrifice through mass protests, public penitence, and an embodiment of a new political spirituality (Cornell and Seely 2016). This was not the spirituality of religion but of a people wanting to redefine their relationships with themselves and others.

Michael Dillon (2017) has shown how Foucault's conceptualization of political spirituality fed into his later work on parrhesia. If spirituality concerns the practices that make a subject capable of transforming themselves pursuant of a truth, then "political spirituality refers to the practices, experience and occasions on which truth is spoken back to power in a discourse that, recalling the ineliminable link between truth, power and the subject, challenges the *doxa* or prevailing orthodoxies currently governing their triangulation" (Dillon 2017, 84). In crafting space for self-formation against a political orthodoxy, parrhesia makes space for political spirituality. Within the "veridical landscape" (84) of truth-politics, parrhesiastic acts force distance between the current and potential self, individual or collective. But these acts also draw on and contribute to a broader ensemble, or "figurative drama" (87), in which they are situated. In what follows I attempt to situate parrhesia within the political spiritualities, and possibly the countergovernmentalities, that form its dramatic ensemble.

## PARRHESIA: A SPIDERY AND SPATIAL NOTION

Parrhesia is not a central concept in classics historiography, nor was it a central tenet of Greek or Roman philosophical or political thought. It was, instead, a "spidery" (Foucault [1982–83] 2010, 45) notion across European history. By it a speaker exposed themselves to risk (whether of humiliation, sanction, violence, or death) in order to proclaim (whether as statement or question) and embody (as performance or askesis) their truth (Elden 2016, 194–204). Parrhesia is thus an act of courage that mobilizes the truth as a dramatic form of asserting power; it achieves "by" saying something, not "in" saying something (Lorenzini 2023, 79). Foucault had long showed that apparatuses made individuals subject to truth (Legg 2016c); here he showed us how courageous interactions with another could make one a subject of truth (Legg 2019b). Reading widely across Foucault's lecture courses, Daniele Lorenzini (2023) has suggested seven conditions that qualify an utterance as parrhesiastic: unpredictable effects; a free speaker; criticism of the interlocutor's ethos; indeterminate risk for the speaker; courage; clear and transparent meaning; and a manifestation of the speaker's truth. Implicit within Foucault's lectures but explicit in the chapters that follow is that there is an inherent spatiality to parrhesia. It depended on a dramatic and often public performance that transformed the status of the subject and created fissile, temporary spaces that produced spaces of philosophical and often political opening.

Foucault was explicit that parrhesia was not the same as freedom or equality of speech (*isēgoria*; Foucault [1982–83] 2010, 150). Likewise, it existed in tension with democracy. The philosophical parrhesiasts that Foucault studied deserted spaces of political democracy when they were overtaken by unrewarding types of risk and rival forms of truth-telling (including rhetoric, flattery, and undirected free speech; Foucault [1982–83] 2010, 202). Parrhesia henceforth found its geography in private councils or public spaces. Democracy paradoxically needs truthful speech but also threatens and regulates it (Luxon 2004). While democracy guarantees (curtailed) free speech, parrhesia introduces another prized quality, the ethical differentiation of the population (Foucault [1982–83] 2010, 157). While in democracy audiences are also won over by rhetoric and logic, the parrhesiast argues and embodies their truth in the face of a difference in status between the speaker and audience that involves a risk (Ross 2008):

> [Parrhesia] is not just the constitutional right to speak. It is an element which, within this necessary framework of the democratic *politeia* giving everyone

the right to speak, allows a certain ascendancy of some over others. It is what allows some individuals to be among the foremost, and, addressing themselves to the others, to tell them what they think, what they think is true, what they truly think is true—this is *khrēsthai logo*—and thereby, by telling the truth, to persuade the people with good advice, and thus direct the city and take charge of it. (Foucault [1982–83] 2010, 157–58)

It is, therefore, just as likely that a parrhesiast will be from lower- rather than upper-status groups, due to them having more to lose and more to demand. This brings us to the broader question of the politics of parrhesia.

Torben Dyrberg (2014) has explored political parrhesia, which he relates especially to the challenging of authority in the public realm in line with a democratic ethos. What made parrhesia political was its addressing of a common concern rather than an individual grievance (68). In terms of its geography, it could take place in a court or office, challenging and provoking political authorities, or it could take place in public assemblies of public spaces, addressing the people. The form of parrhesia would be tailored to the circumstances of each space and to the risk identified. It was not a matter of persuading people (by rhetoric) but of setting up a covenant with the people, sealed by the force of one's embodiment of truth (88).

This leads Dyrberg's political and philosophical analysis toward questions of the autonomy of the political realm that parrhesia helped establish and to its relationship to democracy. This was a product of taking Foucault at his word when he distinguished between the political parrhesia of the assembly and the philosophical parrhesia of Plato, Socrates, or the Cynics' questionings. Given his nearly decade-long exposition of the centrality of biopolitics to governmentalities, the partition is an odd one. We can, rather, agree with Lida Maxwell (2019) that the parrhesia Foucault detailed these philosophers as undertaking was political, whether it was Plato in the court of Dionysius II, Socrates probing the public to an extent that cost him his life, or the Cynics embodying their radically other life as a courageous denunciation of the political order of the polis. That is, purportedly philosophical parrhesia was dependent on and enmeshed within the political context, namely, that of autocracy.

Sergei Prozorov (2017) has shown that Foucault used the example of Cynic practice to demonstrate how biopolitics could become something other than the controlling of populations. Cynic disobedient truth, though not situated in the formal political realm, became political by transforming the world through the public living of another form of life. This did not contest the way that governing apparatuses conducted life but used truth-telling to get subjects to question their own life. For Prozorov the Cynic model of living one's truth marked the paradigm of biopolitics, not its refutation, through the unfettered passage between life and truth. This encapsulated but was more than "resistance":

> The parrhesiastic subject is therefore able to go one crucial step further than any governmentality that seeks to take hold of life and transform it in line with its own truths. It is not merely that resistance acquires a certain primacy in relation to power but that the political subject acquires an autonomous consistency that goes beyond any notion of resistance. Strictly speaking, the parrhesiast does not resist governmental biopower but demonstrates in its very practice of the true life how it has always already failed to transform and govern one's life, while she or he has on the contrary succeeded in doing so by reclaiming its own biopower and applying it to oneself. There is a fundamental asymmetry between biopolitical governmentality and the affirmative biopolitics of the parrhesiast, since even in the worst circumstances the latter is capable of that very productivity or creativity that the former tirelessly asserts but invariably lacks. (Prozorov 2017, 818)

In this brilliant passage Prozorov shows how Cynic life presented Foucault with a route out of dependence solely on the notion of resistance, and toward an affirmative alternative subjectivity filled with insolent life. Both Prozorov and Siisiäinen shift the balance from truth speech to truth acts and life. Foucault himself insisted that parrhesia was truth in action, not *logos* (pure discourse) but *ergon* (work; Foucault [1982–83] 2010, 225). It manifested itself through a "dramatics" of discourse (68), which was as much the study of the act of truth-telling as what the truth-teller was saying (Ross 2008). As such, for Frédéric Gros (2019), "At its extreme, *parrēsia* can be understood as an obligation less to speak what one believes to be true than to make truth visible through one's life" (xix). While the philosophical parrhesiasts that Foucault studied had their words recorded as much as their actions, the archive does not usually record the voice of nonphilosopher parrhesiasts (especially if subaltern).

While the Cynics have attracted much attention in the parrhesia literatures, it is important to remember that Foucault did not value Cynic parrhesia more than Socratic or Platonic philosophical truth-telling (even if you suspect he liked it more). We should also note here the opposition between Cynic affirmative biopolitics (in which Prozorov [2017, 819] sees Foucault producing a microphysical analysis of biopolitics) to biopolitical governmentality.

If this is the case, can we suggest that acts of parrhesia fit into and produce governmentalities?

Lais (2019) suggests that parrhesia aims to keep power relations open, but also that a governmentality critique, regarding a form of governance applied to a population, "can be applied to any interaction among power, knowledge/truth, and ethics to which a structural apparatus can be traced and subsequently tied to technologies of internalisation at the level of self-governance" (81). It is possible that the apparatus of ancient parrhesia was the discipline of philosophy these ancient philosophers were living. In this volume, anticolonialism provides the apparatus that situates parrhesiastic acts within a broader governmentality.

In the postclassical world Foucault was unusually explicit on the transhistorical genealogy of parrhesia and its articulation in successive governmentalities. He suggested that the Christian church cowed parrhesia, forcing obedience to the pastor and the scriptures (Foucault [1983–84] 2011, 334). The Enlightenment saw the reemergence of the parrhesiastic tradition of philosophers criticizing and intervening into their material and contemporary reality (Foucault [1982–83] 2010, 13). Foucault also suggested that Cynic parrhesia was resurrected by the revolutionary movements of the nineteenth and twentieth centuries in modes of life as "the irruptive, violent, scandalous manifestation of the truth" (Foucault [1983–84] 2011, 183) all as part of a battle to change the world (286). Although viewed as personal relations (ethics), these political lives had a relationship to a truth—knowledge claims (veridiction) and the conduct of others (power). Foucault thus explicitly situates phases and forms of parrhesia in the governmentality regimes of pagan antiquity, early Christianity, the Enlightenment, and nineteenth-century anti/revolutionary politics.

In his last two lecture courses, focusing on the study of parrhesia, Foucault was explicit that he was continuing his history of governmentality project. From *The Government of Self and Others*: "You can see that with *parrēsia* we have a notion which is situated at the meeting point of the obligation to speak the truth, procedures and techniques of governmentality, and the constitution of the relationship to self" (Foucault [1982–83] 2010, 45); and from *The Courage of Truth*: "It seems to me that by examining the notion of *parrhēsia* we can see how the analysis of modes of veridiction, the study of techniques of governmentality, and the identification of forms of practice of self interweave" (Foucault [1983–84] 2011, 8). Though governmentality is seemingly singled out here as a separate entity to veridiction and self-formation, these are sets of three practices (obligation, procedure, constitution) and perspectives (analysis, study, and identification) in the broader ensemble previously referred to as governmentality (the conduct of conduct). In one of his last interviews, from 20 January 1984, Foucault recommitted himself to the study of governmentalities, covering the ensemble of practices that inform how free individuals deal with each other (Elden 2016, 195).

From an analytical perspective the categories previously developed in governmentality studies (episteme, identities, visibilities, techne, ethos, and problematizations) can be usefully applied to the parrhesia work to show how the philosopher's acts and lives that Foucault studied can be approached as parts of broader governmental rationalities (drawing on Legg 2019b). The episteme of the parrhesiasts was focused on truth, as a reality to intervene into (Plato), something to be tested (Socrates) or taken to its radical extremes (Cynics). In terms of identities, parrhesia targeted political leaders, the embodied lifestyles of the citizenry, and those vulnerable to the shock of the bestially natural Other life. These targets created different forms of visibility (of the court, the city, and the street) and techne (placing oneself as advisor to the political elite, roaming the streets testing the citizenry, or prostrating oneself in the agora). Parrhesia itself could also be variously problematized. One way was for the risks of speaking to become too great; another was for empty rhetoric to displace parrhesia as a form of speech (equivalent to colonial curfews and acquiescent legislative assemblies in the Indian context). But perhaps the most drastic threat to parrhesia was when a rival form of articulating a different truth emerged. Regarding Foucault's candidate for nineteenth- and twentieth-century parrhesia, revolutionary anticolonialism challenged Congress's professed truth of nonviolence with a different network of claims, actors, acts, and myths.

Foucault detailed how truth claims were taken up in governmentalities of state reason, society, economy, expert knowledge, capitalism, and terror (Foucault [1979–80] 2014, 15). Considering the works reviewed above, we can suggest that ensembles of political spirituality also constituted regimes of truth (93) and that anticolonial governmentalities based themselves on spatial repertoires of parrhesiastic truth claims in the absence of political sovereignty or bureaucratic infrastructures.

### PARRHESIA UNDER COLONIALISM

We will return in the book's conclusion to consider whether the benefits of using such a relatively Eurocentric thinker as Foucault to understand an Indian anticolonial movement is justified. For now, we can position the use of the governmentality approach in four ways. First, the anticolonial politics under study were hybrids of Indian and Western political traditions, and the result of various forms of international interaction (whether the Western education of Indian elites, the wide circulation of Western political texts, or the adaptation of European modes and institutions of state government). Second, the Foucault drawn on here is the author who has been read and reworked for over forty years by Indian and postcolonial scholars, turning him into a tool kit that works in periods and places beyond his imagining for purposes much different from his own (Legg and Heath 2018). Third, the parrhesiastic truth-acts that Foucault examined took place in the political contexts of autocracy and ancient colonialism (Legg 2018), not within the formal realms of democracy. Foucault's late work on ethics thus present an underused resource for advancing postcolonial studies beyond its emphasis on modes of objectification and colonial government (Nichols 2010). And, finally, in his parrhesia work Foucault is calling out for different and other ways in which truth, subjectivity, and power intersected.

While the approach used here will share many of the analytical perspectives used to study regimes of disease, sexuality, or Christianity in the West, the focus on anticolonialism requires a substantial and difficult shift in perspective. Put simply, while colonial governmentality studies of India have made space for subaltern agency or resistance, the space was that of externality and the power exerted was that of problematization. In my previous work these problematizations took the form of clerks petitioning the New Delhi government for better accommodation, rioters and political protesters evading the police gaze, dissenters criticizing the failed improvement of the old city, or women labeled as "prostitutes" defending themselves in court or directly petitioning the chief commissioner (Legg 2007, 59, 111, 135, 159, 181; Legg 2014, 66, 70).

The study of anticolonial governmentalities has to work vigilantly to reverse this geography and upturn the subjects who enact problematizations. People and places that were external to the state and feature in the colonial archive as problematizations become central, and their acts become those of government and conduct. In this analysis it is the apparatuses of colonial governmentality that are marginal, and it is they that problematize anticolonialism (alongside rival anticolonial truth-regimes of nationalism, communalism, or communism). Studying them requires attention to different apparatuses and different landscapes.

As will be apparent already, it is almost redundant to point out the similarities between Gandhi's anticolonialism and Foucault's focus on truth as the mediator of relationships between self and self (ethics) and self and others (politics). Gandhi's life was one of *Experiments with Truth* (Gandhi [1927] 1948), and his aim was for a revolution of political spirituality, bound around a commitment to a new truth (that of nonviolence and love); civilization was, as such, a "mode of conduct" (Gandhi [1909] 2009, 65). He and his followers used Congress to create a state-in-waiting that conducted the conduct of its followers through biopolitical acts of planning and creating a technology of visualizing and intervening into community and individual lives to discipline behavior. This technology of soul-searching constituted an infrastructure of parrhesia whereby people were challenged to think ever harder about how they might fearlessly remake their lives in the mold of satyagraha. But, in radical mode, Congress also demanded that its followers fearlessly speak and act in public, putting themselves at risk so as to provoke the state, and possibly fellow citizens, into violence. Parrhesia here manifested itself through a series of truth tests, or ordeals: undertaking processions and shouting one's truth; breaking the law; picketing vendors of liquor or foreign cloth; and even going underground, problematizing what it could mean to both be within Congress and test the limits of nonviolence. As such, in the Civil Disobedience campaign parrhesiasts disobeyed Congress disciplining and, in the Quit India movement, quit the overground so as to thrive in the risky landscape of the underground.

As rationalities and affects in practice, these parrhesiastic anticolonial governmentalities need to be studied in place. This grants specificity to their "veridical landscape" and situates the acts of parrhesia. But geography can and must play a more pronounced role in the study of anticolonial governmentalities. Where anticolonialism took the form of a mass movement, then its reality was in the people it staged as a nation (Banerjee 2021). Institutions, notably Congress in the Indian case, attempted to direct and craft this movement. But the multitudes' response always exceeded attempts at institutionalization, discipline, and normalization. While Congress might have taken a street or square with relative ease, to take and hold the people of a city was a different matter. To do this the city itself needed to be turned into an apparatus; saturated with a nonviolent ethos; organized and made visible; intervened into so as to mobilize the people who were conceived of as an anticolonial population; and made into a mechanism whereby problematizations of Congress nonviolence could be internalized, condemned, or tactically ignored.

While discourse analysis or intellectual history tend to focus on elite aspiration or perspectives, a governmentality analytics works to bridge rationalities and practices. Categories from governmentality studies as applied to the study of colonialism (Legg 2007, 2014) will structure the chapters that follow. These analytics will show how Congress and the Delhi people fashioned the city into a political technology that mobilized the population in the name of nonviolence but created subjects and problematizations that deviated, increasingly, from the Gandhian creed. Being based wholly on individual participation and self-remaking, each one of these analytical categories is focused on ethics, as part of a thoroughgoing governmentality analysis (from Legg 2007, 12–13):

1. *Episteme*: the use of certain vocabularies and procedures for the production of truth
    - How was nonviolence or violence propagated in Delhi?
    - How were truth claims tailored and adapted?
2. *Visibility*: ways of seeing and representing reality, the practical knowledge of policymakers
    - How were urban neighborhoods mentally mapped and enumerated?
    - How was that which needed to be hidden made invisible?
3. *Techne*: ways of intervening in reality relating to materials, forces, and resistances
    - How were the people mobilized and disciplined?
    - How was nonviolence, and violence, performed?
4. *Identities*: the conception of the governed, the shaping of agency, and the direction of desire
    - What forms of conduct were produced?
    - How did individuals subjectivize themselves?
5. *Ethos*: the moral form that distributes tasks in relation to principles of government; the orientation invested in practices
    - How were elite and subaltern groups differently approached?
    - What were their presumed capacities?
6. *Problematizations*: the crises or challenges that prompt and question regimes of practices
    - When did events overtake plans?
    - How did breakdowns or unexpected events create new disruptions and possibilities?

Even when analyzing a relatively well-resourced and systematized governmentality like that of colonial urbanism, this analysis can become too clunkily structuralist (Philo 2005). For a more decentered and action-based governmentality like that of anticolonialism, the framing risks stretching anticolonial movements beyond recognition. The above categories will be gentle frames through which the stories and places of anticolonialism will be approached (see table 1.1), opening up the stories, people, and places included here rather than shutting them off into analytical silos. There will also be attention to the radical difference of the power relations and archives studied here. Often the accounts that follow string together attempts at courageously expressing the truth of nonviolence and calling the claims of the colonial state into question via ordeals and truth tests: facing down the police in the street, picketing a liquor store, or embodying one's truth in homespun cloth.

Through the interwar years, periods of mass movement inaugurated prolonged periods of parrhesiastic acts in Cynic mode. Congress bodies were not Cynic in their bestial naturalness, but they could be in their militant, insolent refusal of colonial politics and civil society. In periods of cooperation parrhesia continued to drive anticolonialism, continuing with militant protests in the streets, but also in political (in Foucault's typology) forms, such as legislative assembly spaces, and Socratic forms, in the ongoing daily work of questioning conduct via constructive programs.

In the language of the Subaltern Studies Collective, the analysis of episteme and visibility will prioritize elite efforts to direct mobilization; the urban techne marks the intersection of elite planning and popular take-up, while identities and problematization often mark the irruption of subaltern agency into the archive. This agency, and the attempts to channel it, were abundantly recorded in both the colonial archive and nationalist records. What was noted, however, was more the theatrics of these parrhesiastic subjects than their words. Slogan, chants, slurs, and speeches were often recorded, especially if they might provide evidence for a prosecution or propaganda for the cause. But the majority of information was quantitative (number of attendees), tactical (noting the use of pickets, processions, or flags) and geographical (where they were, or were going). While the subaltern are often silent in the archive, they gather, calculate, and move across the page. The recording, or not, of the subaltern marks the recurrent ethos running across these chapters and will be reflected on in the conclusion, in the light of the counterinsurgency discourses discussed in the following chapter.

**TABLE 1.1.** Analytical Chapter Structure

|  | 3. A Disobedient City | 5. Urban Conflict and Collaboration | 6. Quit Delhi | 7. The Underground | 8. Victory? |
|---|---|---|---|---|---|
| Episteme | Nonviolence | Revolutionary violence? | Nonviolence? |  | Tyrannicide |
| Vision | Seeing the mohalla and New Delhi | Imperial autocracy |  | Invisibility | A new Delhi |
| Techne | Meetings, processions, pickets, salt | Constitutional, municipal, and industrial challenges | Force and fire in public |  | Drilling the city |
| Identity | Students and women | Shatrugan |  | C. K. Nair and A. Asaf Ali | S. Datta |
| Problemization | 4. The Gurdwara Sisganj |  | Pili Kothi murder and the underground |  | Victory Day |

CHAPTER 2

# Delhi's Anticolonial Archive

This chapter introduces the resources used to explore Delhi's spaces of anticolonialism in the work that follows. It emphasizes the caution with which we must approach both colonial and nationalist accounts of anticolonialism. Ranajit Guha's (1983b) analysis of the prose of counterinsurgency is appealed to throughout, whereby he explained how both anti- and seemingly pro-insurgency discourses rob subalterns of agency, complexity, and life. I supplement his discourse analysis with attention to the spaces of both our archives and the subaltern and elite politics they relate to us. This, first, shows how national-level organizations (the Government of India and the All India Congress Committee) produced archives through colonial and anticolonial governmentalities that networked together reports of Delhi's spaces into centers of calculation within and beyond the capital. Second, it shows how a broader archive of recollections and collections offers the prospect of escaping, or at least questioning, these elite governmentalities of the archive. Finally, it uses these materials to briefly summarize spaces of anticolonialism in Delhi that have already been explored in published works, almost all of which terminate their studies around 1930, which is where this book begins. While the Subaltern Studies Collective sought out subaltern consciousness, agency, or subject-effects, this volume explores Delhi's anticolonial archive in search of its subaltern geographies (Jazeel and Legg 2019).

The Subaltern Studies Collective was at the forefront of the 1980s turn to contemplating the ways in which the construction of archives impacted the histories we can write, and who figures in these histories. These contributions were contemporaneous to debates over the relationship between specific archives (plural) and the broader discursive archive (singular, after Foucault 1972), the sources for histories "from below" (see Featherstone 2019, 96–99), and the relationship between art, empire, and geopolitics (Said 1978). Later

37

postcolonial scholarship directed attention more to the effects of discourse than to the agency, autonomous or not, of the subaltern. The resurgence of recent interest in subaltern studies accompanied a return to thinking about how we can use colonial and alternative archives to explore the experiences and subjectivization of the non-elite and their silences.

Geographers have contributed to these debates by reflecting on archival distribution and digitization, exclusions and surveillance, and the scale-distorting power of archival collections (Beckingham and Hodder 2022; Duncan 1999; Legg 2016a; Moore 2010). In what follows I combine these approaches with Guha's classic work to consider the archives of anticolonial Delhi. This is not so that we might speculate on the consciousness of the subaltern. Rather, first, each chapter attempts to explore subaltern geographies, including the mohallas of Old Delhi, the residential quarters of New Delhi, and the secret landscapes of the underground. Second, it is so we might engage more fully with the process of subalternity (Gidwani 2009), reflecting on what this book explores, how it does so, and what it does not. This means being conscious of how elite-constructed archives recorded nationalist strivings toward hegemony via anticolonial governmentalities and popular responses to them. It also means taking care to note how subalterns problematized these projects through exceeding, refusing, and ignoring attempts to be mobilized. This engagement supplements Guha's attention to the sources, uses, forms, and times of counterinsurgency discourses with attention to their spaces (see table 2.1). It also updates the threefold discourse analysis, which Guha originally applied to peasant uprisings before the age of mass nationalism, to help us consider the archives of twentieth-century urban anticolonialism.

**TABLE 2.1.** Counterinsurgency Discourses

| Discourse | Source | Use | Form | Time | Space |
|---|---|---|---|---|---|
| Primary | Official: bureaucratic, sleuth, non-official Raj | Governing, action, planning, policy formation | Letter, telegram, dispatch, report, judgment | Event-time: immediate | Archives: local, regional, national, imperial, international |
| Secondary | Primary materials and memory | Historical ordering | Memoir, official annals, amateur or popular history | Deep-time: within memory | The archive: books, memoirs, oral histories |
| Tertiary | Primary and secondary | Left or liberal histories | Academic or political | Discourse-time: history writing | The printed word |

## Primary Discourse: Archives

The primary discourses on peasant insurgencies that Guha (1983b, 47) studied were composed at the time within official registers, spread across chits, memos, letters, and directives that aimed at suppressing uprisings. In this sense they were plainly and openly counterinsurgent; they sat at the core of colonial governmentality, but they also tried to analyze the countergovernmentalities that could string together local acts of resistance into more fully fledged challenges to colonial authority. Subaltern scholarship has shown how the documents of primary discourse can be read against the grain for evidence of agency, politics, and voice, even if mediated and proscribed (Spivak 2010).

The geography of where these records ended up was determined by the constitutional structuring of bureaucratic hierarchies at the time. After the 1919 Government of India Act the detail of counterinsurgency policies was mostly left to the provincial scale and in provincial archives, with summaries produced and high-level policy decisions taking place in New Delhi but rarely in London. As such, few of the sources used here come from the imperial archives of the India Office, stored at the British Library in London.

The central Government of India had a closer interest in Delhi's anticolonialism than in most cities or regions for two reasons. First, most of the Government's ministers lived around four miles from the old city, and periodic threats were posed to the offices and residences of civil servants. Second, the dyarchy reforms of 1919 had left Delhi as a centrally controlled region, with no elected ministers, limited municipal powers, and only one representative in the central Legislative Assembly. As such, the secretary of the Home Department was ultimately responsible for the politics of the capital and took a special interest. The imperial archives of the government became the National Archives of independent India, which store records of prominent trials, reviews of controversial incidents, reports on absconders, and accounts of disturbances filed by the chief commissioner.

The Delhi Administration, under the chief and deputy commissioners, oversaw the running of Old Delhi and its suburbs and cooperated with the Government on matters of shared concern regarding New Delhi. The chief commissionership was created in 1912, with the transfer of the capital from Calcutta, and operated initially through thirteen departments. In 1913 a new "Confidential" department was added to deal with revolutionaries and other matters of political concern; the Delhi State Archive's published guide describes these records as "the best source material for the history of the Freedom Struggle in Delhi" (Delhi Administration 1989, 71). The archives are now stored in the Qutb Institutional Area in South Delhi and provide the majority of material regarding main events, figures, investigations, and reports, all in a thorough counterinsurgency vein.

The aim of practically every document used from the Delhi State Archive and National Archives of India was to explain how the subaltern masses were mobilized, penetrated, and politicized, carefully differentiating between the business classes, the well-to-do, working folk, and the Delhi "underground." Procession routes were described, numbers at meetings estimated, networks of friends, family, and allies noted where possible, and fortnightly reports on political activity composed. Much of this information was passed on to the Delhi Administration, via the police, by the Delhi Criminal Investigation Department (CID). The Delhi State Archive also contains a unique document, published by the CID in 1934.[1] The *Delhi Province Political "Who's Who"* included a preface by CID superintendent C. H. Everett where he introduced a list of "politico-criminals and political suspects" of some importance. Basic biographies, political activities, and physical descriptions were given of dozens of Delhi residents, each of which was allocated a code by which they should be referred to (as used below when contrasting sources on leading figures). It was instructed that the public should not know of the existence of the book.

The Delhi CID was established in October 1912, prior to the assassination attempt on Viceroy Hardinge in Chandni Chowk that December. It operated under the auspices of the Police Department and consisted of one deputy superintendent, one inspector, two superintendents, four head constables, and sixteen constables (twenty-four in total).[2] These men would have their own territories, passing information on their allotted *ilaka* (district) of the province. The force grew rapidly in response to the Delhi Conspiracy Case, after Hardinge's near fatal entry into the old city, Civil Disobedience in 1930, and the growth of revolutionary networks in the following years. By 1930 the CID consisted of one head, one deputy, two inspectors, six sub-inspectors, fifteen head constables and thirty-three foot constables (total fifty-eight); by 1940 the head and deputy were supported by three inspectors, six sub-inspectors, three assistant sub-inspectors, twenty-two head constables, and fifty-eight foot constables (total ninety-four).[3] These men were aided by large ranks of informers.

The records of the CID themselves were procured by the Nehru Memorial Museum and Library (NMML), which sits on the grounds of the former commander in chief's residence in the heart of New Delhi. Founded in 1964, the NMML is a repository of resources on Indian history, and of nationalism especially. The location of the 2,350 CID files, covering 1915 to 1976, here is apposite. The department was the dark heart of the colonial state, paying "sources" in many of Delhi's political movements to inform on their compatriots. While the form and purpose of the CID would merit it a place in the records of the colonial government, its amassed files present a record of anticolonial activity unprecedented in the degree to which it is seemingly comprehensive, and compromised.

Thousands of pages of minutely detailed reports exist covering everything from mass processions to small, private meetings. In interviews I conducted in 2001 and 2003, I would ask participants about CID informers. Most people were aware of them, and dodging the CID was a regular part of daily campaigning, especially during the underground phase of Quit India 1942.[4] Sarla Sharma, who was a communist student activist in the 1940s, remembered inviting the more obvious CID informants in for tea on cold days, welcoming them as fellow workers.[5] If the reports were not secret, they must also regularly have been inaccurate. The bumping up of word counts for greater pay and the setting of vendettas are also possible and probably likely, so these sources have been triangulated with nonofficial sources where possible. While some large files on individuals exist (see the sections on Shatrugan and Subhadra Joshi in chapters 5 and 8), most submissions focused on meetings or events, sketching out diffuse and rich geographies of political activity across the city.

Elsewhere in the NMML, alongside other copies of documents produced by the colonial state, lie a wealth of resources for researching anticolonialism and nationalism before and after independence. Unlike nineteenth-century rural insurgencies, anticolonial movements in the twentieth century created their own archives. While revolutionary, secret organizations necessarily kept limited and often-confiscated archives, Congress produced and collated records of its attempts to coordinate local acts into provincial and national movements. These consist of All India Congress Committee circulars, Provincial and District Congress Committee bulletins, leaflets, and other promotional materials.[6] Delhi Congress leader Brij Kishan Chandiwala recalled local bulletins, containing news about campaigns and instructions for the movement, being written by local Congress leaders and cyclostyled in secret.[7] Des Raj Chaudhry suggested that the cyclostyling machine was kept in a car of auto dealer and Congress supporter Raghunandan Saran so that printing could be done outside the city jurisdiction, while C. L. Paliwal suggested the printing was done in a station wagon while moving around Delhi.[8] Phool Chand Jain later explained that the bulletins were written in Urdu first, then translated, and that authorship depended on whoever was available, especially during the disruption of Quit India in 1942.⁹ National and local sacrifices were outlined to generate excitement in the people, before outlining the program, which Jain described as a kind of "setting."

Guha (1983b, 71–84) explained that accounts of uprisings that were actively pro-rebel could also be counterinsurgent. This occurred if they emptied the subaltern participants of individuality, contradictions, refusals, and the capacity for betrayal in favor of a grand narrative of ideal consciousness and teleological progress toward independence. Across the INC files in the NMML, errant subaltern behavior (violence, aggressive communalism, rowdiness) was tracked and disciplined, while tropes recurred of volunteers prodding a subaltern population into life, rather than harnessing its already existing political interest. Volunteers could feel themselves to be under surveillance by Congress itself, such that comparisons between the colonial police and Congress high command became explicit. Chandiwala, as a fervent Gandhian, practiced cloth spinning as instructed, even when most others didn't: "There were a lot of Delhi-ites and because they always believed that I am Gandhi's man that is why they considered me his CID. They didn't have full faith in me because they had a different way of working. They knew that if Gandhi found out this way then he wouldn't like it. That is why they would stay doubtful of me that if they take me in their midst then I would tell Gandhi and Gandhi wouldn't like this and we will become distant from Gandhi in this way."¹⁰

The NMML also has a large collection of newspaper microfilms, of which *Aljamiat*, *Tej Daily*, *Hindu Outlook*, *Janata*, *Hindustan*, and the *Hindustan Times* were consulted. The latter was the main Congress mouthpiece in the city and was edited by Gandhi's son Devdas from 1937 until his death in 1957. The newspaper editorial offices in Connaught Place, where the Gandhis also lived, was an unofficial Congress headquarters, and was regularly raided as such. While mostly grounded close to their arenas of production, some of these primary discourse texts have been made mobile through reproduction (Chopra 1976; Gupta 1997; Malhotra 1979; Mathur 1979). This allows some remote access to these intensely local geographies, as secondary discourse materials allow more broadly.

### Secondary Discourse: The Archive

Secondary discourse accounts are based on primary materials and recollections, being composed at a historical distance but within living memory. Using hindsight, the events that constitute uprisings or rebellions are ordered and interpreted, whether through memoirs, nonacademic histories, or official annals. They help us understand the networking and strategizing that strung together anticolonial governmentalities. But they also show us how forms of colonial knowledge could transfer seamlessly from policy documents into those purporting to tell us histories (Guha 1983b, 70).

Delhi deputy commissioner Hubert Evans's (1988) memoir, recounting his supposedly heroic efforts to police and manage the unruly city, is an exemplar here (his account of Quit India is discussed in chapter 6).[11] The same might be said of the numerous memoirs of New Delhi life written by Indian and British elites who resided in the capital (generously read by Pothen 2012). Again, participants in and observers of anticolonialism also produced their own reflections of the governmentalities stringing people and actions together, and of the political nature, or not, of participants. Where published, the geography of all of these accounts is as diffuse as the print run and popularity allowed. When written but not published, they often reside in the institutional repositories outlined above. When they exist as stories and memories, they dwell in the homes of the recollector.

The main official annals of anticolonial Delhi are the two volumes of the *Who's Who of Delhi Freedom Fighters* (Chopra 1974; Thapliyal 1985b). The first volume contained around 3,500 very brief life sketches of participants in the "freedom movement" in Delhi (but also of migrants to Delhi from Pakistan), the second volume around 3,000. The aim was to find a way to recognize the contributors to the freedom struggle whose names would not necessarily find their way into accounts of the movement at large. Entry in the volumes could also be used as evidence to claim a freedom fighter pension supplement or state accommodation. Administrative, prison, court, and police archives were used to verify the information. The project was overseen by an advisory committee including Mir Mushtaq Ahmed, who was chair of the Delhi Metropolitan Council when the first volume was completed. He himself features in the volume as a freedom fighter (as does Phool Chand Jain, another member of the advisory committee; see Chopra 1974, 184, 275) as he does in chapters 6 and 7 as one of New Delhi's chief Congress activists.

The volumes undoubtedly constitute a subaltern prosopography of sorts, with thousands of names, dates of birth, movements participated in, and sentences in prison given (although with less detail than in the 1934 CID book, which is not mentioned as a source). These entries are useful for basic fact-checking and are cited in the chapters that follow when used. But Ahmed's foreword to the first volume (in Chopra 1974, i–ii) also neatly collapses all these subaltern contributions into one narrative, which is that of Congress's nonviolence overcoming earlier violent uprisings and revolutionary anticolonialism, overlooking the turn to violence both within Congress and by those who left the fold. Ahmed was replaced by Purushotem Goel as chair of the advisory panel in the second volume. In his preface he homogenized Delhi's freedom fighters very explicitly within a liberal and humanist logic: "During the struggle, various cross-sections of society—rural folks, urban elite, persons of different professions, of all classes, religions or languages and from all political and social strata, became part of an indivisible matrix of liberty from which ambers [sic] of freedom flew far and wide turning into flames and ultimately these ambers destroyed the very foundation of the British Empire, whispering emancipation, freedom, hope, strength and life for India" (in Thapliyal 1985b, i). In terms of memoirs from those explicitly engaged with anticolonialism in interwar Delhi, there are some useful publications from prominent Delhi figures, including Gandhi devotees and Congress organizers (Chandiwala 1954), activists and urban reformers (Jain 2010), journalists (Sahni 1971), and politicians (Raghavan 1994). Others provide context for and details of anticolonialism in Delhi while explicitly distancing themselves from the political memoir genre. The raconteurish memoir of Abdur Rahmann Siddiqi (2011) insisted it was not struck down by the po-faced nostalgia of nationalist accounts, while describing the cultural life of a Delhi in thrall to both anticolonialism and communalism. Likewise, the translators of novelist Intizar Husain's Delhi place-memoir insist it is a counterdiscourse to the language and expectations of nationalism (Husain 2016, xi–xii), constituting a cultural history and geography of the city from antiquity to the 1930s. Other memoirs of place and period allow us to sketch out the lifeworlds in which politics took place (Andrews 1929; Dayal 1975; Thompson 1925).

Published first-person accounts of anticolonial Delhi are far outnumbered by institutional oral history transcripts, especially those consulted at the Delhi Archives (five), NMML (twenty-one), and the University of Cambridge's Centre of South Asian Studies (sixteen). The figures interviewed ranged from leaders of Congress in Delhi (Memo Bai, B. K. Chandiwala, P. C. Jain, K. D. Kohli, C. K. Nair, Radha Rahman, J. N. Sahni) to influential elite figures in the capital (Sobah Singh, Hansa Mehta) and relatively minor political actors. The consulted NMML transcripts date back to the late 1960s and early 1970s, the latest interview being conducted in 1989. They were scripted and directed toward the major periods of mass movement and elite figures but also regularly directed the respondents toward local details, socially marginalized or excluded groups, or tensions. Most were conducted in English, but two substantial transcripts in Hindi, of over twenty thousand words each, have been translated and used here.[12]

Finally, in 2001, while spending six months in Delhi for my doctoral research, I conducted forty-three personal interviews with people who were involved in political activities as youths in the 1930s and 1940s, who were children in political households, or who were just happy to share their memories of life and politics in the capital before independence. My focus was on women and how they were able to act politically from the home (Legg 2003), but the conversations ranged widely. I had only just started going through the CID files at this time, but some of the interviews took place in the evening after a day of reading secret reports on the interviewee at the NMML that afternoon. The very existence of a CID report raised an ethical quandary, suggesting an informant in a political organization, friendship group, or home. Tentatively raising the question with interviewees, most accepted that surveillance and countersurveillance were part of the political ecosystem.[13] After lengthy discussions on the CID, Sarla Sharma was glad to see photocopies of the reports that noted her attending increasing numbers of meetings with leading communist activist Y. D. Sharma, and her file name being updated by the CID from Sarla Gupta when they eventually married.

The geographies of the interviews were also telling. Sharma's home was still in Haveli Haider Quli where she had grown up, a mohalla just south of Chandni Chowk (see Dayal 1975, 112–16). Our interviews in the house (in 2001, 2003, and 2006–7) with her brother, Narain Prasad, brought the old city to life, as did his photographs, which he kindly shared with me. Most other interviewees had left Old Delhi, and we met in the suburbs and extensions of the city to the north of Old Delhi and south of Lutyens' Delhi. Some had been awarded plots in the latter after partition, but others' accommodation attested to the politics of late colonial, not early independence India. Subhadra Joshi (née Datta; see chapter 8) agreed to meet me in 2001, two years before her death at the age of eighty-four, in the flat she had been allocated by the Delhi Development Authority as compensation for the sacrifices made in the anticolonial struggle as part of Delhi's fight for freedom.

## Tertiary Discourse: Historiography

A prisoner of empty abstractions tertiary discourse, even of the radical kind, has thus distanced itself from the prose of counter-insurgency only by a declaration of sentiment so far. It has still to go a long way before it can prove that the insurgent can rely on its performance to recover his [sic] place in history.

—Ranajit Guha, "The Prose of Counter-insurgency"

Tertiary discourses use the materials of primary and secondary discourse to write histories and geographies. They piece together evidence from individual archives and the broader archive of transcripts, memoirs, and memories to understand how rival governmentalities sought to conduct the conduct of the masses. They also highlight and attempt to explain insurrections, resistance, and parrhesia. Guha (1983b, 71) argued that the resulting histories "so far" were counterinsurgent even when they were clearly, and retrospectively, willing the subaltern on to victory. Academic writing from the 1960s and 1970s explained subaltern resistance, as had colonial discourse, through appealing to contexts and structures that rationally explained political choices in the language of Western liberalism or socialism, and which slotted each rebellion into a broader nationalist or Marxist teleology. This tended to underplay regional diversity, factions, ambiguity, and ambivalence, airbrushing place affiliations out of history in favor of ageographical generalizations: "Committed inflexibly to the notion of insurgency as a generalized movement, [the historian] underestimates the power of the brakes put on it by localism and territoriality" (Guha 1983b, 84).

If postcolonial studies risked another sort of generalization, in favor of texts and semiological discourse, the early Subaltern Studies Collective interventions helped weld an appreciation of discourse and ideology to a detailed appreciation of place and territory. In these studies, subaltern consciousness and agency in their political decisions worked against the counterinsurgency impulse, and influenced generations of South Asian scholars, whether directly or not, to further interrogate their archival matter and representation of the non-elite. While there is relatively little historical scholarship on anticolonial or nationalist Delhi that explicitly deploys a subalternist perspective (although see Prashad 2000), much of this literature makes space for considering how and where city elites and middle classes engaged with the non-elite, working populations of the city. This literature will be surveyed, incorporating primary and secondary discourse material that will frame the chapters that follow, always cognizant of Husain's (2016) warning: "No settlement shows its 'self' easily; and Dilli is the one about which [the poet] Mir warned us. It is not just any settlement, it is Dilli! How much of its real face has Dilli shown even to those loose cobblestones who ambled about in its dusty streets?" (3).

The prehistory of nationalism and anticolonialism in Delhi has been much debated, as has the contribution of Delhi's non-elite to its politics.[14] One of the longest ranging accounts of anticolonialism in Delhi bridges secondary and tertiary discourse. It appeared in the second *Who's Who of Delhi Freedom Fighters* volume but surveyed ninety years of struggle using the archives and sources of ongoing academic scholarship. As cited below, Uma Thapliyal's (1985a) overview efficiently summarizes many of the main events in the periods of mass agitation. However, as with the two *Who's Who* prefaces of Ahmed and Goel, the narrative is counterinsurgent in that it threads all activities along one narrative, insisting on Hindu-Muslim unity in Delhi, leading ineluctably toward independence (beginning with the "First War of Independence" of 1857). National leaders "electrified" local activists to rise to the highest level, which they duly did and "carried the torch of freedom lit in 1857 with courage and dignity for 90 years until the moment of triumph on the midnight of 14–15 August, 1947" (xxx).

The uprising of 1857 undoubtedly centered the nation and the empire's attention on the capital of Mughal emperor Bahadur Shah Zafar. The emperor's three sons were murdered outside the city walls, at the *Lal Darwaza* (Red Gateway) of the Purana Qila Fort. Both this site and the gateway near Dariba from which the Afghan Nadir Shah ordered his massacre in 1737 became known in local memory as *Khuni Darwaza* (Gateway of Blood; Dayal 1975, 138–43). The 150th anniversary of the uprising renewed debates over whether the jihad of the uprising was anti-British, anti-foreigner, anti-Christian, or any of these (Dalrymple 2006; Prakash 2007) and what the resulting archival traces can tell us about the interactions of the people, the city, and British and Indian sovereign powers in the city (Farooqui 2010).

The emphasis on 1857 has largely eclipsed previous forms of resistance and the revolt in the city. Mann (2005), however, concluded that tension between religious groups in this period could not usefully be framed as "communal." Margit Pernau (2013, 191) likewise suggested that efforts by Hindu and Muslim communities to distinguish and demarcate themselves in the 1820 and 1830s, in both elite discourse and the practices of everyday life, were not driven by protoreligious nationalism. Rather, they were driven by internal processes of self-identification and the creeping intrusion of regulations by the British Resident, especially regarding annual religious processions, the routes for which were frozen after 1857 (Pernau 2013, 381).

From the late 1860s the population and economy of the city began to recover from the genocidal British violence in the city. While clashes occurred in Delhi in the 1880s, there was relatively little evidence of nationalist politics of the city until the 1900s.[15] Singh (1972, 100–101) has detailed the small number of delegates that Delhi sent to Congress's early meetings from 1888 to the early 1900s. The local concern was to convince the government of Delhi's loyal status. As Edward Thompson (1925) had it: "I am not prepared to discuss the assurances given me by some of my missionary friends that all this anguish had faded away in two generations from the memory of Delhi, the capital of Indian imagination no less than of Indian story. The new capital of our empire is rising on foundations of an unforgotten wretchedness. As in places consecrated by great suffering there seems to linger some ghost whose living body bore a part in it" (78–79).

The announcement of the capital transfer led to what Pernau (2013, 396) called the "nationalization of Delhi," whereby not just the Government but Muslim charities and presses moved to the city.[16] The Delhi Conspiracy Case, investigating the failed assassination attempt during the viceroy's entry into Delhi in 1912, fed the sense that the move from Bengal had not shielded the government from revolutionary anticolonialism as had been hoped (Lal 1999; Singh 1972).

Gupta (1981, 200–204) suggested that politics in Delhi reached a low ebb during the First World War but revived from 1917 with the formation of the Indian Association, Delhi's first nationalist political organization. This was followed by the Home Rule League (HRL) opening its Delhi branch on Chandni Chowk, leading the chief commissioner to suggest in a 1919 memorandum: "This marks the entry of prominent local men into the All-India political arena."[17] Such institutions would prove more effective fora for anticolonial politics than the Delhi Municipal Committee, which was tightly monitored by the deputy commissioner, was impinged on by rival authorities, and lacked the rivalries between British commerce and local interests that transformed municipal authorities elsewhere into hotbeds of anticolonial politics.[18]

One of the few Delhi figures to gain experience of politics in the municipal committee was the later star Mohammad Asaf Ali, a successful barrister who had trained at St. Stephen's College in Delhi (see figure 2.1) and Lincoln's Inn in London (Raghavan 1994). He returned to Delhi in 1915 and was from 1919 drawn to the Khilafat movement protesting the treatment of the Ottoman sultan after the war (which for Siddiqi [2011, 157] roused Delhi from its half-century "coma" after 1857) and from there toward Gandhi, Congress, and his leadership of the local HRL branch (Raghavan 1994, 148–60; Singh 1972,

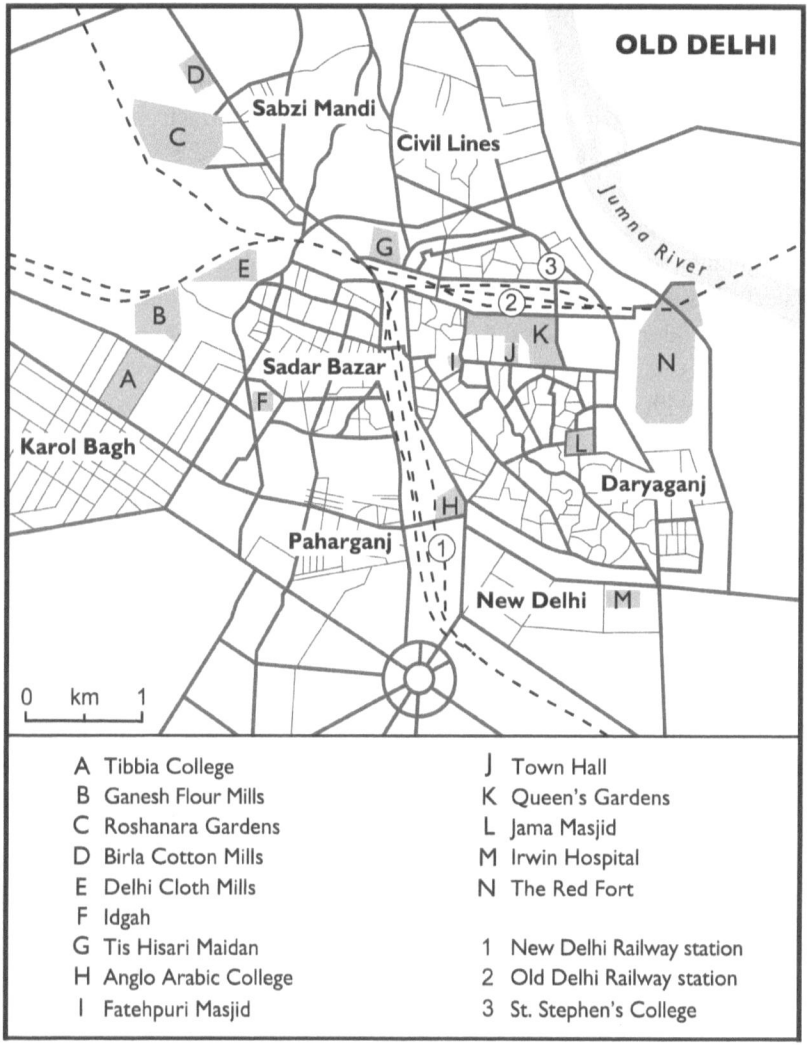

FIGURE 2.1. Delhi landmarks

243). In June 1917 he penned a newspaper article condemning oppressive wartime legislation and chastising the Delhi people for their silence: "The country must be wondering at Imperial Delhi's enigmatic reticence at this juncture, and thinking that the Delhic Sphinx has imparted much of his mysterious silence to the Delhites."[19] Asaf Ali would go on to dominate the local Congress and represent Delhi in local (he was elected to the Delhi Municipal Committee in 1923 [Raghavan 1994, 209]) and national committees and assemblies through the 1930 and 1940s.

Congress and the Muslim League held a joint session at Delhi in 1918 that further excited political support, while price inflation and tax increases stoked popular dissatisfaction. It was in this local context that the Gandhi-led nationwide protest against the Rowlatt Act of March 1919, which extended wartime powers against "anarchical and revolutionary crimes," played out. Contrary to Guha's suggestion that localism and territory tend to be underplayed in accounts of popular uprisings, Gupta (1981, 204) insisted that the Rowlatt satyagraha of 1919 was less a national than a local protest against the colonial state. In this it was very effective, as the chief commissioner noted the following month: "Ten years ago the public of Delhi took but little interest in political events. . . . The people of Delhi as a whole did not appear to concern themselves with such things. . . . The universal character of the *hartal* [general strike] of the 30th of March was, it must be confessed, a surprise to the officials, as it was also apparently to the organisers."[20]

The events in Delhi have been explored in detail by Donald Ferrell (1971) and Sangat Singh (1990; also see Dhanedhar 2011, 13–38). Dr. M. A. Ansari had a directing role, his houses in Daryaganj and near the Fatehpuri Masjid acting as informal coordination headquarters for the four meetings in March leading up to the hartal on the 30th. The arrest of two youths for picketing a liquor store near Old Delhi railway station led to the military being called, which attracted a crowd of up to three thousand. In attempting to retake the area between the station and the town hall on Chandni Chowk, shots were fired, leading to eight deaths and twelve severe injuries. A later crowd approached a military picket near the town hall, fronted by Hindu activist and reformer Swami Shraddhanand. The confrontation between Shraddhanand and the Gurkha soldiers entered Delhi legend, as recalled by the swami himself in the official inquiry that followed: "'*Tum ko chhed denge*' [we will pierce you]. I stood quietly before them and said '*Main khara hun, goli maro*' [I am standing, fire]. At once eight or ten rifles were aimed at my breast and insolent threats went on" (Disorders Inquiry Committee 1920, 189).

Satyagraha meetings continued to attract thousands of people over the next week, and on Friday, 4 April, Shraddhanand cemented Hindu-Muslim unity through addressing a crowd at the Jama Masjid (Singh 1990, 85). Meanwhile, the reaction of the local authorities was traduced in the press, the *Hindustani* newspaper announcing that the town hall was the site "near which the blood of innocent children was shed, and into which their corpses were dragged like the carcasses of dogs. The floor of this building is still stained with the blood of martyrs" (Disorders Inquiry Committee 1920, 145). In the *Inquilab* newspaper Asaf Ali suggested that the area around the clock tower "be named the

*Khuni Chauraha* [Square of Blood] in memory of the Delhi martyrs, just as the *Khuni Darwaza* [Gate of Blood] was so called in order to remind the people of the mutiny" (145–46). Asaf Ali's plan did not take off, but nationally and internationally Delhi had now cast off its loyal status, as Gandhi himself wrote to C. F. Andrews on 5 April: "There can be no redemption without sacrifice. And it fills me with a glow to find that full measure was given even on the first day and that too at the very seat of the power of Satan" (Gandhi 1999, 17:378).

On 13 April 1919 General Dyer opened fire on a peaceful gathering in Amritsar, the members of which were unaware of the ban on public meetings (Wagner 2016). The Jallianwala Bagh massacre in which at least 379 died and 1,200 were injured led Gandhi to call off the Rowlatt satyagraha and focus on building Muslim support through promoting the Khilafat campaign (Arnold 2001, 112). After the reorganization of Congress at the Nagpur session of 1920, Gandhi secured support for a campaign of noncooperation, calling for a boycott of British cloth, elections, and institutions. When the movement was launched in December 1920, Indians working for the government, police, or army were requested to resign, alcohol and drugs were to be rejected, Hindu-Muslim unity bolstered, women and "untouchables" uplifted, and khadi spun and worn.

In Delhi the Non-Cooperation movement targeted the visits of the Duke of Connaught in February 1921 and the Prince of Wales in February 1922. The contrast between two embodiments of sovereignty, imperial and anticolonial, in the city was stark.[21] The *Arya Gazette*, of Lahore, noted on 17 February 1921 that the Duke of Connaught was constantly surrounded by English police, whereas "when Mr Gandhi, the uncrowned king of India, visits Delhi the whole city looks like a bride. He is received by lakhs of people, whose attitude seems to say to the Duke, 'Go and tell the people of England that Mahatma Gandhi and no one else is our real though uncrowned king.'"[22] The Prince of Wales's arrival was met with a hartal on 14 February 1922, in stark contrast to the reception of the king-emperor in 1911 for the imperial durbar and a "Gandhi Day" parade on 26 July 1922 featuring a giant charkha and a display of Hindu-Muslim unity (see Bobb and Gupta 2007, 82–83).

After the killing of twenty-three policemen on 5 February 1922 by a protesting crowd at Chauri Chaura, in the United Provinces, Gandhi suspended the Non-Cooperation movement and encouraged his followers to focus on constructive work and social uplift. Despite this campaign, Hindu-Muslim relations worsened after the Khilafat and Rowlatt unity, with Delhi riots in 1924 leaving seventeen dead.[23] Gandhi visited and undertook a fast to quell the violence in the autumn of 1924, but clashes were periodically triggered by annual festivals (Legg 2007, 119–49). While Congress struggled to sustain itself in the city, three communal clashes between April 1926 and August 1927 left four dead and 116 injured (Hasan 1995, 114). As the senior superintendent of police noted on 17 December 1927, "The people in general are so imbibed with this communal antipathy that the antagonism towards the white races which was so evident a few years ago has completely disappeared and Europeans and foreigners are generally welcomed."[24]

The late 1920s saw a radical resurgence of anticolonial interest of two strands in the city. The first was driven by the spectacular British miscalculation of the all-white touring Simon Commission, assembled in London to advise on India's constitutional future. Simon arrived in Delhi on 4 February 1928, and the leftist congressman Shankar Lal led processions through Old Delhi before the Congress leader and journalist J. N. Sahni brought the protesters to the station at 4:30 p.m.[25] Black flags were waved and "Simon go back!," "Mahatma Gandhi ki Jai! [Victory to Mahatma Gandhi]," and "Commission not wanted!" shouted.[26] B. K. Chandiwala and K. D. Kohli also recalled flags being hoisted on India Gate and "Simon Go Back" being written outside the Legislative Assembly and down the mall of Kingsway, though these do not feature in the official archive.[27]

Simon returned to Delhi and was in the Legislative Assembly chamber on 8 April 1929 to witness the return to Delhi of the second form of violence. Bhagat Singh and Batukeshwar Dutt of the Hindustan Republican Socialist Army (HSRA) hurled bombs and leaflets into the chamber (Lal 1999, 166–236; Dhanedhar 2011, 143–56; Maclean 2015, 13). Gandhi denounced the use of violence, but Congress also worked to tap into the incredible popularity of the resurgent revolutionary movement, which had centered on Delhi again. Although Nehru decried Singh and Dutt in print, he praised them at a meeting in Queen's Gardens on 6 July. When Dutt died on hunger strike, a hartal was announced for 14 September. It was a success: seven thousand people gathered at Delhi railway station, through which the train carrying Dutt's body passed. The confidential fortnightly report on 21 September 1929 concluded: "The general effect of the speeches at this and other recent meetings has been to impress upon the audience that the sacrifice of the hunger-strikers culminating in the peaceful methods would be useless, and that the youths should prepare to sacrifice their lives for the freedom of the country."[28]

On 23 December 1929 the viceroy's train was bombed as it entered Delhi, although he was unscathed. Gandhi moved a resolution at the Lahore Congress Session on 31 December 1929 condemning the bombing and published the condemnatory article "Cult of the Bomb" on 2 January 1930 in *Young India*

(Gandhi 1999, 48:184–86). The HSRA's retort, titled "Philosophy of the Bomb," was distributed throughout Delhi during Independence Day on 26 January 1930 (Lal 1999, 288). Although Congress condemned the bombing, when the perpetrators were eventually brought to trial in the Lahore Conspiracy Case the INC allotted 15,000 rupees for a legal defense in December 1930 and in February 1931 appointed Asaf Ali as defender.[29] This took place during the hiatus of the Civil Disobedience movement, which was launched in April 1930 in response to the British government's refusal to have the Round Table Conference announce dominion status for India as its stated objective (Legg 2023).

There is limited existing scholarship on the Civil Disobedience movement in Delhi. Uma Thapliyal (1985a, xvi–xviii) described the spread of the khadi movement, mentioned the firing at the Gurdwara Sisganj, and listed the prominent campaigners arrested. Dharmendra Nath, another member of the *Who's Who* advisory committee, spent hours with me in 2001 relating his childhood memories of the Quit India movement and translating his writings, in Hindu, to me. By far the most detailed account is that of Reva Dhanedhar (2011, 161–208), introducing the growing support for Congress through 1930, efforts to train volunteers, the mass protests in April, the outrage at Gandhi's arrest in early May, and the emergence of left-right tensions between Shankar Lal and Professor Indra. The chapter is an excellent introduction to the key events in Delhi at this time and, unlike this volume, pays special attention to the role of villages in the movement (209–16).

Dhanedhar ends her study in 1934, the year when Asaf Ali was elected to the Legislative Assembly. Thapliyal (1985a) takes us through the 1930s to the arrests of the Individual Satyagraha campaign and to a more detailed account of Quit India in Delhi. The arrest of the Delhi leadership, the mass protests, and widespread violence, by the police and crowds, were noted as were the sporadic activities of the underground movement through 1943. Anish Vanaik (2019) has provided vital context in terms of property and economy for the politics of the 1930 and 1940s in the city, though anticolonialism per se does not feature in his research. Likewise, anticolonialism frames Nazima Parveen's (2021) and Geva Halperin's (2022) studies of communal Delhi without being the main focus.

In my previous work, the political and communal politics of Delhi were approached as a problematization of colonial governmentality (Legg 2007). These movements were things to be surveilled, stilled, and neutralized by the police, although the agency of Congress and communal organizations was acknowledged as the driving force of change and adaptation by the Delhi Administration. In what follows I use the three types of sources outlined above to inform an approach that explores Congress attempts to string together an anticolonial governmentality in and through the city, while avoiding counterinsurgency discourses that strip the participants of agency and complexity. At each stage it moves beyond elite actors and central public spaces to the subaltern spaces in which minor actors repurposed, questioned, or refused Congress's model of the anticolonial city.

**PART 1**

# DISOBEY

**CHAPTER 3**

# A Disobedient City

## Introducing Disobedience

This chapter explores Delhi as a disobedient city that was often but not always civil. Across each section below, two movements can be tracked. First, and geographically, subaltern spaces are sought out, beyond the main bazaars of Old Delhi. Paradoxically, given how rarely New Delhi has been approached as a space of anticolonialism, the capital is a rich plain for bringing new and sometimes subaltern political spaces to light. Second, in terms of governmentality, the relationship between Congress dictates and the endless inventiveness of the Delhi people is explored. The command to be disobedient, with Congress volunteers serving as what Guha (1997, 145) termed the "people's policemen," was often obeyed, with nonviolent conduct evident in parrhesiastic courageous speech, movement, and acts. But the command to disobey did not lend itself to discipline. Rather, it encouraged an affirmative, Cynic parrhesia in which people reclaimed their own biopower and applied it to themselves and others (Prozorov 2017, 818), sometimes violently. Disobedience, as such, is both what Congress unleashed and what it faced throughout the city.

### ALL-INDIA DISOBEDIENCE

The Calcutta INC Conference in December 1928 accepted the (Motilal) Nehru Report that demanded Dominion status. As a concession to Congress members looking nervously at the popularity of contemporary revolutionary movements (Maclean 2015), however, Gandhi stated that if the British had not accepted these terms by the end of 1929, a civil disobedience campaign would be declared (Sarkar 1983). The viceroy's invitation in October 1929 to the Round Table Conference (RTC) in London was rejected due to the refusal to have that conference's objective set in advance (Legg 2023). At the Lahore Annual Congress Conference in December 1929, the goal of Congress was redefined to be that of *purna swaraj* (complete independence). This would be achieved by the boycott of legislation and a civil disobedience campaign, the timing of which would be decided by Gandhi.

In February 1930 the Government rejected Gandhi's compromise suggestion of social and political reforms, making civil disobedience inevitable (Arnold 2001). Gandhi, and a select group of disciplined satyagrahis, left his ashram near Allahabad on 12 March 1930 and marched the 241 miles to the coast at Dandi. On reaching the shore on 5 April, Gandhi heated the seawater he collected there and produced salt—a simple act, but one illegal under British law due to a state monopoly established in 1878. Gandhi was arrested a month later, on the night of the 4–5 May, but he had been free to hear of the all-India response to "National Week," which began with the remembrance of the Rowlatt disturbances on 6 April and ended with the commemoration of the Jallianwala Bagh atrocities on 13 April. This was a genuine mass movement that included women, students, and the working classes in numbers never before witnessed, although the Hindu-Muslim unity of the early 1920s had dissolved, and many Muslims remained aloof from the disturbances. The movement, though better organized than those of 1919–22, was less strict, with local committees being advised on how to implement the general strategies of noncooperation, foreign cloth and liquor boycott, breaking of the salt monopoly, and actions against the disciplinary technology used to crush the disobedience campaign. Local Congress workers did the most important work, turning such general strategies into local tactics.

Civil Disobedience was such a success that Nehru was able to override moderate Congress pleas to have Gandhi attend the first RTC session in the autumn of 1930. To discuss its results and break the deadlock in India, the viceroy agreed to release the imprisoned members of the Congress Working Committee. Gandhi walked free on 26 January 1931 to face the masses of exhausted volunteers, distressed businessmen, and Muslim representatives who wanted peace. On 5 March the Gandhi-Irwin Pact saw the Government surrender the exceptional legal powers it had bestowed on itself and release all Civil Disobedience prisoners, while Congress withdrew the movement and agreed to enter into discussions on the constitution. These took place in London during late 1931 at the second RTC session. Gandhi failed to secure a breakthrough in London, at a conference he believed was rigged to prevent communal harmony or real consensus (Legg 2023, 65–98). Having refused to denounce cases of Congress civil disobedience that had emerged in his absence, Gandhi was arrested on the morning of 4 January 1932, and revamped political repression was rolled out.

Local "dictators" replaced the presidents of the criminalized Congress committees and instigated the second phase of the Civil Disobedience movement. By March 1932 the movement began to die down as the Hindu, urban, educated elite were arrested and disorganized. From prison Gandhi managed to overturn the "Communal Award" plans for separate electorates for untouchables by undergoing a fast to the death. The movement continued through 1933, but in mid-March 1934 Gandhi assented to Congress members pursuing election to official councils and thus the Swaraj Party was reborn, civil disobedience formally concluded, and a further round of discussions began.

DELHI DISOBEDIENCE

Before moving on to the analytics of the Delhi movement, the basic outlines and background to Civil Disobedience in the city can be set. While revolutionary spectacles in Delhi attracted most attention in 1929, there had also been an increase in the tempo and range of Congress activity. On 5 February Jawaharlal Nehru addressed over two hundred students in Delhi, encouraging them to form a union to represent their views.[1] The Congress Student and Youth League (SYL) was formed as a result, with Muhammad Asaf Ali and J. N. Sahni as president and vice president. A mock parliament was held on 17 February, involving a roll call of Delhi's most important politicians, featuring Diwan (Chair) Chaman Lal, J. N. Sahni as vice president, Muhammad Asaf Ali as prime minister, Professor Indra, Deshbandhu Gupta, and others representing the Labour Party, Hasan Niazmi representing the Conservative Party, and none other than St. Stephen's teacher and historian of Delhi T. G. Percival Spear as home minister.[2] In a meeting on 7 March, Motilal Nehru and Pandit Madan Mohan Malaviya lit a bonfire of foreign cloth and announced a procession for Swaraj Day on 10 March (Sahni 1971, 57). Over six thousand people attended the Swaraj celebrations, including many students who could now be tapped through the SYL, and a growing number of government clerks.[3]

Despite a lull of activity in the summer of 1929, Congress reasserted itself in anticipation of the first Independence Day celebrations of 26 January 1930. Public meetings throughout the city and door-to-door visits by prominent female workers complemented the plans for the day itself, published in the *Hindustan Times* over a week in advance. The full program was published on 25 January, promising a procession, political readings, and a public flag-hoisting at 8:00 a.m., after which people were encouraged to return to their homes and hoist individual flags on their own houses at 10:00 a.m. The stress on the home and the community would recur throughout the Civil Disobedience campaign and helped ensure the celebrations were, as the deputy superintendent of police reported on 29 January 1930, "actually a great success."[4] In the morning Shankar Lal's affiliate Arif Hasvi unfurled the Congress tricolor flag, in front of at least seven hundred people. The SYL, HSRA-affiliated Naujawan Bharat Sabha (NBS), Congress's volunteer organization the Hindustani Seva Dal (HSD), and the laborers' Mazdur Sabha (labor's society) encouraged their members to join in.[5] The emergence for the first time of Delhi's women in mass numbers all contributed to the success of the afternoon procession of an estimated twelve to fifteen thousand people, which terminated in Queen's Gardens (see figure 3.1).[6] While the event itself lasted only a few days, the chief commissioner felt sure that it was another landmark in Delhi's political development, noting on file on 29 January: "In my view the Congress, so far as Delhi is concerned, made a very big step forward; and what happens in Delhi nowadays does have an important influence elsewhere. Congress has been very feeble here of late years, and I think Shankar Lal was probably quite genuine in his expressed delight with the unique results of the day when he said in his speech that these results transcended anything else in his 17 to 18 years experience as a Congress worker."[7]

Following the suspension of Civil Disobedience in March 1931, the chief commissioner of Delhi noted a "swing to the left" within the Delhi District Congress Committee (DDCC) and tensions between Shankar Lal, who represented the mill hands and workers, and Professor Indra, who represented upper-class Hindus.[8] P. C. Jain later recalled Lal's and Indra's different skill sets and incompatibilities.[9] Lal was credited with having mobilized Delhi's youth in the 1920s, especially the working classes. Indra felt that he lacked a space in Congress, despite having moved toward it after earlier experimentation with the Naujavan Bharat Sabha (Youth Society of India), which had been founded by Bhagat Singh and favored revolutionary methods. A Delhi branch was founded in 1926 by Chaman Lal (Maclean 2015, 105, 114). While Indra was an eloquent public speaker, he couldn't mobilize the public like Lal did, although Lal's talents were not to everyone's liking. Jain suggested Lal had a "Jat-like" (here meaning uncivilized, coarse, or harsh) manner, abusing and chastising followers, who rewarded him with their loyalty. This loyalty collapsed during the jail spells of Civil Disobedience, allowing Indra, Deshbandhu Gupta, and Congress's Hindu right wing to gain influence in the 1930s.

By mid-December 1931 unity was restored as the talks in London foun-

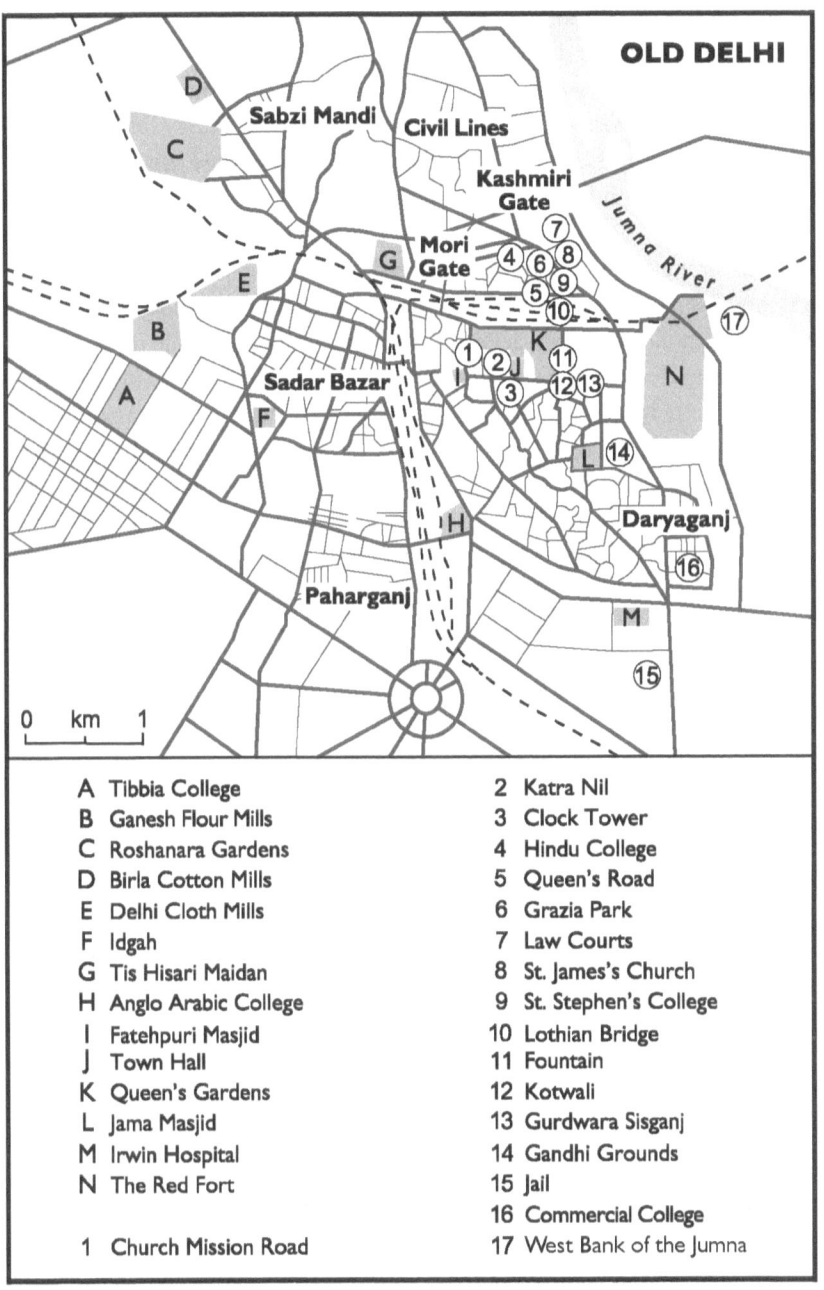

FIGURE 3.1. Old Delhi and Civil Disobedience

dered, leading to a "War Council" being formed by Delhi Congress members that detailed duties to its members for the "coming war."[10] Despite this, Gandhi's arrest seemed to come as a surprise, and on 16 January 1932 the chief commissioner reported that his declaration of the All India Congress Committee (AICC) and the Delhi District Congress Committee (DDCC) as unlawful institutions found "a disunited local Congress which were unprepared and without funds."[11] The following crackdown saw the local administration wield a much strengthened armory of legal and policing weapons to shatter the local movement (Legg 2007, 113–14). The main Delhi figures took up the role of dictator, but all were soon arrested, as the rapid turnover rate of twelve dictators (including three women) in forty-nine days illustrates (Government of India (Secret) 1934): Jugal Kishore Khanna (arrested on 10 January); Srimati Javitri Devi (15 January); Professor Indra (20 January); Farid-ul-Haq Ansari (26 January); Swami Manoharnath (3 February); Mukandlal Johri (4 February); Aruna Asaf Ali (5 February); Durga Das (8 February); Phool Chand Jain (11 February); Rattan Lal Khanna (12 February); Kali Charan (17 February); and Muhammad Asaf Ali (1 March). Beyond this political elite, Civil Disobedience continued, ushering in a new generation of leaders, many of whom would play prominent roles in the next mass movement in the early 1940s.

### Episteme: Truth, Simplicity, and Peace

The Civil Disobedience campaign is nostalgically viewed as the mass mobilization with the greatest consensus over the utility of nonviolence and the least internal divisions over Gandhi's vision of Congress's truth. Two disruptions to this unity were emergent but were overshadowed by the overwhelming success of the movement. First, Civil Disobedience lacked the Hindu-Muslim unity of the Rowlatt satyagraha and the communal cooperation of Non-Cooperation. The communal riots of 1924 had presaged annual conflict in Delhi over religious festivals, and communal organizations did not support the Congress program, although there was still substantial Muslim support. Second, the commitment to nonviolence was fracturing in the face of powerful leftist challengers, who would split Congress in the 1930s. In Delhi the Assembly and viceregal train bombings had stirred interest in revolutionary methods, which Congress had tapped but struggled to reconcile with Gandhi's mission.

For many in Delhi, however, the experiment with nonviolence in the spring of 1930 was adopted enthusiastically. Brij Kishan Chandiwala, who had devoted himself to Gandhi in the 1920s, recalled, "I had reverence for Gandhiji, and whatever he would utter, I would consider it to be right. A passion was born in my heart because of whatever he said against the English."[12] Chandiwala would read *Young India* and relay any of Gandhi's teachings to the people of Delhi, openly admitting to a noncritical application of these teachings. For him (and for J. K. Khanna), the Delhi leadership during Civil Disobedience was largely unchanged from the elite who had emerged in the 1920s and was dominated by Muslims such as Hakim Ajmal Khan, Asaf Ali, Dr. Abdul Rahman, and M. A. Ansari; "It was more-or-less the old people."[13] Many new people came to Delhi in 1930, however, or emerged onto the scene having already been in the city, including Devdas Gandhi, Jugal Kishore Khanna, Memo Bai, Satyavati, Chandiwala, and Radha Raman.[14] But these operated alongside well-established Muslim campaigners, like Dr. M. A. Ansari, Mufti Kifayatullah, and Asaf Ali.

Just as a host of new Congress stars emerged during the 1930 movement, so did new approaches to visualizing and intervening in the city, new political identities, and new problematizations of nonviolence. These would all develop and challenge the Congress episteme, but during the movement itself the main organizers largely conformed to the Gandhian creed. Not many committed their approaches to paper, but a publication by Asaf Ali from 1921 gives us a sense of how one of Delhi's most influential organizers was localizing Gandhi's approach to violence, truth, and the self (see Legg 2018). He would later claim that this was the first work "to give a concrete and positive form to [Gandhi's] non-violent non-cooperation and civil disobedience" (in Raghavan 1994, 26; see also 177–78). Because of this it was dismissed at the time by leading congressmen and Gandhi himself (though he apparently came around to the plan twelve years later; see Raghavan 1994, 178).

Asaf Ali described his seventy-three-page book, titled *Constructive Non-Cooperation*, as "an attempt at non-violent, non-co-operative self-organisation by easy instalments of practical but tentative steps, without coming into violent or any collision with 'the Government established by law in British India'" (M. Asaf Ali 1921, i). In part the plan replicated the broader Non-Cooperation movement, during which it was published, in that it tried to envisage a rival model of political sovereignty within the colonial state that would anticipate and prepare India for full independence. Asaf Ali replicated many of Gandhi's statements from the time (so criticized by Guha 1997). These both stereotyped subaltern groups as prepolitical (Gandhi was depicted as addressing "hunted and vanquished bands of the Indian people" so as to "awaken the slumbering manhood of our country, dispelling the hypnotic spell of national diffidence" [Asaf Ali 1921, 2]) and feared what might result from their politicization (the awakened people would move at "lightning speed" such that "everything should be done to bring moral and social pressure to bear of [sic] our own people to live up to a higher standard of Truth, Simplicity, and Peace" [9, 49]).

The core commitment was to absolute truth, which would be that truth set by Gandhi, namely, nonviolence and satyagraha. The people would need military training so that they might discipline their minds as soldiers do, and to conform to a rigid course of conduct (Asaf Ali 1921, 54). This would require a spatial organization of India that could link the individual up to the highest level of Congress organization (70). Local experiments would be based on traditional village panchayats (councils) and then extended into the cities. Asaf Ali used his home city as an example. Delhi Province was estimated to have a population of 450,000, of whom 100,000 were thought to be children. If the area were divided into twenty-five divisions, each would have four thousand voters (based on adult franchise) who would elect their own representative, who should be a local resident (Asaf Ali 1921, 17). This drew on and fed into Asaf Ali's political campaigns at the time. In a meeting on 17 November 1921, he had laid out the plans for effectively organizing the city: "The city was divided into twelve circles. For each circle was a paid staff of one leader, two advisors and ten volunteers. These would take a census of the people and organise the spinning of cloth. This would take up to three or four weeks. Each area would then refuse to pay any taxes, would ignore the police, magistrates and other officials, but would establish their own police stations and staff."[15]

This was how the truth of Congress would be spread and how the city would be revisualized to enable an anticolonial governmentality that would conduct the conduct of the people, eliciting parrhesiastic subjects who would use the city to reject the state, but to also contest nonviolence as the assumed mode of urban protest.

### Visibility: Seeing the City

Of the hundreds of men and women sentenced during Civil Disobedience, few court transcripts survive. Of those that do, many are blank, due to the refusal of the accused to cooperate with the colonial legal system. Six relatively detailed judgments do survive relating to Delhi. One concerned the trial of "an ordinary bookseller of Khari Baoli in Delhi City," Narain Das Garg.[16] He was prosecuted for having three thousand copies of a pamphlet printed titled *Vilayat men phansi Madan Lal Dhingra ko* (translated for the court as "the execution of Madan Lal Dhingra," the revolutionary who assassinated Sir William Hutt Curzon Wyllie in England on 1 July 1909). Garg was also charged with giving two seditious speeches, in January and February 1930. In the second speech he outlined the challenges involved in mobilizing an urban population in India. He estimated that 20 percent of city populations were government servants (including schoolboys), that 5 percent of urban people were "mad after freedom," but that 4 of these 5 percent had "no means at all." Only 1 percent were thus properly prepared to do everything for India. However, in Delhi, with a population of five lakh (500,000), he estimated that only a hundred or fifty men were ready to make the ultimate sacrifice (presumably because of the greater governmental influence due to it being the capital). Garg politically differentiated the population based on education and means, whereas Civil Disobedience ethically differentiated the population based on parrhesiastic acts. Accessing and encouraging these acts relied on perceptions of Old, and New, Delhi that informed the tactics used to target their spaces, both material and symbolic.

OLD DELHI: THE MOHALLA

The 1920 Nagpur Congress meeting had allowed a national reorganization of Congress institutional oversight, but local bodies also set about their own revisions. It was the duty of local committees to organize the space within their remit—to gather information, knowledge, money, and inspiration from their allotted area and pass this capital back up the geographical network to the coordinating Congress bodies. Outside periods of mass mobilization and radical parrhesia, organizing political space served to recruit volunteers and supporters. Gandhi's unique focus on spinning cloth had provided a new, "constructive" imperative in the 1920s. Rejecting foreign cloth involved a concomitant devotion to spinning khaddar. To spread this message the city had to be effectively organized in order to facilitate Congress propaganda.

Asaf Ali's terminology of spatial demarcations used in 1921 mirrored that of government census operations, which divided territory into "blocks" of around fifty houses, a "circle" of twelve or more blocks, and "charges" of fifteen or more circles. Delhi Province was organized into 3,504 blocks, 316 circles, and 20 charges in 1931, of which 15 were urban (Census of India 1933a, iii). Congress would mirror this means of visualizing the city, but also opposed it on the ground. Having divided Delhi into its fifteen blocks in autumn 1930, the State census enumerators had to then number each individual house. Congress campaigned for the boycotting of the census, resulting in house numbers being wiped out in various parts of the city (Census of India 1933a, iii). During the collection of census data on 26 February 1931, certain Hindu neighborhoods then refused to cooperate with the enumerators, while volunteers picketed the house of a prominent Congress politician so that no information could be collected. Census organizers also had trouble finding people to carry out the unpopular work of enumeration; of the thirty-five members of the municipality who should have helped, only five came forward.

Congress worked to bring the city within its purview through its own organization but also through tapping student organizations to the north of the walled city, labor organizations to the west in Sabzi Mandi, and women's organizations that targeted the home. But Civil Disobedience also gave Congress an opportunity to test its penetration of the city and further encourage this countercartography of the city. A Congress Bulletin for Delhi on 17 June 1930 stressed the need to reorganize the very way the city was conceived, including its dependence on foreign imports and its reliance on the colonial government for settling civil disputes. Panchayats could be organized for the latter, while "mohalla clubs" could be established where the "uninstructed may meet educated peoples for social intercourse."[17]

Mohallas were urban communities, often walled and gated, that traditionally had emerged around noble houses, castes, or professions (Masselos, 1976; Legg, 2019). They were established, coherent units for political campaigning, with Abdul Rahman Siddiqui (2011, 18) recalling his father defeating his great-uncle in 1930 municipal elections after heavy campaigning in his home mohalla; in reward the kutcha (unfinished) roads were paved during his tenure. The same mohalla, Haveli Haider Quli in Ballimaran, was haunted by traces of previous political incursions. A black-doored basement room known as *khilafat* "conjured up for us a djinn or ghost" but was actually the old mohalla headquarters of the Khilafat Committee, "a hideout for the mohalla khilafat workers to hold their secret meeting in support of the Turkish caliphate and against British Imperialism" (Siddiqi, 2011, 23). From the 1920s Congress established their own "offices" in mohallas across the city, although Phool Chand Jain admitted that offices were not specially rented buildings. Rather, "Whoever was a good Congress activist in a ward would put up a board in front of his house that there is a Congress Committee office here, but it was just limited to a board. If we say that we organized and made an office in a muhalla then usually this wasn't the case, there were certainly 2–4 exceptions."[18]

Using these networks, in their June 1930 bulletin the DDCC suggested that "if meetings were organised in a methodological manner in each Mohalla, one educated and experienced person could impart 'Liberal' education to the whole mohalla in a month." By 27 August this process was well underway. In an account summarizing the month's activities, M. A. Ansari's nephew, F. K.

Ansari, reported to the All India Congress Committee that "meetings were arranged in every Mohalla to organise Congress Committees and Seva Dal batches in different parts of the city. Now there are two Congress Committees and 15 volunteer corps in the city. All these corps are affiliated to the Hindustani Seva Dal [HSD] and are given training in the Queen's Garden every morning. The Mohalla Congress Committees have rendered valuable help in the social boycott of liquor vendors."[19]

This system would be targeted, especially during the harsher crackdown of the second phase of disobedience. With the local offices seized, Congress had to utilize alternate spaces. A CID weekly summary on 22 January 1932 reported that fifty Congress volunteers were being accommodated in dharmsalas (rest houses for pilgrims) since its offices had been seized.[20] On 9 January intelligence reports had suggested the disobedience program had been discussed in Professor Indra's house, on 25 January that female workers met in the house of Memo Bai in Katra Nil, while when national Congress president "C Raj Gopal Achariya" (Rajagopalachari) visited Delhi in January he stayed in Birla House in New Delhi.[21] A CID source reported that he complained about the lack of work in Delhi, suggesting the city had once been the foremost in India for Congress work but was now the most backward. This neglected the substantial work done by Delhi activists, but Rajagopalachari's conclusion that Government repression had already triumphed was one that would increasingly be shared in the city as the second round of disobedience played out.

### NEW DELHI: A TERRIBLE CONTRAST

New Delhi was very explicitly designed to present a vision to the world of what a new, third British Empire might look like. Congress targeted this vision discursively, in planned attacks, and on the ground. In terms of the imperial discourse on the new capital, both local and national commentators questioned the aesthetics of New Delhi and the means by which it was constructed. Gandhi himself often referred to the new capital as a general representation of the British Government, not in all its imperial glory but as a parasite. On 27 December 1926 he referred to the new city at Raisina as being built with blood money and that "instead of the blood circulating down to the feet, it is all being sucked by the head. Presently there will meningitis and ——!" (Gandhi 1999, 37:450). On 28 April 1927 he reproduced in the journal *Young India* a letter written to him describing the condition of workers involved in constructing New Delhi. The "terrible contrast" was highlighted between the palaces and the huts to which the Assembly members appeared oblivious, a contrast symptomatic of the disease that was destroying the lives of thousands of people (38:322).

While on tour in England after the Round Table Conference, on 18 October 1931, Gandhi declared how little hesitation he would have in depriving the Government of its houses in New Delhi, claiming, "The extravagance of the Princes was nothing compared to the heartless squandering of crores of rupees on New Delhi to satisfy the whim of a Viceroy to reproduce England in India, when masses of people were dying of hunger" (Gandhi 1999, 54:46). A month later, on 19 November, he would refer to New Delhi as a "white elephant" and suggest that an Indian national government would convert the buildings so that their function represented the whole country, not the elite, such as hospitals to tend for the ill from Old Delhi (54:180). While Gandhi drew attention to the capital, he used it as an example of broader imperialism. Local activists, however, engaged with the vision and materiality of New Delhi and its Indian workers in effective, if forgotten, ways.

On 15 March 1930, two weeks before the start of Civil Disobedience, the Lahore-based *Tribune* newspaper reported plans to "Capture Viceregal Lodge," a "symbol of foreign domination," as soon as Gandhi was arrested.[22] Each province would be asked to send nonviolent soldiers to Delhi, arriving on alternate days, "until the Lodge is occupied and the country made free." A report from the Home Department's Intelligence Bureau on 18 March noted that the idea of a satyagraha attack on the "Viceregal Lodge" (viceroy's house) was not new and had been proposed at the last Congress Working Committee meeting.[23] While Gandhi would lead his volunteers to the seacoast at Dandi, Jawaharlal Nehru would march on Delhi. The plans were blocked for fear of detracting attention from Dandi, but the two keenest advocates, Jamnalal Bajaj and Sardul Singh Caveeshar, revived the proposal as a response to Gandhi's arrest.

Bajaj was an industrialist and nationalist, while Sardul Singh had played a prominent role in organizing protests before and after the First World War against the destruction of the Gurdwara Rakabganj wall during the construction of New Delhi (see Singh 1972, 198–220).[24] In April 1921 Sardul Singh had sent out a call in *Ali*, the popular Punjabi newspaper, for volunteers to march to Delhi to rebuild the wall of the sacred gurdwara. However, before the volunteers, rumored to be seven hundred strong, assembled, the Government rebuilt the wall itself.

Fifteen years later Sardul Singh was still focused on Raisina and similar tactics, but this time his attention was on the completed Government buildings.

In a letter to Jawaharlal Nehru on 13 March, Sardul Singh suggested that the idea of targeting the lodge was originally Gandhi's or Bajaj's, while the march, of an expected seven thousand Akali (reformist) Sikhs to Delhi, was his. Despite the newspaper talk of "making the country free," the intelligence report acknowledged that the taking of the Lodge was unlikely and that the object of the march would be civil disobedience propaganda, to instigate a tax nonpayment campaign and rouse villagers on the way, while the firing or use of force by the Delhi police would further strengthen the satyagrahi's claims to moral superiority. Gandhi himself recalled in August 1940 his dismissal of Bajaj's suggestion, stressing that the salt march was for the millions, not an attack on the elite (Gandhi 1999, 79:124). While doubting the money and support behind the scheme, the Government seriously considered such plans because Gandhi had recently shifted his position to accept the simultaneous starting of the Civil Disobedience movement in different places. The Home Department forwarded the intelligence report to the chief commissioner on 26 March warning that the "absurd proposal" could be revived in the future (see Legg 2007, 95). While the plans were never realized, their discussion highlights Congress's awareness, to the highest level, of the importance of the vision of New Delhi and its symbolic potential, which was as fragile as it was overawing. This became apparent in the plans to target the capital that were put into action.

### Techne: Crafting the Political City

#### NEW DELHI: TARGETING THE CAPITAL

New Delhi came under attack as a vision, the avatar of high imperialism that embodied broader ideology and institutions, but also as an institutional and material space, filled with the machinery of government that could actively be targeted. While in Old Delhi confrontations depended on the large-scale presence and participation of those who lived in the city, this would never be the case within the capital; Eric Hobsbawm ([1973] 1994) suggested that there were few places less likely for a riot than New Delhi. As a space of conscription and audience participation for nationalists, New Delhi was dysfunctional. The elite population and heavy policing made meetings and recruitment difficult, though not impossible. And the combination of high demand for foreign cloth and liquor meant that, despite their efforts, Delhi's Congress Committee admitted that they were freely available in the Civil Lines and New Delhi.[25]

While picketing was a failure, the symbolic capital of New Delhi was so rich that a few successful assaults were made. For example, on 24 April 1930

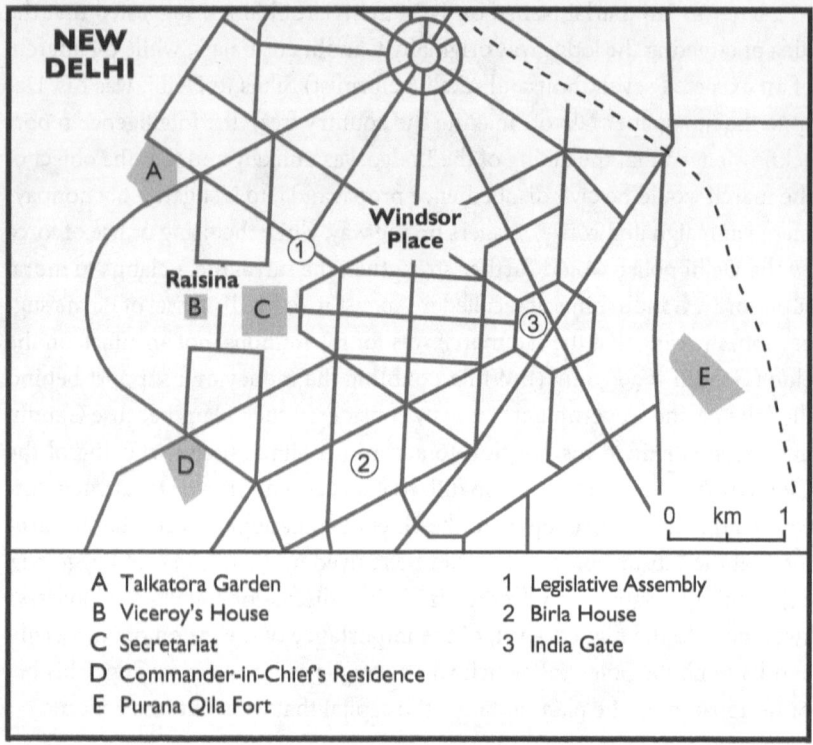

**FIGURE 3.2.** Civil Disobedience and New Delhi

the *Hindustan Times* ran a story on its front page stating "Police Assault Delhi Volunteer: Satyagraha before Assembly Chamber."[26] The account told of seven volunteers who tried to make salt in front of the Legislative Assembly (see figure 3.2). Twelve policemen attempted to remove the vessels used for boiling the salt water, leading to several volunteers receiving scalds and burns to their hands. Late July saw protest meetings in New Delhi's gurdwaras, following the Sisganj incident (see chapter 4).[27] And toward the end of September the New Delhi government was accused of desecrating and burning Muslim tombs and bones on the site of the new Irwin Hospital in the northeast of the capital.[28]

The Legislative Assembly was picketed again in early January 1931 in an attempt to dissuade members, especially the acting president, Mr. Chetty, from participating in certain debates.[29] Mr. Chetty's home in Windsor Place was also targeted, as the viceroy witnessed when driving past on 14 January.[30] While these attempts did attract press and police attention, such success was almost always temporary. Attempts to find spacious bungalows in the new capital in which to house visiting nationalists, so as to take the pressure off Dr. Ansari's abode in Daryaganj, proved fruitless.[31]

The youth of the capital also became involved. On 3 May 1930 the local authorities had to write to the headmaster of the Municipal Board High School to complain about his students parading through the clerks' quarters in the northwest of New Delhi waving the national flag, singing songs, and making "anti-government demonstrations."[32] This was where the less spacious and lower-status accommodation of the capital was located, at the bottom of a counterclockwise spiral from the vast compounds south of Kingsway to the residences of officers, European clerks, Indian clerks, and peons who kept the vast bureaucratic machinery ticking over. The Indian employees housed here regularly petitioned and complained about their accommodation and the inherent racial hierarchies structuring the city (see Legg 2007, 66–75). But they also joined in more political protests.

In March 1929 Delhi's chief commissioner had written to the home secretary, responding to a query about the attendance of government servants at political meetings.[33] He responded that the attendance of clerks and other government servants had been noticeable at recent events. These included the Swaraj Day celebrations of 10 March 1929, at which processions before the meeting of six thousand people had carried banners proclaiming, as translated in the file, "Swaraj cannot be achieved without much sacrifice" and "There is no sin in breaking laws framed by human beings, for the protection of the word of God." The superintendent of the CID had provided, a week after the meeting, the names of fourteen government servants who had attended the meeting. They included clerks from the Indian Stores Department, New Delhi Post Office, and the Public Works Department, as well as the head clerk from the Royal Air Force office in the capital. Government employees attended the Independence Day celebrations of 26 January 1930 in much larger numbers. The CID reported the roles and names of each attendee, listed by their office. From the Public Works Department alone there were overseers, central accounting clerks, horticultural division overseers, a meter reader, a storekeeper, and an electrician. During the Civil Disobedience campaign itself the surveillance would increase, not just over government workers but also over their families. A Congress procession in July 1930 was noted to have included two daughters and the wife of an accountant for the Superintendent of Survey and Land Records, the daughter and wife of a treasurer, the wife of a booking clerk for the North Western Railway, and "three women of" the surveying station master of Shahdara. Evidence was, in most cases, insufficient to press charges, but the surveillance itself gives some sense of the growing support for Congress in the capital.

While the 1932 movement was not as popular in New Delhi as it had been in 1930, it did score one spectacular success. While Congress withdrew from the Round Table Conference with the return to civil disobedience, the conference work continued. Three traveling commissions of inquiry visited India in the spring of 1932 on fact-finding missions. They were the subject of a Delhi Congress Office Bulletin dated 2 February 1932 titled "Smokescreen to Deceive the World: But the World Can See Through It All."[34] The purpose of the constitutional reforms was said to be to "hide the dark deeds of the British Government in India." Particular ire was saved for Lord Lothian, the chair of the Franchise and Finance Commission, and his commissioners, who were described as "foes speaking the language of friends." The voice of the Indian nation, it was said, would roar through the gory and gaping wounds inflicted on Mother India. In contrast, the bulletin suggested, addressing the "Indian Moderates" cooperating with Lothian: "Your lungs are small and you will appeal only in gasps in your Committee Rooms. But your minds are smaller still! Nothing is expected of them. But we have the consolation that you will disappoint nobody! Don't look back, lest you see your Mother writhing in agony! No don't, that will—will it?—distract you."[35]

Lothian was due to be ceremoniously welcomed in New Delhi on Saturday, 30 February, ahead of meetings on the capital. During the previous night "LOTHIAN GO BACK" was stenciled across large portions of the Council Chamber and the Memorial Arch (India Gate) at either end of Kingsway. The *Hindustan Times* gleefully reported: "Workmen were kept busy the whole of Saturday washing stencilled marks in black letters, 'Go back Lothian!' with patrol [sic], Kerosene oil and water which were found all round the Council House part of the Secretariat and the War Memorial. Over the War Memorial, a large flag bearing the same words was also seen flying this morning. The flag was promptly removed. It took workmen many hours to clear the marks from the walls of the Council House."[36]

Radha Raman, an "old stalwart of Congress" (Chopra 1974, 312) who had been active since the Non-Cooperation movement, was eventually convicted for the offense, although the Government recorded a Congress flag being flown from the arch rather than a Lothian flag, while Bhagwan Sarai, younger brother of the long-serving congressman Shankar Lal, was suspected but never convicted of orchestrating the endeavor (Government of India [Secret] 1934, B18). Delhi Congress Bulletin no. 178 on 1 April would report on

"Lothian's trail of blood": "A wave of popular indignation, black flags, bullets, lathis, arrests; these are the signs by which the movements of Lothian and company can be traced throughout India."[37]

The Legislative Assembly was further targeted when picketing infiltrated the building itself. On 4 February 1932 Musammat Devi was arrested for throwing pamphlets in the Legislative Assembly in New Delhi.[38] This followed a decision on 8 February 1932 to switch picketing to New Delhi from the old city; volunteers formed a procession that moved between the two cities, terminating at Connaught Place.[39] After their lunch break on 18 February, Assembly members gathered in the lobby only to have the official whip himself picketed by INC volunteers who pleaded with legislative members to abstain from official business. The quorum of twenty-five members necessary to constitute the Assembly was not satisfied and thus the session had to adjourn.[40]

There was also evidence of New Delhi's workers being targeted. A poster from September 1932 titled "duty of government employees" suggested they look around at the lathis and rifles being used to break heads and make the ground gory with the blood of their compatriots.[41] In the face of a flagging movement the poster attempted to stress Delhi's significance both nationally and historically to political struggle. In terms of the former, amid a list of national figures such as Gandhi, Nehru, and Sarojini Naidu was listed Delhi's Satyavati, placing her (and therefore the city) on a pedestal with the nation's finest. Historically, the contribution of everyday people to the uprising of 1857, to which Delhi made such a vital contribution, was stressed, and used to ask "WHAT do you propose to do in the PRESENT NON-VIOLENT WAR OF INDEPENDENCE?" Government employees were told that participation in the struggle, refusing to participate in "inhuman atrocities committed on your brethren," and contributing 50 percent of their income to the national fund was the minimum demand of them: "SEE THAT YOU DO NOT LAG BEHIND YOUR BRAVE SIRES OF 1857! THIS IS THE CHANCE! THIS IS THE CHANCE! NOW OR NEVER IS YOUR WATCHWORD!" Unlike the first phase, there is little evidence of government employees participating in 1932; the majority of mobilization took place around the old city, reviving the templates established in 1930.

## OLD DELHI: MAKING PUBLIC SPACE

In the month between the beginning of Civil Disobedience (5 April) and Gandhi's arrest (4–5 May), many of the techniques that would be used to territorialize and deterritorialize the city through nonviolent means were established. While the local Muslim population remained largely aloof and the police felt that the subaltern "underworld" had been kept in check, the par-

**FIGURE 3.3.** Swadeshi League Procession in Delhi. Courtesy of the British Library Board (Asia, Pacific and Africa SM 27, *Hindustan Times*, 27/2/1932)

ticipation of Delhi was remarkably successful. Organizers played on memory (especially of 1919), and daily rituals were created through meetings, flag-raisings, songs, and, particularly, the community work of women and the role of the newspapers (see figure 3.3 for a view of a later Swadeshi League procession passing through Delhi, led by women workers of the league, carrying placards advocating the use of swadeshi goods, and figure 3.4 for a depiction of leading female workers of the Swadeshi League, who had partaken in the procession and a public meeting, with the first figure on the left being Mrs. J. N. Sahni, who presided over the meeting). Photos of women filled the pages of the *Hindustan Times*, Delhi's English-language nationalist newspaper (alongside the *Arjun* in Hindi, edited by Professor Indra, and the *Tej* in Urdu; see Jain 2010, 17). The processions themselves were also spaces of artistic creativity depending on the focus of protests each day. P. C. Jain recalled "jail day" processions including demonstrations of jail cells and prisoners in jail uniforms, carrying dressed "dummies," adorning carts with pictures, and mocking the police, each procession reminding the watching crowds that the movement was alive and well.[42]

FIGURE 3.4. Swadeshi League Procession in Delhi. Courtesy of the British Library Board (Asia, Pacific and Africa SM 27, *Hindustan Times*, 27/2/1932)

The newspapers did not simply report on such public rituals; they scripted performances and advocated political acts. Through describing the songs, poems, actions, and speeches of particular meetings, and describing where and when the next meeting would take place, the activities of organizing Congress minorities were presented as both the standard and the ideal the population should normalize and aspire to.[43] Salt production was also key, the location of its manufacture (by the River Jumna) adding extra drama and religious significance for the (mostly Hindu and Sikh) participants. All these locations provided testing grounds for nonviolence, through breaking the law and placing protesting bodies between the lawbreakers and the police.

Particular sites were central to publicly and symbolically claiming the city, none more so than Queen's Gardens, the site of a mass meeting after a procession of over 350 supporters on "Civil Disobedience Day" on 12 March to mark the beginning of Gandhi's trek to Dandi.[44] The program for National Week was published in advance in the *Hindustan Times* and drew on the history of processions in Delhi and the more recent anticolonial struggle. It was declared in print that eleven years after the Rowlatt disturbances of 6 April 1919, "history had repeated itself" as Delhi again "did itself proud" in its range of protest activities.⁴⁵ The activities began with an early morning meeting at Queen's Gardens, a flag-raising by Shankar Lal, and song recitals by prominent female volunteers.

Being a landlocked province, Delhi could not easily produce salt, but Shankar Lal announced that a jatha (a small group, usually associated with Sikh processions) of volunteers would use a patch of saline marsh water on the banks of the Jumna. P. C. Jain recalled salt being made from soil on the west bank of the Jumna at Salimgarh, next to the fort.⁴⁶ Chandiwala suggested that the main salt production camp was established at Loni Village at Shahdara, on the east bank of the Jumna across from Old Delhi.⁴⁷ Jathas toured Chandni Chowk and the area around Fatehpuri Mosque before heading across the river, returning in the early afternoon with packs of "contraband" salt that were sold throughout the city. J. N. Sahni (1971, 72) recalled that hundreds of people followed the procession to the river in which the inedible mixture of "sand, salt and putrid soil" was produced, all under the surveillance of the assistant district magistrate and senior superintendent of the CID. A second batch of volunteers paraded through the entire city then left for the river at 3:00 p.m., returning for the mass meeting in Queen's Gardens at 6:00 p.m., during which Pandit Madan Mohan Malaviya addressed a reported twenty thousand people.

As these events showed no sign of abating over the following days, the police began the confiscation of illegally produced salt. Reporting the events of 8 April, the *Hindustan Times* headline proclaimed "Delhi Satyagrahis Triumph over Police Violence: Exhibition of Police Raj" after a disturbance at Shahdara. Superintendent Bishan Singh of a nearby police post reported that about nine volunteers had arrived at 11:00 a.m. and were joined by a crowd of 125 by 1:00 p.m.⁴⁸ The volunteers linked arms and formed a cordon around the salt solution. As the police broke the cordon, Singh reported that a "scrummage" of "regular wrestling" ensued as the unarmed police attempted to confiscate the salt. The struggle lasted an hour, during which the *Hindustan Times* claimed that volunteers reacted nonviolently, even when manhandled and dragged through brambles and scrub.⁴⁹

At 4:00 p.m., the daily time set to stop production, the two-hundred-strong crowd carried the salt and injured volunteers back to the city, passing the withdrawn police and proclaiming victory, singing "Bande Mataram" (the Congress anthem) and "Mahatma Gandhi Ki Jai" (Victory to Mahatma Gandhi). A daily ritual became established: volunteers were dispatched to the river, demonstrations were held on the waterfront, the produce was carried to the city and paraded through the streets, then the crowd was channeled into Queen's Gardens. Unsuccessful attempts were made to attract Muslim support through reports of a volunteer's Qur'an being snatched from him. The Jama Masjid Committee denounced this as Congress mischievousness and rebuked the man for taking the Qur'an with him, the chief commissioner claimed in a telegram to the government in Simla on 10 April.[50] The chief commissioner remained concerned, however, that Congress would tap into a wider, subaltern spectrum of the city, writing to the home secretary on 10 April:

> I do not like the demonstrations at night in front of the Kotwali. The Kotwal, a tough Khatri from the NWFP [North Western Frontier Province], who knows Delhi well, is evidently rather worried about them.[51] But up to the present there is no sign of the *emergence of the underworld*. The Muhammadans are holding aloof, with the result that Muslim hooligans (the worst element of the population) have not stirred, though efforts are being made to get at them. But we must keep pace with the movement and be careful to check developments, so that they may not gather head.[52]

On 9 April a procession was met by 180 armed police who arrested more than thirty Congress leaders including Devadas Gandhi, Shankar Lal, Deshbandhu Gupta, Dr. Yudhvir Singh, Radha Raman, Mahomed Arif Hasvi, Fariq-ul-Haq Ansari, and Durga Das Vaid.[53] A huge protest meeting of an estimated fifteen thousand assembled in Queen's Gardens at which the few remaining Delhi leaders spoke, while a hartal the next day drew up to seventy thousand people onto the street. However, for the next fortnight there would be few large demonstrations or successes. Congress workers attempted to capitalize on a Delhi Cloth Mills strike between 23 and 26 April. Although 3,721 out of 5,686 workers went on strike, the grievances and settlements were all internal to the factory.

The movement flared again on 5 May when news of Gandhi's arrest reached Delhi. The events of that day came to focus around a shooting incident at the Gurdwara Sisganj, the reverberations of which were so significant they are treated separately in chapter 4. After this flare-up, protests continued at a community scale (as explored in the next section) as broader attention turned to preparations for the opening of the RTC in London. The arrest of further senior members of Congress in Bombay led to huge processions and meetings on 4 August that deployed the by-now-traditional routine. This included a 7:00 a.m. flag-raising, smaller processions through the streets announcing a hartal, and a larger procession in the afternoon with the special feature of a massive charkha (spinning wheel) to parade (reminiscent of that from 1922, depicted in chapter 2, as discussed below). Finally, an evening meeting was organized, which the *Hindustan Times* suggested seventy-five thousand people attended (figure 3.5 depicts volunteers carrying national flags and other mottos during the Hartal Day procession in Delhi). The prospect of further trouble after 16 September, when "Independence Week" was planned to start, led the local authorities to declare the Congress Committee and the Satyagraha Ashram unlawful associations. The confiscation of their buildings and the arrest of 109 members marked the first of a regular series of provocation arrests that would continue until the pact of 1931. Jawaharlal Nehru Day on 6 November led to a spate of arrests, as did the processions celebrating Satyavati's release from prison on the 26th. Protests against women's jail conditions in late December led to a surge of arrests over Christmas while intensified picketing during January 1931 and the release of more political prisoners led to further conflict.

**FIGURE 3.5.** Mammoth procession on Hartal Day in Delhi. Courtesy of the British Library Board (Asia, Pacific and Africa SM 27, *Hindustan Times*, 7/8/1930)

The final mass event of the first Civil Disobedience period was on 26 January. As Gandhi walked free, the *Hindustan Times* reported that Delhi was "Decorated from End to End."[54] The DDCC demonstrated that the routine of interaction it had established with the Delhi population was one of not only protest but also celebration. To encourage people to show their support, early morning rounds of the city were made at 8:00 a.m., a "mammoth procession" undertaken at 2:00 p.m., and an evening meeting held in Queen's Gardens at 6:00 p.m., at which the crowds were congratulated for their support in more than a year of concerted effort and told to celebrate the movement of the freedom struggle into a new stage of dialogue.

The second round of Civil Disobedience in Delhi from January 1932 followed the set pattern. After the initial peak of 505 arrests in the first month and a half, due to Gandhi's arrest and Independence Day on 26 January, the local movement slowly faded. Liquor picketing was reported on 19 March and 15 May, while salt was produced during a protest on 12 March.[55] A Congress Bulletin for the "Gandhi Day" protests on 4 March encouraged students to abandon their "petty exams" and participate in the greater examination of their country, to shake off their lethargy and come onto the streets in the thousands, organizing flag salutations in every city ward at 8:00 a.m., processing all day long through different wards before converging at the clock tower at 6:00 p.m.[56] The CID log for that week reported a meeting of five hundred people but little more.[57] More concerted efforts were announced in a bulletin of 5 April, outlining plans to celebrate National Week from 6 to 13 April, the first date commemorating the turning of Jallianwala Bagh into a "lake of blood by the WHITE MILITARY," the latter the Rowlatt Acts and Swami Shraddhanand's stand against them in Delhi.[58] The full repertoire of urban protest was outlined, with each day having a theme and time-tabled events:

- 6 April, Swadeshi Day: 8:00 a.m. flag salutations in every ward; 9:00–4:00 p.m. foreign cloth boycotts; 6:00 p.m. processions urging boycott; 7:00 p.m. boycotts of foreign cloth in every ward
- 7 April, Khadi Day: 8:00 a.m.–4:00 p.m. hawking of khadi and taking khadi pledges; 1:00 p.m.–3:00 p.m. charkha and takli competitions; 5:00 p.m. khadi procession
- 8 April, Sugar Day: 8:00 a.m.–4:00 p.m. pledges against foreign sugar; 4:00 p.m. picket sugar dealers not signing Congress pledge
- 9 April, Petrol and Kerosene Day: 8:00 a.m.–5:00 p.m. propaganda against use of British petrol and kerosene
- 10 April, Drugs Day: propaganda with chemists and doctors against using British drugs

- 11 April, Personal Household Goods, Office Requisites, Tobacco, Tea, and Coffee Day: 8:00 a.m.–5:00 p.m. pledges by traders and users to not use British manufactures of such goods
- 12 April, Women and Children Day: 8:00 a.m.–5:00 p.m., women to collect pledges, hold demonstrations, distribute leaflets, and process through the city in *kesaria* (saffron) dress
- 13 April, Jallianwala Bagh Day: 8:00 a.m. flag-hoisting in all wards; 9:00 a.m.–11:00 a.m., manufacture contraband salt in different wards; 4:00 p.m. bare-headed procession; 6:00 p.m. bare-headed mass meeting and two-minute silence

The CID reported the week as a political failure. Although a thousand people attended the concluding procession and some bricks were thrown at the police, the crowd was dispersed with only nineteen arrests being made.[59] The last major event of the movement was the All India Congress Session that was held in Delhi on 24 April, having been arranged by secret invite (Sahni 1971, 101).[60] People flocked to Delhi from all over India, estimated in the CID weekly report at 800 people, including 220 Sikhs and 360 delegates.[61] Huge numbers were arrested as a preventative police measure, causing the *Hindustan Times* to report on 24 April: "Earlier in the day Delhi presented an appearance of what must be described as a war-camp rather than a peaceful city."[62] A procession from the Gurdwara Sisganj had led the police away from the kotwali down to a bluff meeting on the banks of the Jumna. The proximity of the Sisganj to the kotwali was exploited, as was the passionate connection Akali Sikhs felt for the building after the 1930 shooting. In a letter the following day to the Government, the chief commissioner reported, "Things started with a stir and buzzing in the Sisganj Gurdwara, and eventually a big Sikh jatha . . . emerged, carrying one Congress and one Akali flag, and began to demonstrate very determinedly against the kotwali, making a great noise. Crowds commenced to gather in consequence, and there were all the elements of an ugly situation."[63]

They were all arrested, removing the threat of the "pests" to the kotwali, and the focus moved into the center of the old city. Through prearrangement and lanes of communication, the session was held at the Ghanta Ghar (clock tower) in Chandni Chowk. L. C. Jain (2010, 25–26) recalled Congress organizing a large *baraat* (celebratory procession) with music and dancing that stopped at the Ghanta Ghar for half an hour. When the police were distracted, a volunteer reportedly found their way into the clock tower, climbed the staircase, and hoisted the Congress flag. The "national anthem" was sung, speeches made, and initial resolutions passed, although the police descended before business could be concluded.[64] The sub-inspector asked some of the main delegates to surrender themselves and enter the police lorry. As they did so, two dozen supporters were reported to have jumped on top of the lorry and started waving the resolutions to the police. Arrests continued throughout the morning, including those of batches of women from Delhi's "respectable families."[65] Although arrests would continue until the new year, a bulletin from 15 May struck a quietly desperate tone, circulating this hymn:

> From all that terror teaches
>
> From lies of tongue and pen
>
> From all the easy speeches
>
> That comfort cruel men
>
> From sale and profanation
>
> Of honour and the sword
>
> From sleep and from damnation
>
> Deliver us, good Lord.[66]

## OLD DELHI: MAKING COMMUNITY SPACE

The account of Civil Disobedience so far has been of activities at a grand scale, in clashes, large meetings, processions, and arrests. In terms of temporal and spatial scale, the attention has been overwhelmingly on the occasional and on central public spaces. This tends to focus on power as possessed by elite groups, whether hegemonic or not, deployed to rouse or suppress the masses, not on the political initiatives of the subaltern themselves.

Following the arrests between March and May 1930 and the shootings on 6 May, the focus in Delhi moved from the concentrated to the dispersed. This was not the discovery of a new mode of functioning but the reliance on the scale and range of activities that predated and supported monumental acts of confrontation. While Chandni Chowk was an essential political theater, relatively few people lived and dwelled on the street itself. Beyond the grand bazaar lived the people who thronged into the streets and produced the politics that Congress organizers were desperate to tap into and discipline. Two main techniques were used: the first was to make salt, and the second to stop the purchase of foreign cloth and liquor.

During the initial stages of Civil Disobedience, the production of salt did not only take place at the riverside. Salt water was carried into the city in large cauldrons and boiled next to the clock tower in Chandni Chowk.[67] However, by the end of National Week, salt production had multiplied throughout the city. This was part of an attempt to tap into popular support, recruit people into the movement, and systematize Congress support throughout the city, rather than simply scoring high-profile demonstrations in the main bazaars. The chief commissioner, to whom this seemed illogical, reported on 12 April 1930, "Today such demonstrations as were made, were made by small, disconnected groups, indicating some absence of unified control."[68] On the contrary, it was because of the burgeoning system of citywide control that within two days the police were investigating cases of salt production in over twenty separate places throughout the city. On 17 April protesters produced salt outside the jail in which those arrested on 9 April were being tried, while the *Hindustan Times* reported salt production in Minto-Dennis Park near Kashmiri Gate on the same day. On 21 April the paper reported that production had percolated into finer scales within communities:

> Every day the satyagrahis who make contraband salt in the city are changing their "field of operation." Today they have gone to Subzi Mandi, with Mr Idris as their head. It is believed that the frequent change of places has been attended by an appreciable success in their programme in so far at least as the propaganda work in favour of breaking salt laws is concerned. Enquiries at the Congress office go to show that the number of private homes in which contraband salt is made is daily increasing.[69]

This flitting between "fields of operation" shows Congress refusing to be drawn into the spaces of police violence. These temporary re- and deterritorializations helped give Congress a sense of omnipotence throughout the city. The *Hindustan Times* reported on 26 April that salt production had taken place near the Law Courts at Kashmiri Gate on the 23rd and in Maliwara on the 24th, and would take place at Lahore Gate the next day. Delhi Administration daily telegrams to the Home Department reported a small jatha of five men touring the city and making salt on 18 April, two small parties making salt on the 24th, and some very slight manufacture on the 25th.[70] The sites of salt production were mobile, but so were the sites of sale. During National Week the "Satyagraha Party" toured the city with banners advertising their sale of "contraband salt" in the city's bazaars.

This period also, however, saw attention shift away from salt production to the picketing of liquor and foreign cloth distributors. The chief commissioner noted this shift, from 15 April onward, and suspected its aim was to attract more students. He also noted that the salt campaign seemed to be failing to retain the interest of the public, to the extent that on 13 April C. Krishna Nair had to cancel the auctioning of salt manufactured by Gandhi himself due to inadequate bidding.⁷¹ The picketing of retailers of foreign cloth was dominated by women, with Gandhi preferring women for this role because nonviolent picketing, unlike salt production, was less likely to result in arrest (and disrupt their roles as mothers and wives).⁷² It took place not only in high profile areas but throughout the city. The "lady volunteers" vowed, the *Hindustan Times* reported, to "organise mohalla committees to do propaganda for Swadeshi and prohibition and to organise meetings in various places with a view to bring about complete boycott of foreign cloth and liquor in Delhi city."⁷³

In the opinion of the local police, the boycott of foreign cloth superseded all other forms of community campaigning by 12 April.⁷⁴ This built on a long-standing national campaign, the swadeshi movement having spread from Bengal in the early 1900s. Gandhi bifurcated the swadeshi campaign in relation to cloth. First, the constructive khadi movement was to be continuous, the spinning of cloth on charkhas in the home providing a space for contemplation of the political cause, which would also reduce the drain of wealth to the textile mills of Lancashire and equip supporters with white clothing by which they could be identified in public as supporters of swadeshi and the Gandhian cause. Second, during Civil Disobedience foreign cloth vendors could be picketed. Both tactics were forms of embodying Gandhi's truth, the first through a repetitious and spinning askesis, the second through parrhesiastic tests in the face of intimidation and violence at foreign cloth retailers.

The geographies of spinning were diffuse and rarely noted in official archives, although most interviewees mentioned wearing khadi, while many spun it at home, or wore that spun by female family members. This was the result of well-established campaigning in the city. For instance, on 27 February the *Hindustan Times* featured images of women participating in swadeshi league processions. There could also be more targeted and coercive campaigns. Chandiwala recalled Delhi's lawyers refusing calls to wear khadi.⁷⁵ A poster depicting a donkey seated on a throne and wearing foreign clothing was pasted outside the courts. On 12 April, as the campaign against foreign cloth accelerated, the Delhi Bar Association announced its plan to have its members wear khaddar and support the boycott.⁷⁶ On the following day, foreign cloth was burned on the riverbank, the traditional site for cremations in the city.

While mostly the result of diffuse Congress campaigning, there was one coordinating hub for spinning work in Delhi. This was the "Gandhi ashram" in Daryaganj, a "barrack" where Chandiwala was sent by Gandhi to propagate spinning in the city.⁷⁷ Using public donations the ashram distributed charkhas to the people of the city and expounded the value of spinning. It also served as a fulcrum between constructive and disruptive cloth work. The ashram pro-

**FIGURE 3.6.** Picketing of Delhi foreign cloth shops. Courtesy of the British Library Board (Asia, Pacific and Africa SM 27, *Hindustan Times*, 18/4/1930).

duced a large charkha and spindle and took it on processions through the city. Chandiwala attributed this and other "strange" processions, including of camels and donkeys, to the ex-Khilafat campaigner Abdulla Churiwala. P. C. Jain, however, attributed the vast charkha to Dalel Singh Surana, who colored the charkha like a cannon and claimed the cannons of cotton would blow away the British (confirmed in Surana's entry in Thapliyal 1985b, 399). The ashram also trained volunteers on picketing cloth stores, until it was closed down on 17 September 1930 having been declared illegal, alongside the INC offices. Picketing of foreign cloth vendors continued, however (see figure 3.6, which depicts women volunteers who were picketing foreign cloth shops in Chandni Chowk, here seen as part of a procession passing by the clock tower). Chandiwala recounted sitting down outside designated shops, including the Mohan Brothers shop in Chandni Chowk, distributing pamphlets, castigating the owners for selling foreign goods, and spinning cloth in the street, for which he was eventually arrested. P. C. Jain suggested, however, that prominent names were reluctant to picket, delegating this work to volunteers so they could focus on writing, moving around the city, and doing things more "stimulating."[78]

"Close picketing" was described around Chandni Chowk by the *Hindustan Times* from 15 April, while fifty men and women toured the city encouraging picketing on the 18th. On 20 April the newspaper reported that "almost all" places in the cloth market, to the west of Queen's Gardens on Mission Road, and in Chandni Chowk were being picketed. By the end of the month the chief commissioner had to report that foreign cloth retailers were feeling the effect of picketing "with some acuteness."[79] By May 1930 the DDCC could report that since April the cost of foreign cloth had decreased by 25 percent and that picketing would continue, despite attacks on some satyagrahis (including one Muslim Congress volunteer) in Chandni Chowk by Muslim traders.[80] In late June the civic center on Chandni Chowk was claimed as a space of swadeshi when the foreign cloth traders around the clock tower shut down.[81] Women's meetings continued at the clock tower for the next fortnight, ensuring traders could only reopen if they traded in Indian-made goods.[82]

However, from the very beginning of the campaign, it had been clear that picketing would be deployed throughout the city, not just in its ceremonial spaces. This was not just an elite-coordinated, top-down mobilization, but one that emerged from the people and mohallas of the city. The latter self-organized into surveillance networks, tracking foreign cloth traders' attempts to surreptitiously continue their trade. P. C. Jain recalled: "The people of the muhalla would inform us that the goods are lying here. If any new clothes godown was opened then the people of the muhalla would tell us that today the carts have gone there. The cart drivers would also help us a lot. If they would take out the goods and keep it in some other place then they would come and tell us that babuji look a godown has been made there, the goods have gone there, so we would quickly write the name of that place on our 'list.'"[83] Volunteers would be sent to picket, and if they were arrested then residents would get a message to Congress organizers and replacements would be sent, most of whom would be Hindu women. As traders switched to moving cloth between properties at night, the pickets also became nocturnal.

Memo Bai, a female activist who came to prominence in 1930, later recalled that although the office of the female Congress workers was in Chandni Chowk, and that her set task was to picket the Delhi Mills Cloth Shop on the same street, the majority of picketing took place throughout the city.[84] Smaller trading centers at Mori Gate, Kashmiri Gate, Paharganj, and Sadar Bazar came to be targeted, under the surveillance of community Congress committees. Women's participation in picketing was not incidental or symbolic but rather, as the DDCC reported on 15 May, "The successes of the campaign for the boycott of foreign cloth [were] solely due to the determined picketing of shops by ladies at very great personal inconvenience."[85]

Just as salt production underwent a change in "field of operations" in late April, by early August Congress cloth picketers were not only focusing on trading centers but had drawn up "impressive programs targeting different wards."⁸⁶ Specific communities were targeted, for example, Katra Nil near Queen's Gardens and the Cloth Market, because it was a wealthy area. However, because it was not a trade center, different loci of attention had to be selected. For 17 August the local Swadeshi Society announced a program of social boycotting (despite this being against Gandhi's wishes [Guha 1997, 135–37]). It announced a Khaddar Day during which nobody in the locality would be allowed to stir in the streets unless they were wearing homespun cloth. The same rules applied to people coming into the area to visit temples, a substantial number as the day chosen was that of Shri Krishna Joyanti (Krishna festival). The day began with temple prayers at 6:00 a.m., a procession through Chandni Chowk to the Jumna, returning to the ward between 12:00 and 4:00 p.m. to picket those not dressed in khaddar, and ending with the picketing of temples whose deities were not dressed in khaddar materials in the evening.⁸⁷ P. C. Jain also recalled picketing a Ramlila procession to insist that those playing the roles of Ram and Ravana would wear khadi, as would the priests in the procession (wedding processions were also targeted).⁸⁸

As more and more of the Congress leaders were arrested, the cloth activism became more locally orientated. Memo Bai recalled "Spinning Clubs" in small lanes and communities, while committees targeted larger areas, such as Daryaganj, Sabzi Mandi, and Karol Bagh.⁸⁹ Jugal Kishore Khanna also recalled every ward having workers, local leaders, committees, and presidents. Specific wards in rotation would offer satyagraha, while support would be maintained in nonactive periods by picketing and prabhat pheris processions.⁹⁰ On 18 September 1930 the chief commissioner reported that Congress had been specializing in ward and mohalla meetings, hoisting the national flag in any area that paid 500 rupees to Congress funds.⁹¹ By 4 February 1931 this was reported as a daily activity.⁹² Likewise, on 18 December, when the movement was tiring, the main form of advertisement of the Congress program was reported to be women and children touring the bazaars advocating swadeshi.⁹³

The DDCC reported on 29 June 1930 that as well as campaigning at temples and Jumna ghats (access points to the river) and forbidding people wearing foreign cloth from entering the temples or the river, women had been securing swadeshi and temperance pledges through house-to-house picketing. While swadeshi picketing occurred at the level of the ceremonial bazaar and the community-based mohalla, it also at times (like salt production) targeted homes themselves. Reporting on the first month of Civil Disobedience, a Congress note on cloth picketing stated, "In addition to picketing their shops, we picketed the houses of the defaulters, disallowing any member of their family to come in or go out, and not permitting sweeper, kahars [palanquin bearers] or anybody else to enter the house. This practice so far has been very successful and helps us in recovering fines from the defaulters."[94]

The DDCC noted on 15 May, "Now the ladies propose to try for and achieve a more substantial triumph. They are drawing up a programme of constructive work by house to house visit, which will be started almost immediately." Swadeshi picketing at the home scale served two functions. First, it was a tactical response to attempts by foreign cloth retailers to continue their trade. In May 1930 it was reported that such traders attempted to move their goods to safer trading areas, concealed in holdalls, bedding, suitcases, and purdah palanquins. In response, Congress reported setting up round-the-clock patrols to detect such cases. This took the total number of volunteers on permanent pickets at rail stations, banks, and godown markets to 325, though the reporter was pained to admit that these volunteers couldn't be secured from Delhi proper and had been paid a special allowance to come to the city from Meerut and Bulandshah. Such activities were still reported in August, and women were specially allotted to house-to-house work, even though "belaboured by hired goondas," so they could confront "burqa ladies" who would take materials into peoples' homes to trade.[95] The second function, with much wider implications, was that of house-to-house visits and picketing, which allowed the focus to shift from boycotting to khadi and swadeshi, which continued in domestic spaces, though largely unreported, throughout the first phase of Civil Disobedience.

The second phase likewise featured picketing in both prominent and community spaces. On 5 February 1932 the *Hindustan Times* reported on its front page "Lady Picketers Arrested" after Shrimati Jai Lakmi (listed as the mother of Radha Raman), Srimati Narbada Devi, and Mrs. Deshbandhu Gupta were arrested in Chandni Chowk and the cloth market. This was repeated on 7 and 10 February, while 25 February and 29 May saw mass processions of female swadeshi workers move through the center of the city.[96] In late February 1932 Asaf Ali (dictator from 18 February until his arrest on 1 March) redirected the boycotting field of operations to the community and home scale, as in 1930. As a police report written on 16 January 1931 testified, when justifying the employment of residential police protection for foreign cloth traders, "This is attributable to a systematic visiting of the houses of retail dealers by Hindu women for the purpose of advocating the boycott of foreign goods."[97] House-to-house picketing and propaganda were also noted in the fortnightly reports of the chief commissioner on 19 January and 18 June 1932. When most

FIGURE 3.7. Boycott vs. Buy British. Reproduced with permission, NMML/CID/IX/371

other forms of protest had died down, it was women's picketing that was still reported, on 1 August and as late as 19 January 1933.

Women were valued for their supposed moral force in shaming retailers of foreign cloth, but also for the impact their arrest could have. A Delhi Congress Bulletin of 25 February reported with outrage the arrest of a "hunger satyagrahi," an unusual hybrid of the nonviolent picket and the hunger strike. Premsukhdas of Dwarkadas Cloth Market had apparently caused a "hunger satyagrahi lady" to be arrested from inside his house: "Thus has the hard hearted money-grabber violated the most sacred conventions of Hindu society. He has not only handed over to the police a lady who was under his roof, but one who had remained without food or drink for a whole day, and who was marched off to the prison from her tapasya [penance or ascetic practice]. Can human morality fall lower?"[98] An undated cyclostyled sketch of a valiant Indian woman, bound and pleading for a boycott of British goods, was also submitted in the same file (figure 3.7).[99] She faced a British bayonet without fear, as the soldier trampled kisans (peasants) underfoot.

Women were further encouraged to act in a Congress Bulletin issued on "Gandhi Day," 4 March 1932, marking three months since his arrest. All "sisters" were called on to act that day "and to flood the streets of the City with 'Kesaria' [saffron], the colour that stands for courage and self-sacrifice."[100] Picketing was therefore a powerful part of the broader nonviolent techne. It could call forth the violence of the state, exposing the sham of its civilizing mission. But it also raised the prospect of satyagrahis or their followers succumbing to violence, problematizing the Congress creed (Mantena 2012). This chapter will conclude with the example of Mrs. Kohli's picketing, which was felt to have crossed the line of violence.

## Politicized Identities

### STUDENTS

The Civil Disobedience movement led to a new generation of political leaders in Delhi. It also allowed for the ethical differentiation of non-elites who distinguished themselves by their courageous anticolonialism in the city. But it further led to the emergence of newly politicized collective identities. One of these brought students together, many of whom had been radicalized by the revolutionary movement and were a source of Congress anxiety (Maclean 2015). Until it was banned in 1931, Congress's Hindustani Seva Dal effectively targeted Delhi youths, including students (Raza and Roy 2015). P. C. Jain recalled being introduced to the Seva Dal in the 1920s by Shankar Lal, expecting just to work on one task but being given another each day: "I would think every day that this is just today's work, do it, but then some other work would come up the next day. Then some work would come up on the third day and this way by doing work continuously my taking part in the national movement began and then there was no break from it, that work kept increasing."[101] Jain identified the students as being particularly fearless, as organized by campaigners and student union organizers, C. L. Paliwal among the latter.[102]

Delhi's colleges were concentrated to the north (Civil Lines) and east (Daryaganj) of the old city, providing a cluster of recruiting grounds that Congress was quick to tap; Gandhi had visited Hindu College in November 1929 and received a purse of 5,753 rupees (Chandiwala 1954, 55; see also Vatsayan et al. 2000). Before Gandhi had even begun his salt march, the Delhi CID had been voicing their concerns over the "infection" of students and their teachers. On 6 March 1930 the additional superintendent of police, CID, informed the deputy commissioner that over five hundred members of Hindu, Ramjas, and Commercial Colleges and of high schools had attended the Independence Day celebrations.[103] Eight students were under special investigation but, more worryingly, so were four teachers, two professors, and even the principal of Commercial College in Daryaganj. Six of the suspected students were affiliated with the SYL, while a further six were members of the NBS, HSD, or Congress. Gracia Gardens, between St. Stephen's and Hindu Colleges near Kashmiri Gate, became the students' own "Queen's Gardens," being used on 20 March by two hundred students to encourage a mass protest should Gandhi be arrested when he reached the eastern coastline.[104] The following day a report was submitted to the Government by Delhi's CID suggesting that Congress was targeting young men in particular, holding open-air meetings near Hindu College and another near schools and colleges in Daryaganj: "In addressing the young students, the preachers said that Gandhi has already received the applications of 80,000 young men who have volunteered themselves to die for the liberation of India. Delhi alone has got 3,000 men ready, and they may launch civil disobedience any moment. He told the students that it was not the occasion for spending their time in making merry, but they should concentrate themselves in helping Gandhi to liberate India."[105]

The students were encouraged to dismiss those who ridiculed them because "a handful of ill-clad un-armed people were marching against the strongest empire in the world. He said it was not with arms that they were going to win the battle, but it was by will-power." The informer had listened to student conversations at the meetings and reported the common consensus that British days were numbered in India. Schoolmasters were said to be helping, passing around boxes every morning and encouraging students to contribute money toward national Congress funds. The chief commissioner instructed his superintendent of education to chase up such allegations, adding in his letter of 7 April: "I know how difficult it is for Principals to control their students but they should I think have less difficulty in controlling their staff."[106]

These inquiries showed that students had been participating in the buildup to the movement. In the former there had been meetings in what was known as "Student's Park" near Kashmiri Gate. A telegram from the chief commissioner to the Home Department reported students being encouraged to enroll as picketing volunteers on 15 April, but also being blamed for low meeting turnouts on the same day and being appealed to directly by "Gandhi's emissary" Krishna Nair on 18 April.[107]

Student activities continued to worry the local authorities, as demonstrated in a letter sent from the superintendent of education to the principal of St. Stephen's College on 3 May 1930.[108] The letter stressed that students had been spotted at protest meetings, but also acknowledged their effect on the landscape, referring to their meeting ground as Student's Park. Principal Mukarji replied on 6 May that he would keep an eye on his boys and sent assurances that the college stood for law and order. However, he pointed out that in such a strongly politicized environment, tact and sympathy were required to make sure students did not go "beyond their limits," and strong discipline against transgressors could often make the situation much worse.

Students from Hindu and Commercial Colleges continued to be reported making political speeches into July, with the CID requesting the local administration get four students dismissed.[109] The Delhi Provincial Students Conference further affirmed its links with Congress. Between 7 and 9 August it was addressed by Asaf Ali and Satyavati, who participated in the singing of nationalist songs and ceremonial flag-raisings. Satyavati was one of the pivotal figures of the Delhi scene, bridging student, leftist, and Congress organizations, while inspiring an entire generation of women to shed purdah and take up the anticolonial struggle. Such inspiration had taken place among the students of Indraprastha College, Delhi's women's school, founded in 1924. But the spaces of women's political education were also the homes, mohallas, and bazaars of the city.

## WOMEN

It is the women of India who are going to bring Swaraj to India. Wherever I go I find hundreds and thousands of women attending public meetings, joining processions and picketing liquor and foreign cloth shops and taking part in other activities of the Congress. It is a sight for gods to see.
—DA/Confidential/1930/55/Conf C.

The above was taken from a speech in Queen's Gardens on 26 August 1930 by cofounder of the Swaraj Party Vithalbhai Patel. He lambasted young male students who continued their studies instead of coming out of their houses and protesting. As demonstrated above, the women's movement cannot be separated from the broader Civil Disobedience campaign in Delhi, nor can the movement's success be dissociated from the mass engagement of women. Women didn't just participate in Delhi; they led. This was all the more affecting because of the strong tradition of purdah, especially in upper-class families, that had prevailed in Delhi.

This was a period of rapid change in the gender politics of India. While many women created bold new public and political roles for themselves, many thousands more adapted their roles within and beyond the home (Legg 2003). These roles were often those of refusal, each marking private and personal but no less risky acts of parrhesia. Chandiwala recalled wanting to join Gandhi on his salt march, but his mother went to Gandhi's ashram to plead with him not to allow her son to join him, forcing Gandhi to agree.[110] More common were those women who refused demands to refrain from participating, especially risky in high-caste families from which women had not previously had public roles. P. C. Jain recalled intending to offer himself for arrest in February 1932, but his wife, Chameli Devi Jain (see figure 3.8), insisted that she had looked after their children during his previous arrests and she wanted to offer herself up this time: "Listening to her say these words I was completely astounded and as if uncertain I started looking at her. I said with composure that you are from a Rajasthan family. Your life has been spent in a lot of Purdah."[111] Despite family upset (Legg 2003), Chameli Jain was arrested and went to jail, causing a sensation and making her son into a schoolyard celebrity (Jain 2010, 17).

Although Gandhi had initially attempted to limit women's participation in the 1930 movement, they had joined the salt march and come out onto the street anyway (Kishwar 1986; Thapar-Björkert 2006). Women of every class and caste participated, although those from Congress families took many leadership roles. In order to deal with these often high-caste female protesters, the Delhi Administration innovated in January 1932 by forming a female police force, including women of low caste (see figure 3.9; Legg 2007, 114).[112]

**FIGURE 3.8.** Phool Chand Jain and Chameli Devi in Delhi, 1923. Reprinted with permission from L. C. Jain family and the Book Review Literary Trust

On 5 February 1932 the *Hindustan Times* reported "Lady Picketers Arrested" (as mentioned above) while picketing cloth vendors near the clock tower in Chandni Chowk. One of those arrested, the wife of Delhi publisher Desh Bandhu Gupta, complained that she had been arrested by men while female constables stood by.[113]

This chapter has clearly shown that women influenced all public aspects of Civil Disobedience. They had been incredibly effective at the mohalla level and house-to-house organization and campaigning, and had been at the forefront of cloth and liquor picketing campaigns. They also formed minority but

FIGURE 3.9. "The Policewoman Reaches India," University of Nottingham Manuscripts and Special Collections, Special Collections Periodicals, *The Graphic*, 26/3/1932

very visible components of the general activities of mass mobilization during the early stages of the campaign. The *Hindustan Times* drew special attention to the prominence of women, especially when events were subject to police violence, such as an 8 May 1930 moment of "police madness" during a meeting at "Gandhi grounds," behind the Commercial Bank on Chandni Chowk.[114] It reported a ladies' jatha arriving under the leadership of Shrimati Jai Rani, "Commander of the Lady Volunteers" at the meeting. Mrs. Sen Gupta attempted to speak, but a lathi charge by the police broke up the crowd. Women had earlier been assaulted in the events leading up to the Sisganj shooting, during which they were said to have made up at least a thousand of the fifty to sixty thousand people on the street, and their efforts in the following weeks earned them, and one woman in particular, special mention in a Delhi District Congress Committee Bulletin of 15 May: "The part that the ladies of Delhi have been playing in the national movement under the intrepid and untiring leadership of Shrimati Satyavati Devi cannot be appreciated too highly. The successes of the campaign for the boycott of foreign cloth [were] solely due to the determined picketing of shops by ladies at very great personal inconvenience."[115]

*Satyavati: Delhi's Joan of Arc?*

Pointing to the dead-body which was actually being cremated, she told her audience that such results were only to be expected from a tyrant Government. She referred to the Mutiny of 1857 as having taken place in these very days (months of May) and exhorted her audience to honour the blood of their Indian martyrs —to rise up and secure freedom at all costs for their country. She even went to the length of suggesting that they should bare their chests and receive bullets.
—NA/Home(Political)/1930/432

The above account was lain down as evidence in the trial of the Crown vs. Satyavati Devi on 27 May 1930. Satyavati was born in 1907 and grew up in Ludhiana but had a deep attachment to Delhi due to the leading role of her maternal grandfather, Swami Shraddhanand, in Delhi's 1919 Rowlatt satyagraha (see Sharma and Kishwar 1998 for a brief biography). She moved to Delhi in 1923 when she married a manager at the Birla Cloth Mills. Her mother, Ved Kumari, was an active Congress worker and was arrested in 1931, 1933, 1940, and 1942 (Vachaspati 1977). Her maternal uncle was "Professor" (occasionally "Pandit") Indra, the influential Congress organizer and editor who was imprisoned in 1927, 1930, and 1932 (Government of India [Secret] 1934, 12). While he was a Hindu reformist to the "right" of Congress, in the 1930s his niece moved farther to the left.

After Shraddhanand was assassinated in 1926, Satyavati had risen in prominence among reformists and nationalists. In 1923 she had anticipated Gandhi by seven years through suggesting that the salt tax (which had just been doubled) was more offensive than the Rowlatt Act.[116] She was committed to Congress's empowerment of women, to which she brought her own energy. K. D. Kohli recalled Satyavati "pulling" his wife (see below) and others out of the home and initiating them into politics.[117] C. L. Paliwal suggested that it was she more than any other who brought Delhi women out of their homes.[118] An interviewee recalled her going into women's homes and convincing them to leave with her, the boldness of which (and her early death from tuberculosis in 1945) earned her the title of Delhi's "Joan of Arc" (Vachaspati 1977).[119]

Her conviction in 1930 helped establish her, in the CID's eyes, as "one of the most prominent left-wing Congress leaders of Delhi" (Government of India

[Secret] 1934, s-14) and a prime mover of the Civil Disobedience movement. J. N. Sahni (1977) later suggested that she was one of the great unremembered stars of the Delhi scene and that throughout she had wavered between violence and nonviolence, the charkha and the bomb. The fortnightly report concerning her arrest in May 1930 explained that it was because she "proved so violent in her speeches and so unflaggingly troublesome."[120]

The case laid against her was that she had been organizing large processions of women and going around the city distributing seditious matter against the Government. Gatherings of more than five people had been prohibited in the city since the disturbances following the arrest of Gandhi on 5 May. But Satyavati continued to "organise procession[s] of ladies going through the main bazaars of the city addressing all manner of people. Her extortions are directed to inflaming the minds of the people against Government."[121] On 12 May the body of a man killed during the police shooting the day after Gandhi's arrest (see chapter 4) was cremated on the banks of the Jumna River before a large crowd, which Satyavati took the opportunity to address (see epigraph above). Her speech was reported as preaching hatred of the very worst type against the Government, with its object being to inflame the masses against the Government.

The noncooperation element of the Civil Disobedience movement meant that the accused were supposed to refuse to participate in criminal proceedings against them. Satyavati did, however, file a written statement. In it she said that she was only one of millions of women who had been "compelled to come out from their traditional seclusion and muster under Mahatma Gandhi's standard to fight the nonviolent battle of freedom for India."[122]

This brief case report is overflowing with the rich historical allusions she made in her speech. The "Mutiny" of 1857 was evoked, which nationalists would rebrand as the First War of Independence. In exhorting the crowds to "bare their chests and receive bullets," Satyavati was invoking her grandfather Swami Shraddhanand's famous 1919 stand against Gurkha soldiers outside the town hall on Chandni Chowk. In much of this campaigning, as with her cremation speech, Satyavati's language and incantations were laced with violence: the dead body on the cremation pyre was dramatically claimed as a symbol of tyrant imperialism; the blood of India martyrs was to be honored; the crowd should offer up their body; and this was all in the name of non-violence.

Satyavati was released from prison in time for the second phase of Civil Disobedience, in which she coordinated women and cloth picketing in public (see figure 3.10 for one of the few images of Satyavati, here captured mid-speech in Chandni Chowk). The CID also reported her as the Delhi "Dictator"

FIGURE 3.10. Satyavati addressing a meeting in Chandni Chowk, 1932 (Vachaspati 1977)

who organized processions and telegraph wire-cutting, funding revolutionaries, and printing "red leaflets" (Government of India [Secret] 1934, S-14). Between Civil Disobedience and the outbreak of war in 1939, Satyavati continued to explore the tense line between Congress and socialism, violence and ahimsa. Nonviolence was also coercive, however, as the following study of "Mrs. K. D. Kohli" will illustrate.

### Mrs. Kohli's Glance and Liquor Picketing

Chandrawali Kohli was the wife of influential newspaper publisher K. D. Kohli. Her activities, touched on above, earned her a place in the Delhi Province Political "Who's Who" (Government of India [Secret] 1934, K-15). This noted her threatening of policemen with social boycott unless they resigned (as a result of which the Police [Incitement to Disaffection] Act was introduced into Delhi). By June 1930 a Congress bulletin would congratulate the work of the "dictator of the ladies Council" Mrs. Kohli, the successor of Satyavati.[123] Kohli was arrested and sentenced that summer in a case that brings to light the incredibly fine orchestrations that women, and men, were stringing together as they teased and tested the spatial boundaries between violence and nonviolence.

Alongside the much more widespread picketing of foreign cloth was that of liquor stores. Alcohol was viewed as another Western, corrupting import that deprived the national body of much-needed economic resources and the individual body of precious health and energy (see Thapar-Björkert 2006, 115–20). Women especially would picket stores and insist that customers contribute their money instead to Congress and an independent India. Since 1929 liquor picketing had been taking place, at not only shops but also the homes of liquor vendors.[124] By August 1930 it eclipsed the picketing of foreign cloth vendors, with Chandiwala recalling picketing being led by women at Bholnath's (P. C. Jain remembered it as Bhole Ram) store at Mori Gate, Baratuti's near Bara Hindu Rao, and Daulat Ram Narula's shop at Sadat Khan.[125] P. C. Jain recalled the latter hiding in empty sacks to evade female picketers but being found by them and publicly shamed. He also, however, recalled women picketers, led by Mrs. Kohli, being surrounded by youths one evening outside an alcohol godown at Baradari and the police having to intervene.[126] But Kohli was also capable of using men, and their potential for violence, when necessary.

Chandiwala recalled significant differences between cloth and liquor picketing that may help explain the following incident. Many cloth vendors had agreed to stop selling foreign textiles and canceled their existing orders. Alcohol vendors, however, were tied into contracts that would be expensive to leave and that the government insisted they honor: "That is why 'picketing' would keep happening for the alcohol shops. Funeral processions of the shopkeepers would also be taken out. Many times their 'hai-hai' [shame-shame] would also happen, but there would be no great effect on them. There was quite an effect on the clothes sellers."[127]

Chandiwala reported a sense of intermingling and brotherhood with cloth sellers, using friends to exert moral suasion and win them over. As a result the Mohan Brothers cloth retailers on Chandhi Chowk were said to have donated a mansion in Okhla for a new Gandhi ashram. This followed Gandhi's insistence that picketing be done without animosity and with love. The liquor picketing was, however, more aggressive. P. C. Jain reported volunteers doing hai-hai at the shops of Bhola Ram and Daulat Ram, with slogans shouted that drinking alcohol was haram (forbidden). In response, the women picketers were harassed; Jain suggested that "alcoholics" were used to attack the women, labeling them "whores" who were redundant in their own homes.[128]

The women picketers, ten to fifteen in number, were unrepentant in the face of these attacks. On 13 August 1930 an attempt by liquor contractors in Sadar Bazar to restart their trade was met by vigorous picketing.[129] Chief among the picketers was Mrs. Kohli, and the question of animosity or love was central to the problematization of nonviolence that resulted. The details of the case provide fascinating insights into the micropolitics of picketing and the precarious borderline, as perceived by the government, between violence and nonviolence.

On 27 August a case was lodged against Kohli and Parbati Devi, another prominent female campaigner. Devi later acted as president of a mandal (board) to remove untouchability among women, served on the Mahila (Women's) Congress Committee in the early 1930s, and remained a prominent protester into the 1940s.[130] Charges were filed against Kohli, Devi, and fifty-eight men while those against an additional eleven women were dropped, although the fortnightly report suggested that similar actions by women would not be tolerated again.[131] The case stated that liquor picketing had begun on 12 June but that the shops remained open until the 25th. The following day the private residences of liquor traders were picketed, leading to the shops closing on the 27th. The Excise Department, however, insisted that the licensees open their shops (confirming Chandiwala's account), calling them to his office and demanding they pay their license for July and August and recommence trading. The licensees consorted and decided that one shop would be opened on 13 August to see what happened. One Ganga Pershad's shop was chosen; the other contractors gathered in the shop to observe. Before long the women protesters arrived and started picketing. Others began to gather around the shop, and the police were informed. Despite attempts to disperse the crowd, it continued to increase until at 10:45 p.m. the police were told that a larger crowd, some armed with sticks, surrounded the shop and that "violent speeches" were being delivered within the crowd. The fortnightly report had also suggested there had been talk of burning down the shop.[132]

Mrs. Kohli was leading a batch of women picketers and told the crowd to sit down in the road and refuse to move, which eighty to a hundred people did, with other male followers standing at a distance. Their placement would prove to be vitally important. The police told the crowd that with the contractors locked in the shop and traffic being blocked, there was a breach of the peace and they should disperse. The contractors had even knocked down an internal panel in an almirah (cabinet) to get into an adjoining room and try to escape from there, but they found themselves surrounded. The crowd refused to disperse, so armed police moved in and arrested seventy-one people.

The case against Kohli and Devi was that they had clearly defied section 144 of the Criminal Procedure Code (CrPC), which banned public groupings of more than five people. It was also suggested that Parbati Devi had addressed the people standing at a distance and asked them to come forward, "as death was the end of all." Mrs. Kohli had been "singing some songs," and at this time it was alleged that two stones were thrown from a house adjoining the liquor shop. The first class magistrate, Mr. A. Isar, argued: "I think anyone with any knowledge of mob psychology would agree with [the] insp[ector] that this was a breach of the peace." The police had not arrested the women at the time as it would have caused a further disturbance of the peace in the crowd, which by this point was estimated to have reached ten thousand.

It was felt that the women had confined the contractors inside the shop and had thus also breached section 342 of the Indian Penal Code (wrongful confinement). The men were said to have been caused much fear and "mental trouble" inside the store and could not leave it for nine hours. The question of how the women manufactured this confinement nonviolently was key to the prosecution. This was the magistrate's explanation:

> One can easily conceive of a situation where an accused person in order to abet such an offence need not say or do much. His very presence if he knows why he is present there and knows what is going on is sufficient encouragement to the actual offender and may amount to sufficient intimidation to the victims of the offence. Thus only 2 or 3 ladies may be sent to picket a residence. The inmates may not be embarrassed by these 2 or 3 ladies and if restrained from going out of the house or from entering it they may brush them aside or use other force necessary to protect their legal rights, but if a dozen strong men are sitting at some distance from the 2 or 3 ladies and it is known to the women that these men are their sympathisers and will if necessary help them and it is known to the inmates of the house that in dealing with the women picketers they might have to deal with the male guard, can there be any doubt that the men have facilitated the commission of the offence of wrongful restraint by the women and are consequently abetters [sic] of it.[133]

As such, the women were posited as nonviolent conduits, strategically placed outside the liquor store, for the violence of their male counterparts who were some distance off. The magistrate continued to argue that the crowd "abetted" the women's intimidation. People in the crowd were said to be uttering threats, and as such they were not just observers.

It was therefore found that the women abetted wrongful confinement by their "presence and conduct," while each had also defied CrPC section 145 (joining or continuing in unlawful assembly, knowing it has been commanded to disperse). Their action was found to have been high-handed, unjustifiable, and fraught with great danger to public peace. No matter what the cause was for picketing, it was felt there could be no excuse for refusing to allow the men to leave. The particulars of the case were explicitly linked by the magistrate to expose the violence within nonviolence:

> This action of the accused and all that followed was far from the much talked of non-violent methods of the Congress volunteers. The unfortunate contractors were confined in a small room with no exit and but for the ability to break open an almirah and go into the adjoining premises their plight would have been worst [sic] than what it actually was. The refusal of the accused to disperse in the middle of the night and under the circumstances was extremely foolish. At any time the crowd might have burst into violence and drawn upon itself counter-violence on the part of the Police resulting perhaps in loss of life and property.[134]

This statement emphatically links nonviolence to violence of two types. One was the violence of coercion, which nonviolent picketing clearly constituted. The second was the violence that it threatened to provoke in the police, which became inverted in this space of law to be a condemnation of the women, not of the police itself. The participants were sentenced to four months of rigorous imprisonment. Their crimes were public assembly, wrongful confinement, and refusal to disperse. No physical violence had been enacted, but, it was argued, the force of their placement had made the women into conduits of coercion. This fine dance on the precipice between violence and nonviolence was repeated in innumerable pickets, standoffs, charges, and protests throughout the Civil Disobedience movement. But the event that came to dominate the movement in Delhi lacked the subtle play of force, nonviolence, "presence[,] and conduct." At the Gurdwara Sisganj, on 5 May, violence was perpetrated by both the police and the public. The key questions here were how much violence, and why?

## CHAPTER 4

# The Gurdwara Sisganj

*Problematizing Nonviolence*

### The Ordeal

The nonviolence of Civil Disobedience risked calling forth the violence of participants and of the state but also of bystanders. Joining processions, picketing liquor or cloth vendors, breaking the law by making seditious speeches, or manufacturing salt were parrhesiastic acts; they required courage, involved real risk, and were dependent on their setting for the dramaturgical effect of their truth claims. In this sense they were tests. Of another order were ordeals—moments when violence was called forth and people (not just the courageous enactors of parrhesia but bystanders and followers) suffered. These ordeals provided the martyrs for Congress propaganda and were valued as recruitment tools. But the use of state violence also triggered official inquiries by colonial and Indian bodies to establish the truth, justify what had happened, and record the violence that triggered the response. These events and their aftermaths problematized the government by exposing colonial violence. But if nonviolence slipped into violence, then Congress's claim to be in control of Civil Disobedience would itself be problematized.

The events outlined below took place within one of the many overlapping sacred landscapes in Delhi. The city and its environs contained Sikh shrines and gurdwaras of national significance, which had already been pulled into political controversy. Memories of the incursions into Rakabganj Gurdwara's grounds in New Delhi (and the rift those incursions created between the local government and Delhi's "Sikh aristocracy"; Singh 1972, 215) had been stirred at the start of the Civil Disobedience movement.[1] But the Sikh community of Delhi was still relatively loyalist, especially the influential Sikh "contractors" who had built New Delhi.[2] This loyalty was shaken by the events of 6 May, though less among the Delhi Sikh "aristocracy" than among younger Sikhs, especially from beyond the city.

When news of Gandhi's arrest reached Delhi on 5 May 1930, Congress volunteers were dispatched through the city to propagate a hartal. By 3:00 p.m. most Hindu shops throughout the city were closed, and crowds gathered to protest outside the kotwali in Chandni Chowk while tongas, trams, and motorcars were stopped in the street.[3] A meeting in Queen's Gardens announced an early morning procession the next day to register the city's outrage at the arrest.[4] On 6 May the hartal was a success; a procession of an estimated hundred thousand people toured the city, as organized by Congress and the Naujawan Bharat Sabha, the Student and Youth League, and the Hindustani Seva Dal. The nature of the violent outbreaks that followed was heavily contested at the time, in reports that followed, and in the archives that resulted and with which we have to work. A brief sketch of the events will be given by triangulating the rough outline that was agreed upon by most sides. Two contesting reports into the most violent event, the shootings at the Gurdwara Sisganj, will then be contrasted before looking at how the Sisganj became a contested site of truth-making strung between four small- versus large-scale binaries, regarding (1) community (Delhi Sikhs and the broader panth [Sikh nation, or global community]); (2) the Government of India (the local and central state); (3) religious institutions (the local Gurdwara Committee and the Shiromani Gurdwara Parbandhak Committee); and, to a much lesser extent, (4) Congress (local activists and national figures, especially Gandhi).

Two outbreaks of violence were involved on 6 May. The second, later event took place at the Gurdwara Sisganj on Chandni Chowk, the very location of which was a testament to former imperial oppression. It marked the site where the Mughal emperor Aurangzeb had executed the ninth Sikh guru, Tegh Bahadur, for refusing to convert to Islam and defending the rights of Sikhs and Hindus to choose their own religion. The gurdwara constructed on this site in the late seventeenth century (INTACH Delhi Chapter 1999, 51) abutted the Mughal kotwali, the home of the kotwal (magistrate), the chief urban official in the Mughal city (Blake 1991, 23). Here the guru had been held hostage after surrendering himself to the Mughal authorities before being executed outside the kotwali on Chandni Chowk. This embedded an anti-imperial site of countermemory (Sikh vs. Mughal) directly next to the building that would become the center for urban policing in the colonial period (see figure 4.1).

The first, earlier event, however, took place in the north of Old Delhi. This area of the city was already associated with the historical geography of the city's oppression, Kashmiri Gate being the famous ingress through which the

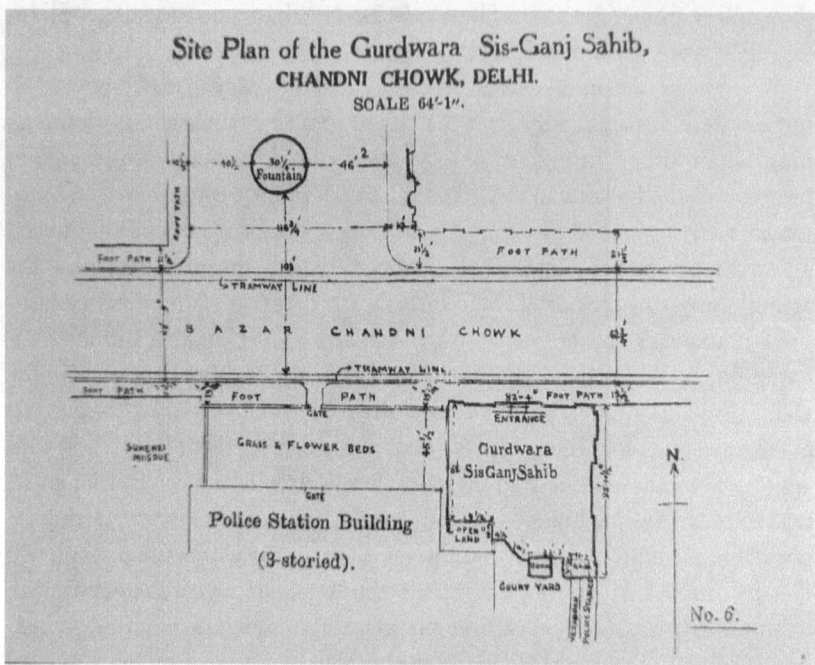

**FIGURE 4.1.** Site plan for the Gurdwara Sis-Ganj Sahib (Gurdwara Sis-Ganj Firing Committee 1930; courtesy of National Gandhi Museum and Library)

British retook the city in 1857. By 1930 the area was also home to the office of the CID, which had informants throughout the crowds that gathered nearby on 6 May. The CID senior superintendent, Mr. A. Senior, was able to witness from his office window the clash between the crowd and a car, which sparked much of what followed.

The district magistrate's cutchery (courthouse) near Kashmiri Gate contained the civil and criminal courts, the Treasury, and a police office.[5] Indian workers in the compound had been encouraged to boycott their employers, and protests were made against cases tried there, although such cases had been heard in the jail since 10 April to avoid exactly these sorts of protests.[6] From the vast ranks of protesters in the city on 6 May a group of volunteers headed toward the compound. They comprised an estimated thousand women, rallied by Delhi's leading female satyagrahi. A contemporary later recalled that "the late Satyavati, granddaughter of the late Swami Shraddhanand, came with a batch of women volunteers and formed a cordon with a view to preventing lawyers from entering district courts, which were then located in Kashmiri Gate."⁷ The women were dressed in red saris (red being a color usually worn at weddings and considered a good omen) and were protected by a ring of male volunteers. The chief commissioner later claimed that the police were provoked by an "aggressive mob" that gathered around the compound and assaulted a European officer driving through the area, who only escaped through "a judicious mixture of rapid advancing and reversing" in which several members of the crowd were injured.⁸ Following reports of such attacks, the police were sent into the area to disperse the crowds at 12:00 noon.

The official report into the violence that ensued suggested that thirty to forty people were injured, but the women were shepherded to safety.⁹ J. N. Sahni's (1971, 75) memoir, however, recalls the police mercilessly beating, lathi charging, and shooting at the crowd. The Delhi District Congress Committee (DDCC) reported of its volunteers that "lathi blows were mercilessly showered on them and more than ten of them received injuries including Mrs Sahni [the first figure on the left in figure 3.4] and the Mother-in-Law of Pandit Jawarhar Lal Nehru."¹⁰ Many lawyers were perfectly positioned within the courtyard to observe the police charges outside, and on 9 May a report was submitted to the president of the Bar Association by a subcommittee of lawyers appointed to investigate the police actions.¹¹

The report stated that the police threatened the picketers with lathis, chased some through the compound, and continued to hit some volunteers as they lay on the floor. A member of the Bar was attacked near St. James's Church even though he had nothing to do with the movement, while a ten-year-old girl received a fractured arm in one of the many witnessed "deliberate, indiscriminate and brutal assaults" that were totally indefensible and in "utter defiance of the law." On 12 May the president forwarded the resolutions of the subcommittee to the home secretary, stating that unwarranted and unjustifiable force had been used without warning, with no medical aid on hand, and that the attitude toward women and children was reprehensible and cowardly. The terminology used here anticipated that of the gurdwara report into the violence that followed.

The same crowd that was alleged to have attacked the car-bound European officer was involved in a further incident to the south, at the intersection of Queen's Road with Lothian Road Railway Bridge (see figure 3.2). Two cars containing the deputy commissioner, Senior Superintendent of Police (SSP) Mr. R. C. Jeffreys, the city deputy superintendent of police, and an inspector were stopped by a crowd of over five hundred who struck the cars with stones and sticks.¹² The "mob" was charged by lathis, and the cars escaped to the kotwali, where they were allegedly met with a brief shower of stones from the neighboring Gurdwara Sisganj as police tried to clear away the protesters.

At 4:00 p.m. four lorries of policemen were returning from a false callout to the pumping station near the River Jumna. Having picked up a fifth lorry on the way back, they entered Fountain Square on Chandni Chowk, opposite the kotwali. The police claimed they were heavily stoned from the nearby Majestic Cinema building and, as they approached the kotwali, from the Gurdwara Sisganj. The fifth lorry was left stranded, and SSP Jeffreys led a force out into the square to rescue the crew. With the rescue squad finding it difficult to return to the police headquarters, the police force on the veranda and ground floor of the kotwali opened fire on the gurdwara and the crowd in the street. The exact nature of the events over the next twenty minutes is contested, but the end result was that four members of the public were killed (listed as three Hindus and one Muslim) and 190 injured. No policemen died and only eighteen required hospital treatment.

As with 1919, the gurdwara violence took place on Chandni Chowk, and, as then, the official inquiry (necessitated by the CrPC) took place in the town hall. It was appointed by the local government and conducted by a local magistrate between 16 and 27 May. However, on this occasion the state marshaling of history was challenged by an alternative account that rendered the gurdwara as a site of alternate truth-making. The "Gurdwara Sis-Ganj Firing Enquiry Committee" (henceforth the Firing Enquiry) was established on 15 May by the Shiromani Gurdwara Parbandhak Committee (SGPC). They lay claim to being an official inquiry through their recognition, via the 1925 Gurdwara Act, as the state-sanctioned and official managing body of all gurdwaras.[13] This inquiry carried out its public sittings, with the permission of the municipal secretary, in Queen's Gardens, having been denied permission to use the town hall because it was being occupied by the official inquiry. Thus, the Civic Centre, reconstructed in the 1860s and intended as the new public heart of Delhi, became the site not only for physical clashes between the local authorities and nationalist groups but also for discursive contestation between two rival truth claims. The Sikh committee meetings were popular and open, with the morning and afternoon sittings attended by over one thousand people (Gurdwara Sis-Ganj Firing Committee 1930, 9). The local magistrate Abdul Samad's meetings were open to the public, but not one submission was made, as the inquiry took place during the ongoing Civil Disobedience campaign, which demanded noncooperation with the state.

## Juridical Truth: The Magistrate's Report and Manly Spirit

EVIDENCE

On the evening of 7 May the Government wired J. N. G. Johnson, the chief commissioner, "noting with pleasure" the "spirit and behaviour of the police" in difficult circumstances, asking for a public communiqué regarding the Sisganj shooting, suggesting a magisterial inquiry under CrPC, section 176, and offering to obtain a magistrate from the United Provinces or Punjab for this purpose.[14] Johnson replied the following day saying that a communiqué would be forthcoming and that he had already appointed his own local magistrate.

On 16 May the district magistrate, A. H. Layard, had written to Sardar Abdul Samad Khan, a first class magistrate, confirming that, since several people had died of injuries received on the 6th, it must be subject to a specific investigation.[15] This was within his broader inquiry into violence during Civil Disobedience, conducted under the conditions of section 176 CrPC. Layard considered that it should be conducted as follows: in public, letting this be widely known; not as a judicial proceeding, with no pleaders, cross-examination, or questions from relatives of the deceased; with no prosecution, accused, or inquiry into police conduct; with "no rush to record evidence"; but with an emphasis on where and when injuries were received. The interviews were carried out on 22–23 May and the completed findings forwarded to the chief commissioner by Layard on 27 May, with a note explaining that the only course possible to protect the men in the lorries by the fountain and the rescuing squad was to open fire on the gurdwara and the "mob outside."

Mr. Abdul Samad began his two-and-a-half typed pages of findings with an outline of occurrences as he saw them on 6 May. The basic facts were as described above, but the accompanying explanations slipped straight into tropes of counterinsurgency primary discourse (Guha 1983b). Around noon a huge number of demonstrators "in a very excited mood" crowded Kashmiri Gate and the surrounding area and started assaulting European officials. Police from the kotwali thus dispersed "this truculent mob" with lathis before the police officers gathered back in the kotwali. Here they claimed to have witnessed stones being thrown from the gurdwara, so its manager was sent for, who promised no such "mischief" would happen again. SSP Jeffreys, "seeing the miserable condition of his men in the lorry blocked at the fountain[,] dashed towards them under a heavy shower of bricks for rescue followed by a party of police who had no fire arms. He found his men in it seriously injured and rolling in a pool of blood." Sub-Inspector Tara Chand led police into the gurdwara to bring out the stone throwers, before which he removed his shoes, though some constables had rushed into the gurdwara wearing footwear, "but not into the sacred part." Most Sikh detainees were let go, while the night-posting of police at the gurdwara was in plain clothes. In summary, "taking into consideration the above circumstances, I come to the conclusion that the firing at the Sisganj Gurdwara and the fountain was inevitable and had there been a slight hesitation on the part of the police in the firing, the SSP and his party including those in the lorry who had no fire-arms would have undoubtedly lost their lives. In the end I am unable to with-hold myself from expressing that the manly spirit shown by Mr. Jeffreys in saving his men is creditable."[16]

In this report the crowd is an unthinking mob, truculent, excitable, and mischievous. Against them stood the police and, especially, Mr. Jeffreys, embodying the righteousness of state violence and performing the courage of his truth. Though Abdul Samad found himself unable to sign off without a personal endorsement of Jeffreys, the tone of the findings very much represented the seven statements given by police officials, with the European officers and the city magistrate, Mr. A. Isar, speaking under oath. The general narrative across the statements is largely harmonious, though each includes specific features that work with or against the official narrative.

### TESTIMONIES

The statements confirmed doctors were dressing injured members of the public at the kotwali; thus the "mob" outside may have included concerned friends and family. The calm of the driver at the cutcherry was contrasted with that of the driver of the lorry at Fountain Square, who deserted when the crowd gathered. The car of Mr. Isar (who also tried the cases of Narain Das Garg, Satyavati, and Mrs. Kohli described in chapter 3) had been stopped and abused by a crowd on arriving at the kotwali at 6:30 a.m., where he would later see a constable, running into the kotwali, being hit by bricks three times: "At the last blow he fell down face downwards between the two pillars of the entrance to the Kotwali and he lay there in a pool of blood." Others reworked the condemnation of the violent masses.

The kotwali sub-inspector Abdul Wahid noted the "great excitement" in the city, that the crowd at the cutcherry shouted revolutionary slogans and surrounded the car in a "very menacing attitude." He rescued the SSP and deputy commissioner from the "fury and attacks of the infuriated mob" at great risk to his life, during which he and the SSP were injured. Wahid was about to depart but, on seeing that Devi Dayal, the DSP, was in danger, he informed Jeffreys, who "like a true brave man" went back for the DSP "whom we found in a very precarious condition and rescued him with much difficulty from the hands of the infuriated mob." His praise continued in describing Jeffreys's rescuing of the fifth lorry from Fountain Square outside the kotwali: he dashed out before his party of constables; Chandni Chowk crowds had assumed a "menacing attitude"; the SSP and his men were under great risk, so "the least hesitation on the part of the Officers in the Kotwali in taking steps to prevent the horrible catastrophe would have certainly ended in a very horrible disaster."

The central statement came from Jeffreys, the senior superintendent of police who had been coordinating the day's activities and whose courage was the object of clear adoration by his staff, and the magistrate adjudicating the official inquiry. Jeffreys's own account mixes forensic detail with bursts of machismo, but also with theatrical and affective flair. He recalled seeing the fifth lorry, stuck in Fountain Square:

> All around it was a mob attacking it. I at once gave a shout to my men to come out and rescue their comrades and I led a charge across the Chandni Chowk to the lorry. The crowd at once began to flee and I saw that the lorry had been wrecked and that men were standing right against the lorry and even climbing on to it and flinging down stones and bricks on the unfortunate people inside. We rushed at this mob and I was able to strike one man with my fist, but as I was 10 or 15 yards ahead of the main body of the police the mob was able to escape all serious damage and arrest. We pursued the mob a few yards down the Kauria Pul Road and then returned to rescue the men in the lorry. As I reached the lorry one occupant who had obviously been injured and who was probably half unconscious climbed out very slowly and in a dazed condition. I looked inside the lorry and saw 3 or 4 men who were in much the same condition. There was a great deal of blood. The lorry was full of stones. The driver had apparently escaped.[17]

The shooting on the gurdwara was described as "a minor business," being occasional and not directed at any individual. This wholly failed to address the sacred geography of the gurdwara. In its report the Firing Enquiry concluded as follows, which indicates the distrust between the two inquiring bodies, and the sacred geography they were negotiating:

> **Note by the Committee.**
> In our presence when we went to the Gurdwara after visiting the Kotwali, a man went up the steps of the Gurdwara with his shoes on, and there came a loud noise of protest from all the people present there. He looked to be a CID

man and he seemed to have done it to rebut the theory of the sanctity of the Gurdwara premises. (Gurdwara Sis-Ganj Firing Committee 1930, 70)

## Embodied Truth: The Firing Enquiry Report and Excessive Violence

### EVIDENCE

A member of the SGPC had visited Delhi on 8 May and interviewed twenty witnesses (Gurdwara Sis-Ganj Firing Committee 1930, 25). The following day the Gurdwara Sis-Ganj Firing Enquiry Committee was established in Amritsar and visited Delhi on 18 and 19 May. The committee members, as described by the report, were the chair, Mr. K. L. Rallia Ram (educationist, president of the Punjab Indian Christian Conference, and member of Lahore Municipal Committee); Sardar Gulab Singh (bank director and Sikh member of the Legislative Assembly, representing West Punjab); Professor Ruchi Ram Sahni (retired professor of chemistry from Lahore); Sardar Buta Singh (former deputy president of the Punjab Legislative Council); and Maulana Abdul Qadir Qasuri. The latter was president of Lahore's Provincial Congress Committee and was arrested in this connection before the inquiry could progress. Another Muslim member was sought but could not join in time for the visit to Delhi. On 15 May the committee had written to the chief commissioner requesting his help "in arriving at the truth" by producing witnesses, cross-examining any witnesses the committee produced, and doing all other things that would help the committee arrive at the whole truth. The chief commissioner's registrar replied on the 17th saying that whatever the committee required would be explained in a personal interview, which took place on the 18th (and lasted twenty minutes). After the inquiry's public sessions, a second, two-hour-long interview was granted, at which the SSP and city magistrate were present. After this the committee was allowed to inspect the kotwali grounds, but not to question any members of the police while they were there.

Before meeting any witnesses the Committee had "decided to inspect the Gurdwara with a view to have a general idea of the place and its immediate surroundings" (Gurdwara Sis-Ganj Firing Committee 1930, 5). Five diagrams were included in the report, including a plan of the street area (figure 4.1) that was complemented by photographs of the buildings demonstrating how close the kotwali (on the right) and gurdwara were (figure 4.2).

The manager of the gurdwara pointed out the big stone pillars behind which those in the gurdwara had hid during the shooting, the bullet and buckshot marks on the walls as well as on the "Nishan Sahib [the Sikh religious standard] the cloth round which had been pierced by the shots in numerous

FIGURE 4.2. Gurdwara and kotwali (Gurdwara Sis-Ganj Firing Committee 1930; courtesy of National Gandhi Museum and Library)

places, and the locality where the portrait of Guru Gobind Singh was hung up behind the glass panes of an arched window. The glass panes had been shattered by the shot fired from the Kotwali and the portrait itself was damaged in places" (Gurdwara Sis-Ganj Firing Committee 1930, 5).

The folds of the Nishan Sahib around the mast had been cut open, and a number of spent shots were said to have been found within. Various objects were found shot through by buckshot cartridges and revolver bullets. Although the police, soon after the shooting, had collected as many of these shots and bullets as they could find and taken them away, the manager had collected those remaining. Committee member Gulab Singh was deputed to count the bullets and buckshot marks on the walls facing the kotwali. He found 686, excluding those that had hit the Nishan Sahib or did not leave a mark. The report followed this with a description of the historic significance of the Sisganj site "in the eyes of the Sikh Panth (Community)," being sacred as the site at which the ninth guru, Guru Tegh Bahadur, had been beheaded in 1675, with the gurdwara being completed in 1803 (Gurdwara Sis-Ganj Firing Committee 1930, 6).

This placement of the gurdwara's geography and history on the second page proper of the report is significant. While claiming that the committee visited the gurdwara "before proceeding to examine witnesses and record their statements," in a very real sense their depiction of the "general idea of the place" was the statement on which all those that followed rested, and the building itself was the key witness. It bore more wounds (686) than any other site in Delhi, but its wounds were also deeper, affecting every member of the panth. These were not just bullet wounds, but wounds to religious precedence (the wearing of shoes in the gurdwara), to religious honor (the touching of a men's *kesha* [sacred hair]), and of profanation (the damaging of the Nishan Sahib and portrait of Guru Gobind Singh).

The committee had seen the magistrate's report, which was submitted to the chief commissioner on 26 May, and agreed with some of its factual account of events leading up to the shooting, as relayed above, but contested many of its interpretations. For instance, the committee admitted that the crowd had been highly agitated but insisted there were relatively few cases in which they transgressed the law of nonviolence (Gurdwara Sis-Ganj Firing Committee 1930, 10). They admitted that some Europeans were roughly handled near the cutcherry, while their discourse on the subaltern occasionally aligned itself with that of the official report in describing the people on the street as "being in a state of intense excitement, as one could expect from a mob on such a day" (10). But, in general, the report undid the depiction of a seething mass, giving the crowds intentionality and reason in their placement and movement through the city.

Focusing on a fact only hinted at in the magistrate's report, many of those injured by police action at the cutcherry had been brought to the kotwali for treatment or detention. As such the "mob" at the gurdwara could have been "sight-seers" (those enjoying the buzz of the hartal); "others, perhaps, were in an angry mood and wanted to know what was going to happen to their friends and associates. Yet another section might have gone to the Kotwali with a view to look after their injured friends and relatives and render them such relief and assistance as it was in their power to do" (Gurdwara Sis-Ganj Firing Committee 1930, 10).

This set in motion a self-perpetuating cycle of violence and concern swirling around the kotwali that would propel it toward "the final tragedy that occurred there": more people "began to throng this part of the city"; the police made charges on the crowd to disperse them; the number of casualties in the kotwali increased; thus more people, it was suggested, thronged that part of the city (Gurdwara Sis-Ganj Firing Committee 1930, 10). As events moved into the final act of this tragedy, the two reports' versions of events diverge. The pivotal disagreement was whether stones had been thrown from the gurdwara and whether the lorry in Fountain Square had been out of reach of any brickbat that could have been thrown from the gurdwara.

Regarding the first point, every witness denied that anything was thrown from the gurdwara, while the SSP during his interview had said that brickbats had come from the gurdwara side in "tons" and "clouds" (Gurdwara Sis-Ganj Firing Committee 1930, 12). The committee found it hard to disbelieve an officer of such high standing and experience as the SSP, but nor could they "swallow the statement easily, particularly as we did not notice a single leaf or flower or blade of grass to have been injured in the flower garden in front of the Kotwali where the Policemen are said to have received 'tons' of brickbats" (13).

The committee offered two explanations, both of which reversed usual colonial depictions of the subaltern by suggesting that it was the representatives of the state who were irrational. The first was that the brickbats came so heavily at the police from the fountain side that their " 'tons' and 'clouds' . . . must have darkened the atmosphere a little, and made it difficult for them to judge rightly" (Gurdwara Sis-Ganj Firing Committee 1930, 13). The second was that the SSP was, naturally, in a very bad state of mind, having had a strenuous few days and having been, by his own admission, hit four or five times: "In such a mood of mind, psychologically, however good and well intentioned a man might be, he could not well be expected to judge things rightly. As we know, he acted just in the heat of the moment" (13). Moving from the SSP to the police more generally, the report suggested that the police were tired, in sullen mood, their pride wounded, their prestige lowered, and "they wanted only an opportunity or any pretence, real or imaginary, to wreak vengeance upon the crowd which had no doubt annoyed them a good deal and to make an impression" (14). The police had failed to adhere to section 127 of the CrPC, having not issued a warning that they were about to open fire; it appears that the police acted without the orders from an officer.

The Firing Enquiry thus came to their conclusions, which stand in direct contrast to the gendered and affective concluding paragraph of the magistrate's report (which they had seen) but also references the conclusions made by the president of the Bar Association (indiscriminate, reprehensible, cowardly, in defiance of the law) regarding the attacks earlier in the day: "Now, considering the duration, the number of marks on the walls, and the way the Police fired into the Gurdwara, we have no hesitation in saying that the firing was **indiscriminate, vindictive, and excessive**" (Gurdwara Sis-Ganj Firing Committee 1930, 16, emphasis in original).

Evidence was used to bolster the three claims above, stating that shooting was

- *Vindictive*: no distinction was made between the guilty and the innocent. Anybody who could not find shelter was a potential victim.
- *Indiscriminate*: markings were found where nobody could possibly have been standing; even the upper arches and domes of the building had been hit (see figure 4.3). Nor had punitive accuracy been maintained in firing on human bodies; one fourteen-year-old boy was hit in the intestines and another in the arm.
- *Excessive*: due to its duration of, with intervals, at least twenty minutes. The superintendent claimed that people in the gurdwara continued to throw "brickbats" during this time and thus firing was legitimate. At this argument the committee could not withhold their incredulity: "It is inconceivable that in a place which was quite exposed to the firing of the Police from three directions anyone but a lunatic could have had the temerity and the foolhardiness to throw a brickbat and come forward against men who had rifles or revolvers in their hands and who were actually firing at the time." (Gurdwara Sis-Ganj Firing Committee 1930, 16–17)

The gurdwara was violated not only from without but also from within. The final diagram in the report showed that bullet marks were found in sacred parts of the building, while the police were alleged to have entered the con-

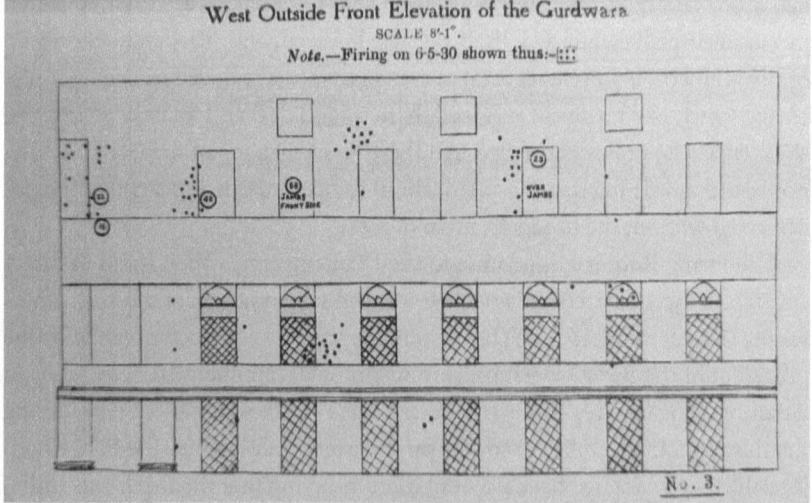

**FIGURE 4.3.** West outside front elevation (Gurdwara Sis-Ganj Firing Committee 1930; courtesy of National Gandhi Museum and Library)

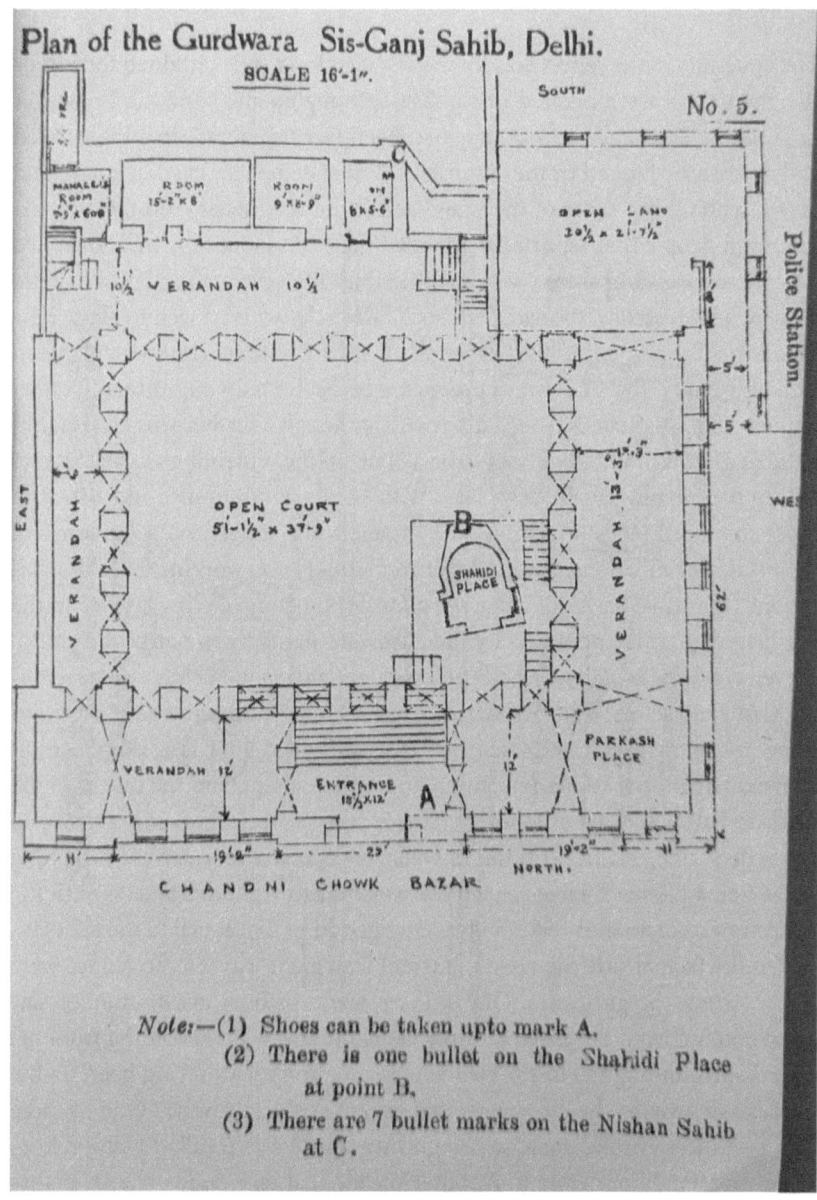

FIGURE 4.4. Plan of the Gurdwara Sis-Ganj Sahib (Gurdwara Sis-Ganj Firing Committee 1930; courtesy of National Gandhi Museum and Library)

fines wearing their shoes before dragging a man by his hair out of the gurdwara (figure 4.4).

## TESTIMONIES

The appendix to the report was forty-five pages long and contained forty-four statements. All were printed in English, although some contained passages in Hindi, which suggests that they had been translated and thus interpreted and necessarily filtered by the committee. The statements varied in length and detail, with all but three of the witnesses listing their occupation. Given the thousand people that reportedly attended the open inquest, it was not stated why these forty-four were chosen (other than the seven wounded witnesses at the Civil Hospital), though their social diversity worked well to show how broad the affected communities were. Of the forty-four witnesses, eighteen explicitly stated that they were practicing Sikhs, with an additional five surnamed Singh suggested to be Sikhs as well, although a further witness, Raghunath Singh, was pointed out not to be a Sikh. Of the remaining witnesses, seventeen had names usually associated with Hindu communities and two with more commonly Muslim names. The witnesses also ranged widely in terms of their stated occupations. Seven identified themselves as working for Sikh institutions (the SGPC, an Akali jatha, *sewadars* [volunteers offering service to the gurdwara], guards appointed by the gurdwara manager to patrol the gates). Eleven could be broadly termed professionals (five in medicine, two academics, two contractors, and two with the press), ten as owners or managers in trade (two managers in the construction of the new capital, four shopkeepers, a businessman, a soap manufacturer, an iron merchant, and the owner of the Café-de-Paris) and ten as laborers (two factory workers, two in service, two cap sellers, one *beldar* [working in construction], a motor driver, a cigarette seller, and a painter). They ranged from victims to witnesses and, as with the magistrate's statements, their evidence ranged from the factual to the affective.

On the factual side the most recurrent statement was that no stones were thrown from the gurdwara. One witness saw no stones at all; another saw some coming from the cinema, while yet another saw them coming from the crowd surrounding the lorry. Two witnesses admitted to having been on the procession around the city before the events at the gurdwara. One of these was asked to form the guard at the gurdwara gate and recalled being told to remain perfectly nonviolent. Another recalled, after a police charge before the shooting: "The people left [the gurdwara] in a sullen mood. The people shouted, had Mahatma Gandhi allowed them, they would have done something" (Gurdwara Sis-Ganj Firing Committee 1930, 45). The statements also attest the arbitrariness of the violence; many had been in Chandni Chowk and had taken refuge in the gurdwara when the shooting began and had then been either wounded or arrested.

Throughout the witness statements there are also glimpses of the experiences of the day and the attempts to recollect the affective experience of violence. A fifteen-year-old factory boy called Buttu was near the gurdwara because he was out seeing the *tamasha* (fun). But the most common emotions evoked were those of horror and shock. Captain (Dr.) Mul. Singh, who had offered medical assistance to the injured in the kotwali, rushed to the gurdwara after the shooting: "I rushed to the Gurdwara and what I saw there I shall never forget. Many people were being dragged and pushed out from inside the Gurdwara, wounded or unwounded" (Gurdwara Sis-Ganj Firing Committee 1930, 30). The gurdwara manager recalled being roughly handled and spoken to by Tara Chand (who denied this charge in his magistrate's statement), and Ram Singh, who beat him with lathis, forcibly took him to the kotwali and said to him, "Sonny, we will teach you a lesson" (34). Commenting on the police action, a female doctor, Devi Kuntal Kumari, insisted: "The firing was indiscriminate and unjustified. My impression was that the Policemen had lost their senses" (58). Another man, Mithan Lal, who had taken refuge in the gurdwara during the firing, recalled: "During the time I was in the Gurdwara, the people were terror-stricken" (61). Perhaps the most affecting of the statements were those that enveloped the raw emotions of loss within the factual discourse of testimony, such as the statement of Bibi Hardei, listed as a widow, and resident of mohalla Dariba, Kucha Sethan:

> My son Ami Lal was shot at, as he was getting into the Gurdwara. He received three shots, one in the abdomen and two in the thigh. He was carried to the General Hospital, where he died. He was thirty years of age. Here in the Hospital he told me that he had been shot at while he was going up the steps of the Gurdwara. When he lay dying he said he was glad to die at the feet of the Lord. ("Bhagwan ke charnon men mara hum.") He used to go to the Gurdwara very often. He lay unconscious for some days toward the end. (Gurdwara Sis-Ganj Firing Committee 1930, 53)

Fact and affect aligned around two central themes in the statements, charting the damage done to both individuals and buildings. As such the testimonies captured the trauma of transgression of two types of body: one, corporeal and individual; the second, social and collective, via transgressing the boundaries of the gurdwara building itself. Regarding the former, the statements provide a violent union of truth and body, not through habitual self-formation but through what Veena Das (1995) referred to as a "form of a memory inscribed on a body" (176).

Five witnesses were able to show the committee evidence of lathi blows on

FIGURE 4.5. Some of the persons injured by firing into the gurdwara (Gurdwara Sis-Ganj Firing Committee 1930; courtesy of National Gandhi Museum and Library)

their bodies. Bhai Beant Singh, for instance, claimed the police had started beating the crowd with lathis, without warning, and that the marks could still be seen; his statement was signed off by the committee with "The witness showed the Committee the marks of the blows" (Gurdwara Sis-Ganj Firing Committee 1930, 36). The committee also confirmed seeing other injuries from lathi blows on legs, feet, and heads. More serious were the gunshot wounds. The forty-year-old Khazan Singh was hit by two or three pieces of buckshot to the head and was carried, unconscious, to a nearby dispensary. Another reported having a bullet extracted from his leg, which committee member Gulab Singh confirmed by examining the wounds. A student at MB High School in New Delhi, Davender Singh, hid behind a column in the gurdwara during the shooting but was hit on both his thighs; one shot pierced through the leg while the other was extracted afterward by a doctor. The committee appended a note showing that they had examined the boy and confirmed that there were two marks on either side of one thigh where a shot had passed straight through. Construction worker Chiddu was shot in the arm and leg in the gurdwara, while Bhai Prem Singh, a driver for an Englishman, remarkably survived being shot through the chest. A young cap seller, Biro Singh, who had been passing by the kotwali and took refuge in the gurdwara, was hit in the abdomen. The committee made inquiries at the hospital and learned that his intestines had been ruptured and repaired. A similar incident was recalled by Dr. K. L. Brahmchari, who, between 4:00 p.m. and 5:00 p.m. on 6 May, "saw a boy named Biro Mal outside the Gurdwara, whose intestines had come out. I had him carried to my dispensary, where the intestines were put in and skin was stitched up by myself and Rai Sahib Dr. Hari Singh. The boy died three or four days ago in the General Hospital" (Gurdwara Sis-Ganj Firing Committee 1930, 58). While the hospital and surname of the victim differ in the last two cases, they may be referring to the same incident, though confusion remains about the fate of the boy.

Death was here marked on bodies, but bodies were also used to convey the shock of death itself. Mian Fazal Ilahi, a forty-five-year-old box maker from Sadar Bazar, recalled going out on the 6th to look for his seventeen-year-old son, who had been sent out to buy some *churian* (bangles) for his sister but had not returned home. He heard in the street that his son had been fired upon and that his body was being brought to his home: "When I heard the news I fainted and I do not know what happened afterwards. The people who communicated the news to me told me that they had kept me up from falling down. They also told me that they had brought my son from the Fountain" (Gurdwara Sis-Ganj Firing Committee 1930, 58).

If these accounts chart violence done to individual bodies, others recounted the violence done to the gurdwara building and, through it, to the collective body of the Sikh panth. Bridging the two categories were those incidents that did individual and religious violence to people in the gurdwara. One New Delhi contractor, Sardar Bahadur Sardar Dharam Singh, arrived at the gurdwara after the firing and heard reports of a man dragged from the building "by his keshas (sacred hair)" (Gurdwara Sis-Ganj Firing Committee 1930, 64). This was witnessed firsthand by retired professor S. K. Sharma, while another statement claimed that Tara Chand not only abused the gurdwara manager, Bhai Budh Singh, but also slapped him in the face and caught hold of his beard. This wasn't mentioned in Budh Singh's statement, though he did recall "a *Gora* (white-faced) Officer dragging Bhai Hari Singh by the sacred hair" (34). Bhai Hari Singh's statement, however, contradicted this, suggesting it was Bhai Maya Singh who was dragged out of the gurdwara, before the shooting, by a European sergeant. Maya Singh confirmed this in his statement, after which Hari Singh rescued him by delivering a *mukka* blow (with a closed fist) to the sergeant.

More of an insult to the gurdwara itself was the wearing of shoes by the police within the building. Captain (Dr.) Mul Singh suggested fifty to seventy policemen had been seen within the gurdwara wearing shoes; Professor Sharma put the figure at twenty, while the contractor Dharam Singh confirmed the police were going about freely with shoes on into all parts of the gurdwara. Lest there be any confusion on this issue, during the first witness statement by Giani Gurmukh Singh of the SGPC, the president (presumably referring to the chair) of the committee had asked, for clarification, whether no one was allowed in the gurdwara with shoes on, to which he received the unambiguous reply: "Nobody is allowed in the Gurdwara with shoes on" (Gurdwara Sis-Ganj Firing Committee 1930, 27). Bhai Beant Singh, secretary of the Akali jatha, though experienced in the military, spoke of his severe mental shock at seeing the gurdwara desecrated by the police bringing their shoes into the *smadh* (shrine) of Guru Tegh Bahadur.

Perhaps of greatest offense to the wider community, however, was the violent sacrilege committed against the gurdwara itself. While the police were searching the gurdwara for protesters after the shooting had concluded, Captain Singh reported how they turned their attention to the *kothri* (a small private room for the safe-keeping of the Holy Granth Sahib) "where Sri Guru Granth Sahib was lying" (Gurdwara Sis-Ganj Firing Committee 1930, 31). The syntax here captures the sacred geography of this place. "Sri" is the title used for venerating deities (translated as "holy") but is also a polite greeting when used to refer to humans (equivalent to "Mr."). While the Granth Sahib is the sacred Sikh text of 1,430 pages, it also considered to be the final, eleventh guru who was, in this case, in refuge in the kothri from the hail of bullets and buckshot raining down on this Sikh temple. The police proceeded to break the lock of the kothri with their lathis, while others were trying to break the gate to the room. The sense of the Granth Sahib as a subject rather than object was reinforced by the manager's protestation against the attempt to open the kothri, "because there was none in that room except Sri Guru Granth Sahib" (Gurdwara Sis-Ganj Firing Committee 1930, 31).

But the offense went further than breaking into the kothri. Captain Singh suggested that before the shooting, when stones had reportedly been thrown into the gurdwara from the kotwali, that one stone had fallen on the rumals (sacred vestments) of the Sri Guru Granth Sahib, after which it was removed to the kothri. Bhai Maya Singh reported shots striking the Nishan Sahib (see figure 4.4). The report had also highlighted the damaged portrait of Guru Gobind Singh Sahib, as witnessed by the iron merchant Sardar Nanak Singh and the contractor Sardar Dharam Singh. Fellow contractor Sardar Bahadur S. Wasakha Singh, who was also president of the Gurdwara Committee, spoke of seeing the torn portrait of Guru Gobind Singh, on which the marks of shots were visible, and which was surrounded by broken glass. That evening he sent emissaries to Amritsar and Lahore to alert the SGPC, setting in motion the upscaling of the firing from a local incident to an attack on the Sikh nation. As he put it: "We felt that it was a great insult to the Gurdwara and thereby to the Sikh religion; and not only did we alone feel it, but as the Gurdwara belonged to the Panth, therefore, every Sikh felt this insult. The Manager was trembling all over because he had been so much affected by the occurrence that he could hardly express himself" (Gurdwara Sis-Ganj Firing Committee 1930, 47).

## Scales of Commemoration

While the two inquiries into the shooting constitute remarkable documents in their own right, they were but two fragments of a broader archive that was emerging around the struggle to define what had happened on 6 May. At the center of this struggle was the question of scale. As the significance of the violence became clear, the initial actors in the tragedy (the Delhi Administration, the Gurdwara Sisganj management, the Delhi Sikh community, and the Delhi Congress organizers of the May protests) were joined from offstage by their national-scale counterparts (the Government of India, the SGPC, the national Sikh community, and the Indian National Congress). These local-national pairings would upscale the Sisganj shootings, bringing in resources and publicity that helped wrestle the event into rival camps of interpretation. But these inpourings of attention and interpretation would also lead to tensions between scales, as the sensitivities of Delhi's governmental and social environments were ignored. These tensions and upscalings will be highlighted as the tragedy unfolded across the nation.

### UPSCALING

The local authorities had been aware of how dangerous the gurdwara could become as a magnet for dissidence and a site of countermemory. The local Congress committee attempted to capitalize immediately on the shooting by organizing a large funeral procession for two of the dead on 7 May. But it was canceled after they were told it would contravene CrPC, section 144 (prohibiting the carrying of lathis or assemblages of more than five people) that had been declared. The chief commissioner, J. N. G. Johnson, stated in his message of 8 May to the home secretary, Herbert Emerson, which accompanied the draft communiqué that had been requested of him: "From past experience in Delhi the dangerous results of such processions are only too well known."[18] Johnson was likely referencing the occasion, three years earlier, when the corpse of Abdul Rashid, the assassin of Swami Shradhannand, was captured during its funeral procession and toured around the city, causing further rioting.[19]

Shortly after the shooting the Punjab provincial government had telephoned the chief commissioner asking for an account of events. This concern related to the Punjab's large Sikh population and concentration of Sikh holy sites. Of a Punjab population of nearly 29 million, the 1931 census listed returns by Sikhs at just over 4 million, though they made up one in four of the population in the Jullunder and Lahore Divisions, the latter of which included the sacred Golden Temple complex at Amritsar (Census of India 1933b, 278). On 8 May Johnson telegrammed a condensed version of his communiqué to Sir Henry Craik, the finance minister for the Punjab in Lahore, exonerating the police action and insisting that the firing was the minimum that was necessary to safeguard the police.

This message was passed to the governor of the Punjab, Geoffrey de Montmorency, who telephoned the home secretary. On 10 May Home Secretary Emerson reported on file that a recent meeting at the Akal Takht, the primary seat of the Sikh faith located at the Golden Temple complex in Amritsar, had been addressed by Sikhs from Delhi, presumably those dispatched by the president of the Sisganj Gurdwara Committee shortly after the shooting. They were decided, presumably in contrast to Johnson's report, to have given "a very exaggerated account of what had happened" and had worked the audience "up to a very excited state."[20] Three Sikhs from Amritsar had been sent to Delhi and returned on 9 May, bringing with them the buckshot-riddled portrait of Sri Guru Govind Singh, photographs of the gurdwara's broken windows, and lead that they "alleged" had been extracted from the gurdwara's woodwork. A meeting was held in the evening of the 9th in Jallianwala Bagh, the site of the British massacre in 1919. The Punjab government promised to do all it could to prevent a jatha marching to Peshawar to garner support for a larger protest and promised to distribute a translation of the chief commissioner's communiqué into Gurmukhi (the language used by the Punjabi Sikh community). On

11 May the *Daily Akali* newspaper in Amritsar published an account of events in Delhi as told by the Sikhs who had returned from Delhi on the 9th.[21]

At this time there was a great deal of traffic between the Punjab and Delhi. The preliminary visit to Delhi by an SGPC representative had been made from 8 May; Giani Gurmukh Singh had collected the first twenty witness statements but had been told by the chief commissioner that no unofficial inquiry, anywhere in the world, would be allowed to cross-examine police officers (Gurdwara Sis-Ganj Firing Committee 1930, 25). On 12 May "Baisakha Singh" (listed as Wasakha Singh by the Firing Enquiry), the president of the Sisganj Gurdwara Committee, and fellow Delhi contractor Sardar Bahadur Sobha Singh met with de Montmorency in Lahore, having first visited Amritsar. After a long discussion with them, de Montmorency reported to Delhi's chief commissioner that he "sent them back to Amritsar to do what they could to allay public feeling among Sikhs," where they would also meet his Sikh minister Sir Jogendra Singh, who de Montmorency had "primed" using facts from Johnson's communiqués. Both the Delhi and Punjab governors clearly felt that the Delhi Sikh community, especially with its contractor leadership, proffered a conservative base with which to challenge the more radical Akalis from Amritsar, who de Montmorency felt had done their best to "set abroad highly sensational and lying rumours."[22] Their ambition was to further upscale the shooting from a local to a provincial to a national scandal, planning that every gurdwara in the country should recite a prayer on the 18th of each month about the Sisganj affair, asserting that

1. The authorities in Delhi fired without justification on the sacred gurdwara, killing Sikhs there
2. The Government was refusing to hold an inquiry or punish those at fault
3. It was therefore prayed that the guru may destroy the British nation and its Government in India

De Montmorency said he would try to stop the plan but doubted he could, and that such a prayer "in remote Gurdwaras amongst ignorant crowds of Sikhs would have a very bad effect." As such he made suggestions for urgent action in Delhi, having told Baisakha Singh to visit the chief commissioner on his return, possibly with a deputation of local Delhi Sikhs. From this point, however, the Delhi Sikh community found themselves very much positioned as witnesses, not inquirers. Johnson had anticipated this. In his letter to de Montmorency on 13 May regarding his plan to meet with Delhi Sikhs, he wrote: "The trouble is that they now seem to count for so little in the matter, of which the SPGC and the Amritsar people would appear to have assumed complete control." On the 18th he sent a further letter suggesting that Baisakha Singh and Sobha Singh had been able to achieve nothing; the GPC at Amritsar had refused them, and the prayer plans were going ahead: "Both were genuinely grieved and indignant at this behaviour. I gather from various sources that the Delhi Sikhs of varying shades of opinion are vexed and consider that the Amritsar people have treated them in a very cavalier fashion."²³ This was made very clear when the Firing Enquiry arrived in Delhi. The Local Gurdwara Committee had arranged for the public meetings to be held in a local hotel, but the chair shifted the venue to Queen's Gardens where a shamiana (awning) was erected, and the proceedings were conducted by the Lahore-based committee (Gurdwara Sis-Ganj Firing Committee 1930, 7).

The SGPC, while clearly stoking discontent and upscaling the shooting, were also responding to genuine shock in the Sikh community and beyond. The viceroy and chief commissioner received a steady stream of telegrams and letters expressing hurt and outrage at the shootings. While the government files do not speculate on whether these messages were being coordinated or were responding to wordings in the press, there was a recurrent focus on the need for an independent inquiry and that the guilty be punished, though each articulated the offense done to the Sikh community, and the reputation of the British, in specific ways.

The first recorded message was a telegram to the viceroy on 8 May from Sher Singh Gyani, editor of the *Daily Asli Quamidard* of Amritsar, stating that the whole Sikh community had been perturbed, that an impartial inquiry was required, and that guilty officers should be punished, "or serious consequences will be with govnt." In a letter from Delhi's Arya Samaj to the chief commissioner on 12 May, the police action was described as barbarous and a nonofficial inquiry was demanded to "allay the public feelings of discontent and horror."²⁴ On the same day two telegrams had been sent to the viceroy, from the Sikh-protectionist Singh Sabha in Abbottabad, Punjab, and from the president of the Central India Gurdwara Prabandhak Committee, expressing grief and sorrow; both demanded an independent inquiry. Two days later a telegram was sent to the viceroy from the manager of the Gurdwara Panjasahib Hasanabdal, a holy temple thirty miles from Rawalpindi in the Punjab, sited around a rock said to bear an imprint made by Guru Nanak. A meeting had been held with local people and those from the frontier province with Afghanistan, who had insisted that Sikhs should never bear such illegal actions, that an inquiry be held, and that guilty officers be punished.²⁵ On 16 May the Gurdwara Committee Bhai Joga Singh Ji of Peshawar City in the North-West Frontier Province wrote to the chief commissioner of their pain at hearing of the shooting and on behalf of the Sikhs of Peshawar requested that there be an immediate inquiry "to pacify the burning Sikh hearts," and that the offenders be dealt with severely.[26]

On 18 May the president of the Shri Guru Singh Sabha of Hosiarpur in the Punjab reported that they had reviewed the data available in the communiqués of the chief commissioner and from the SGPC members who had visited Delhi and concluded that the police did fire on the gurdwara for reasons that were unclear, that the perpetrators of the firing and "desecration" should be held to account, and that they were awaiting the SGPC inquiry findings. Time was doing little to assuage these sentiments as the rival inquiries were taking place. On 26 May (the day the chief commissioner received the magistrate's findings) the home secretary forwarded to Delhi a telegram sent to the viceroy from the Sikh Sangat Sargodha in the Punjab on 19 May condemning the "callous sacrilege" at Delhi that had been "absolutely gratuitous[,] purposely provocative[,] and unprecedented since British occupation."[27] Official denials were condemned as brazen-faced and calculated to add insult to injury, while the most fervent and emotional prayers were said to be rising from every Sikh heart for the surest and speediest destruction of the tyrannical governmental system.

In the face of this growing anger the chief commissioner found himself unable to turn to the local Sikh community for help. Baisakha Singh and Sobha Singh had not produced a varied and convincing local deputation, in the face of declarations being issued from Amritsar that appeared to be intimidating potential supporters, so Johnson wrote to de Montmorency on the 19th that he would rather keep the "friendlies" and moderates onside for now. From further afield Johnson was also receiving suggestions from the maharaja of Patiala, the most prominent Sikh voice among the hereditary rulers of the Indian states. On 21 May Patiala had written to the Government of local Sikhs' complaints and suggested the Government convey regret at some of the language used in their communications and select representatives to visit Delhi and put forward their specific complaints. Johnson replied the following day with a flat refusal, suggesting the time had come to start containing the difficulties the Government was experiencing and for a judicious stiffening of attitude. Emerson forwarded a report to Johnson on 26 May suggesting that "firebrands" among the SGPC wanted a *morcha* (agitation) at the Sisganj Gurdwara unless their demands were met (that the Government express regret, that responsible officers be dismissed, that the injured be compensated, and that the gurdwara be repaired).[28] This would depend on the finding of the magistrate's report.

## READING THE REPORT/INQUIRY

The Government received the magistrate's inquiry at the end of May, and Emerson wrote to Johnson on 4 June with his comments, which were at best muted in support and asked for further clarification of key facts. Johnson fell back on the decisionism that political emergencies demanded (see Hussain 2003): "The police were justified in opening fire, even without the orders of a superior officer, if a sudden emergency had arisen which rendered it necessary for them to defend themselves and to save their comrades who were in jeopardy of their lives. That such emergency had arisen the evidence in the papers before me appears to have established."[29]

Johnson eventually came up against the irremovable offense committed against the building itself. "Now I can well understand the pain that must have been caused to all staunch and devout Sikhs by the news of the firing on a building which possesses such a very special sanctity in the eyes of all Sikhs as does the Gurdwara of Sisganj."[30] Sikh anger, however, should be directed not at the police but at "wickedly-disposed" members of their own community who had desecrated the gurdwara by using its building materials as weapons and itself as a base for assault on the forces of law and order "with the inevitable result," that is, the shooting.

While the magistrate's findings had been published by the Government on 4 June, the Sis Ganj Firing Enquiry Committee's report was published in time for discussion at an All Parties Sikh Conference on 7 June and a meeting of the SGPC on the 9th. Preparatory meetings in Amritsar had been attended by up to three thousand people, including Akali activists, Hindus, and Muslims. The prayer plan for 18 May had not come to much, but loyal Sikhs had been expressing their concerns to the deputy commissioner in Amritsar.[31] The conference, however, did not produce the unanimity that the Punjab government had feared. It included representatives of the SGPC, the Shiromani Akali Dal, the Chief Khalsa Diwan, the Central Sikh League, representatives of the Nirmala, Namdhari, and Nirankari Sikh traditions, various other *diwans* (congregations) and Singh sabhas, and members of legislatures. One resolution was passed against the firing, but only by 57 to 56 votes, after which the conference had broken down, with Sir Sunder Singh Majithia walking out after he had been called a *toady bacha* (literally, a sycophantic child).[32] Various resolutions by loyalist parties were debated, and the Delhi Sikhs were noted for resisting extremist demands. The resolutions were that the Government should express regret and protect the sacred places of all religions; there be exemplary punishment; and the gurdwara be repaired. Various Akali Dal members attacked the SGPC, insisted the gurdwara bullet marks should not be repaired as long as the British remained in India, and demanded a morcha at the gurdwara and pressed for jathas to be dispatched.

On 16 June the SGPC sent a copy of their report to the viceroy, emphasizing its conclusion that the firing was indiscriminate, excessive, and vindictive. It had since held meetings in Amritsar on 9 June and Lahore on 15 June where minimum demands had been agreed to redress offenses to the Sikh panth, which would be published on 22 June. They were that the Government should express unqualified regret at the sacrilege, officials be punished, reparation be made, and the position of the kotwali be altered so as to make any future outrage impossible.[33] On 2 July the viceroy replied, backing the chief commissioner's statements, but as a token of goodwill the Gurdwara Committee was offered a grant of 25,000 rupees to help with repairs. This formed the Government's final public statement on the matter, seemingly satisfying many moderates but leading the more extreme agitators to pursue other means and parties of protest.

### BACK TO DISOBEDIENCE?

The gurdwara shooting did not easily lend itself to Congress mobilization, given that violence on the part of the protesters had never been conclusively ruled out. In response to the viceroy's statement the SGPC formed a funded "Sisganj Committee" in mid-July to coordinate further action. On 12 August de Montmorency reported to Emerson that two parties from the SGPC were touring the Punjab collecting Akali volunteers and money to concentrate in Lahore between 17 and 25 August. Some Sikhs had already gathered at Jallianwala Bagh in Amritsar and in Lahore, where they were engaged in picketing. While Congress had attempted to capitalize on the shootings in the immediate term, they seem to have been happy to stand back and let divisions grow between the government and the previously loyal Sikh community. Congress also had mixed relations with the Sikh community, springing from perceived incompatibilities between Gandhi's nonviolence and the committed martialism of Sikh culture, as well as difficulties that emerged in the 1920s between Nehru and the Akali Dal movement (Jalal 2000, 404). However, the Akalis saw Civil Disobedience as a means to advance their demands for greater Sikh autonomy. On 4 June Emerson had forwarded to Delhi a note by the maharaja of Patiala expressing concern that the extreme wing of the SGPC was pressing to join Civil Disobedience.[34] Johnson himself, in his reply to the Government's queries over the magistrate's report on 7 June, stated that both the Delhi Administration and the Sikhs themselves knew that a section of their community, over whom others lacked any control, had played a "specially truculent part in the Civil Disobedience movement in Delhi."[35] At the All Parties Sikh Conference in early June there had also been pro-Congress speeches reported.

Yet when the Akalis and Congress workers came together in August 1930, tensions quickly surfaced. De Montmorency reported that the Akalis were thoroughly sick of picketing and that quarrels had broken out in Amritsar between the two parties. The Akalis apparently felt they were being used as tools by Congress volunteers, who wanted them to go to jail instead of Hindu volunteers, without providing enough money to feed them.

The union in general seemed short-lived and enthusiasm for commemorating the shooting faded by the end of the year. In November there were reports that the SGPC and Shiromani Akali Dal were trying to stoke the agitation, to incite anti-British prayers in gurdwaras, and to interest Sikh soldiers by showing them the bullet marks on the gurdwara. It was true that these marks had become a memorial of sorts, and that the gurdwara gatekeeper showed them to visiting Sikh pilgrims, but there was no evidence of this being part of a political program. Senior members of the SGPC and Shiromani Akali Dal visited the gurdwara in early December in the hope of organizing a morcha. However, the Delhi Gurdwara Committee took this opportunity of having the national players on their home ground to say, in no uncertain terms, that they did not agree with the proposal and that it would not get assistance from local Sikhs. They were told that jathas of Punjabi Sikhs would soon be arriving, so the SGPC was bound to commit to the morcha, whether local Sikhs helped them or not. On 31 December two members of the Legislative Assembly, Sardar Harbans Singh and Sant Singh, wrote to the viceroy warning him that his response to the shooting had been inadequate and that a new inquiry should be instituted to quell the "present climax" of Sikh resentment.[36] The chief commissioner reassured Thompson that there was little local appetite for further action and recommended a polite but distant response.

On 5 January 1931 the Punjab government informed Emerson that the Sikh League had passed a resolution requesting the SGPC drop the Sisganj agitation and focus on securing adequate Sikh representation in the future reformed constitution. With Civil Disobedience being suspended, all eyes were now on London and the Round Table Conference. Sant Singh wrote to the viceroy on 15 January informing him that his attention was now focused on London, and that any reply to his previous letter could agitate the Sikh community, so he would be happy not to receive it. As the Punjab government had put it, "the matter is thus practically dead," and no jathas materialized in Delhi.³⁷

It was in this context that one last upscaling was attempted. Gandhi himself visited the Gurdwara Sisganj between his release from jail on 26 January and the signing of the Gandhi-Irwin Pact on 5 March. On 26 February he addressed the gurdwara, making a speech that was reproduced in the nationalist all-India periodical *Young India* on 5 March. He spoke of his "painful interest" in the details of the police shooting, which had been recounted for the audience by the previous speaker. Stressing his grief and resentment at the transgression of the sacred precincts of the gurdwara, Gandhi linked this local event to a national community. But this was a nationalist, not a Sikh community; he suggested "we are today fighting not for one Gurdwara but for the bigger Gurdwara, which is the common sacred possession of us all, viz., *purna swaraj*" (Gandhi 1999, 51:186).

Gandhi's truce with the viceroy meant that the first anniversary of the shooting in May 1931 was not marked by a major commemoration. While a resolution was passed at the gurdwara regarding the shooting, Congress's energies were focused on preparing for Gandhi's trip to London. The 1932 anniversary, however, took place after his return from London and arrest, sparking the second phase of Civil Disobedience. On 29 April the chief secretary of the Punjab, C. C. Garbett, wrote to the chief commissioner of Delhi that the Shiromani Akali Dal were planning to commemorate the 6 May shootings.³⁸ Garbett was convinced this was a Hindu Congress plan to get the Sikhs more involved in the ongoing protests against the Government and shift attention away from a Hindu-Sikh dispute over a contested gurdwara/dharmsala in the Punjab town of Daska. He went on to reiterate the problem or potential, depending on perspective, of the anniversary:

> The solution of the Hindus is to create a diversion and the Sisganj Anniversary appears to give them an opportunity. If they can get enough people to demonstrate before the SisGanj [*sic*] Gurdwara, there must be a clash as there is only a partition wall between the Gurdwara and the Kotwali and any really large crowd of Sikhs will block the entrance to Delhi's chief police station with the inevitable result of clashes, beatings, pulling of sacred *keshas* and perhaps (if Kali is kind) firing. Thus they would then hope to establish a really good Sikhs morcha against Government. Daska would be forgotten and the Hindu papers would chant *Te Deums* laudatory of Sikh efforts in the cause of their faith and commination [*sic*] services regarding the sins of Government in repressing its bravest and most deserving subjects.³⁹

As with the case of Mrs. Kohli, the dividing line between violence and nonviolence was a spatial one here, being the partition wall between the kotwali and gurdwara. But it was also a temporal one, interlinking 6 Mays over the years, and a relational one, linking the temple in Delhi to those throughout the Punjab and beyond.

Chief Commissioner Johnson responded that local Sikhs were still opposed to a morcha at Delhi, as they had been in late 1930. He planned to detain 186 Akalis who had been arrested in April in connection with the attempt to hold an AICC session at Delhi in jail until the anniversary had passed. As it happened the "wealthy contractors of New Delhi" used their influence to dissuade local participation in the planned commemoration, and the gurdwara shooting did not enter popular memory after the more dramatic and violent events of Quit India 1942 and partition in 1947.

This undid the work undertaken assiduously for six months in 1930 that had attempted to use the rich historical geography of the site to turn an anti-(Mughal) imperial site into an anti-(British) colonial one. As a report on Giani Kartar Singh's speech at Amritsar's Golden Temple in December 1930 put it: "He observed that whereas the body of the Guru was beheaded under the command of the Moghal Emperor from the Delhi Kotwali, sacrilege had now been done to the Gurdwara of the same Guru by firing from the Kotwali."[40] Ultimately, however, the Sisganj affair had problematized Congress's claim to be mobilizing a nonviolent but disobedient city alongside problematizing the government's use of violence. A comparable event occurred in 1932 but was successfully prevented from becoming a public problematization of state violence.

### A Non-Event: The Hauzwali Masjid

The government learned from the Sisganj affair and was able to respond much more quickly to accusations of religious affront the following year. Its measures were effective and demonstrate how effectively the government could prevent Congress from upscaling a local to a city- or even nationwide event.

The return to Civil Disobedience in February and March 1932 had seen increased cooperation between Hindus and Muslims with the Working Committee of the Jamiat-ul-Ulema-i-Hind (an anticolonial organization led by Islamic scholars) announcing its intention to work with Congress in early March. This was under the coordination of the Muslim Congress leader Abul Kalam Azad and Mufti Kafiyat-Ullah, the Jamiat president who had unsuccessfully campaigned for collaboration during the first phase of Civil Disobedience.[41] Muslim protesters had been particularly vocal, making speeches at the Jama Masjid and parading through Chandni Chowk, which resulted in a clash with the police on 29 January.[42] An official report stated that such occurrences were unacceptable, and a much stronger police force confronted a similar procession of two to four thousand people from Jama Masjid Mosque on 12 March.

The city magistrate reported antigovernment slogans "Long Live Revolution, Down with Ordinances" and banners proclaiming "Long Live Mufti Kafayat Ullah," who had been arrested the previous day.[43] In the ensuing disruptions two constables were stabbed prior to a lathi charge on the remaining protesters, who escaped into Queen's Gardens to the north and a series of small alleys to the south.[44] The police would later report that this triggered a shower of brickbats from a small lane named Kucha Rahman, which the police then entered, knocking down the door of one house to gain access to a veranda above. It later emerged that this house was in fact Hauzwali Masjid, a small local mosque.

Conscious of this becoming another Sisganj incident, the police produced a departmental inquiry within twelve days, complete with dozens of statements from locals claiming that anyone not familiar with the locality would not have known that the building housed a mosque. The kotwali sub-inspector, Abdul Wahid, evoked comparisons with the gurdwara predicament of the policemen in Fountain Square two years earlier: "The police were at this time in a great fix and could not go out of the lane. The door through which one has to pass for going to that room was given a push on which it fell back." As with the police entering the Sisganj, so it was insisted that "the mosque area was not entered by the police and every due respect and consideration was shown for the sanctity of the mosque."[45] It was also stressed that the police were not familiar with that part of the city and that most of them were Muslim.

Aware of how the gurdwara's report had used local testimonies to bolster its authenticity, fifty pages of statements from local residents were appended to the report. These backed up the police claims that the building was not identifiable as a mosque from outside, with no minar (tower) or mihrab (a wall niche indicating the direction of Mecca). One reported, "As a rule the mosque is only used by the people of the Mohalla and the outsiders unless they were specifically told would not know that there was a mosque." Just as the Gurdwara Inquiry Committee had produced a detailed plan of the Sisganj, so the government report included a detailed plan (figure 4.6) drawn by M. Fazluddin of the Public Works Department (who would draw another plan regard-

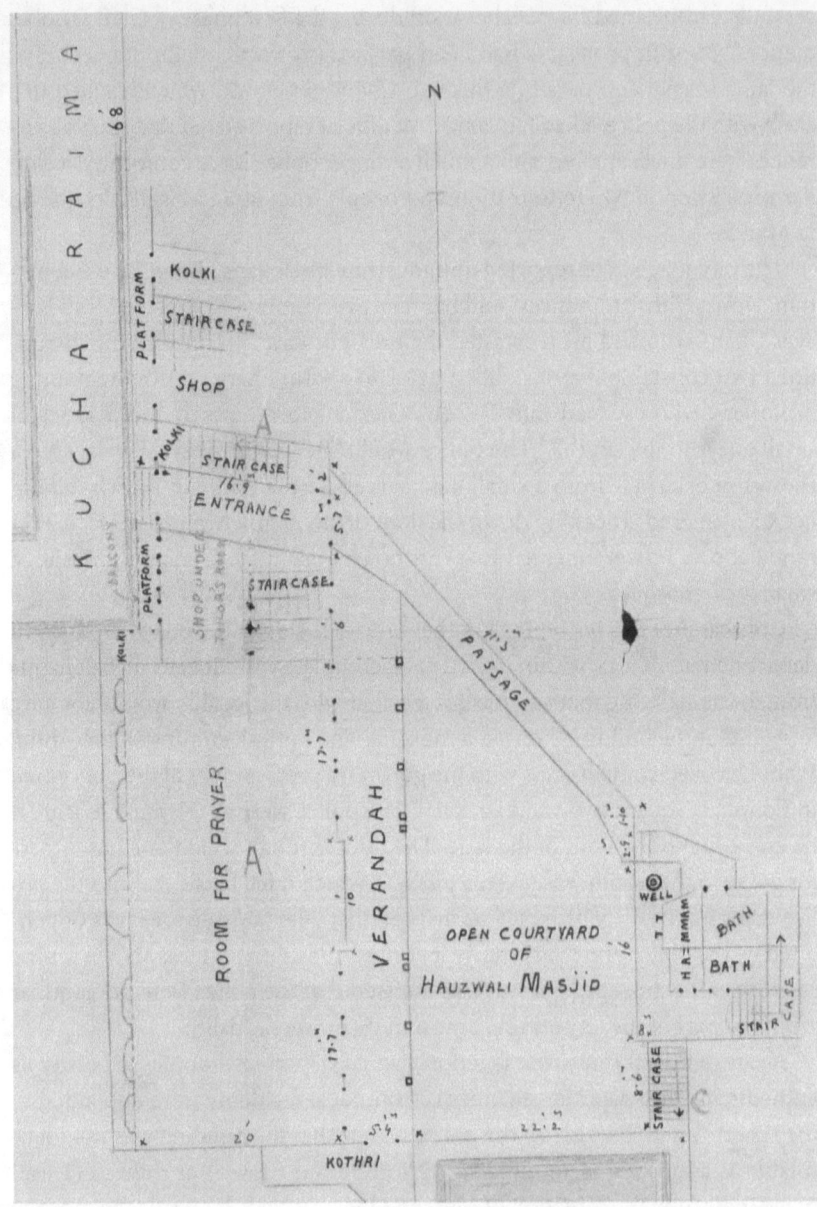

**FIGURE 4.6.** Map from the Departmental Enquiry into the Incident of the Mosque in Kucha Rehman. Reproduced with permission of the Delhi State Archives, file no. 1–26(B), Year 1932, Home (Misc.), Chief Commissioner Confidential, Department of Delhi Archives, Government of NCT of Delhi (India).

ing the Pili Kothi murder in 1942; see chapter 6).[46] The plan served to demonstrate the overlapping residential and religious geographies of the area and to reinforce the nonculpability of the police.

Unlike with the Sisganj shooting, the local government succeeded in containing the Kucha Rehman affair. On 14 March an adjournment motion in the Legislative Assembly had challenged the police account, but the home member was able to quote extensively from magistrate reports acquitting the police of wrongdoing.[47] The motion was defeated by 50 to 47 votes. A week later, on 21 March, the CID reported that Delhi's Khilafat Committee had commissioned its secretary, Hakim Ajmal Khan, to lead an investigation into the incident and to report within a week.[48] Posters throughout the city spread news of the inquiry, but, despite a meeting of three thousand *ahrars* at the Jama Masjid on 26 March that carried a resolution of protest against the Hauzwali incident, plans to mark 1 April as "Mosque Day" came to nothing. The Jamiat-ul-Ulema signaled the suspension of its more radical campaigns in mid-April with a resolution passed at a meeting of two thousand in the Jama Masjid that they would seek to expel the Government by constitutional means. On 12 May Congress issued a bulletin identifying Sub-Inspector Wahid as "defiler of Kucha Rahman Mosque" and as preferring to defile his religion than offend his English "MAI-BAPS" (parents, or master).[49] However, on 17 May Chief Commissioner Johnson declared the matter closed, with no uptake by the Muslim community in Delhi or beyond noted.[50] This was in keeping with the general absence of civil disobedience in the summer of 1932.

From September 1932 the movement was relatively featureless, and by December the chief commissioner could report that "Delhi's political life is at the lowest degree now."[51] The mid-1930s would see Congress face the challenge of functioning as an anticolonial association while also collaborating, from 1937, with the new constitution. Delhi was, however, carefully excluded from the privileges of the Government of India Act (1935). As a centrally administered capital territory it would have no elections to the Delhi Administration. Its only national-level representative would be its one member in the Legislative Assembly. This position would be assumed by Mohammad Asaf Ali, building on his fifteen years of city campaigning, including the role of dictator of Delhi Congress from 18 February to 1 March 1932. A bulletin was issued in early February that, while its authorship was listed collectively as Delhi Congress, bore many of the hallmarks of Asaf Ali's elevated prose and abstract political critique in the language of citizenship, sovereignty, and violence. Even if not penned by him directly, it anticipated the rhetorical campaigns that Congress would deploy in the city as the national party entered into collaboration with the Raj. Each paragraph opened with the address: "Citizens of Delhi." While Gandhi had been in London, Viceroy Willingdon's government was condemned for having spent four months

> arming itself; gathering information; issuing orders; organising its forces; and preparing itself for one last attack which should finally crush the Congress out of political existence. Without any cause or provocation Government has set at nought all civilized laws, thrown off even its cloak of benevolent despotism and with a shameless display of naked terrorism is trying to destroy the only effective political organisation of the people. *Is the Government going to win? Are the civilian forces going to triumph? A million voices answer NO, and three million echo 'NEVER.' For the Congress is the people and the people are the Congress. Every house is a Congress house, every man a Congressman, every heart a Congress heart.* And the Congress cannot be DESTROYED so long as the Indian people are not destroyed; and the Indian people cannot be destroyed. They have survived countless invasions; and they cannot succumb to this futile attack. THE CONGRESS IS ALIVE. IT LIVES. IT SHALL EVER LIVE.[52]

**CHAPTER 5**

# Urban Conflict and Collaboration

Nearly a decade separated the end of Civil Disobedience and the beginning of the Quit India campaign in 1942. Between these two mass revolts Congress engaged with the reformed colonial state, switching conflict for collaboration. This, at least, is one of the neat chronologies that political histories of the 1930s provide. In Delhi as elsewhere, however, the 1930s saw the techniques of disobedience adapted rather than disbanded. This chapter will explore the geographies of this politics in the new and old Delhis, which continued to be targeted as recruiting grounds and symbolic spaces. In terms of anticolonial governmentality, with colonial restrictions on political associations eased, different forms of parrhesia had to be sought out, whether railing against the constitution, municipal neglect, or capitalist exploitation. While the Hindustan Socialist Republican Association (HSRA) faded as a rival for Congress supporters, the question of leftist politics dominated the battle for anticolonial loyalty before and after the outbreak of world war in September 1939.

During the early 1930s Civil Disobedience had given Congress both justification for its claim to speak for "all-India" and an emblem with which to enthuse its followers. After the withdrawal of the mass movement, and the beginnings of an uneasy collaboration with the Government, a new series of challenges faced Congress as the largest nationalist political institution. Following the Government of India Act (1935) and inspired by the moderates' and big-business interests, Congress sought election and representation in provincial and central legislative assemblies. In July 1937 it triumphed, taking 711 of the 1,585 Provincial Assembly seats, with majorities in five out of the eleven provinces (Sarkar 1983, 254). This placed Congress in the ambiguous position of working with limited powers in a system it had denounced since the opening of the Round Table Conference in 1930. It also found itself trying to quell worker uprisings in provinces it controlled, while also retaining the use of language designed to appeal to worker communities (Joshi 2003). Local policy debates also took place in the context of intra- and interparty tensions that forced Congress, as Sarkar (1983, 351) has put it, to recognize that it was no longer simply fighting the Raj but becoming the Raj itself.

These strains pulled in two different directions. One was toward communalism, with tensions between religious groupings provoked by the constitutional deals reached. Having withdrawn from the Round Table Conference negotiations, Congress could claim that these tensions were external and that it continued to speak for all Indians, regardless of caste or religion. This line would become harder to hold into the 1940s. A separate strain was much more openly internalized into Congress in the 1930s. In 1934 an alliance of the left started to form against the pro-Gandhian council entryists of what was explicitly dubbed the Congress "right." Suggestions of a leftist support group, floated in 1933, were taken up in May 1934 when the Congress Socialist Party (CSP) was formed. In line with the Comintern's "United Front" approach adopted in 1935, the CSP worked within Congress itself (Sarkar 1983, 339). Its broad ideology stressed collective over individual action and was more amenable to violence, whether against objects or subjects, than the INC. The CSP represented in concentrated form the left wing of Congress, which included Nehru and Subhas Chandra Bose, the latter of whom formed the "Forward Bloc" in May 1939 within Congress to consolidate the various leftist groups. The declaration that India was at war on 3 September 1939, without any consultation with Indian leaders or promise of reform, led Congress to withdraw from Government over 29–30 October and plot its third period of mass mobilization.

In Delhi Congress had responded to the suspension of Civil Disobedience in April 1934 by reorganizing and recruiting. In early June alone, twelve hundred members were enlisted, a figure that rose to two thousand by mid-July 1934.[1] P. C. Jain explained that new elections led to fierce campaigning to recruit support, and as a Congress secretary he would work for three to four hours a day in his division of the city, organizing meetings, hearing complaints, and taking out processions.[2] Although the public seemed unresponsive to INC flag-hoisting ceremonies and other familiar Congress routines, a celebratory gathering of two thousand people in Queen's Gardens followed the election of Mohammad Asaf Ali on 14 November 1934. In a constituency with no reserved seats and a two-thirds Hindu population, Asaf Ali won by 3,424 votes to 949, despite attempts to stir controversy regarding his marriage to the younger, and Hindu, Aruna Ganguly (Raghavan 1999, 223). Asaf Ali would give Delhi a national voice during the mid-1930s while also joining struggles to maintain Congress unity within the city. Congress coveted the CSP's ability to mobilize protests over manufacturing and municipal exploitation, but also had to attempt to mediate religious disputes, while reorganizing its penetration of the city's wards and mohallas. In terms of regional imagery, Delhi was pictured in the 1930s as the center of the Indian legislature and the host of a "repressive regime" that provided continuity between the Civil Disobedience of the early 1930s and Congress's next, and last, anticolonial mass mobilization, in the early 1940s.

### Episteme: Echoes of Revolution

The mid-1930s saw Congress grapple with the challenge of the left, especially its appeal to Indian youth. It challenged Congress in its method of (revolutionary) political change, its models of masculinity and femininity, and, especially, the violence of its methods and imagery. The rise of the Congress left led to the diluting of the commitment to nonviolence within the organization. For the local government, there was delight when evidence of this shift came to light.

On 2 August 1936 ninety-five copies of a poster titled "Karanti Ki Gunj" (Echo of Revolution) were seized from the Delhi Congress Office by the CID following a tip-off, along with an original stencil-cut for the posters and a cyclostyle machine. The central Home Department noted on file that it could not be overemphasized how disconcerting this would be for Congress.[3] The charge of sedition and making unauthorized news sheets was laid against Raghbir Singh, a twenty-six-year-old from a village near Meerut. In addition to three "Echo of Revolution" posters found in Singh's possession, a further one was found titled "Lal Dhandora" (Red/bloody proclamation).

In passing judgment on the case the content of the posters was summarized. The "Lal Dhandora" poster claimed that the British Government throttled weaker peoples to benefit its own, that it provoked communal trouble, and that every Indian should refuse to pay land revenue. The first "Echo" poster denounced the deceitful government and discouraged any tax payments. The second poster encouraged every resident of Delhi, whether peasant, laborer, or zamindar, to refuse to pay a single pie (one-twelfth of an anna, which was a one-sixteenth of a rupee) to the "tyrannical Government." The final poster repeated these claims but concluded that "streams of blood should flow to ensure [the Government's] annihilation."[4] These were taken as sufficient evidence of sedition and being unauthorized news sheets. Evidence of the search was presented, during which a DDCC meeting was taking place on the roof; the general secretary was said to have come down mid-search and sarcastically congratulated the police for finally finding the printing machine, although he denied this in court.

Gandhi's support for collaborating with the new constitution and his lack of support for socialism came to be questioned, even by loyalists. On 9 January 1935 "Source D" reported to the CID that Gandhi had been interviewed by a panel from the "Delhi Provincial [Congress] Socialist Party," consisting of J. N. Sahni, Farid-ul-Haq Ansari, Satyavati, Mukand Lal Johri (an "enthusiastic and jovial" worker, sentenced in 1930 and 1932; Chopra 1974, 192), the industrialist Lala Shri Ram, and others.[5] Ansari insisted that Congress would waste its time running for Assembly elections after the passing of the Government of India Act that year. Gandhi concurred, suggesting he had only agreed to council entry to avoid further factionalism even though it could present opportunities to repeal repressive measures. More provocatively, Satyavati asked what the difference was between the village schemes of the Socialist Party and those of Gandhi. He replied that the defect of the Socialist Party was that it had no permanent creed. Gandhi's permanent aim was not to destroy capitalism or start a revolution but to change mentalities, create tolerance and love, and ameliorate the condition of peasants and laborers. There were still capitalists and zamindars in Russia, he insisted, and there always would be. Gandhi insisted that Congress should not formally link with socialist parties due to their abandonment of nonviolence but that socialists should remain within Congress.

Over the following years Gandhi loyalist Brij Kishan Chandiwala cooperated closely with Congress Socialists in the city. He warned Gandhi that he was losing the support of socialists, so in the spring of 1939, he organized a two-day meeting at his house between Gandhi and Delhi socialists. Gandhi was reportedly aggressive, insisting he was more socialist that the local campaigners. Chandiwala also referenced a meeting at Shahdara (this may have been a much later DPCC meeting in July 1947) where he insisted that he loved socialists like J. P. Narayan. "But these people are not socialist, I am socialist. All the things they say are on paper. They incite people but don't do any work. If they work then everyone will join them."[6] Chandiwala believed that Gandhi won many socialists over to his perspective. The 1930s had indeed seen Congress find inventive ways to use the specificities of Delhi's urban landscape to build support between the mass movements of 1930–32 and 1942. Socialists within Congress, however, had also shown themselves to do much more than simply say things on paper.

## Visibility: Seeing the City

REORGANIZING SPACE

Central to Congress's attempt to recruit members after the suspension of Civil Disobedience was the continued countergovernmentalization of the city (for later works on organizing surrounding villages, see the concluding section on Shatrugan). Mirroring Asaf Ali's proposals of 1921, the chief commissioner reported on 15 December 1934 that to increase Congress membership, "Delhi City has been divided into 16 wards while for the rural area of the Province five divisions have been formed and a small committee of workers has been allotted to each ward and division."[7] The new year, in accordance with Gandhi's wishes, saw the focus shift to the rural realm, with extensive village touring under the guidance of Satyavati, along with Memo Bai and Gandhi's "emissary," Krishna Nair. A further push in late March saw the rural area divided into five thana subdivisions for more systematic targeting.[8]

However, a "mass meeting" during Gandhi Week in October 1935 was attended by only four hundred people, leading several speakers to condemn the "apathetic attitude" of the Delhi population.[9] While the spectacle of Congress's Golden Jubilee celebrations between 22 and 28 December attracted crowds of up to five thousand, the recruitment drives met with little success, and the flag-raising at the end of the week attracted only 250 people.[10] If the audience for Congress activities was seemingly apathetic, so the party itself was riven by deepening ideological fissures, with impacts on how the city would be visualized and engaged.

By late March 1935 the chief commissioner reported disputes between the left and right of Congress.[11] Under increasing pressure from the left, moderate Congressites sought popular support through electioneering, following the decision at the Faizpur Congress Session of December 1936 that Congress would run for seats in local government. They simultaneously, however, protested against the imperial autocracy of the Government of India Act (1935) that allowed the elections themselves. The full range of Congress protest techniques, including daily meetings, a hartal, street canvassing, processions, and poster distribution, were redeployed as both election and protest tools from March 1937 (see the account of the 1 April 1938 hartal below). Congress's citywide organization was also still operational; regular *prabhat pheri* parades were used to spread information about ward activities and rouse people for the remaining mass protests, while in April 1937 two wards near the Jama Masjid had adopted resolutions setting out a program that shows how communities were being visualized in the hope of mobilization. Activities included

1. Holding INC flag salutations twice a month
2. Hosting debates on the second and fourth Saturdays of each month
3. Touring wards with members once a month to assist the poor, distribute medicines, etc.
4. Preparing lists of all the societies and organizations in wards and efforts to seek their cooperation
5. Helping inhabitants understand the legitimate rights of a citizen
6. Arranging public Congress meetings in the wards
7. Hanging notice boards wards with announcements written in chalk when necessary
8. Enlisting as many four-anna members as possible
9. Making special appeals to Muslims[12]

Following the 1938 AICC session in Delhi, which included a meeting of twenty-five thousand people on 29 September, the local Congress Committee found itself overwhelmed by initiatives that were not of its own making.[13] While it did respond to these initiatives, it also maintained its own momentum through continual enrollment and meetings, as the five or so meetings or flag salutations per fortnight throughout 1938 and early 1939 attest.[14] National Week in April 1939 and rural agitations during August led to surges of activity, but the year was dominated by speculation over the advent of war. Local movements only regained momentum during discussions of the proposed civil disobedience campaign that edged its way closer to reality during the spring of 1940.

### THE CITY OF IMPERIAL AUTOCRACY

The second Civil Disobedience campaign had been crushed by the disciplinary technology of government. These tools were not readily lain down in Delhi due to the importance placed on protecting the capital. While the autocracy of the state had been opposed using civil disobedience in the early 1930s, it had to be tackled legally and discursively during the period of collaboration. These debates articulated an attack on not only the local administration but also how the capital was visualized. Against the image of a benevolent city administering a liberal empire, local campaigns positioned it as a bloody capital curtailing the liberty of the people.

The activities of the Delhi authorities were questioned in the Legislative Assembly on 11 September 1936 when it was stated that during the last two years there had been eighteen raids made in search of proscribed literature and fifty-nine in search of terrorists.[15] Of these seventy-seven searches, only fifteen produced incriminating matter, from which only one person had yet been convicted. Over the following two years the local authorities maintained their strict control over the Delhi district, yet Congress members were quick to criticize such measures and associate them with the Government, often using the imagery of New Delhi to target popular sentiment.

On 29 August 1937 Professor Indra had spoken at a Congress rural conference near Mehrauli where he had prophesied that the tricolor flag of Congress would soon fly over New Delhi. The theme was taken up by his niece during one of her village tours with the CSP on 11 March 1938. Since her release from prison in September 1933, Satyavati had campaigned for the uplift of women and Harijans (Dalits) but moved in 1934 to closer association with Delhi labor unions (Government of India [Secret] 1934, S-14). During her village tour Satyavati encouraged peasants to realize (during the season of harvest and celebration) that they were the producers of wealth and thus of strength. Were these workers to join with Congress, she continued, then "just as these peasants of Delhi are today running to the feast of sugar and rice, in the same way they would pass through the streets of Delhi with the flag fixed on their lathis and take possession of the Viceregal Lodge (cheers)."[16]

Satyavati even suggested that such a possession could be figured as a *retaking*. On 9 April 1938 a procession of five to six hundred stone breakers moved from Jhandewalan near Paharganj to the southwest of the walled city, through Khari Baoli to Chandni Chowk and then onward to Diwan Hall near Pipal's Park. At the Jhandewalan meeting Farid-ul-Haq Ansari had urged the government to stop using crushing machines in Delhi, to safeguard the stone breakers' jobs. Satyavati urged the breakers to form a union and, a CID report suggested, proclaimed, "The labourers should realise that it were [sic] they who constructed big palatial buildings and so they should have ever [sic] right to live in them." This theme was taken up in later meetings: on 12 June 1938 at the Annual Conference of the Thela (goods carriers) Union in Multani Dhanda, Paharganj, the CID reported Hukam Singh saying, "He was waiting for the time when he would see the tri-coloured flag flying over the Viceregal Lodge where the Viceroy drew twenty-five thousand salary"; on 23 June 1938 Satyavati reportedly addressed sixty to seventy villagers in Naraina, saying, "Crores of rupees were spent on the Viceregal Lodge and on the construction of the roads in New Delhi, but nothing was done for the comfort of the villagers by constructing pucca roads for them. She called the Government to be tyrannical."[17]

The chief commissioner had complained in March that such rural agitations were becoming less nonviolent and more racially motivated and claimed on 22 June that referring to the British as "red-faced monkeys" and "dacoits" justified the use of special powers.[18] The Delhi-based *National Call* newspaper did not agree and, after further people were externed or banned from political speeches in May and June, published an article titled "Preferring Jail to Freedom of Delhi" on 25 June 1938.[19] It reported that the Delhi District Congress Committee had formally written to Congress president S. C. Bose, Gandhi, and Sardar Vallabhai Patel protesting that political prisoners had not been released in Delhi, while in provinces run by Congress Ministries they had been freed.

On 8 February 1938 the CID had received a copy of a letter from "Source 78," who reported that the letter had been drafted by Satyavati and J. N. Sahni and forwarded, without much debate, from the Delhi District to the All India Congress Committee. The request was that measures, including nonviolent civil disobedience, be authorized to "terminate the anomaly of autocratic government in Delhi."[20] The letter expertly connected Delhi as a demographic, political, and constitutional space of exception (see Hussain 2003), by which the legal provisions of the Government of India Act (1935) were used to deny Delhi democratic representation. It drew on a longer history of protest regarding the constitution of the capital. In 1919 Asaf Ali had drafted a memorandum to be presented in London during the preparations for the new Government of India Act requesting "self-determination" for Delhi by expanding the province (Raghavan 1994, 145). This proposal had been revived in an unofficial report published in 1928 by a "provincial redistribution committee," including Sahni, Deshbandhu Gupta, and Asaf Ali himself. It proposed the merger of parts of Delhi Province with those of Agra, Meerut, Ambala, and Rohilkhand to make a larger province with better representation. The proposals were revived during discussions at the Round Table Conference, but Chief Commissioner J. N. G. Johnson dismissed them, in a letter to a conference committee secretary on 2 May 1932, as "sheer nonsense" due to the need to keep the capital under direct control.[21]

Sahni and Satyavati's letter argued that the "miniature Province of Delhi," with an area of 573 square miles and a population of seven lakh (700,000, 500,000 of whom were urban), had displayed plentiful evidence of political maturity.[22] It had participated in Congress's staging posts of politicization (Home Rule League, Khilafat, Rowlatt satyagraha, Non-Cooperation, Civil Disobedience) and had held INC sessions in 1918, 1924, and 1932. Despite this, while the Government of India Act had included other provinces in "autonomous Government," Delhi had been deprived of any form of responsible government (continuing the political categories of dyarchy established in 1919; see Legg 2016b). As a centrally administered area its ultimate authority was the central government, and the chief commissioner did not even have an advisory committee: "While huge Provinces are administered by elected ministers, Delhi is administered by an autocrat." The Delhi Municipal Committee lacked an elected chair, the elected members were counterbalanced by nominated members, and the New Delhi Municipal Committee was wholly official and nonelected. What this meant was that the combined overseeing authorities were top-heavy with European officials, feeding into a reactionary, autocratic, and antediluvian Delhi Administration.

The exceptionalism of Delhi's situation was positioned between a physical geographical and a political geographical metaphor. First, the letter suggested that "Delhi is like an Isolated Island, where politically awakened and otherwise fully advanced citizens are positively marooned." None of the constitutional changes affecting the rest of India had touched the "old and stagnant spirit" of the Delhi Administration. As such, it continued to extern and intern political organizations and workers and restrict civil liberties to "ridiculous degrees of illegality." The rural population was said to groan under the burden of heavy land revenue, usurious exploitation by money lenders, and police harassment. These realities were pulled together with the image of the island to end with an explicit and politically geographic metaphor: "Either Delhi should march with the rest of the country and establish its children's right to what their ability, talent and industry and the country's general advance can bring them or Delhi will ultimately be reduced to the position of a political Andaman Island within the country."[23]

A *National Call* article from 25 June 1938 reported that the number of incarcerated in Delhi's jails was increasing. "The conditions in Delhi are becoming unbearable.... We are governed in this Imperial capital of India by autocracy. The Chief Commissioner is the sole authority for taking action against political workers which is done upon police reports."[24] With Delhi *itself* being a jail, Congress argued that being convicted for Civil Disobedience was preferable to the repressive conditions of Delhi.

A Congress protest meeting of nine hundred people in late June advertised a hartal proposed for 22 July 1938.[25] Between this meeting and the hartal a further twenty-five people had been restricted or externed, including Congress leaders Brij Kishan Chandiwala and Krishna Nair. In a letter to the chief commissioner in late July, Asaf Ali further pinpointed the local nature of the problem, stating: "the Police of the Province has inherited some unfortunate traditions, including an unhealthy zeal in overtaking even peaceful political activities, if they appear to them to indicate a departure from the orthodox constitutional quiescence." In reply Chief Commissioner Jenkins fell back on the standard Orientalist rhetoric that had been used to construct the image of the impassioned, communally minded Indian, stating, "People are now incapable of discussing anything temperately; the slightest grievance results in references to blood, death, self-sacrifice and so on."[26]

By 20 July 1938 meetings were being held in different wards in the city, the highest number for any fortnight that year.[27] The hartal itself on the 22nd was a success, with the chief commissioner himself estimating that 85 percent of Hindu shops closed, including, unusually, some in Gol Market and Connaught Place in New Delhi. The *Hindustan Times* reported sixty-nine arrests, including that of the president and vice president of the Provincial Congress Committee.[28] Although only about 10 percent of Muslim shops closed, reflecting the growing distance between Congress and the Muslim League after the former's electoral victories in 1937, the Birla and Delhi Cloth Mills' combined workforce of ten thousand went on strike. A meeting of three thousand people at the clock tower in the afternoon was followed by an eight-thousand-person gathering in Queen's Gardens in the evening.[29]

Attempts to instigate civil disobedience continued throughout August, following reports earlier in the month in the *Arjun* newspaper that the general secretary of the AICC had granted the DDCC permission to begin a campaign.[30] However, the AICC advised that preparatory work would be necessary and that there were many forms of protest besides civil disobedience.[31] No mass disobedience campaign came about, being overshadowed by growing communal tension, the AICC session in the city in September 1938, and both municipal and industrial disputes. But the campaign had exposed the unique political environment in which the other campaigns were taking place. Following the arrest of Satyavati for her village speeches on 21 August, the president of the DPCC Nur-ud-Din Behari, issued a statement that expertly linked this illiberal basis of colonial rule to the geography of Delhi, stating:

> It is a fact that the Delhi Province is a Central administered area; but it does not mean that the people of this province should remain under perpetual slavery and be treated like chattels. The state of affairs obtaining in this province is such as can never be tolerable to self-respecting citizens. We have no civil liberty worth the name here.... The Congress stands for complete independence; but we have not got even a semblance of independence here. Is it pos-

sible for the country to attain freedom while the Capital and the 350 villages surrounding it are kept tied with such bonds of slavery?[32]

## Techne: Crafting Non-Mass Politics

CONSTITUTIONAL DISPUTES

The Faizpur Congress Session of December 1936 had resolved that Congress should run for seats in the upcoming provincial elections. But it had also insisted that this did not disqualify ongoing protests against the Government, in favor of Swaraj, and against ongoing abuse of civil liberties (Kuracina 2010, 113, 38). Specifically, it had called for a nationwide hartal on 1 April 1937 to express hostility toward the new constitution, which would come into effect on that day (a year before the local hartal described above). On 16 March the central government circulated a letter to all provincial governments outlining how it felt the hartal call had been responded to.[33] The traditional Congress repertoires were called upon: converging on government offices in rural areas; combining hartals with processions, burning of effigies, and protests at legislative buildings in provincial cities; and cooperation with student, trade union, and peasant societies. The Congress Socialist Party had also supplemented these measures with calls for strike committees in industrial areas to make the hartals complete and militant.

The declaration of Congress's victories in February 1937 led the Government to doubt how enthusiastically moderate Congress supporters would participate in this hartal. Chief Commissioner Jenkins agreed, writing on 29 March that he expected Delhi's Hindus to strike but its Muslims to hold aloof. While it was decided to police the hartal as gently as possible, Jenkins also pointed out, in a note written on the day itself, that "a hartal in an important city is always undesirable and something dangerous, because it may easily lead to anti-Government rioting, or to communal rioting, at best, it probably involved intimidation on a large scale" (a realist reading of nonviolence; Mantena 2012).[34]

Delhi was coincidentally hosting a national AICC convention in March that brought in big names like Nehru and Gandhi, who advertised the hartal planned for 1 April. On 30 March a meeting was attended by five hundred people in Queen's Gardens, billed as "Martyrs Day" to commemorate those killed nearby during the Rowlatt protests of 1919.[35] Asaf Ali issued a plea to "Mohammadens" to join Congress, while Phool Chand Jain announced that the procession planned for 31 March had been pushed back to 4:30 p.m. to allow Muslim student supporters to conclude their Asr prayers. A procession, headed by a gas lamp and Congress flags, was then taken through the city to advertise the hartal. It circled the inner city, moving from the clock tower at the town hall through Chandni Chowk, Fountain Square, Dariba Kalan, Jama Masjid, Chawri Bazar, Bar-Shah-Bullah, Hauz Qazi, Lalkuan, Tahawar Khan, Nia Bans, Khari Baoli, and Fatehpuri Mosque before terminating at the Congress office on Chandni Chowk, although only twenty-five to thirty people remained at the end. The processionists crossed the spectrum of Congress support in the city. From the left were Bahal Singh (who bridged Congress, revolutionary parties, and communists in the mid-1930s), Chando Bibi (a widow and strong Congress supporter who joined the CSP in 1934), and Satyavati. From the center were Shiv Om (of Gandhi's Harijan colony), influential women like Parbati Devi (arrested with Mrs. Kohli in 1930 for liquor picketing), Memo Bai ("one of the leading lights" of the 1930 protests, but with "revolutionary tendencies"; Government of India [Secret] 1934, M13); and Ved Kumari, the daughter of Swami Shraddhanand and mother of Satyavati.

The confidential fortnightly report suggested that the hartal was not complete.[36] Most Hindu shops, cinemas, and some printing presses were closed while Muslim businesses, the mills, and transport were unaffected; some objectionable picketing led to sixteen arrests. The contradiction of the policy (having Asaf Ali pleading for the hartal while representing Delhi in the Legislative Assembly) may have affected the turnout, but the events of the day itself gave plenty of cause for complaint against the ongoing repression of public liberties in the city.

On 9 April a note was passed to the chief commissioner from the Home Department, congratulating him on how the hartal had been dealt with and the behavior of his senior superintendent of police, Mr. James A. Scott.[37] Scott was a hugely divisive figure in interwar India, having been in charge of the police when leading nationalist Lala Lajpat Rai was lathi charged in Lahore in October 1928. Lajpat Rai died of injuries received that day, and an attempted assassination of Scott was carried out by Bhaghat Singh and his colleagues (although they mistakenly killed Assistant Superintendent of Police John Saunders), for which Singh was, in turn, executed.

In contrast to Scott's glowing review from the Government of India, Asaf Ali had given notice the day after the hartal of his intention to move an adjournment of business motion in the Legislative Assembly. This allowed him to perform one of his many acts of political parrhesia in the regulated representation chamber at the heart of the Indian Empire. He proposed a discussion of police behavior during the hartal, namely, the rough treatment of a "respectable congresswoman"; the insulting of the Congress flag; and the provocation of peaceful demonstrations by the citizens of Delhi (Raghavan 1994, 226).[38]

The adjournment motion was heard on 2 April, bringing the affective atmosphere and external events of Delhi into the circular legislative chambers at the heart of New Delhi. The *Tribune* of Lahore reported on 4 April that the Congress benches "were gay with profusion of miniature tricolour flags placed on desks in front of each member and showing vividly against black blush seats," while members also wore tricolor buttonholes. The chair of the Assembly, Sir Frank Noyce, raised a point of order regarding the demonstrations in the house, but the (Congress) president, Mr. Bhullabhai Desai, denied it on the grounds that there was no restriction on dress or emblem within the house. Desai then went on to narrate the events to which Asaf Ali had objected. The "respectable congresswoman" was Asaf Ali's long-term collaborator Satyavati, who was said to have told officers she would not resist arrest should their case be put to her "but they put their hands on her shoulders when she was willing to be arrested (Shame, Shame)." The second claim was that a constable had confiscated a Congress flag, "put it under his feet and tore it up (Shame, Shame)." All of Asaf Ali's resolutions were accepted, and he was allowed to put forward his case. He argued, "Unfortunately for the capital it had been entrusted to the care of a pinch-beck Hitler."[39] He insisted Satyavati had been grabbed so heavily as to tear her blouse. He also showed a torn flag to the house and insisted it had been broken off of a car and trampled underfoot. A voice from the chamber cried out asking to know who had been in charge, and whether it was the same Mr. Scott connected with the beating and subsequent death of Lala Lajpat Rai (to "angry cries of Shame").

Mr. J. A. Thorne was representing the Home Department and read out brief defenses based on material provided by the chief commissioner, consisting of a report made by SSP Scott. Regarding the first charge, Scott wrote that Satyavati had been arrested at 7:00 a.m. at the Delhi Cloth Mills, where she and a large crowd were reportedly encouraging employees to abandon their work.[40] Before Satyavati arrived, Scott claimed workers had been able to access the mill but she had brought Birla mill hands and others from Bara Hindu Rao and had started blocking the gate. Scott's recollection of his staff's implacably (and implausibly) calm actions ran as follows:

> She then began to incite in a loud voice the employees inside to cease work, actually touching and pushing back some of the workers who were approaching the entrance; thereupon the Assistant Superintendent of Police considered

it necessary to arrest her. The crowd swarmed round on both sides and there was the possibility of an ugly scene. She was still jostling with some workers and the Assistant Superintendent of Police laid his hand on her shoulder and told her that she was under arrest. On this some of her followers ran forward and the Traffic Inspector placed his hand on her shoulder and indicated that she should stand near the gate until a Police lorry should arrive from Sabzimandi. She told him not to touch her and he left her. The crowd was then quietly pushed back but portions commenced to throw brickbats.[41]

As so often with Satyavati, accounts of her protest emphasize her violent embodiment ("loud," "touching," "pushing") and her effect on her subaltern followers ("swarm," "ugly," "jostling"). Against this the supposed gentleness of the police (laying and placing hands, gently pushing crowds) seems all the more affecting, and unbelievable (as with the Sisganj dispute). The lorry eventually arrived and Satyavati was carried off, as the crowd reportedly stoned the police.

The other two charges were summarily dismissed by Scott. The flag incident ("if it could be called such") supposedly consisted of the police noticing some Congress and red flags being carried by the crowd and on a car, while some were on the floor. Scott calmly ordered they be left, but "a slight confusion in the crowd" distracted his attention during which the car's flag was lost. After this Asaf Ali approached Scott "obviously in a very bad temper and demanded to know in an extremely provocative and unbecoming manner why the Police were acting in so provocative a fashion."[42] He apparently became further enraged when the police moved the crowd on, though Scott insisted that "no violence was used by the Police and on any ordinary day no notice would be taken of the incident." The final charge regarding police conduct was said to be too general to reply to, but for most of the day, Scott concluded, "not a single baton was raised."

These protests saw the local Congress committee responding to a national call and challenging the response of the capital authorities. It had also, however, launched its own campaigns against the international vision of a benevolent New Delhi. In the old city it targeted not the vision but the technological functioning of the local authorities.

### MUNICIPAL DISPUTES

June 1936 saw Delhi Congress Socialists turn their attention to the city's tonga drivers in an attempt to widen their appeal, codifying local complaints within the overriding logic of anticolonialism. These workers had formed a Tonga

Owners Union in July 1935 and gone on strike over police harassment. Following a speech by Jawaharlal Nehru to an audience of five thousand in Queen's Gardens in late May 1936 propounding swaraj through socialism, the Congress Socialists organized a meeting on 19 June.[43] Speeches at the meeting claimed the cause of the tongawallas and announced a hartal for 1 July. Posters by the Tonga Owners Union appeared over the next fortnight naming the Delhi Municipal Committee (DMC) as "tongueless animals" for not defending the tonga owners, criticizing the New Delhi Municipal Committee for banning tongas from some of its roads and condemning the Society for the Prevention of Cruelty to Animals for persecuting the underpaid tonga drivers.[44] A mammoth procession was organized that took in the North Delhi industrial suburbs and the heart of the city while a weeklong strike was successfully organized that ended on 15 July. Though centrist Congress activists had appropriated the movement and "joined in enthusiastically," this had been an agitation claimed and instigated by the Congress Socialists.[45]

Due to the perception that the Municipal Committee had reneged on the promises made after the July 1936 strike, Delhi's tonga drivers instigated a hartal on 5 April 1938 and gathered at Roshanara Gardens in Sabzi Mandi.[46] This meeting was appropriated by a collaboration of Congress and Congress Socialists, who collected another group of striking confectioners that had gathered at Queen's Gardens and led them out of the city to join the tonga drivers in the north.[47] At 3:30 p.m. the combined protesters were led back into central Delhi by Delhi's socialist elite: Hukam Singh, Baba Ram Chandra, Satyavati, Chando Bibi, Memo Bai, Shakuntla Devi, Durga Das Vohra, and Phool Chand Jain. In this procession the chants used were less easily divided into those that were "socialist" or "nationalist" because the laborers' employer was an arm of the colonial state. Thus the Marxist cry of "Labourers of the World Unite!" was followed by shouts of "Tyrant Government may Perish!," "Delhi Municipality may Perish!," and "Bribe Takers should Perish!"

Later protests would target the physical as well as the administrative governmentalization of Old Delhi. The most basic level of biopolitical provisioning was targeted on 8 June 1935 by a public meeting in Queen's Gardens protesting municipal provision of water. The city was likened to a desert, with centrist Congress speakers including Jugal Kishore Khanna, Farid-ul-Haq Ansari, Desh Bandhu Gupta, and Memo Bai. A Rate-Payers Association was established to, as the CID report on the meeting put it, "remove all the discrepancies and corruption existing in the Delhi Municipal Committee and to assert the rights of the Delhi citizens."[48]

More sustained protests targeted the Delhi Improvement Trust (DIT) between March and May 1938 (Legg 2007, 181–82). While this was an essentially local protest, political agitators manipulated it into a national-scale debate. More violent cries pervaded the protests of May 1938, including "Beware of toadies," "May India become free," "Long live revolution," "May the committee which wanted to ruin Delhi perish," and "May the British Government perish," although moderate Congress strains could be detected in shouts such as "Hindus and Mahomedans are brothers!"[49] However, while acknowledging that the meetings had led to "racial hatred" through suggestions that profit from the urban improvements were being shipped over to England, the chief commissioner also reported that such meetings had led to "religious fanaticism" following rumors that temples and mosques would be interfered with.[50]

A procession on 3 June 1938 of 350 people actually headed into New Delhi and picketed the DIT office in Connaught Circus during which placards and shouts reiterated the earlier complaints.[51] This physical movement outside the confines of Old Delhi symbolized the expansive nature of the antimunicipal agitations. The chief commissioner commented in mid-June that, having exhausted the potential for strikes in the textile sector, the "professional agitators" were looking further afield.[52] Following their machinations, a strike by New Delhi dhobis (washermen and women) and the coolies (assistants) at Old Delhi railway station had been organized. While sporadic protests against the DIT peppered the rest of 1938, in the last fortnight of December a new remonstration emerged against the introduction of waterborne sanitation. The "Anti-Flush Union" comprised three prominent Congressmen who proposed a social boycott of the system should it be introduced (see Prashad 2001).[53] The chief commissioner acknowledged in February that such complaints were both "comic" and "serious" because the system was required to meter the supply and thus charge for the water. As such, the protests were not just antimodern or against the unfamiliar but also a strategic deployment against the governmentalization of the cityscape in favor of the traditional means of water collection. An Improvement Trust Union was revived in late May 1939 to oppose slum clearance, with its political affiliations remaining unchanged. As the chief commissioner reported, "In these matters public opinion in Delhi is about a century behind the times, and the most virulent opposition is directed by persons with Congress affiliations."[54]

In May 1939 the disparate bodies protesting the DIT united with the Anti-Flush Union to become the Municipal Reform Committee, which launched a three-month-long series of protests. The committee's first campaign targeted electrical supply, arranging a five-minute blackout on 21 May as a protest against high electricity charges. The committee augmented its scope of action through hosting an Improvement Trust Union meeting on 8 June and representing the milk, tonga, and thela unions in a demonstration at the town hall on 6 July, followed by a tram boycott the next day. The hartal on the 6th was a partial success, and the influence of radical socialists was indicated by the retrieval of HSRA material during a police raid.[55] The last recorded protest was against the restriction announced on the number of calls to be made from private telephones in late July, but as tension mounted over the possibility of world war, such protests were either wound down or no longer reported.

INDUSTRIAL DISPUTES

The split between left and right within Congress had led to a series of rival yet interlinked institutions emerging in the mid-1930s.[56] In their earliest form these took the shape of societies such as the socialist "Youths Study Circle" formed in May-June 1934 by Satyavati, Professor Indra, and Aruna Asaf Ali, wife of Delhi's legislative representative. The socialists began to move further and further away from the DDCC, with rumors of a split beginning in June 1934.[57] Due to lack of support, by April 1935 the Delhi CSP had closed down.[58] Developments in Delhi's labor scene were, however, laying the seeds for the CSP's later reemergence. The Delhi Labour Union had been broken up in 1932 but was restarted in 1934 with the backing of the All India Trade Union Congress. In April the Labour Union drew up ten demands relating to pay, working hours, and conditions of dismissal.[59] The Delhi Cloth Mills (DCM) laborers took up the union's demands and, on refusal, went on strike between 26 April and 4 May 1934, with 50 percent and 83 percent of the day and night forces respectively striking on the first day.

Congress had ensured that some of its members were placed on the Labour Union's committee. The nonviolent tactics adopted by the strikers, such as lying in front of the lorries that brought replacement workers to the mills, hint of Congress influence and the innovative ways in which workers turned the Congress repertoire to their own ends (Nair 1998). Furthermore, a protest meeting held in Queen's Gardens on 3 May established a picket of hunger strikers who used familiar meeting grounds in which to protest labor conditions. Following rumors on 5 May that hunger striker Laxmi Chand had died, his female relatives picketed the DCM for the return of his body. A further rumor that these women had been molested led the female workers to picket the mill, in scenes reminiscent of the cloth picketing of 1930–32. While Congress managed to infiltrate this industrial dispute, it would face competition in the future not just from CSP members but from external left-wing organizations that challenged its claim to speak for the city's industrial workers.

Within four months of their closure the CSP was being reorganized in Delhi. A meeting was held for Congress Socialists from the Punjab and United Provinces on 3 August 1935 while the chief commissioner noted the increased activity of the CSP by September.[60] Its presence in Delhi was further fortified through the CSP's role in a dispute at the Birla Mills in November 1935. At a meeting in Roshanara Gardens in Sabzi Mandi on 19 November, workers voiced their grievances over wage cuts and working hours and formed a representative committee that included several Congress Socialist Party members. A strike was instigated on 24 November, beginning with only 172 workers but spreading to include 1,394 of the 1,456 workforce.[61] Street processions and meetings in Queen's Gardens further fortified the strike, which lasted until 9 December. The success of the CSP in infiltrating a labor dispute was thrown into sharp relief at the INC Golden Jubilee toward the end of December, which mill workers boycotted because of Congress's lack of support in recent disputes. The jubilee also saw Lal Chand, one of the founding members of the Youths Study Circle, arrested for distributing "red leaflets" at the Swadeshi Exhibition.[62] This was just three weeks after Satyavati was alleged to have hosted Yusaf Lal, a communist from Calcutta. The new year saw an Ayurvedic dispensary being established as a meeting place for Delhi socialists and renewed efforts to organize the Delhi CSP between February and May 1936.[63]

The most intensive period of industrial agitation occurred between September 1937 and January 1938. On 14 September 1937 a strike was instigated at the Krishna Gold and Silver Thread Factory, which had also gone on strike in August 1936 over the arrest of employees for alleged assault on the manager. The superintendent of industries at the time reported to the deputy commissioner that "outside influences appear to continue at work which gives rise to the fear that trouble may recur as a result of such influences."[64] A year later this prophecy was confirmed when Chando Bibi and the Congress Socialist workers of the Delhi Workers League made contact with the operatives and encouraged a strike on 15 September 1937.

The strike lasted over a fortnight and forced the moderate members of Congress to realize the need to make an impact on the industrial scene. Chando Bibi and close colleague Ajit Das Gupta organized meetings in Bazar Sita Ram in central Delhi, encouraging the workers to demand their rights and picketing the factory along with the dismissed workers. A strike committee was formed with Baba Ram Chandra, the Congress Socialist, as secretary, which spread the strike to four other thread factories, bringing the total number of workers on strike, from an initial walkout of 30, to 684. In an attempt to further network affiliated industries, the local INC appointed a subcommittee to guide the strike, including the moderate Jugal Kishore Khanna but also the left intermediaries Brij Kishan Chandiwala and Satyavati. Various other institutions, including the socialist Delhi Worker's League and Delhi Textile Unions, were also attempting, in the words of the superintendent of industries on 25 September, "to exploit the ignorant workers for their own ends and striving for labour leadership."[65] Under such pressure the factory owners settled on 3 October, promising more holidays, better pay, and safer working conditions.

During the winter of 1937 socialist institutions redoubled their efforts to arouse popular support, echoing turns elsewhere in the country that increasingly associated the state with factory owners, not as a barrier against their excessive demands. On 4 October the Textile Labour Union under Baba Ram Chandra formed a procession of 150 people leading from Sabzi Mandi to Queen's Gardens, during which chants of "Long Live Bhagat Singh!" and "Release Political Prisoners!" were mixed with socialist mantras such as "Long Live the Revolution!," "May Capitalism Perish!," and "Break the Shackles of Slavery!"[66] In early November left-wing Congress members toured the city calling for an anti–land revenue protest and terminated at the chief commissioner's private residence.[67] The chief commissioner went on to report that the first fortnight of December saw "professional agitators" trying to start more strikes.[68] These attempts blurred with those of the INC to maintain its support, with Congress ward and mohalla meetings in the Sabzi Mandi industrial area being taken over by the socialists Chando Bibi, Basant Singh, Baba Ram Chandra, and Shakuntla Devi.[69]

In January 1938 Delhi hosted the All India Trade Union Congress during which the "extreme socialists" of the Delhi Workers League reportedly captured the Textile Labour Union, and by the end of the month the growing discontent in Birla Mills had been capitalized upon.[70] The workers went on strike on 25 January 1939, and the discontent lasted until 18 February. Citing the familiar complaints over wages, dismissals, and working hours, the workers were contacted by Chando Bibi as the new president of the Delhi Textile Labour Union on 29 January. It was two weeks until the INC established its own subcommittee to consider the strike situation, composed of the moderate Kishore Khanna, the leftist Phool Chand Jain, and M. A. Farooqi, the future communist. After the strike settlement, socialist meetings continued. On 26 March 1938 Baba Ram Chandra stressed that socialists and the INC must work together, but it was the labor unions who would fight for the peasants and the working class while the INC would fight for all people residing in the country.[71]

This tension was one played out across India, within the Delhi Congress Committees, but also within particular lives and biographies.

## Problematization: A Subaltern and Socialist Identity

The Congress Socialist Party was a force to be reckoned with and proved itself to be efficient at mobilizing and recruiting the urban working classes in a way the traditional Congress machinery had not been. Vying blocs and parties had emerged within Delhi to reenvisage the old city, expose the autocracy of the capital region, and mobilize around issues from the constitution to municipal and industrial disputes. While recurring characters warp and weave through these narratives, it is difficult to give a sense of how individuals were changing throughout these times. This is largely a product of the archive; few thorough memoirs or personal collections survive from Delhi's left, especially of the non-elite.

But an alternative biographical archive does exist in the voluminous papers of the CID. Though, of course, massively compromised and fragmentary, files would be kept on individuals into which were deposited copies of daily political summaries, informant source reports, and overview commentaries in which the individual was mentioned. From this we can get a sense of the (at least perceived) evolutions in the political life of campaigners through sources that are clearly biased, partial, translated, and transliterated. Through these biases, however, we can encounter detailed reports into the lives of campaigners who proved, in the nationalist historiography, to be minor figures. The nature of compilation also makes for an intriguingly decentered biographical archive. A whole sheet describing a week's political activity might be preserved because it mentioned the subject's name once, but in so doing it gives a sense of the milieu in which they were operating and the company they were keeping (or not).

In what follows I would like to give an overview of the file concerning a male Congress volunteer named Shatrugan, from 1937 to 1941. He makes a fascinating figure here in at least two respects. First, he has virtually no presence in the annals of Delhi's freedom fighters, either from the period or since: no entry in the colonial 1934 *Delhi Provincial Political Who's Who* (Government of India [Secret] 1934); nothing in the official postcolonial *Who's Who of Delhi Freedom Fighters* of the 1970s (Chopra 1974; Thapliyal 1985b); and only fleeting mention in other files. Second, his zones of operation were mostly outside the old city, focusing on the suburb of Qarol Bagh and the district of Najafgarh. This account therefore takes us to a different geography and a subaltern biography (Anderson 2012). It marks the period of shift in one life from Congress supporter to Congress socialist and finally back to Gandhian nonviolence. It hints at how one man careered between these two poles, and beyond them, tracing the problematization of Congress from within by its attempt to internalize the potential and problem of socialism. In so doing it also takes us to the outbreak of war (both in Europe and between the left and right wings of the Delhi Congress) that presaged the next round of mass movement in the early 1940s.

### SHATRUGAN, QAROL BAGH, AND NAJAFGARH

File 31 of installment IX in the Delhi CID files begins with the briefest of introductions to its titular subject: "Shatrugan." He is listed as the son of Bikram Singh, resident of Chhapparwala Kuan, Qarol Bagh, Delhi. Qarol (or Karol) Bagh was part of the Western Extension of Old Delhi, partly funded through the new capital project in the 1920s and 1930s, having been designed to absorb some of the anticipated growth in the city's population (no mention is given of his family's previous home). The extension was planned poorly and the subject of protests in the 1930s due to its inadequate and unsafe basic infrastructure (Legg 2007, 183–90). Shatrugan's file consists of chronological excerpts from documents in which he appears, or that mention the areas he operated in. There is no linear narrative to his life, or even mention of his caste and background (standard features in most police files) here. His wife, "Mrs. Shatrugan," was mentioned only twice. The first was on 27 June 1937 when she participated in a Congress flag salutation in Qarol Bagh at 7:30 a.m. It took place near their home in Chhapparwala Kuan, where she sang the "usual songs" and unfurled the flag. The second time came toward the end of the file while Shatrugan languished in jail, having been detained as part of the Quit India movement, during which time a maintenance charge of twenty rupees was paid to his wife.

However, as a result of his political efforts, on 24 September 1938 Shatrugan achieved a special sort of anticolonial honor: he was added to the "Supplement of Abstract of Intelligence," which listed CID suspects residing in Delhi.[72] He did not achieve a rating of ** (continuous surveillance throughout India) or * (continuous surveillance within Delhi), meaning that only his movement to or from Delhi was noted. Were he to leave the city, his number and area, not name, were to be telegrammed to his destination; in this abstract world, Shatrugan was "Delhi No. 37." Unlike in his personal file, all entrants in the abstract table had their serial number supplemented by their name and parentage (and caste), description, and remarks. The CID information confirmed the details above but supplemented Shatrugan's caste as Brahmin. The description reads: "born about 1912; height about 5'5"; sallow complexion; black eyes; black hair on head; trimmed moustache; no beard; one finger of the left hand disfigured; walks quickly; wears Gandhi cap, shirt, dhoti and coat of khaddar." The report blends many common features of Congress leaders (high caste, homespun clothing) with special identifiers (a physical marker on his hand and performative marker in his gait). The remarks read "Congress and Kishan [peasant] worker." These descriptors mark Shatrugan's two compatible roles but also hint at his acceptance by socialist Delhi between his first entry in February 1937, the outbreak of war in 1939, and his arrest in 1940. He seems to have undergone radicalization while he was, ironically, restricted from public political activity by the chief commissioner for three months in Delhi.

The first entry from 26 February 1937 listed Shatrugan giving a speech in favor of a Congress nominee for Delhi Municipal Committee elections.[73] Although this is his first locatable mention in the CID files, he was already speaking among luminous company, including Congress elite members such as Jugal Kishore Khanna, Dr. Yudhvir Singh, Phool Chand Jain, and Satyavati, the latter of whom insisted that Congress was for the poor. She would be arrested five weeks later due to her picketing of mill workers during the anti-constitution hartal of 1 April 1937 and sentenced to one month of SI (simple, not rigorous, imprisonment); Shatrugan was also arrested and received two weeks of rigorous imprisonment. Three weeks after his release Shatrugan spoke at a meeting of the Congress Workers' Union in his home ward (XVI) of Qarol Bagh. He and others exhorted the crowd to organize under the Congress flag to attain freedom. He also referred to the controversy over the construction of a low-caste Hindu temple near the site of a graveyard and Muslim shrine at Basti Nabi Karim (see Vanaik 2019, 192–221), evidence that the government was trying to stoke Hindu-Muslim tension while also "sucking the blood of the people." A speech by M. Abdul Manan compared the condition of the workers historically (grain had been more affordable during the reign of Ala-Uddin Khilji [1250–1316]) and geographically (workers were denied the sort of welfare provided in other countries, while in India the unemployed were denied benefits and the masses were denied education to prevent them standing up to the government).

On 11 July 1937 "Source La.D.1" submitted a report, filed under "terrorist," which listed Shatrugan as one of five holders of extreme views who had been involved in terrorist activities in the past. On 26 July he was reported to have been in a meeting with the leftist (and later member of the Indian National

Army) Hukam Singh and other members of the Congress Workers' Union, at which plans were laid for the assassination of Scott (of Lajpat Rai infamy and the rough action during the April 1937 hartal).

A source report on 10 July marked a substantial shift in Shatrugan's field of operations. The Village Sub-Committee of the Delhi Congress Committee met in its office on Chandni Chowk under the presidency of Mst. Ved Kumari, Satyavati's mother.[74] There were sixteen members, four of whom were also women (Satyavati, Chando Bibi, Atma Devi Suri, and Memo Bai). Rural areas were divided into *halqas*, which served as functional equivalents of urban mohallas, each having supervisors for Congress propaganda, an inspector, and a monthly conference. Just as the mohallas often mapped directly onto the circles used to divide bureaucratic wards, halqas often coincided with tax or police divisions of the countryside. Shatrugan was allotted Najafgarh, twelve miles to the west of Qarol Bagh, which had historically developed around the country seat of a Persian noble (Mirza Najaf Khan Baloch) from the Mughal court. For CID surveillance purposes this zone was referred to as Police Station Najafgarh. Other workers were appointed for Mehrauli, near the Qutb Minar to the south; Nangloi, to the west of the city but north of Najargarh; Narela to the north; and Shahdara, on the east bank of the River Jumna opposite Old Delhi.

Shatrugan started visiting his halqa regularly, traveling out by car on 25 July 1937 with other members of the Congress Workers' Union. A speech he made on the 29th was noted as objectionable and prosecutable, although on 1 August the chief commissioner decided to wait for action given the "fluid state" of the political situation (Congress Ministries had recently been formed). Shatrugan continued to divide his attentions between his allotted village and his residential ward, organizing a procession of twenty people around Chhapparwala Kuan on 1 August, which Nehru had named Congress Ministries Day. Resolutions were made to celebrate the Congress Ministries, demand the revocation of Delhi's repressive laws, condemn high-handed local officials, investigate local communal incidents at Basti Nabi Karim, and continue to campaign for Congress in every village, which Shatrugan did throughout August.

In accordance with the schedule issued when Shatrugan accepted Najafgarh as his halqa, on 5 September a conference was held in the village of Jafarpur Kalan, listed by the CID as falling within the jurisdiction of Police Station Najafgarh. The resolutions sought to connect the villagers to the concerns of the city and the broader polity. Local issues raised include remission of land revenue to compensate for crop failure, the replacement of the local tahsildar (revenue officer), compensation for land taken during recent road works, demands for the eradication of *begar* (forced labor), and the need for villagers to join Congress. Specific to Delhi "the speaker [Shatrugan] deplored that the labourers who had built the paradise like city of New Delhi had been ousted from the New Delhi" while the autocratic nature of the administration was invoked, which fed into the broader appeal for Delhi to become a fully autonomous province.

Such pleas were repeated in weekly and sometimes daily meetings and flag unfurlings. A speech by Satyavati on 23 September in a Mehrauli village expressed sympathy with the oppressed in China (Beijing had fallen to the Japanese in July 1937) and demanded compensation from New Delhi for military maneuvers in the locality. The demands were repeated in a speech to a village near the Delhi Cantonment on 12 November attended by Shatrugan, Satyavati, Swami Sarupa Nand, Krishna Nair, and Brij Kishan Chandiwala. The villagers they met "strongly protested" against the losses experienced by them due to military troops and said that their women could not work the fields for fear of being arrested by military men. Villagers were urged to meet at the private residence of the chief commissioner on 24 November to get their land revenue remitted. In a later speech "Shatrugan said villagers should attack the residence of the Chief Commissioner but Satyavati intervened and said it was against their creed to attack anybody."[75]

While Satyavati would later adhere less tightly to the command for total nonviolence, at this stage (and in public) the nonviolent line was being strictly upheld. Many other meetings encouraged villagers to converge on the chief commissioner's house on 24 November 1937, but none went so far as Shatrugan's outright incitation to violence. This was all the authorities needed, however, and the five speakers at the cantonment event on the 12th were placed under a restraining order by the chief commissioner, forbidding them from political agitation, processions, or meetings in Delhi for three months.[76]

## A RADICAL BREAK, AND RETURN

Shatrugan seemingly obeyed the order as his next report comes over four months later. While there had previously been hints at "terrorist" activity in his reports, and definite evidence of working with Satyavati on socialist policies, he seems to have returned from his political break freshly radicalized. The winter of 1937–38 marked a peak of industrial activity and mobilization (see above), which must have stirred Shatrugan, even if he could not participate. On 24 March 1938 he reemerged on the public political scene during a meeting in the village of Dichao in his Najafgarh halqa. He condemned the restraining order on Satyavati and "forecasted revolution in India in the same way as it had come in the trail of oppressions in Russia." He then participated in the stone breakers' protests mentioned earlier, leading the procession from Jhandewalan into the old city, shouting traditional Congress slogans such as "Down with Imperialism!" and "Inquilab Zindabad!" (Long live the revolution!) but also the communist mantra "Laborers of the World Unite!" To press home the coming together of the Congress and socialist message, the procession was headed by two flags, one for Congress, the other a "red flag."

Shatrugan continued to work in both country and city but with a renewed socialist vigor. In addition to the procession just mentioned, he attended a Qarol Bagh meeting on 11 May 1938 where Professor Indra protested the inadequate resettlement after slum clearance at Basti Harphul (see Vanaik 2019, 114) and the corruption of the Delhi Improvement Trust; he suggested complainants send their resolutions to the authorities or the Legislative Assembly. But Shatrugan took a more radical line: "He further added that it would be better to shoot the poor people than to perpetuate such oppressions upon them[;] the time was nearer when the peasants and labourers would rule the country."[77]

Meetings continued around Najafgarh in the summer of 1938 during which Shatrugan had to square his increasingly revolutionary (and, for Gandhi and others, inherently violent) outlook with the urgent Congress need to discourage communal violence. In August 1938 a controversy had emerged over a contested site in the center of Old Delhi in which it was claimed a mosque had been built on the site of an old Shiv(a) mandir (temple) (see Vanaik 2019, 209–19; Baul 2020). Shatrugan addressed a meeting in Qarol Bagh on 4 September, the day after a Hindu sadhu had been stabbed at the contested compound, suggesting that it was Congress that would diffuse the situation, and the police and municipality were to blame for the disruption to public tranquility. He repeated this message in Najafgarh on 9 September, proposing the government as the problem and Congress as the solution to communal violence. He further recrafted the message in Najafghar village on 12 December during a Congress meeting attended by 125–150 people, upscaling to the national level to try to explain what was also happening in Delhi: "The Government wanted to make separate blocks in the country and to act upon the policy of divide and rule. Its policy was to make a separate block of the inhabitants of the Indian States and then to make the Hindu and Muslim blocks separate from each other. The Indian should now unite together and should achieve their well deserved freedom."

The Shiv Mandir dispute would continue for over two years, despite Congress's best efforts. Their inability to effectively intervene may, in part, have been due to the factionalism that partly disabled the Congress committees in the late 1930s, dividing it between a left wing headed by Shankar Lal and a right wing headed by Professor Indra. The CID struggled to fathom the overlapping categories and factions that had emerged within Congress by early 1939. On 8 January a meeting was held to select fifteen delegates from Delhi for the Congress session to be held at Tripuri in March. A list of proposed delegates was divided between "Congress" (meaning moderate) candidates such as Jugal Kishore Khanna, Bhagwan Sahni, and Satyavati (who was listed as part of Indra's party while being socialist) and Shankar Lal's party including Bahal Singh (listed as a socialist), Ram Chander Sharma (listed as Congress), and Shatrugan (without note). On 29 January Subash Chandra Bose secured the presidency of Congress, defeating Gandhi's preferred candidate in a direct snub to those within the party he termed "rightists." He failed, however, to carry Congress Socialists with him at Tripuri, so he resigned the presidency and formed the Forward Bloc Party within Congress.

If Shatrugan had begun 1939 as a radical, after Tripuri he seemed to move back toward the center of the party. On 1 May he presided over a meeting at the home of Professor Indra that included moderates like Krishna Nair, Memo Bai, Dr. Sukh Dev (Indra's brother-in-law), Ved Kumari (Indra's sister), and Jugal Kishore Khanna as well as more traditionally radical members like Phool Chand Jain. The meeting resolved to implement the policies of the AICC and not those of the Forward Bloc, which Shatrugan openly condemned on 7 June. July saw the Delhi Congress Socialists launch a successful push for greater support, hosting meetings between 2 and 3 July that attracted between 1,000 and 1,500 spectators.[78] On 24 July the CID reported that Bahal Singh had been named general secretary of the "Actives," a representative of socialist workers, while two smaller groups had been organized to target rural and industrial workforces.[79] But, despite this push, a working agreement across the Delhi Congress divides seemed to hold into the summer. On 7 August a DDCC meeting included moderates Jugal Kishore Khanna and Seth Kidar Nath Goenka alongside leftists Shankar Lal, Bahal Singh, and Shatrugan. Forward Bloc's calls for an immediate civil disobedience campaign were debated, as the declaration of the Second World War edged nearer, with Shankar Lal fully in favor.

This truce, however, was shattered during Delhi Provincial Congress Committee (DPCC) elections of October 1939. "Source 78" reported on 3 October 1939 that the DPCC, as constituted by the AICC, consisted of fifteen delegates, encompassing both left- and right-aligned members, including Shatrugan.

The PCC itself was made up of twenty-five members. Professor Indra called a meeting on the 2nd at the Delhi Congress office stressing the need to overcome differences and work together. However, Shankar Lal and Nur-ud-Din Behari said they could under no condition work with Indra's "party" and the forthcoming election should be determined by votes (of the DPCC members), not compromise. Nur-ud-Din Behari suggested Indra's party had defamed them and passed votes of no confidence in them. M. Abdulla and Bahal Singh pressed them to compromise, at which they made to leave, but they were convinced to stay.

Indra admitted to being in a minority and agreed not to interfere with the election. As such M. Imdad Sabri put forward the following nominations, which were all leftists, and were accepted: Shankar Lal (president); M. Nurud-Din Behari (vice president); Bahal Singh (general secretary); and Ram Singh and Hukam Singh (joint secretaries). M. Abdulla said that as no member of the "other party" had taken office, they should be included in the working committee. He suggested Lala Desh Bandhu Gupta, Professor Indra, Dr. Yudhvir Singh, and Onkar Nath, but the first two were rejected by Shankar Lal, who suggested members of his own party. The resulting membership contained fourteen leftists, nine rightists, and Shakuntla Devi, who had been proposed by both camps and was described by the CID as having imbibed revolutionary tendencies from her family (Government of India [Secret] 1934, s18).[80] At this Professor Indra left the meeting, saying they had wasted their time, and the moderate Dr. Shaukat Ullah Ansari resigned his membership in the DPCC.

The coup seems to have also reinforced Shatrugan's retreat from the left of the party. At a DPCC meeting on 2 November Bahal Singh suggested the AICC should declare a "War of Independence" in light of the viceroy's statement on 10 October that India was at war, alongside the empire. Singh was contested and defeated by the DPCC, especially by Shatrugan who was now listed as a "Gandhite." The CID reported in early January 1940 that the Delhi Congress left and right had been split over which Congress candidate would be proposed for the municipal elections on 23 January, with Shankar Lal leading the leftists.[81] The AICC had to be called in to monitor the elections, causing the resignation of Nur-ud-din Bihari, vice president of the DPCC. Shankar Lal did not involve himself with the unsuccessful Independence Day celebrations on 26 January but had been busy continuing his purge of "rightists" within Congress. On 25 January 1940 he had decided to expel the Gandhian Krishna Nair from the DPCC for alleged misappropriation of 250 rupees from the Congress famine relief fund; to seek further details from the DMC regarding allegations made against Desh Bandhu Gupta; and to ban Shatrugan from assuming any elected Congress body for a year for falsely accusing Imdad Sabri of enrolling bogus Congress members.

Despite being caught in the dragnetting of conservative Congressites, Shatrugan survived the accusation and participated in meetings through the new year. He was able to attend a meeting of all senior Congress workers called by Acharya Kriplani, general secretary of the AICC, on 28 April at the Gandhi ashram north of Delhi. The Congress elite turned out, including Bahal Singh, Phool Chand Jain and his wife Gulab, Jugal Kishore Khanna, Memo Bai, Ved Kumari, Chando Bibi, Onkar Nath, Hukam Singh, Ram Charan, and Shatrugan. Kriplani said that a nationwide satyagraha campaign would soon be starting and that all provincial Congress committees had to start preparing their supporters, but Delhi had done nothing as yet. "Source 78" reported: "The people so gathered there said that there was a great corruption prevailing there on account of party feelings and until and unless it was not removed it was impracticable to start any work there. People asked Kriplani to bring an end to the party feelings." Kriplani said that the AICC had previously sent an auditor and inspector to Delhi with a warning, only to find the Congress offices closed. He blamed Bahal Singh, as general secretary, for the disunity and corruption and told him to resign his post. Singh insisted he would continue his work until early May, after which the AICC could do as it pleased.

Full celebrations were organized for May Day 1940, in collaboration with the Congress Socialists and members of the Forward Bloc. A ninety-person procession carrying twenty-five red hammer-and-sickle flags followed the well-trodden Congress route throughout Old Delhi, returning to Queen's Gardens in the evening. Placards displayed five main mottos:[82]

1. Workers of the world unite
2. Break the chains of slavery
3. Workers will lead struggle for freedom
4. Public Guard
5. May capitalism perish

While Singh had recruited outside leftist support for this celebration of international socialism, the Congress Committee and its presence in the city was in difficulties. On 19 August the chief commissioner responded to central government queries regarding preparations for any civil disobedience movement.[83] He reported that Congress had been riven by Shankar Lal's temporary supremacy in the city and that it now found itself without funds, volunteers, or rural propaganda. But it had a seasoned collective of campaigners and funders to call on, should it be able to organize itself. He listed the most important members as Mohammad Asaf Ali, Desh Bandhu Gupta, Dr. Shaukatullah Ansari, and Dr. Ashraf, the latter being the only one with leftist connections. Another sixteen significant members were listed, again, with hardly any leftist members, although a few had experimented with the left but returned to the moderate center ground, including Shatrugan.

Nine days after the chief commissioner's report, Shatrugan delivered a speech in Nangloi for which he was later arrested and prosecuted under rule 34 6 jj (inciting the nonpayment of land revenue) of the Defence of India (1939). He was sentenced to a year's rigorous imprisonment on 14 October, but Jugal Kishore Khanna represented him in court on 11 November and secured his acquittal. He returned to public speaking and was reported speaking at a meeting in Nangloi alongside the future star of the Quit India movement, Aruna Asaf Ali. They spoke on traditional Congress lines regarding the need to remove untouchability, end poverty, and spin khaddar.

Between the resignation of the Congress Ministries over the war and the beginning of the Quit India movement, Gandhi announced that Individual Satyagraha, in which people would offer themselves up for arrest as a symbolic protest, would be sanctioned. These took place in three waves, beginning in November 1940, January 1941, and April 1941. One month into the second phase, Shatrugan announced to the deputy commissioner that he would be offering satyagraha. When he reached the appointed spot, on 6 February, he was arrested as he left his car, shouting anti-war slogans to a crowd of 250–300 people. He was prosecuted and sentenced to two consecutive eighteen-month periods of rigorous imprisonment, to run concurrently. This saw him miss much of the Quit India movement, the largest uprising against the British in India since 1857, and one that tested Congress's commitment to nonviolence through geographically dividing the right and left into those above and below ground.

**PART 2**

# QUIT

## CHAPTER 6

# Quit Delhi

*The Overground*

As with the disobedient city, when Delhi told the British to quit, it did so in a language that was often but not always civil. The spatial repertoire of nonviolence was in evidence and roused much of the city in August 1942. But the Quit India movement split Delhi in a way Civil Disobedience had not. This was not a horizontal divide between old and new Delhis but a vertical one between under- and overground cities. These cities shared populations, but the overground city was generally that of the Congress center and right, while the underground was the city of the left. That geography divides this and the following chapter, which cover respectively the overground and underground cities that Quit India made of Delhi. These are simultaneously fictive and real cities, both chapters returning to many of the same spaces (on the "unvisible" city, see Miéville 2009).

If the chapters share a political moment and material spaces, there are real differences in the governmental analytics at play. The overground movement, the subject of this chapter, did not produce radically new ways of visualizing Delhi nor of producing new political subjectivities. The formal Congress program was rolled out, to great effect. Though the new and more radical politics of Quit India attracted much attention, this chapter shows how the overground techne was still effective at drawing out the violence and contradictions of the colonial state. The following chapter explores the new forms of (in)visibility and (revolutionary) identities demanded by the underground (while Mohammad Asaf Ali was quickly arrested, the movement saw the ascendency of his absconding wife, Aruna).

Violence remained the main problematization of Congress mass mobilization. This chapter concludes with an incident that problematized the August uprising in Delhi, with uncomfortable parallels to the Chauri Chaura incident of twenty years earlier (arson, and the murder of a policeman). The entire underground city itself, however, is posited in the following chapter as a problematization, of both nonviolence and the truth relations of satyagraha. While the former incident could be dismissed as an isolated act of disobedience, the latter constituted a systematic quitting of the Congress commitment to nonviolence and the open manifestation of one's truth.

### Introducing Quitting: From Individual Satyagraha to "Do or Die"

On 3 September 1939 the viceroy announced that India, following Britain, was at war with Germany (Sarkar 1983, 375). No significant consultation had taken place with Indian members of government. After a month of protestation, on 17th October, all the viceroy offered was more vague promises of Dominion status in the future and a greater role for Indians in the viceroy's council. Between 29 and 30 October Congress resigned its official posts and channeled its attentions into increasing popular support, while the government debated a "Revolutionary Movements Ordinance" to augment the substantial disciplinary powers it already possessed. On 8 August 1940 the viceroy reiterated the offer of October 1939, which Congress once again rejected.

Following a period of contemplation similar to that of early 1930, Gandhi announced the Individual Satyagraha campaign. Still reluctant to hinder the war against fascism and unsure of the degree of Congress support, Gandhi selected individuals to offer themselves for arrest in symbolic protests against the Government of India.[1] This was the epitome of directed and disciplined parrhesia, with selected individuals scripted into courageous speech. Three surges of jailings, first in November 1940, then again in January 1941 and April 1941 (Malhotra 1979, 29), characterized a campaign that did little to affect the functioning of Government but did provide Congress with a means to increase awareness of its activities outside of office. The stalemate continued until 7 December 1941 when Japan declared war on Britain and invaded Malaya, leading Congress, between 23 and 30 December, to withdraw the movement (Mathur 1979, 12). January 1942 saw the Communist Party of India (CPI) announce its support for the colonial government, as an ally of the USSR, while on 15 February the British stronghold of Singapore fell to Japan.

As the Japanese forces pushed closer to India, the internal situation appeared bleak; rocketing defense spending had led to an inflation-fueled economic crisis, Congress maintained its guarded political criticism, and British MPs, along with U.S. president Franklin Roosevelt, pushed the Government of India measures to secure India (Bose and Jalal 1998, 159). Sir Stafford Cripps arrived in March 1942 seeking a concord with Congress, yet by 2 April his attempts at negotiation had failed. Denied once again their demand for central control of government, the declarations of Congress, and more specifically those of Gandhi, began to take on a more combative, though nonviolent, tone. From April onward the nation awaited the AICC session at Bombay in August 1942.

On 14 July the Congress Working Committee passed a resolution demanding the removal of British power, under the threat of another nonviolent mass movement (Mathur 1979, 20). Unable to delay further demands for a mass agitation, Gandhi legitimated a movement that demanded the British "Quit India," even if India had not mastered the art of nonviolence (Arnold 2001, 211). India had to "Do or Die"—to become free or to die trying. So would be instituted "a Gandhi-led un-Gandhian way of struggle" (Chakrabarty 1992, 791).

Officially, Congress issued a twelve-point program that established tactical continuity with previous protests. The list emphasized the importance of hartals, salt protests, noncooperation, student activity, withdrawal from government service, targeting the armed services and the Indian states, encouraging women to participate, wearing "Do or Die" badges, spinning, overcoming communal divisions, and personal or regional autonomy within the realms of nonviolence (Mathur 1979, 160–63). However, a widely circulated pamphlet from the Andhra Congress Committee proposed a more extensive range of activities (159–60), which can be categorized as in table 6.1.

**TABLE 6.1.** Congress Quit India Activities

| Technique/Target/Aim | Action |
| --- | --- |
| Traditional satyagraha | No-tax campaigns, hartals, picketing, no-confidence votes on Government servants, resignation of army and police staff |
| Rural areas | Inform village leaders that British rule has ended, replace or disown dissenting leaders |
| Autonomous government | Establish independent post offices, law courts, inform shopkeepers that the panchayat system of local government has replaced that of the British, establish Government seals of Free India, use silver coins instead of British currency notes |
| Communications | Cut telephone and telegraph wires, remove rails and demolish railway bridges, travel without train tickets and stop trains nonviolently |

Besides tactics to noncooperate with the state, the instructions also reactivated established ways of visualizing and mobilizing the people. A nationalist leaflet attributed by the Government to Congress included recommendations to divide Congress jurisdictions into thanas (wards) to which daily reports and instructions could be made available (Chopra 1976, 307). Within these thanas, finance committees and rendezvous points would be arranged. Women would be encouraged to perform *prabhat pheris* within the thanas to encourage enlistment, while distributing leaflets from house to house (see also Nair 2007, 109). Finally, at the most intimate level, efforts were to be made through private talk to instigate feelings of rebellion against the Government.

The All India Congress Committee gathered in Bombay and approved the July resolution on 8 August 1942. The British premeditated response was devastatingly effective in disabling the elite and restoring "order" to the public sphere (Legg 2007, 115). The arrest of nearly the entire Congress elite, from 9 August, and police crackdowns throughout the country led to a nationwide outcry. Though in some senses this decapitated the movement, it also freed up local supporters to act in more inventive and less disciplined ways. Viceroy Linlithgow admitted to Prime Minister Churchill, on 31 August, that the nature of the revolt was the largest since the "Mutiny" (Chopra 1976, 1). Sarkar (1983, 394–395) categorized the movement into the overlapping phases as shown in table 6.2.

However, these three phases were geographically specific. Many maintained a degree of autonomy at the local level (Chakrabarty 1992). The movement was strongest across northern India (Pandey 1988), while each region had different traditions of protest, felt the threat of the Japanese advance differently, and had variably politicized workforces. The various chapters in Pandey's (1988) pivotal collection on 1942 explore the diffuse and wide-ranging disruptions in the district of Medinipur, the violent successes of Gujarat, which strengthened Congress support, and the elite-led skepticism in Madras.

**TABLE 6.2.** Phases of Quit India

| Dates | Characteristics | Tactics/Events |
|---|---|---|
| 9–mid-August 1942 | Urban, violent, massive | Hartals, strikes, and cla clashes with police; involvement of the urban middle classes |
| Mid-August–late September | Rural | Militant students spread into the countryside; communications targeted and peasant rebellions encouraged |
| End of September–late 1943 | "Terrorist" youth activity | Communications attacked and Government property sabotaged |

Nair (1998, 277) has elsewhere insisted that we should not presume the seductive power of nationalism for workers, showing that their support for Quit India in the princely state of Mysore was tactical and used to further their own collective aims. As elsewhere, the arrest of the INC leadership was met with strikes and violent attacks on colonial infrastructure, while longer-running strikes were less well attended but still relatively long-lasting.

While Mathur (1979, 28) acknowledged an "underground" movement of sabotage, wire cutting, bomb throwing, dacoity, and arson during the Quit India campaigns, even the "open" movement was characterized by damaging Government and municipal property, "hooliganism," and attacks on the British. Radical nationalists and internationalists, many of whom retained their links to Congress, proposed more violent protests than the measures contained in the Andhra circular. While attacks on communications would continue, industrial disruption would be prioritized, as would incendiary attacks on government buildings, petrol pumps, and arms and ammunition stores (Lal 1975, 112). While strengthening the urgency of Congress claims, these techniques undermined the moral force of Congress's nonviolent ethos. As Pandey (1988) put it, Gandhi and Congress had become symbols, not leaders, for a movement that coalesced myriad disobedient subjects (those who refused the command to be nonviolent, or communists and peasant workers who refused the command not to participate). When the movement was finally suspended, the Congress elite congratulated the peoples' fortitude but berated their abandonment of nonviolence in familiar terms of elite-subaltern condescension: " 'Wild with rage,' 'maddened with fury,' 'frenzied' and 'insensate': it is a collection that competes with any colonial lament over an uprising among the Indian peasantry" (Pandey 1988, 14).

In others ways the past was also present in the movement. Masselos (1998) has argued that despite the move toward violence during the Quit India movement, "The genealogy of the past was not superseded in the linearity of Quit India, it was present and alive. Quit India was familiar and it was different" (68). While using violent techniques of protest, the movement was still led by local Congress organizations and relied on "underlying patterns of behaviour derived from the city experience in its demonstrations, festivals and crowd gatherings and events" (91). For Khan (2016, 101) Quit India was a much different form of Civil Disobedience, with students supplanting elders as the inspirational leaders; its politics more amorphous; penetrated by the aesthetics of modernity; a more radically internationalist movement; and one perpetually teasing the boundary between ahimsa and violence.

### Episteme: Nonviolence?

The divisions within Delhi Congress organizations that had emerged in the 1930s were intensified by the outbreak of war and ahead of the turn to Quit India in 1942. On 14 June 1939 Lala Shankar Lal presided over a private meeting of eighty people at the offices of the Municipal Reforms Committee on Egerton Road. A CID source reported the formation of a "forward bloc of leftists" within Congress with Maulana Nur-ud-Din Behari as president. Within weeks they were coordinating different "radical groups" within and beyond Congress, including communist and student groups, and pursuing the national agenda being set by Subhas Chandra Bose, to the annoyance of "right wing" Delhi Congress members. On 20 January 1940 a CID report was composed regarding "Leftist Activities in Delhi" ahead of Independence Day on the 26th. On the verge of steps toward a new mass movement, local Congress followers were still politically divided: "Repercussions of this all India wide difference between the leftists and the rightists can be felt locally also and both of them are struggling to maintain their hegemony in the office."[2] This was also a deeply philosophical divide regarding the ethical route to independence. Within leftist circles there was said to be "condemnation of the cult of nonviolence and spinning clause in the new pledge of Independence" as these were considered to be obstructionist tactics of the rightists.

The latter were in the process of fighting the leftists for Congress tickets to contest municipal seats. While the left felt the commitment to nonviolence to be anti-revolutionary, the Government felt they were facing an insurrection. In February 1942 J. A. Thorne, of the central Home Department, considered the chief commissioner's suggestion that municipal commissioners in Delhi who participated in satyagraha should be removed from their positions, because it demonstrated "a defect of character which unfits [them] to be a member."[3] Tottenham, the home secretary, was nervous at this, but Thorne insisted that a distinction could be made between "symbolic" satyagraha and those who would interfere with the operation of the war.

The growth in the number of those who would not just interfere with governmental operations but seek to violently sabotage them shocked Congress traditionalists and provided rich propaganda material for the Government. On 18 January 1943 a house was raided in Old Delhi after a tip-off. It was being rented by Khushi Ram, listed as a "Congress peon" (a messenger or junior member) who was arrested for being in possession of Congress literature.[4] The haul was huge; 19,650 copies of forty different items. The diversity of formats, topics, and languages demonstrates how keenly Congress had been trying to stimulate the Quit India movement in the five months since its launch. Of the forty items, twelve were in Urdu, twelve in Hindi, three in both Urdu and Hindi, eight in English, and four in either Urdu or Hindi. Over 1,500 copies were found of five of the items, nineteen numbered between a hundred and a thousand, and under a hundred copies were found of the remaining sixteen items. The predominant formats were handbills (fifteen items) followed by the bulletins and pictures (six each), pamphlets (five), books (three), posters (two), and leaflets, flags, and newsletters (one each). The items were usually printed, though some were cyclostyled or, in the case of posters, stenciled.

They thematically fell into familiar groupings by title. Five generic Congress items included regular newsletters, miniature Congress flags, transcripts of talks given on "Congress radio" and printed handbills in Urdu and Hindi titled "Congress Special Bulletin-Yeh Congress Aur Mulk Se Bewafai Hai" (This is disloyalty toward the Congress and the nation). Six further items focused on general mobilization, from a book in Urdu titled *Hamari Aj Ki Larai* (Our fight of today), to Urdu handbills titled "Bharat Viro Kab Jagoge" (When will the brave people of India rise). More specific Quit India items included stenciled Hindi posters of the totemic cry "Karo Ya Maro" ("Do or Die") or, in English, "Liberty or Death"; quotes from Gandhi and Vallabhai Patel; and pictures of the imprisoned Nehru and Abul Kalam Azad bearing the words "Hamare Neta Kahan Hain" (Where are our leaders?).

Common motivating themes were appealed to: three on imperial economics questioned the devaluing of Indian silver on the London markets, discouraged accepting currency notes and postal stamps, and highlighted the devaluing of the currency; two addressed the violence of the state, both within its jails and on the street, since the Quit India movement began; and two handbills in Urdu and Hindi focused on Congress's rural heartland, insisting that "Dehati Bhai Aur Zaraat-Pesha Log Hakumat Ki Machine Ko Bilkul Rok Sakte Hain" (The villagers and cultivators could completely stop the Government's machinery). Some of the items addressed the wider world, disparaging communists and addressing Muslim politics, while others advertised local events such as Martyrs Day and the hunger strike of Krishna Nair (see chapter 7), or targeted specific groups, like Delhi's large population of governmental workers. Though this is clearly a diverse tranche of Congress literature, a note on the Home Department file on 24 March made their key feature, to governmental eyes, crystal clear: "their complete omission of even lip service to non-violence."

This transition in Congress more broadly was embodied by the shift in leadership not just in Delhi at large but within its new political power couple. Mohammad Asaf Ali had dominated Delhi's politics in the years between Civil Disobedience and the outbreak of war through his performances in the Legislative Assembly and in the public politics of the city. Being a committed Gandhian, when called on he offered himself for arrest in both the Individual Satyagraha and Quit India campaigns. His wife, however, took a very different path. Having associated with Congress Socialists in the mid-1930s, Aruna Asaf Ali found fame after hoisting the Congress flag at Gowalia Tank Maidan on 9 August due to the arrest of the Congress leaders in Bombay. She evaded arrest and spent the duration of the Quit India movement underground, orchestrating activities in Delhi and the northwest of India (including the Punjab, Sind, North-West Frontier Province, and Delhi; Chopra 1976, 351; see also chapter 7). In so doing Aruna Asaf Ali was directly and openly disobeying Gandhi's commands and the Congress creed. She embodied the parrhesia of Quit India in her life, her body, and her movement but also in her statements, which see her negotiating the complex dilemma of her courageous but newly violent truth.

Aruna Asaf Ali was publicly implicated in Congress violence by the Government. She replied in hiding, "by the only means available in tyranny." A cyclostyled copy of a letter, bearing Asaf Ali's signature "from somewhere in India," came to the notice of the CID in Delhi on 22 February 1943. The "force" she represented was said to be incompatible with that of the viceroy's savagery, and she condemned his suggestion that the world would judge Congress poorly for allowing violence. The only world judgment would be against tyranny and for striving people: "This is yet a sealed book for you; the generations of your children will read it; most probably you too will with some ashy recollections." Gandhi was said to have forged a test for the people: should they seek to destroy tyranny without aiming to kill or injure? Yet the government had found Congress guilty of organizing violence. Against this Asaf Ali insisted that Congress had no plan and set out to explain both the political and spiritual infrastructure of the uprising, insisting that the viceroy was

> seeing ghosts of a disturbed fancy.
> The non-violent Revolution is something pervasive like the water under the hills or the earth that flows whit[h]er it can into a thousand streams. No canals are dug.
> No plan was imposed from above on the Revolution that broke out on 9th Aug. There was the living reality of India with its great memories, there was the passion of the people to be free, there was twenty-three years' work of a master who is sensitively tuned to the re[a]lity and passion. That was all. Let

me tell you something about the passion of a people that has endured for at least five times as many centuries as yours. Passion is an elusive substance. Hounds cannot tra[c]k it no[r] bullets kill it. Your men have killed tens of thousands, burnt, pillaged and raped, smashed up organisations, arrested I do not know how many lakhs, but have not new men and new organisations cheerfully volunteered themselves in the service of this passion. Happen what may, this passion will haunt you until your system breaks. You may succeed in smashing up this Congress but, even before you have been able to do so, a newer and vaster Congress will arise. There is to be no respite for you.[5]

The "potter" working the clay of this passion was the revolutionary technique arrived at by a people who had given up arms. Instead they went on strike, suspended trade, expelled civil administration, and dislocated communications. The technique was that of creating a "vacuum" in the country such that the alien forces must surrender—the technique not of seizing power in a few towns but of expelling tyranny from the whole country—"the technique not of capturing power but of shattering it," that is, a technique of the people as a whole. The common man had revolted.

The remainder of the letter, however, expressed Asaf Ali's ambivalence over nonviolence. She recounted the violence of the colonial state in the face of Quit India, listing innumerable rapes, the torture of women, and firings on crowds amounting to "scores of Jallianwalabag." If the people of India had been violent in response, she claimed, Gandhi would have been administering a free people by then. But she was not unhappy, as the discipline he had instilled in people allowed the movement to continue even when its organization had been smashed. Yet, if the government continued to goad the people, who could say if there "might not be some setbacks in the story of the unarmed common man"? Asaf Ali continued working toward these setbacks until she finally emerged from the underground in February 1946.

## Techne: The Overground

### INDIVIDUAL SATYAGRAHA: COMPELLED PARRHESIA

The early 1940s saw Delhi struggle to overcome the left-right, Hindu-Muslim tensions that had plagued it in the late 1930s. The lack of support from Shankar Lal's leftist DDCC meant that the 26 January 1940 celebrations were muted. Despite regular flag salutations over a month in advance, Congress's National Week between 6 and 13 April was not widely observed.[6] On 5 November a hartal was held following Nehru's arrest, which the CID reported as a failure, while a meeting of three thousand people was told that Congress was awaiting instructions from the national working committee.[7]

On 29 November Mohammad Asaf Ali launched the Individual Satyagraha campaign, making an anti-war speech in Queen's Gardens to an estimated audience of ten thousand. Raghunandan Saran, with Radha Raman as assistant, selected and organized satyagrahis for arrest.[8] Asaf Ali was followed by those of leading congressmen Nur-ud-Din Behari, Bahal Singh, Farid-ul Haq Ansari, and Desh Bandhu Gupta.[9] A hartal the following day was, however, only partially successful.[10] In 2001 Roop Narain recalled how he was selected by Brij Kishan Chandiwala to offer himself up in Hauz Qazi. He staged a protest, shouting, "Not a pie donation, not a sepoy to join the army," for which he was arrested.[11] Meanwhile the newly elected DDCC, including Satyavati, Aruna Asaf Ali, and "behind the scenes" organizer Premjas Rai (Chopra 1974, 306), focused on constructive work until the next instructions to court arrest.

The series of arrests continued but failed to spark enthusiasm in the Delhi people. A speech by Congress president Abdul Kalam Azad on 1 January 1941 reportedly attracted only 2,500–3000 people. On 15 January the chief commissioner reported to the Home Department that eight people, including two women, had been arrested for Individual Satyagraha but that not only had two of them had been "imported" by Congress from the neighboring district of Rohtak, but the majority "were people of small status who could hardly be said to possess the qualifications" laid down by Gandhi for selecting individual satyagrahis.[12] Yudhvir Singh later recalled these qualifications as being a member of Congress, wearing khadi, having regularly spun for ninety minutes daily, believing in the abolition of untouchability, and supporting Congress's aims.[13]

A further four arrests in late January took the total convictions to twenty-three, and regular arrests continued throughout the spring. Efforts continued to stoke support in the capital, with Mir Mushtaq Ahmed being arrested in Connaught Place on 7 April 1941 for shouting anti-war slogans. Ahmed would become leader of New Delhi's Congress Committee, and the district magistrate who sentenced him noted his contacts in the capital.[14] He had until recently served as a translator of Persian in the Imperial Record Office, his brother worked in the Supply Department, and his sister was married to a clerk in the office of the private secretary to the viceroy.

In general, however, the Delhi Administration felt it was a "poor type of persons" offering themselves up, not leading Congress figures. By June 1941 the chief commissioner confidently reported that the movement was "losing its vitality."[15] The use of tear gas against the Guru Tegh Bahadur Commemoration procession on 23 November 1941 led to a local outcry and demands for an inquiry (Legg 2007, 145). But a protest meeting held on 6 December attracted just over five hundred people.[16]

As confidence in the Government's economic and foreign policy plummeted, Congress's popularity began a slow recovery, with a healthy showing for Independence Day on 26 January 1942.[17] Beyond the main bazaars the mobilization techniques of 1930–32 were also resurrected, with the DPCC reporting prabhat pheri processions, decoration of bazaars, and flag salutations in wards throughout the city.[18] While a speech by Nehru in early February attracted an audience of twenty thousand, other nationalist factions were also active.[19] Stories of men being abducted at night for war recruits began to circulate, while communities fortified their mohallas with lockable gates (as much through fear of rival religious communities as of the police or CID, however; see Legg 2019a).[20]

Congress used the cultural landscape of the city to tap into memories of previous, more successful and unified campaigns. In the second half of March 1942 the traditional meeting ground of Queen's Garden hosted nineteen Congress meetings. The largest of these, on 30 March, commemorated the shootings at the town hall twenty-three years before during the Rowlatt satyagraha.[21] National Week was a success between 6 and 13 April, which simultaneously commemorated the first such week during the Civil Disobedience of 1930, the beginning of the Rowlatt disturbances on 6 April 1919, and the Amritsar shootings on the 13th.[22] A month later, "Gurdwara Firing Day" was observed on 6 May to commemorate the Sisganj shootings in 1930.[23] General meetings continued, including some in New Delhi between April and July, which led to a campaign to rename the garden at the center of Connaught Place "Nehru Park." By the end of July street-corner meetings were occurring every day, visiting national leaders had delivered speeches, and a thousand people met in Connaught Place on 20 July.[24] All these efforts were to brace the public for the "last battle for freedom" that would emerge from the AICC meeting in Bombay on 8 August 1942.

#### QUIT OLD DELHI

The political momentum that had been established in Delhi during late July was carried through into early August. "Tilak Day" was observed on 1 August, anchoring the new movement to one of the founders of mainstream Indian nationalism, while a Sikh meeting at New Delhi's Gurdwara Bangla Sahib on 5 August compared the British Empire to that of Aurangzeb, whose repression of non-Muslim populations, it was thought, had led to the decline of the Mughal Empire. Tilak Day had included nine salutation ceremonies introducing the main figures of local politics, most of whom would be arrested within a fortnight of the Quit India movement beginning. The list included Memo Bai (arrested on 9 August), Farid-ul-Haq Ansari (also arrested on the 9th), Mohammad Asaf Ali (9th), Mir Mushtaq Ahmed (9th), Brij Rani (15th), Satyavati (20th), and Aruna Asaf Ali, who evaded arrest. Students also revived memories of earlier political activity by holding a rally of over two hundred people in Gracia ("Student") Park on 6 August (see also Vatsayan et al. 2000).[25] L. C. Jain (2010, 29) and his fellow students at Hindu College later attacked the loyalist "toady" St. Stephen's College, cutting their phone lines, helping make them in J. K. Khanna's opinion the "vanguard" of the 1942 movement.[26]

Phool Chand Jain recalled that he and other Congress workers had been preparing posters and instructions along the lines of Civil Disobedience, until AICC bulletins arrived announcing the decision to cut telegram lines and break rail tracks. In a statement made to the police after his arrest on 11 December, Jathu Bhai Vohra stated that at a meeting before the Bombay Session, it was agreed that Satyavati be appointed Delhi "dictator," and that should the government launch an offensive, the movement would go underground (Chopra 1976, 279). A secret source report also disclosed to the Government, in November 1942, that extensive preparations had been underway in Delhi since early August, with Deshbandhu Gupta organizing funds and attempting to arrange a strike in the mills (310). The established means of visualizing the city and its population was deployed, with Congress centers established where possible in mohallas in which they did not exist.[27]

The successful priming of the city, as established over the previous twenty years, was noted in Justice Wickenden's later report into the Quit India movement: "it is significant that Delhi reacted so violently at a very early stage and the leaflet campaign got started earlier and on a bigger scale than elsewhere" (Chopra 1976, 310). This response, however, emerged from the people as much as the elite. Just as local neighborhoods created countersurveillance networks against foreign cloth traders in 1930, so they self-organized after the arrests and police firings in August 1942. As Phool Chand Jain recalled:

> Because of curfew being imposed many people were also killed in muhallas through bullets which benefitted our movement. Then groups of people were formed in our muhallas. People from the muhallas would contact us to give them some program. Out of them some people would be those who we knew other-wise locally, so we would distribute work to everyone. Then when our

contacts with them increased then through them we would move forward and then moving forward would also get caught. Before getting caught we would tell each other that if I am caught then this person will work instead of me. Then if that person was caught then another person would work in that person's stead. This way a chain would be formed.[28]

News of the Bombay arrests in the morning of 9 August soon filtered through to Delhi.[29] The chief commissioner declared the INC Working Committee, All India Congress Committee, and Delhi District Congress Committee illegal, after which thirteen local Congress members were arrested, leaving four wanted members "underground" and the rest in Bombay. The *Hindustan Times* reported that Congress's central office on Chandni Chowk, Swarajya Bhawan, had been declared illegal and raided by the police, where Farid-ul-haq Ansari, Professor Nigam, and a servant who worked in the office had been arrested.[30]

The Government's provincial summary of events in Delhi reported only a procession by students and communists and a "partial hartal."[31] The fortnightly report further downplayed the hartal as it occurred on a Sunday, when many Hindu shops would have been closed anyway.[32] However, a detailed intelligence report revealed the depth of local activity. Small groups of Congress volunteers were dispatched throughout the city, advertising a procession in the afternoon and an evening meeting in Queen's Gardens. These groups coordinated community Congress committees, which mobilized their own support bases. As the intelligence report continued: "Accordingly the Ward Congress Committees formed small processions which passed through their respective jurisdictions persuading the shopkeepers on their way to close their shops though with little success and interfered with the traffic on the roads, raised anti-British and anti-Government slogans and assembled at the Queen's Gardens where they were joined by students and labourers."[33]

The eventual procession included two thousand people (Thapliyal 1985a, xxii) while ten thousand attended the meeting in the evening.[34] Socialists played a prominent role at the gathering, exploiting the links they had forged during the anticapitalist and antimunicipal protests of the 1930s. However, traditional Gandhian Congress members were still in strong enough positions to veto suggestions of attacking lines of communication and government property.[35] Laborers, government servants, and tonga and tram drivers were incited to go on strike and gather at the clock tower in Chandni Chowk at 5:00 p.m. the next day, with speeches referencing the successes of the Axis powers in the war and Britain's leeching of resources from the Indian economy.[36]

The Delhi Cloth Mills and Birla Mills went on strike from 10 to 17 August, and striking textile workers, joined by students, swelled the processions through Delhi's main bazaars, terminating at the clock tower at 9:30 a.m.[37] Though largely nonviolent, some shops and cars en route were stoned.[38] More dramatically, and despite the blockades around the border between Old and New Delhi being strengthened by the senior superintendent of police at 9:30 a.m., the protesters infiltrated the new capital and picketed Connaught Place (see the next section).[39]

After an evening gathering of an estimated eight thousand people, a statement made to the police in December 1942 recalled a meeting at the house of publisher and elected city father Yudhvir Singh (Chopra 1974, 426). Here Satyavati and the Congress organizer Premjas Rai passed on information from Bombay (279).[40] This instructed supporters to continue hartals and excite the urban and rural populations. However, orders were also given to break down lines of communication, create revolts in the police and military, and "create rowdyism."

The Quit India movement in central Delhi came to a head on 11 August, after which the protests would diffuse away from central Delhi and from nonviolence. The events of the 11th can be divided into three overlapping phases and geographies in which first, small groups moved Delhi's main thoroughfares and public spaces (7:00 a.m.–12:00 p.m.); second, the police and military forcibly retook the main public spaces of the city (12:00–12:30 p.m.); third, agitation spread throughout the suburbs and periphery of Old Delhi (12:30–9:00 p.m.).

First, in the morning specific areas of the city were targeted in the hope of getting as many people into the center of the city as possible. From early morning bands of aggravated protesters toured the industrial suburbs to the northwest, attempting to enforce the strikes and entice factory workers into the city's heart. A small group attempted to break into Delhi Cloth Mills at 7:00 a.m., allegedly with the intention of attacking the two European sergeants posted there, but was turned back by a dispatched police force.[41] At approximately 7:45 a.m. a crowd gathered in Gracia Park outside Hindu College but was dispersed by a police force of over fifty men.[42] The students split into smaller groups and moved down Hamilton Road, Kashmiri Gate Bazar, Dufferin Bridge, and Lothian Road toward the city center.

In central Delhi the crowds were growing by 8:00 a.m., with groups of students and laborers stopping trams in the street to obstruct the flow of traffic.[43] By 8:15 the city magistrate estimated that over eight thousand people had gathered along Chandni Chowk, some of whom began setting fire to trams and cutting electrical wires.[44] In separate personal interviews both Roop Narain

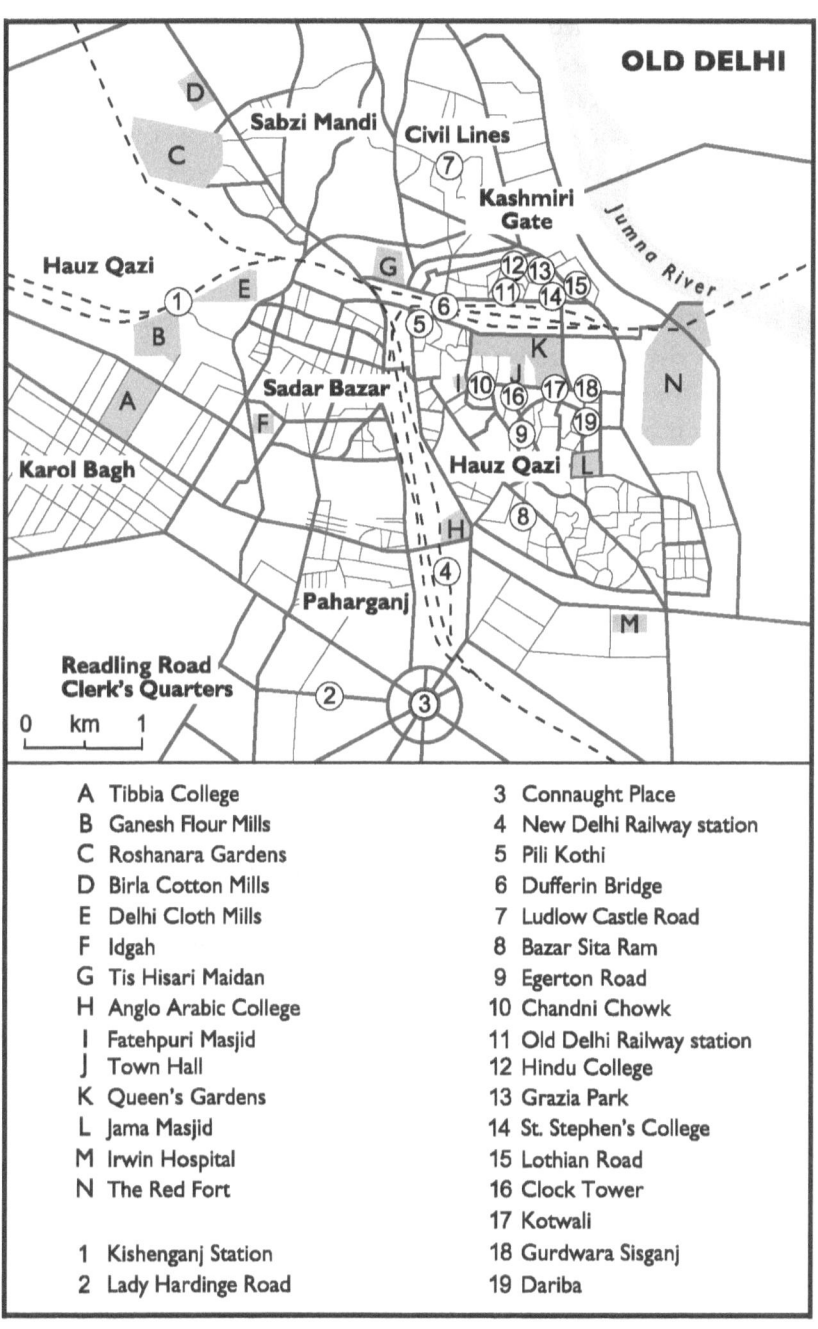

**FIGURE 6.1.** Quit India and Old Delhi

and Dharmedra Nath recalled a popular social memory of the "Hakim and the Doli."[45] A doli, or palanquin, was a covered carriage typically used by women in purdah that was carried by bearers while a Hakim was a Muslim physician (see Husain 2016, 148). Just before 10:00 a.m. a doli approached the clock tower (see figure 6.1) on Chandni Chowk (also see Dayal 1975, 23). The tower was under heavy police guard as an established center for political gatherings. The doli pushed through the police guard, and at 10:00 a.m. emerged a figure in a burka. Dramatically removing the veil, local Muslim Congress activist Hakim Khahil-ul-Rahman, replete with flowing white beard, mounted the steps of the clock tower and made a brief speech before being arrested.[46] The *Hindustan Times* confirmed that Rahman had hoisted a Congress flag at the clock tower but suggested he led a procession up Chandni Chowk to the kotwali, where he offered himself for arrest.[47]

The rest of the crowd became increasingly agitated as the procession approached the Gurdwara Sisganj and the kotwali. Bricks had been thrown through the windows of shops that remained open, so the district magistrate ordered the crowd to disperse, to no effect. This led Kilburn, the senior superintendent of police, to launch a police lathi charge out from the kotwali, splitting the crowd in two around 10:00 a.m. The crowd was intransigent, and R. W. L. Adams later recalled the police opened fire "in self defence," having been cut off from their superiors in the struggle. The police retreated to the kotwali gate under the orders of Kilburn yet continued using "controlled fire."[48] The magistrate reported the use of nineteen rounds of ammunition, killing two people.[49] A temporary and fragile clearance resulted around the kotwali, which was now surrounded by the crowd. As the city magistrate later reported: "The members of the crowd went in the bye lanes but after a little while again came out and continued to throw brick bats wherever they could on Policemen on duty and military vehicles passing that way."[50]

Meanwhile, a military truck that attempted to clear the street at 11:15 a.m. was stoned and overturned.[51] A quarter of an hour later, a U.S. Air Force lorry being driven by three white soldiers carrying 250 gallons of petrol was stoned near Dariba and set alight.[52] Under the cover of the crowd that was still surrounding the kotwali, at 12:00 noon a group of three hundred protesters forced the evacuation of the town hall and set one wing alight, pelting workers who fled the site (although Phool Chand Jain suggested it was municipal workers themselves who set their offices alight).[53] The police picket that guarded the "Shiv Mandir" (Baul 2020) site near the town hall was also attacked and torched. The fire brigade engines that arrived shortly after, and their protective convoy of two tanks and motorcycles, were stoned and set on fire also. Throughout the morning, the police and army had been overwhelmed.

The second stage saw the local government fall back on the military (Legg 2007, 118). Kilburn, now trapped in the kotwali, had been unable to contact the troops in the fort because the telephone lines had been cut. However, a Hindu merchant had taken a message from Kilburn to Deputy Commissioner Hubert Evans in Kashmiri Gate, stating that the crowds in Chandni Chowk were out of control (Evans 1988, 236). Before making his way south with the armed police, Evans telephoned the fort requesting Major Webber lead the army's striking force out onto the crossroads that faced down Chandni Chowk.[54] The armed police led the march south from Kashmiri Gate at, as Evans recalled, "the tempo, half the tempo, of a dead march" (237). This was, however, to little effect, as Evans later recalled, recounting his subaltern targets in full counterinsurgency naturalizing (scampering, wriggling, heaving) mode (see Guha 1983b, 46): "They fired and fired again with their smooth-bore muskets enough times to demonstrate that their volleys were too feeble: there was some scampering back, there were twenty wriggling bodies on the ground, but no lanes were opening in that heaving mass. I called back the policemen; it was now for the soldiers" (Evans 1988, 237).

The police blocked the side streets and provided rear support as the army moved down Chandni Chowk from the fort, firing successive rounds into the crowd, which slowly began to disperse.[55] While the technology and violence of the military seemingly achieved its "moral effect" (Legg 2007, 103), the army commander had admitted he had no experience of civil unrest and that several of his troops vomited with fear during the advance (Evans 1988, 237). On reaching the kotwali, Kilburn and the police emerged and helped clear the street. While Delhi's main thoroughfare had been retaken, agitation in the periphery of the city remained active. The result of police firing was reported in the press the following day as twelve dead and thirty-five injured, but the report also listed the result of extensive arson in the city and counterviolence against the police.[56]

The third stage saw the movement, and violence, dispersed throughout the city in the afternoon and evening of 11 August. Protesters sabotaged, torched, and destroyed the physical embodiments of the colonial authorities, including tax offices, railway stores, postal services, and telecommunications, as in 1857 (see Lahiri 2003), what Guha (1983a, 18) termed the elementary aspect of negation.

One group of protesters had headed toward the four-story Railway Clearing Accounts Office on Queen's Road near Dufferin Bridge, known as Pili Kothi. The murder of a policeman was the most devastating problematization of Congress's already tenuous claim to be orchestrating a nonviolence movement (see the concluding section of this chapter). But violence against objects, if not subjects, was widespread throughout the city. At 3:00 p.m. the police received reports that a group of protesters had moved through the Civil Lines and set fire to the income tax office and nearby petrol pumps on Ludlow Castle Road in the Civil Lines. To the southwest of the old city, Evans (1988, 236) challenged a crowd that had stormed a police substation, set fire to two signal cabins at the railway junction, and attempted to reach the durbar railway cabin at New Delhi railway station. Evans's force later used twenty rounds of ammunition at 4:00 p.m. to protect a sub–post office at Sadar Bazar Bridge before dealing with a disturbance at Kishenganj railway station.[57]

As the focus of the protests diffused out of the city during the early afternoon, military pickets replaced the police posts at the exits from the walled city to the Civil Lines and New Delhi. This followed a small batch of students finding their way to the Secretariat at 11:00 a.m. but did not prevent students from damaging electrical wires in the Reading Road clerks' quarters, setting fire to the house of a European Railway servant at 7:00 p.m. or severely damaging the ceremonial platform at New Delhi railway station.[58] The police had also been dispatched to Shahdara village, to a godown in Teliwara where a bonfire of military uniforms had been created, and to the Ganesh Flour Mills, where a further protester was shot dead. CrPC 144 was issued at 8:00 p.m. forbidding assemblages of more than five persons in the urban area, while a curfew was issued between 9:00 p.m. and 6:00 a.m. throughout specified parts of the municipal area that would last until 19 August. By the end of the day, nine more people had been killed and fifteen wounded.

While 12 August saw great disruption, there was nothing on the scale of the previous day. As the government's provincial summary of events concluded, the police and army pushed protesters out of the city center and into the surrounding suburbs.[59] Student protesters continued their activities in the northwestern section of New Delhi, causing damage in the Reading Road and Punch Kuin Road areas from 8:00 a.m. By 8:40 a.m. a group of students from Ramjas College had moved on to Qarol Bagh, the Western Extension of Old Delhi, where an octroi (tax) post, a warden's post, Sarai Rohilla railway station, and other properties were torched while telegraph wires and poles were also destroyed. The armed police, on arrival, responded with twenty-one rounds of ammunition in the act of saving five "European or Anglo-Indian adults" who were under attack, one of whom had had his house destroyed.[60]

A similar pattern recurred between 10:00 a.m. and 4:00 p.m. consisting of fleeting, violent attacks on the periphery of Old Delhi. A police sergeant, while patrolling Punch Kuin Road between New Delhi and Paharganj, was stoned at 10:15 a.m. and fired in self-defense, as recurred at 12:30 p.m. An electric sub-station was burned in Paharganj at 12:00 p.m., while a sub–post office was destroyed in Sadar Bazar at 1:00 p.m. A European officer fired in self-defense on Ibbetson Road at 3:00 p.m. while the army striking force targeted disturbances in Sadar Bazar and Paharganj throughout the afternoon. Later that afternoon activity switched to Old Delhi, during which a police picket in Bazar Sita Ram opened fire on a crowd at approximately 4:00 p.m., while police and Congress processions clashed on Egerton Road at 6:15 p.m., during which the police fired again to disperse the procession.

By 13 August the Delhi authorities could confidently print an official communiqué in the *Hindustan Times* stating: "In the Old City, peaceful conditions are rapidly returning under the strong police and Military forces now stationed there. A few shops are reopening. In New Delhi all is quiet."[61] This intentionally downplayed the violence and the micropolitics of ongoing activity, which was surveilled by press, government, and Congress reports. The *Hindustan Times* listed twenty-five as dead from gunfire by 14 August, including bystanders killed during a police shooting spree in Parhaganj on the 13th, among whom were a tailor waiting for a tonga and a water carrier, while a man was hit by a stray bullet while lying in bed at home.[62]

A regrouping of remaining organizers on 15 and 16 August led to an attempted relaunch of tried and tested techniques on 17 August, as the CID reported: "The Congress in Delhi is making attempts to arrange Congress processions to be taken out daily from unusual places at untimely hours in order to keep the movement on."[63] At 5:30 p.m. a procession of between three and four hundred people marched from the clock tower to the kotwali, where it dispersed, while a meeting of around five hundred people took place in Queen's Gardens at 6:15 p.m.

As more shops opened, although schools and some mills remained closed, a local magistrate listed the ways in which Congress was continuing to rally support, utilizing many of the nonviolent techniques outlined in the Andhra circular and other Congress literature.[64] Congress members were touring the city, door to door, enlisting support as well as distributing pamphlets, posters, handbills, and flags that advertised meetings and especially targeted the Secretariat staff in New Delhi.

Such methods were used to advertise a procession at 5:30 on 18 August that toured Chandni Chowk from Fatehpuri to the kotwali, distributing Congress badges stating "Do or Die" and "Death or Freedom." The CID reported chanting and cheering on both sides of the bazaar when Radha Raman, who had been selected to head the procession, offered himself for arrest. The CID also reported that Congress had been spreading various rumors, concerning the alleged death of Mahadev Desai (Gandhi's secretary) and Delhi's Mohammad Asaf Ali, a supposedly seriously ill Nehru, shootings by the police during curfew hours, and women being called to picket the Council Chamber in New Delhi.[65]

On 21 August Satyavati, Premjas Rai, and Brij Kishen Chandiwala, three of Delhi's old vanguard of Congress workers, were finally arrested.[66] Chandiwala suspected a tip-off to the police from a "comrade" who had just visited and recalled Satyavati being caught despite trying to flee the house via the roof. Even before his arrest Chandiwala attested to the impact of the Government's actions on the coordinated activity in the city: "Actually every person was doing their own work. No one was doing anything openly, everything was happening underground. All that time the thing was of how to run the movement. Most people did whatever came in their minds."[67]

The organizational void that the arrest of Congress leaders had created would be filled by Aruna Asaf Ali and Jugal Kishore Khanna, who had escaped arrest while representing Delhi in Bombay on 9 August and found their way back to the city on the 13th. Following Satyavati's arrest, Asaf Ali and Kishore Khanna were appointed as Delhi's new "High Command" (Chopra 1976, 279). At the house of Radha Raman's sister on Egerton Road, in the heart of Old Delhi, they started to plan the next stage of the Quit India protest, one that would radically depart from the Satyagraha mold of the previous mass movements and would take the organization "underground."

This turn enabled Congress workers to evade not only the police but also strict ahimsa, as the sections that follow will demonstrate. Not all Congress workers approved of the underground tactics, but the traditional mobilization techniques had lost their power just a fortnight into the movement. Attempts to publicly commemorate just one month of the movement faltered. Although the director of the Intelligence Bureau reported that Bombay and Delhi were among the few places to instigate a revival of interest around 9 September 1942, he also noted that the movement was quickly put down.[68] This was despite a meeting at the Gurdwara Sisganj on 30 August at which Sikhs were encouraged to join the movement, and the Muslim Jamiat ul Ulema-I-Hind declaring its support for Congress on 4 September.[69] There was some limited picketing, the distribution of unauthorized newssheets, and fifty-nine arrests in the first fortnight of September. Crowds toured around Fatehpuri

Masjid and Sadar Bazar on 7 September shouting "Don't forget the ninth!" but caused no major disturbance.[70] There was little activity in the walled city for the rest of the month, the exceptions being a failed attempt to bomb the kotwali from the nearby Sunehri Masjid on 18 September and a procession of eleven donkeys through the city to represent the members of the Governor-General's Council on 20 September (the police impounded the donkeys; Raghavan 1994, 289).[71]

The director of the Intelligence Bureau concluded on 19 September, "Below the surface, there is little doubt that the spirit of lawlessness is being sedulously kept alive by the promotion of *satyagraha* tactics, traces of which have been becoming increasingly evident of late, particularly in Delhi, Bombay, the Central Provinces and the North West Frontier Province."[72] The nature of this underground activity had been accurately foretold in a secret report by the assistant central intelligence officer on 18 September, who had spoken to the detainees in Delhi's jails. He claimed that Satyavati and Premjas Rai had admitted inciting people to destroy government property and concluded that "the entire membership of Congress have given up their faith in non-violence."[73]

QUIT NEW DELHI

On 15 August 1942 the Intelligence Bureau of the Government of India sent an extract from its secret reports to R. G. Mellor, the senior superintendent of Delhi's CID.[74] The focus of the report was how nationalist activity in the old city was spreading into the new city to the south. It listed the Congress workers requiring attention, including "Radharaman" (Radha Raman), "Phulchand" (Phool Chand) and "Gulabchand" (Gulab Chand) Jain, Satyavati, Chandulal (arrested during Civil Disobedience and as an individual satyagrahi; Thapliyal 1985b, 70), Raghunandan Saran (individual satyagrahi; Thapliyal 1985b, 248) and "Jayant (Son of Prof Indra)." They were said to meet, with others, in the India Coffee House on Queensway in New Delhi, while on the night of 13 August they were said to have met at India Gate (see figure 6.2). In the geometric center of New Delhi, the seventy attendees included clerks from the Supply Department, where plans for picketing government offices has been laid. A CID note on file replied that these locations would be looked into and that plans were afoot to place "agents" in various Government offices to report on disaffection. A further report on 11 September suggested that Delhi's most influential nationalist women, named as Mrs. Gadodia, Mrs. Sahni and Mrs. Kohli, were also meeting in New Delhi's India Coffee House. The last two of these were said to be connected to both Congress and revolutionary networks,

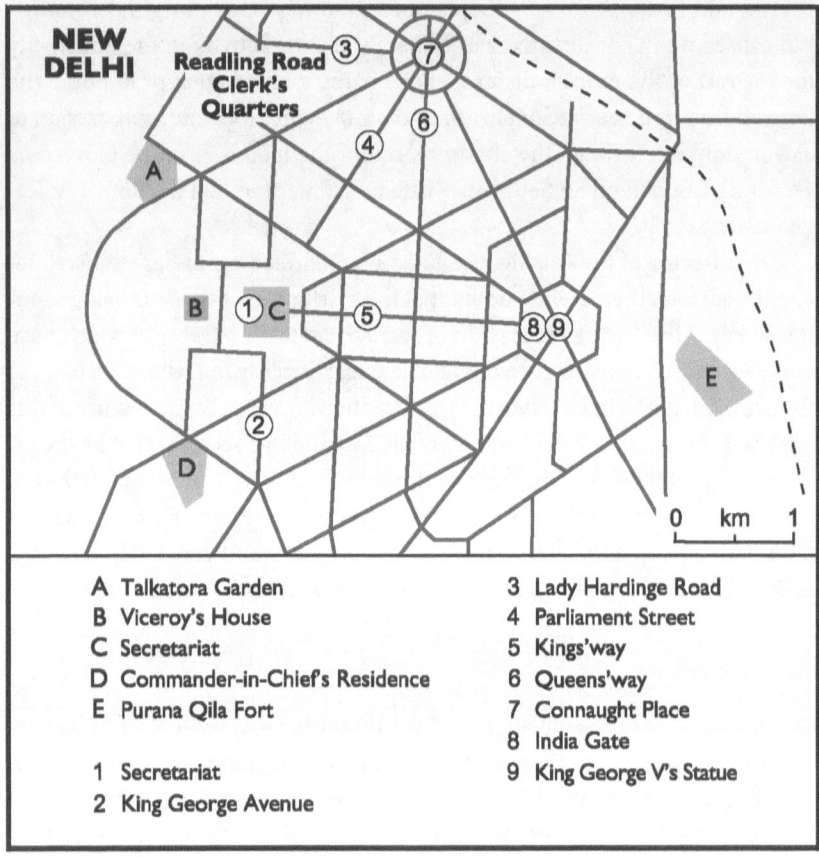

**FIGURE 6.2.** Quit India and New Delhi

the latter of whom were thought to be planning a scheme for terrorizing the Government in Delhi. Mrs. Gadodia, wife of a very wealthy Old Delhi trader, was said to have facilitated the transfer of a large sum of money to Aruna Asaf Ali in Bombay. The result of this and much broader campaigning was the successful targeting of the New Delhi overground.

During the war years the capital was the host of both American troops and press (Datta 2019a), which only made it more tempting as a political target. As above, occasional incursions were made into New Delhi from the old city to the north. But the capital was also more systematically targeted, as a symbolic, bureaucratic, and flammable space. First, the visualization of New Delhi as a liberal capital was challenged repeatedly over the first five months of the Quit India movement. As noted above, on 10 August students had made their way into New Delhi and converged in Connaught Place.[75] From there they headed south to the Secretariats but were pushed back by the police and returned to Connaught Place. During "considerable rowdyism" (Mathur 1979, 76) bricks were thrown through the windows of Lloyds Bank and surrounding shops while a bus belonging to the Convent of Jesus and Mary was also stoned.

The *Statesman* made much of this penetration of the capital, announcing on 11 August "Demonstration in Connaught Place" and, two days later, stressing the protection that had been required along the border between the new and old cities. Marking the significance of the incursion, Delhi's superintendent of police, other officials, and Deputy Commissioner Hubert Evans had converged in Connaught Place.[76] Evans later reflected on the significance of the switch to the capital: "Whether New Delhi as the seat of imperial rule would be the next target, or a target at all, of the revels was to be seen; but the odds were against this. It sheltered no canaille [rabble], it hated the profane crowd" (Evans 1988, 235).

Vishwa Bandhu Gupta, the son of Desh Bandhu Gupta, commented in a personal interview in 2001 that this political geography of the two cities was very much apparent to Congress. He suggested that planting a Congress flag in Chandni Chowk would go unnoticed as "everyone" had them anyway, while hosting one in Connaught Place or near New Delhi police station on Parliament Street was a big deal (for which he himself was arrested in 1945).[77] Regarding New Delhi more broadly he suggested: "Since this was the greatest symbol of the British Empire, the seat of power, any protest taken out here carried more value in terms of media attention and in the sense of talking points and situations which inspired workers. If you could succeed in a protest in Connaught Place for example that was considered to be a bigger thing than doing the same in Old Delhi."[78]

As the students had found, however, certain parts of the capital were policed more than others, especially the Secretariat and the elite houses south of Kingsway. Rajmohan Gandhi suggested in an interview that there were certain parts of Delhi that were out of bounds: "Whenever one entered the area of British officers, one knew one was entering forbidden territory, passing an invisible wall."[79] Yet Connaught Place was described by him as an "Indian place," being the location of the *Hindustan Times* offices and his home (being the son of Devdas Gandhi, the newspaper editor and son of M. K. Gandhi). The outer ring of Connaught Circle was, for him, a "nationalist space" in the commercial heart of New Delhi (see figure 6.3). The role of this area in the underground movement will be discussed in the next chapter, but it was not the only part of the capital to be targeted by the overground movement.

**FIGURE 6.3.** A 1946 protest meeting in Connaught Place. Photograph by Narain Prashad, Delhi; reproduced with permission

Because (not in spite) of the high officials living in the "forbidden territory" of central Delhi, these areas became prized targets because of the media coverage they could attract to the despotic capital. Picketers outside the houses of four members of the Executive Council and outside various shops in New Delhi were arrested on 9 September, while further arrests were made at the Assembly Chamber on 14 September after Aruna Asaf Ali and J. N. Sahni organized picketing by male and female students.[80] A casual Congress supporter who was drawn into the Quit India movement, Mool Raj, later confessed to the CID how he had been introduced by Manubhai Shah to Aruna Asaf Ali and Jugal Kishore Khanna after they had gone underground. He recalled: "She said that New Delhi being the Capital of India and is [sic] a place where so many Americans are residing at this time the demonstrations would prove most effective and would be known to America through American correspondents." Mool Raj's efforts to coordinate villagers and other volunteers came to naught, but a ward organizer, Ved Gian Chand Chopra, recounted to the CID how he had sourced two volunteers from Paharganj and taken them to the Legislative Assembly by tonga by 9:00 a.m. on 14 September.[81] His volunteers joined students to shout slogans at the gates and were later joined by seven or eight women who arrived by taxi.

While Chopra's volunteers were arrested, the ladies picketed until 2:00 p.m., when eight of them were arrested. They were convicted under section 7 of the Criminal Law Amendment Act (XXIII of 1932, "Molesting a person to prejudice of employment or business") and fined 200 rupees or given two months' imprisonment. The CID noted: "This picketing has proved detrimental to the interests of the Government in as much as the foreign Press correspondents who had come to report the Assembly proceedings (majority of them being Americans) got an opportunity to witness for themselves Congress demonstrations. They were talking to picketers, taking notes and photographs." While censorship bodies in New Delhi could refuse to pass on what was written, the CID suggested, the reporters had been heard saying they would convey what they had seen to American diplomatic authorities: "Some of these American correspondents were surprised at the treatment accorded to the picketers, particularly girls, by the Police in dragging the first batch to the Police vans."[82]

Early 1943 would see two spectacular assaults on the symbolism of the imperial capital. Manubhai Shah, who had been born in Gujarat and served in technical and administrative roles at the Delhi Cloth Mills, has recalled participation in the first scheme (and his later turn to violence in Delhi more broadly).[83] With the help of Devadas Gandhi at the *Hindustan Times*, signposts were printed with alternative names for the main roads in New Delhi, the nomenclature of which associated the most prestigious roads with the most prestigious figures of British and Indian history. On the night of 31 December 1942 Shah and a band of helpers pasted the new signs throughout the capital, renaming Parliament Street as Jawaharlal Nehru Road and King George's Avenue as Sardar Patel Road, for example. Students and workers from Delhi Cloth Mills were used to paste the new signs, as was R. P. Puri, who confirmed this story in a police interview (Gupta 1997, 83).[84] While Shah was actually caught by the police, he escaped after paying the arresting constable 100 rupees.

> SHAH: Nahin, nahin, main to larka hun; volunteers hun. Yeh to sab Congress wale badmash hain. Un logon ne humko garbar kar diya; our yeh kardiya; mere chacha mujhe danteen ge.
> POLICEMAN: Nahin, sale, tum log badmash hai, tum sub long tung kar diya hum ko; yeh jala diya, yeh kar diya; voh ker diya.[85]

[SHAH: No, no, I am a boy, a volunteer. All these Congresswalas are miscreants/badmash. They have made us bad, and have done this, my uncle will scold me.
POLICEMAN: No, saale [brother-in-law, but used as an insult], you people are miscreants, all of you people have troubled us, burned this, done this, done that.]⁸⁶

Shah and Puri were also involved in the next project, which Puri claims took place on New Year's Day 1943. The aim was to break the nose on New Delhi's statue of King George V and place a black robe over it. In a later interview Puri recalled thinking, "I think there is some custom, when Christians die, I think, they put some cloth and write something on it."⁸⁷ The statue was situated behind India Gate at the end of Kingsway, the ceremonial heart of New Delhi. A robe was prepared that was thirty feet long and six feet wide, on which was written "King George V, Looter and Plunderer of India! Death to the Tyrant," beneath which was placed a picture of Gandhi and the AICC logo.⁸⁸ However, in practice, the ladder proved to be too short to reach the statue, the participants fell into the pool below, and the police descended, although nobody was arrested.

Over the first year of the campaign New Delhi was targeted not only as a symbolic space but also as a bureaucratic space with a working population who could potentially cripple the machinery of the Government if successfully recruited. A Congress Bulletin logged by the Delhi police in late August 1942 condemned government employees as traitorous collaborators. The city functioned here as both a symbolic and material landscape for anticolonialism: "Those who are still left in New Delhi are trembling in their shoes. . . . Every student, every employee of the Government of India, every labourer should set an example to these criminals by acting as courageous and responsible Indians. Processions should be taken whatever the consequences. The offices should be picketed. The residences of these craven men should not serve as asylums for them. Get ready to act, if you are not already acting."⁸⁹

Others within government had, it seems, already heeded these messages. Regarding his trip to Bombay for the 9 August launch of the Quit India movement, Jugal Kishore Khanna recalled that Mohammad Asaf Ali had received a tip-off from a Shri Mahindrapati who was feeding information from New Delhi's Home Department to Congress.⁹⁰ Both he and Khanna tried to convince the AICC elite that the government was planning mass arrests after the resolutions had been passed at Gowalia Tank Maidan, but Sarojini Naidu and others laughed the reports off. Khanna's contact was said to be a "dispatcher" of government circulars who would read them before sealing them in confidential envelopes.⁹¹ Chandiwala also recalled their detailed knowledge in advance of the arrests, including that Gandhi would be held in the Aga Khan's palace, leaked specifically from a telegram operative in New Delhi. But the national Congress leaders laughed and dismissed his source as *chandukhana* (which literally translates as "opium den" but refers to gossip from a disreputable source).[92] As such, the Delhi leaders who had decided to go underground (see chapter 7) avoided being arrested in Bombay because they heeded the leaks coming from the capital.[93]

Further sources in the Government of India Press in New Delhi fed through information about government circulars being printed to be sent to the secretary of state for India in London.[94] According to Phool Chand Jain, "Government workers would come and tell us that today in our place this is happening, in the ministry this is happening today, the Home Ministry is doing this today. To the extent that sometime they would even get copies of 'circulars' and give them to us. Two or three boys of Delhi were also caught in this act."[95]

One of the organizers of the attempted firebombing of British shops in Connaught Place in January 1943 (see below) was later claimed to be working undercover within the government.[96] This situation was closely monitored by both the central and local administrations. The former produced a "Government of India Workers Delhi Situation Report" on 20 August, noting the distribution of leaflets appealing to Secretariat staff around New Delhi.[97] The latter, on 18 September, expressed concerns about the activities of clerks in the Accountant General's office.[98] S. C. Gupta of the Supply Department later recalled organizers grouping workers into blocs with a representative in each section who would distribute literature in the office space itself.[99] These actions only compounded the pressure that was already bearing on the workers in New Delhi.

The central intelligence officer had produced a report on the "Effect of the Congress Movement on Secretariat Staff" on 5 September. It stated: "There is little doubt that the Congress movement has shaken the loyalty of the Ministerial Staff attached to the Headquarters of the Government of India to a considerable extent." Workers were seen to willingly discuss politics, whereas before they had been portrayed as apolitical. Clerks had now become "more willing to complain about the treatment and the lack of consideration they receive from their officers, work at high pressure, longer hours in office and meagre chances of promotion." A follow-up report on 19 September acknowledged the intense pressure that had been exerted over the last fortnight and noted the distribution of leaflets stressing that without the support of the people of New Delhi, the Government would fall. Appeals were made to "cast aside your false selfishness and sense of security and become the torch-bearer

Some one shouts Koi Hai! and there we are. We are the flunkeys—literally of Empire. We do not know our degradation—like the domesticated cow or horse we go on unmindful of what has happened to our human dignity. Who is responsible? Not we. But you, who shout Koi Hai! We work little and are clothed very well.

**KOI HAI?**

This page of pictures gives you an idea of how we Chaprassis of the Imperial Secretariat, live. We are classified as Peons, Daffadars, Jamadars and Daftries. Our clothes are resplendent. Our salaries range from fourteen to thirty-five rupees. But our clothes cost the Government from twenty to forty-five rupees. Per week eating costs us about Rs. 8-9. That means about Rs. 34 per month. Are we not well provided for? In a way, yes. For we get the clothes and the pay for sitting down infinite hours or occasionally going from one room to another. We make use of the long hours by spinning and knitting. Our homes are dirty and we may have been better men had we stuck to our villages. But doing nothing has a great attraction, has it not?

**FIGURE 6.4.** "Koi Hai?" (Is anyone there), *Janata*, 17/2/1946

of Independence."¹⁰⁰ These attacks would be sustained long past the end of the Quit India movement. An article from 1946 (figure 6.4) ventriloquized the uniformed staff of the Secretariat as confessing: "We are the flunkeys—literally of Empire. We do not know our degradation—like the domesticated cow or horse we go on unmindful of what has happened to our human dignity."[101] Their well-dressed servants of the Raj in New Delhi are contrasted with images of poverty in village life.

As well as a symbolic and bureaucratic space, New Delhi as a material space was the subject of incendiary attacks. A fire was started in the record room of the south block of the Secretariat on 12 August 1942 followed by another in the Supply Accounts Office of the Assembly Chamber on 1 September.[102] This was followed by a fire in the Central Ordinance Depot of the Delhi Cantonment Army base on 16 September, and two letter box burnings in the capital.[103] This continued to be an acknowledged aim of Delhi's Congress command; from November onward a priority was to damage and burn the Government records in the Imperial Secretariat. Chemical solutions in small bottles were believed by the CID to have been prepared; only the lack of sufficient amounts of chemicals was preventing a wider arson campaign.[104]

Delhi Provincial Congress Committee's newsletter of 23 December 1942 hailed ongoing national and local campaigns of disruption and arson. The viceroy was said to have lied in suggesting that the movement was "in hand": "for we believe that palsied hands corrupted with dead authority cannot hold down a people's revolt against a Government which has the sickening and perverted capacity of breeding its own anti-bodies within the body politic of the country it governs."[105] In and around Delhi, telephone and telegraph lines were being disrupted while many more letter boxes had been burned in Lady Hardinge Road, Connaught Circus, and elsewhere in the capital. This was part of what Phool Chand Jain recalled as the "dal lifafa dekh tamasha" (put in the envelope, see the show) movement, whereby gunpowder-filled envelopes would be used to start fires in letter boxes or foreign shops.[106]

In addition to the nonviolent street renamings and the attempted statue maiming of early 1943, another outrage in the capital was orchestrated on the night of 3 January by M. M. Shah. At the stroke of 9:00 p.m., when the New Delhi Municipal Tower "hooting" would drown out the noise, Shah and his accomplices intended to smash the windows of eleven British shops in Connaught Place and set them alight.[107] Over thirty students and mill workers reportedly helped, although none of the eleven shops damaged caught fire.[108]

The last major violent outrage took place in New Delhi in early March 1943. On the night of 7 March crude bombs exploded in the auditoriums of three of the four English cinemas in New Delhi, while an unexploded device was found in the final cinema the next morning.[109] Three of the cinemas were located in Connaught Place; the explosions injured one British soldier and one Indian woman.[110] Asoka Kumar Dutt later admitted his role in the explosions, along with students from Ramjas, Hindu, and Commercial Colleges, who had decided to put into action a plan originally suggested by Aruna Asaf Ali (see also Jain 2010).[111]

As the Quit India movement began to wind down, the deputy commissioner came to consider claims of compensation from those whose property had been damaged during the disturbances. On 5 October 1942 the central Home Department had stated that where the property of a Government servant had been damaged or destroyed, the presumption should be that the attack was due to their occupation and that generous compensation should be given where possible. In June 1943 the deputy commissioner assessed the claims, which included cases where Government employees had clearly been targeted. Lance Corporal W. Canning of the 151 Parachute Battalion, for instance, registered losses of 1,750 rupees, claiming: "During the recent riots in Delhi my wife and home was [sic] subject to rather a rough time at the hands of the hooligans taking part. My home was at Karol Bagh. The mob took my wife into the street, they then proceeded to loot my house and carry away what goods they could carry. After stealing everything, they continued to set fire to my home resulting in the complete loss of everything. My wife was left without clothes, money or food etc."[112]

Canning could be posed as a representative of the central, autocratic, imperial state, as could the destroyed property within the New Delhi Municipal Committee, which suffered losses totaling 5,000 rupees. These were dwarfed, however, by the losses of the Delhi Municipal Committee, which were thirty-five times higher, totaling 175,193 rupees (£516,972 or 44,976,564 rupees in 2017).[113] Major costs came from services that had been targeted, such as the 12,100 rupees damage to the Municipal Fire Brigade (stoned at noon on 11 August) or the damage to street lighting costing 15,000 rupees (after most of the streetlamps were reported on the 12th to have been smashed). The list of buildings requiring repair charted a landscape of arson and sabotage, from the torched town hall to the housing of the fire brigade, a TB clinic on Queen's Road, air raid shelters, and tax offices. While this violence was within the limits of Congress guidance, the violence against individuals was not.

### Problematization: Murder at Pili Kothi

In 1930 the Gurdwara Sisganj shooting problematized both colonial and Congress governmentalities. It exposed the unhinged violence of the police, but it also highlighted the violence of some, if not all, of the local participants and the inability of Congress to control the event or its narrative. As Congress's partial claiming of the event demonstrated, however, the state could easily be portrayed as the perpetrator. In contrast, the Quit India movement left no major monument to nonviolence in the city but bore the marks of various experiments with violence. This can be seen in the representations of the first few days in general and the portrayal of the Pili Kothi incident in particular.[114]

The local authorities tended to interpret the outbreaks of violence as an inevitable consequence of subaltern indiscipline following the arrest of the Congress elite. The city magistrate reported on 11 August that morning crowds "got up to mischief" when the local leaders did not turn up, most of them having been arrested.[115] A CID report on 17 August admitted that the arrest of the leadership had left the crowds without anyone to lead the movement "in the correct channels," and as such it was easy for instigators to incite the "mobs," which were "inherently not non-violent."[116] Against such depictions, the local press had few of the rhetorical tactics available to it that had been deployed so effectively against the "Police Raj" during the Civil Disobedience campaign. The *Hindustan Times* condemned the "repression" of the government and listed the occasions on which firepower had been used, but this was muted by the admission of violence on both sides. The newspapers did, however, offer alternative views of the sequence of events, in which, for instance, the crowd on Chandni Chowk only stoned Kilburn and the police after the initial lathi charge, not before.[117]

Nationalist newspapers, unable to launch an unambiguous attack on state violence, resorted to listing (and in a sense celebrating) the extent of the damage caused by the protesters. The papers evoked the sensory dislocation that the disturbances had created. The *Statesman* reported that on 11 August the clock in front of the town hall had stopped at 12 o'clock while a siren had been ringing all day (the "hooter," which gave an owl-like "wail" to signal the start and end of each day; Siddiqi 2011, 113), unable to be turned off because the stairs leading to it had been destroyed by fire.[118] The city was filled with the smell of burning paper and tires, while the *Hindustan Times* had reported on 12 August that letter boxes throughout the city had also been destroyed and their contents burned. Most electric lamps had been smashed, and after the curfew, "the city was in complete darkness." Little positive could be said, however, about the events at Pili Kothi, and it was official reports that used sensory and affective language in reporting on the violence. It had less in common with the violence at the Gurdwara Sisganj of 1930 than it did the fatal incidents at Chauri Chaura in 1922 (Amin [1995] 2006).

As with the Gurdwara Sisganj incident, the basic facts here are agreed, but unlike May 1930, there was little contestation over who was to blame for the violence. The Clearings Accounts Office in Delhi was known as the Pili Kothi. It was located on Queen's Road in North Delhi, near the railway lines within the northeast of the walled city (see figure 6.1). Hari Narain, the office head clerk, reported to the police that sixty to seventy "Congress volunteers" arrived at 12:30 p.m. on 11 August and set fire to the building and a fire brigade substation.[119] This version was contested, however; Phool Chand Jain would later suggest that it was the clerks of the building who encouraged the crowd to torch it.[120] Nirad Chaudhuri (1987, 703) was living near some Bengali clerks from the office at the time and noted their glee as they saw the flames rise. Yet J. N. Sahni recalls being asked to help two young women escape from the area after Satyavati had convinced them to torch the building.[121]

Superintendent Pirji Mohammad Sharif arrived from Kashmiri Gate police station with four constables to investigate.[122] He attempted to call for extra police from the kotwali, but the lines had been cut. The crowd returned and, according to a constable's report, stoned the police as they attempted to protect the office. The police were forced inside the building, but the records in the basement were then also set alight, forcing them back out to confront the growing crowd. On leaving the building the police were split up and, upon regrouping, discovered that the superintendent had been murdered and left naked on a nearby road. By 1:30 p.m. Kilburn had heard about the trouble and sent further troops.[123] After clearing Chandni Chowk, Evans (1988) arrived to find McClintock, an assistant superintendent of police, "firing with deliberation" (238) at the crowd.

In the Delhi court papers resulting from the trial, eight statements were collected, five from the police and three from eyewitnesses, that agreed on the basic sequence of events, though with subtle differences in the depiction of the violence and its causes. At midday the head clerk from the Railway Clearing Accounts Office arrived at Kashmiri Gate police station and informed them that fifty to sixty Congress volunteers had tried but failed to burn down the office. Foot Constable Mohd Iqbal, Head Constable Amar Singh, Superintendent Pir Mohd Sharif, and six others set off by car for Pili Kothi. By then the crowd had dispersed, but, despite the junior staff suggesting he leave, Sharif insisted on guarding the building and the office staff. After he had gone inside to telephone in his report, 100–150 protesters arrived and started attacking European cars and torched a fire engine. "Pirji," as Foot Constable Hamid Ali referred to him, forced the crowd back from the office, firing occasional gunshots. They were eventually forced back into the office, so the police evacuated the staff and took refuge inside for thirty minutes, until the records in the cellar were set on fire through a smashed window. After this the crowd dispersed and Sharif led his men to the railway compound, hoping to reach the railway hospital. Some made it over a wall into the hospital while Sharif struggled to open a gate, after which he led the remaining police into the compound. There he and Head Constable Amar Singh were caught by the crowd. They made an escape but, after being chased, were caught near Dufferin Bridge on Phuta Gate Road and beaten. Sharif died of his injuries while Singh passed out and only awoke later in Irwin Hospital.

So precise were the witness accounts that a detailed microgeography of the violence could be mapped for the court. On 18 August M. Fazuldiin, subordinate officer of the Public Works Department, filed a cartographic depiction of the events described in the witness statements (as he had ten years earlier, regarding the Hauzwali Masjid affair; see figure 4.6). Like much court and police material at this time, it was annotated in Urdu.[124] The map is that of a chase, its line of flight narrating a murder (figure 6.5). Across the precisely rendered objectivity of the buildings, street, and railway plans was traced a line of frantic mobility and the ultimate site of violence. An English translation of the thirteen "marks of distinction" on the map was provided, beginning with the Railway Clearing Accounts Office where shots had been fired (number 1 at the base of figure 6.5). Number 3 transects the map, marking the route by which the "deceased" attempted to escape and the accused gave chase, through the hospital gate (number 2). The hospital wall over which they clambered was marked (number 4 in figure 6.6) and the railway lines they crossed included. Number 5 marks the spot where the murder took place, the clustered numbers 6 to 12 where witnesses were stood, and number 13 where Amar Singh was struck and rendered unconscious.

The reports all concurred that there were three culprits behind the death. They were varyingly described but with agreed-upon main characteristics: a Sikh with light skin and a black *danda* (staff); a youth dressed in fashionable English dress; and a Sikh in dirty clothes carrying an iron bar with a curved tip. The Sikh with the danda struck Sharif with his staff and then kicked him in the back with his knee. The viscerality of witness statements is shocking, the violence being clinically translated into blow-by-blow evidence for the trial (as with the witness testimonies of the Sisganj Firing Inquiry report). Head Constable Amar Singh was interviewed in the hospital, confirming that he had been struck by the Sikh with the danda and that the assaulters had torn off his clothes. Witness Abdul Majid described how "Pirjee" fell after the first strike, lying half on the pavement and half on the *patri* (rail track). The "fashionable youth" picked up a stone and struck it on his head, after which the second

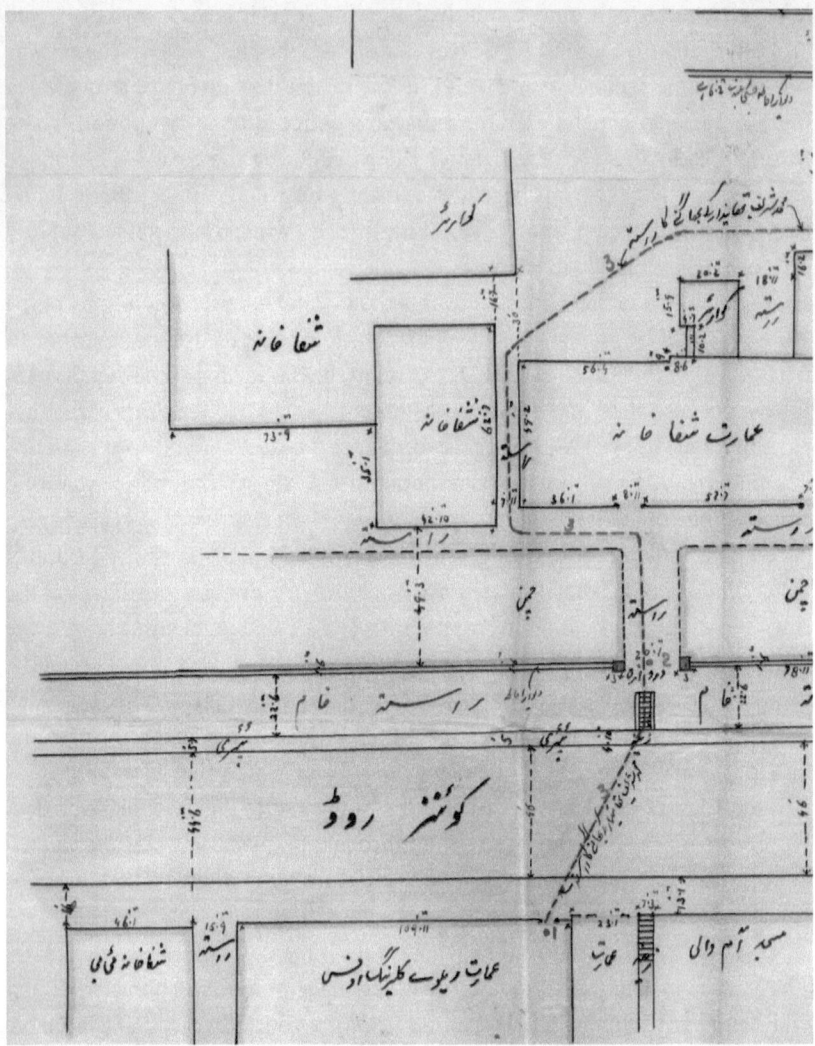

FIGURE 6.5. The Court Map of Pili Kothi. Reproduced with permission of the National Archives of India, Delhi Court Papers. Serial 3, Crown vs. Feroz Uddin and Jagat Singh

Sikh man hit him with his iron bar. Witness Ghulam Mohd from the railway hospital confirmed this report, suggesting that "the head was mostly crushed with the stone." He also stated that Sharif was stripped after he had been killed and that his naked body had then been dragged to the roadside using his belt. Sub-Inspector Mohd Khan reported finding Sharif's body by the road, covered with wounds, and surrounded by bloodstained stones and bricks.

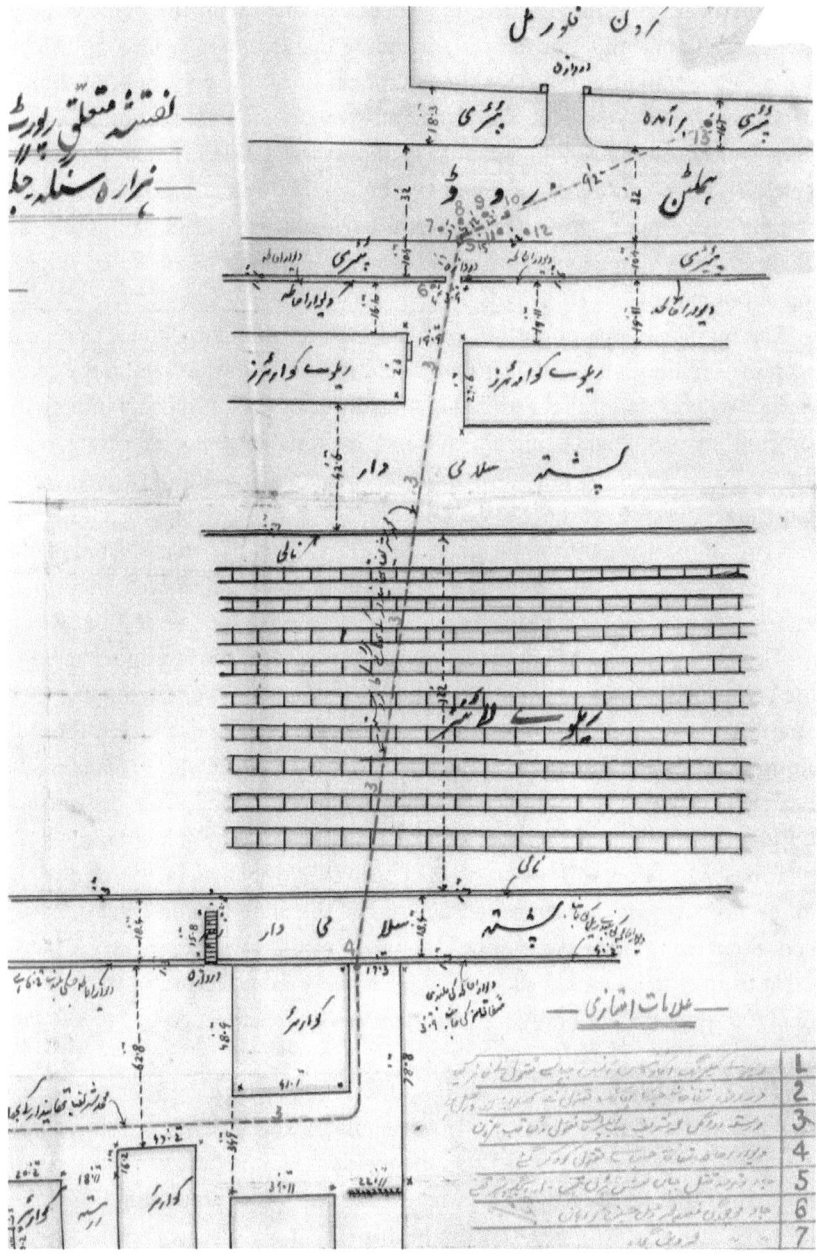

FIGURE 6.6. The Court Map of Pili Kothi. Reproduced with permission of the National Archives of India, Delhi Court Papers, Serial 3, Crown vs. Feroz Uddin and Jagat Singh

A medical examination form lodged as evidence with the court papers listed Singh as having nine injuries, including marks on the head, a split right ear, a swollen and injured right shoulder, bruises on the back of both shoulders, a swollen left forearm, a bruised and swollen left wrist and thumb, and injury marks on the right hand. Sharif's report form, titled "Unnatural death by violence," noted marks of injury on the dead body's face, forehead, eyes, and the whole of his body, and to the report's category 11 question ("blood, liquid or clotted? Where oozed from and to what amount?") it answered "Flowing out of mouth."

The reports therefore portray a violent mob attacking the police as representatives of the state. Europeans were said to have not been safe in the area, while two policemen that escaped changed out of their uniforms into civilian clothing in a neighboring mosque and the home of someone who worked for the Delhi Administration. All of the reports stress that this was not a communal riot, despite most of the victims (and witnesses) having Muslim names and two of the assailants being Sikhs. The third assailant had a Muslim name (Feroz) while the crowds, who took part in stoning the police, were described as being Hindu, Sikh, and Muslim.

The statements also include a counternarrative, though minor, in both the police and witness statements. The police statements repeatedly mention Sharif firing on the crowd, for the thirty minutes of the assault on the Pili Kothi and in their attempt to make it to the railway hospital.[125] This is made especially clear in the nonpolice statements. Ghulam Mohd, from the railway hospital, had been hit in the eye, while Ali Hussain, also from the railway hospital, described how various people had been shot by Sharif, including one hit in the stomach. He also suggested that one of the Sikhs claimed that if Sharif continued firing shots at the crowd then they would not "let him go." A statement from witness Baboo suggested Sharif had fired at Feroz, on the railway lines, but had missed, implying the attack was one of revenge and retaliation rather than that of an unreasoned mob.

This was the line taken by the *Hindustan Times*, which mentioned the fire at Pili Kothi and stated that the crowd had attacked after the sub-inspector had produced his pistol.[126] As such, the incident was portrayed as another of the arsons that had taken place in retaliation for Kilburn opening fire at the kotwali earlier in the day. However, in this case it was the Government who could publicize the violence perpetrated against Pirji Mohammad Sharif and the sentences given to those convicted. When extra police had arrived at Pili Kothi, twenty men were arrested on the spot and a further fifteen over the following days. Of these, five were discharged, five acquitted, one released on payment of a security, one given a year's rigorous imprisonment (RI), another given eighteen months of RI. The remaining twenty-one received two years of RI for, first, being among the rioters and, second, forming an unlawful assembly to set fire to the building.[127]

In pronouncing his judgment the special magistrate, Rao Saheb Mian Jagdish Singh, launched a scathing critique of the goondas (hooligans) and "loafers" who had committed the crime, just as the lawyers at Kashmiri Gate and the Gurdwara Enquiry Committee had criticized the Government in 1930. The hooliganism of the goondas was said to have destroyed the public sense of reason under the "pretext of patriotism."[128] In his damning conclusion, the magistrate stated:

> What but sabotage crime and death could emanate from a crowd consistent of such elements. The crowd had lost reason, no mind had the genuine, no soul had the virtue to dissuade the mob from its path of destruction and sabotage and persuade them towards law and order. Such work is a blot on Indian Patriotism, and even Mahatma Gandhi—the author of this movement, would feel nothing but disgust and dis-appointment at this monstrous behaviour of the mob. Never before and on no preceding occasion had the mobs shown such an ugly character in Delhi.[129]

Here we see counterinsurgency subaltern discourse in full force, analyzing a crowd through their elements, a people who had lost Reason and order, and a monstrous mob. The magistrate's report further portrayed Superintendent Sharif as having asked the crowd to desist from attacking Pili Kothi and that, while they were casting "brickbats" at the police force, "S.I. Mohd. Sharif firmly and calmly faced the crowd."[130] When the police were forced out of the building, the report stated that they ran to the nearby railway hospital and that it was while "running for his life," not firing at the crowd, that Sharif was killed by stones and lathis. As such, although a great distortion of the facts, it was a policeman who was positioned as the nonviolent victim of anticolonial violence.

In summarizing the events at Pili Kothi in its fortnightly report, the local administration complimented Sharif, who had "most courageously attempted to save the building."[131] The wording recalls the admiration expressed for the "manly spirit" displayed by Mr. Jeffreys during the Sisganj incident of 1930, but here Congress could not contest the verdict. While there is no doubting the violence and cruelty of the repressive measures of the state, Congress had no moral vantage point. In recalling the Quit India movement, Delhi journalist J. N. Sahni (1971, 190–91) could only conclude: "Government replied sabotage with lawlessness, violence to property with violence to persons." Even his claim that "it was India's last great rebellion with violence directed towards everything touching the administration except human beings" (191) had to be qualified with "except stray incidents" (190).

## CHAPTER 7

# The Underground

*Problematizing Nonviolence*

> How can anyone demonstrate the power or force of truth unless he [sic] dedicates himself to truth? Truth, therefore, is absolute necessity. It cannot be abandoned, whatever the cost. Truth has nothing to hide. There is no question, therefore, of satyagrahis maintaining a secret army.
>
> —Gandhi, "Hind Swaraj"

### The Lie of the Land

Both of these chapters on the Quit India movement document repertoires of parrhesia. In the previous chapter, these acts largely took place within the expanded remit of the Congress campaign and constituted a mostly overground movement. This chapter focuses more on parrhesiastic acts that rejected both colonial and orthodox Congress rule. The distinction between the over- and underground was not simply that one was open and the other was hidden. The activities in the last chapter were mostly organized in secret and out of sight. Rather, the under/overground distinction was a truth relationship. We can see this play out in two of the key facets of mass political movements: arrests and violence. First, satyagrahis would not evade arrest and would often seek it out. When arrested they would often refuse to cooperate with the legal system and would not contest their sentence. Underground activists, on the other hand, evaded capture, and many gave detailed statements when arrested. Much of what follows is based on their confessions. Second, while overground campaigns may have resulted in violence, they were premised on nonviolence; the object of the underground *was* violence, against objects and sometimes against subjects.

As such the underground problematized the Quit India movement. This is not to say that it criticized it or was external to it. Rather, it exacerbated tensions already present within the Congress system and forced changes in its anticolonial governmentality (following Barnett 2015). While it is the violence of Quit India that garners much attention, it is perhaps its truth relations that more fundamentally challenged the Gandhian ethos. As Shruti Kapila (2021, 145) has put it, "Truth was a visible form of the political, whereby all that was hidden came to the surface to display the ordering that made the practical world." The underground was a secret landscape that compelled those who knew about it to lie. They could not speak of its members, methods, or places, and if asked about it, they should not tell the truth. It compelled courageous acts without courageous, public, open speech.

This is not to say that members of the underground or of secret revolutionary networks were untruthful. Foucault ([1983–84] 2011, 183) himself picked out revolutionaries as the embodiment of modern parrhesia, "the irruptive, violent, scandalous manifestation of the truth." But revolutionary and satyagrahi forms of parrhesia were incompatible. In the Quit India movement revolutionary politics were ascendant and captured the nation's imagination. Gandhi himself implored Aruna Asaf Ali to give herself up for arrest and even met her in secret when he was released from prison, but she refused him (Asaf Ali 2006). Mohammad Asaf Ali remarked on 3 October 1942, in prison, that the cloaks and masks of the underground were demoralizing because they avoided the consequences that honest and sincere action faced, although he accepted his wife was doing what she felt best for the country (Raghavan 1994, 290). P. C. Jain recalled her as Delhi's leading if secret proponent of parrhesia: "Arunaji played a huge role in running the whole movement in Delhi. Actually the one who should be called a fearless woman was Arunaji."[1]

Aruna Asaf Ali was the breakout star of the Quit India movement in Delhi and embodied the revolutionary spirit of courageous if covert life, mobility, and speech (Bakshi 1994). Born Aruna Ganguli in 1909, she had been educated at Catholic and Protestant schools and was working as a teacher when her aunt introduced her to Mohammad Asaf Ali (Raghavan 1994, 202; Raghavan 1999). They were married in 1928, the nineteen-year-old Aruna to Asaf Ali, over twenty years her senior, she a Hindu and he a Muslim (Gopinath and Farooqui 2014). She moved to Delhi and was in the Legislative Assembly gallery in 1929 when Singh and Dutt cast their bombs into the chamber (Asaf Ali 1947, 42–44). After her husband's arrest in the 1930 Civil Disobedience campaign, Aruna also joined the campaign and was jailed the same year, in 1932 and in the 1940 Individual Satyagraha campaign. She recalled being inspired to leave both her home and her "cowardly hesitations" by Satyavati, who took her to Shahdara to make salt in 1930 and continued to inspire her through speeches and her courageous campaigning (Asaf Ali 1977). Gopinath and Farooqui (2014) note the lack of evidence of political activity by Asaf Ali in the 1930s (although she headed the Delhi Women's League and campaigned against trafficking of women and children; see Legg 2014, 80–85; Raghavan 1994, 204). In 1942 she accompanied her husband to Bombay and, after his arrest, unfurled the Congress flag at Gowalia Tank Maidan and then went underground, while her husband went to jail, leading to a near permanent separation. As she later recalled: "I discarded the prison-house of the domestic world to which all Indian women are dedicated. My home was no longer my world. I was unfortunately very cruel to my husband but somebody had to pay the consequences of the break with the past. I broke away from home and wandered about among socialist minded people all over India" (Asaf Ali 2006, 31).

When interviewed in 1968, P. C. Jain was asked why the Quit India movement took the turn toward destruction when previous movements had not.[2] He listed several reasons. Individual Satyagraha had only shown that this technique achieved nothing. The literature circulated by Aruna Asaf Ali, J. P. Narayan, and others suggested that Gandhi had left people to "do or die" as they felt best. The youth were angered by the August arrest of the Congress leaders and vowed to avenge them, using destructive, not constructive methods (it was they who sustained the underground, rather than being mobilized by it; see Khan 2016, 184). This was, for him, the beginning of the "dal lifafa dekh tamasha" (put in the envelope, see the show) movement. The first trick of the tamasha was to make an entire city disappear.

**Invisibility: Delhi's Underground**

Undergrounds are meant to be invisible, but this does not make them unseen. They have to be accessible by some, unveiling themselves to admit supporters and taunt or terrify their opponents. Their visibility in the archives is, to an extent, the result of failure, whether because they were observed or because a member betrayed them to the overground. But undergrounds are also objects of postcolonial nationalist pride and nostalgia, something to be preserved in memory and dictated into history. This can string the researcher between two problematic poles. From the perspective of failure, this edges the researcher closer to the uncomfortable position of "spymaster" (Duncan 1999), acting as the CID, or colonial government more generally, did in trying to "crack" or decode the distant, muffled, and encrypted signals from the underground. From the perspective of nostalgia this edges the researcher closer to the uncomfortable position of acolyte, celebrating the genius of the absconders and orchestrators of the underground. These positions map, not wholly, on to the main archival sources used throughout this chapter: the richly detailed source reports and statements from detainees procured by the CID, and the memoirs, transcripts, and interviews of nationalists after independence. As with Lara Cohen's (2022, 15) investigation into a very different types of (American) underground, this involves "burrowing" into ephemeral sources without presuming a single, locatable object. This attempts to honor the elusiveness of an underground that wanted to stay hidden, recuperating its spaces and subjects while acknowledging that such recuperation is impossible.

The object here is to examine the underground as the predominant form that Quit India assumed beyond the initial month of protest. The aim here is not to plot and map it, undoing its invisibility. Rather, it is to explore some of the dynamics of the underground as a way of understanding how the landscape of Delhi was used in the ongoing acceptance of violence against objects and, in some cases, against subjects. After exploring the unexpectedly deep underground in New Delhi, the periods and places of the broader underground will help us understand how its invisible landscape was produced.

In a personal interview, Roop Narain stressed that although New Delhi was well protected and that most of the civil servants "did not have the courage" to sacrifice their livelihoods, "in the underground movement of course New Delhi was affected[;] literature was reaching all those places."[3] The New Delhi landscape also provided endless sites for organizing the Congress underground. From November 1942, with much of the Delhi Congress elite arrested, most of the remaining organizational work was conducted underground. Roughly in line with Sarkar's (1983) chronology, November saw Delhi's rural project founder (as described in the last section of this chapter) and attention switch to New Delhi. The central intelligence officer (CIO) in Lahore listed four main activities anticipated in Delhi, all of which were to some degree connected to the new capital. First, there would be the continued distribution of subversive literature, attributed to Devadas Gandhi and his assistant editor at the *Hindustan Times*, which was based near Connaught Place and provided a meeting ground for underground organizers. Second, the group was thought to be planning the murder and assassination of high officials, from both the local and central governments. Third, attempts would be made to burn the records of the Imperial Secretariat. Finally, staff in the Home Department of the Secretariat would be approached to obtain classified information. These tasks were distributed among different groups as classified by geographical location. The Old Delhi groups would maintain contact with rural areas and organize processions and demonstrations. The New Delhi groups consisted of professionals who could publish Congress bulletins, maintain contact with Secretariat staff, and organize sabotages in Government of India offices.[4]

The capital provided a useful space for the organization of an underground because it was so sparsely populated. Jugal Kishore Khanna recalled of the underground leader J. P. Narayan, who had escaped from jail following his Quit India arrest: "In Delhi/New Delhi he used to wander freely and on occasions when he stayed with us, I noticed he used to bring newspapers and books etc., from stalls and shops in Connaught Place. In those days he had a flowing beard and big moustache and it was not possible to recognise him."[5]

But the residential landscape also proved to be surprisingly supportive. Kishore Khanna later stated: "We got shelter from high Government servants in New Delhi. We could not have possibly stayed in the streets in old Delhi, it was not possible. All the absconders generally stayed in New Delhi and in places which were safe and, of course, where cars and so on could go inside right up to the porch so that we could alight and go inside. They could be the houses of rich people and Government officers."[6] It was the support of government officials, many of whom earned over 3,000 rupees per month, that the movement sustained itself until April 1943, he suggested. Others recollected government officials who had resigned their posts in protest, but others who had helped, within their limits, ranging from influential New Delhi–based industrialists like G. D. Birla to junior officials.[7] Even Sobha Singh, the influential Sikh contractor who had helped smooth over the Gurdwara Sisganj shooting protests in 1930, found his house being occupied by Aruna Asaf Ali, his son Kushwant Singh remembered.[8] Those who opposed the growing violence of the underground movement might still offer support, like the lawyer Ganpat Rai who refused to shelter Asaf Ali and Kishore Khanna but agreed to hand over money from his pro-Congress friends via his contacts with the movement.[9]

Manubhai Shah, who had worked on the New Delhi street sign, George V statue, and shop raid protests, recalled moving through the nonofficial New Delhi underground landscape with his fellow absconder: "There is not a single place in Connaught Place where we had not lived a night—Mrs Asaf Ali and myself were mostly hiding together."[10] He claimed that for the autumn of 1942 people all over India knew that the Delhi underground was coordinating Congress across the country. The capital provided some obvious resources, like its wealthy supporters and desolate material landscape, and some less obvious. Manubhai spoke of raids on the army stores at the Red Fort (one of two bases near the capital) that provided the underground with detonators, revolvers, and rifles. New Delhi was a rich source for the underground but was just part of a wider landscape, as its recurrence in the examples that follow make clear.

## Making Invisibility

There was a delicate and fine art to producing an invisible underground. The aim here is not to make the underground visible but to consider how it was made invisible. This will necessarily be a fragmentary analysis, but the fragments can be located in the geography of Delhi's urban landscapes (the old city and the capital; the rural underground is described later). Here we will look at how techniques clustered around mobilities, locations, and infrastructures (human and nonhuman).

### MOBILITY

The underground was not a stable structure beneath the surface of everyday life; what happened underground was *constant* movement (Laursen 2021). Perhaps *the* feature of the underground was its mobility and the capacity of its inhabitants to move. As Ajit Singh's testimony will prove, in the rural underground a bike was vital; it was his attempt to catch a train home from a failed arson attack that got him arrested.[11] A statement provided by Gobind Saran Gupta relayed how, heading back to Delhi after the Bombay declaration of August 1942, he had met Jugal Kishore Khanna on the train. Apprehensive of his arrest at Delhi station, Khanna left the train at Muttra to pass the night with Gupta and left by lorry the next day for Delhi.[12] M. L. Parashar also recalled that Maulana Nur-ud-Din Behari had not been so lucky; the police boarded his train back from Bombay at Tughlaqabad station and arrested him, while Parashar hid in a bathroom.[13]

For traveling between New and Old Delhi, and within the former, a car was essential. This was apparent in the police statement made by Mool Raj, a forty-year-old insurance agent who lived in Connaught Circus and had become a four-anna member of Congress in 1941.[14] He met Mir Mushtaq Ahmed, secretary of the New Delhi Congress Committee, in 1942 and became involved in regular flag raisings in New Delhi. Before the August declaration in Bombay, Mool Raj had met Mohammad Asaf Ali on the veranda of Connaught Circus where he had explained the forthcoming struggle to him. In September he was approached by M. M. Shah, who revealed the new tactics of the movement and promised to introduce him to the high command. He was picked up in a car and recalled being driven to the end of Prithi Raj Road, turning right, and stopping at the first bungalow. In the large compound of the government contractors' bungalow other cars arrived, bringing further workers. Raj met Aruna Asaf Ali, who co-opted him to work within the capital. Being the leader of the Delhi underground, Asaf Ali lived life on the move. As her collaborator and supporter Phool Chand Jain recalled, "Arunaji didn't take any part herself [in violence]. But she would roam around a lot. She would be at one place in the morning, at another at night, she didn't stay at one place. She didn't stay at any one place at night. If she had caught hold of a 'centre' today then she wouldn't go there again, that is why she could be successful for so many days, to go on."[15]

Other accounts tell of the circuitous routes one had to take to get to Asaf Ali herself. Girwar Narain recounted having known Mohammad Asaf Ali throughout the 1930s and having met Aruna through him.[16] After she went underground she arranged for a man to pick him up from his flat overlooking Chandni Chowk on Katra Sat Narain and take him by foot to a tonga at Turkman Gate, from where they went to Irwin Hospital in New Delhi. A car picked him up from there, containing Asaf Ali and Kishore Khanna. They went to Surendra Nath Jahar's house on Babur Road and were admitted to the quarters via a back door. Four days later he was picked up again and taken to Asoka Road by car with Asaf Ali and Kishore Khanna and then to a house at 28 Feroze Shah Road in the capital, where Asaf Ali asked him to procure two hundred iron cylinders for bomb making.

### LOCATION

There were clearly safe places and zones that were used by the underground, but not too often or too regularly. Phool Chand Jain recalled storing bundles of bulletins for distribution in the bushes of "Company Bagh" Gardens (the old name for Queen's Gardens; Dayal 1975, 32), where Congress workers from each district in the city would be told to come at a certain time to collect bulletins to distribute in their allocated area.[17] This meant that if one worker were arrested, they would not know who the other workers were. In early September Aruna Asaf Ali wanted to meet all the distributors together, however, and commanded Chand Jain to organize a meeting. Despite Jain's misgivings, he told the distributors to converge in Company Bagh Gardens and follow him, at a distance, when he left. He led them to Kadasiya (Qudsiya) Ghat at the Jumna, having told Asaf Ali to meet him there. However, on arriving he found the area filled with "undesirables" whom he suspected of being CID. He got a message to Asaf Ali not to drive over, told the workers what they should do in their areas, and dispersed. On apologizing to Asaf Ali, she told him, "You fear a lot." This may have been with good cause; the next time he checked on the bundles in Company Bagh, he was arrested by the CID and detained in the Red Fort for interrogation.

Domestic locations were also used, and feared. As part of working his way closer to Krishna Nair (see the next section), in late August 1942 (the later informer) Raj Narain met with Desh Bandhu Gupta at the house of Surendra Nath, to which Asaf Ali and Kishore Khanna soon arrived.[18] As soon as the meeting started in a closed room, one of Bandhu Gupta's relatives suspected a cyclewala (presumably a messenger) of being a CID informer. The group immediately split in two; they left in separate cars and went to "a place near the Harijan colony." This was north of Delhi and where Gandhi often stayed when visiting. It was an obvious place to meet and was under close surveillance for illegal activity so was used relatively rarely.

Delhi's two urban landscapes had their relative merits. Old Delhi was more likely to have willing supporters of the underground than the official and often government employee–populated landscape of the capital, but it was difficult to move around without being observed, very possibly by CID informants. This was a product of the dense landscape, but it also presented its own opportunities, especially as a three-dimensional space. As previous chapters have shown, Congress had divided the city into wards and mohallas, many of which had their own Congress representatives who could gauge the loyalty of each locality, suggesting safe places for those underground to seek temporary refuge. Should they need to flee, it was difficult to find a car in which to make a speedy escape, but the cityscape itself provided its own escape routes. S. N. Banerjee, whose father was a superintendent of police, recalled how "Hansraj Pearless" had been staying near the Jama Masjid. He was visiting from Lahore and was a suspected revolutionary, so the police were sent in large number to arrest him: "He simply jumped from one roof to the other because all the houses in that gali [small lane], they were adjacent. There were nearly 300 policemen had gone to arrest him. And they were so much afraid that nobody was going for the stairs to the third floor where he was staying."[19]

While we might question the number of policemen involved in the raid, the use of the Delhi rooftops for making speedy escapes is well documented. Paths across the rooftops were used and invoked in everyday life, including in a petition against prostitutes (see Legg 2014, 60) and as means of conversation and dissemination between women (Legg 2003, 20). For women in purdah the rooftops provided a space to talk and for women within a community to gather and move between houses. As one interviewee remarked, while the view of women in purdah was that they led secluded and sheltered lives, the truth for many was that it was they who were jumping across rooftops at night to assemble for meetings.[20]

Supporters' houses were the core locations of the underground. The domestic here functioned as a node in much wider and multiply connected anticolonial networks. In the archives they rarely feature as more than locations, with perhaps the briefest description of the geography of the house or compound. But these locations do build up a picture of the diversity of sites used to support the movement. Kishore Khanna, for instance, having finally made his way back to Delhi by lorry, stayed in the house of Radhe Raman's sister on Nai Sarak, the road connecting the Jama Masjid and the town hall in the heart of the old city (Chopra 1976, 279). Messages from Bombay at the end of August were delivered to Sushila Devi at the house of Vijay Kumar near Kashmiri Gate to the north of the city (279). In September Krishna Nair was called to a Ved's Ayurvedic pharmacy in the center of the city to be tempted into the campaign of violence (284). While Sucheta Kripalani, when visiting Delhi in December 1942, stayed at Dr. Basu's house on Nicholson Road, north of the railway in the old city (384).

The detailed CID statements are rich in locations because they served as evidence to connect testimonies and secure convictions, thus providing a rich cartography of individual experiences of the underground.[21] Raj Narain, in informing on his work with Nair, told of student meetings in Hindu College in north Delhi; secret meetings in Shaukat Ullah Ansari's house on Rajpur Road in the Civil Lines; taking students from their hostels to Dr. Yudhvir Singh's house (at Kucha Brijnath near Chandni Chowk); meeting Asaf Ali and Kishore Khanna in the house of a doctor who lived in Qarol Bagh behind a nursing home; and going with students to the Shankar Ved [Vaid] Girwar Narain's Ayurvedic Pharmacy on Chandni Chowk to meet Kesho Dev Malviya. Gobind Saran Gupta recalled procuring underground work from Raghbir Singh who lived in a small gali near the Latifi Press in Faiz Bazar and educating workers in propaganda at Dr. Chopra's house on Panch Kuin Road between the new and old cities.

During their period as Delhi's high command, Asaf Ali and Kishore Khanna would visit people throughout the old city and its suburbs: meeting Dayal Sharma to debate how to disaffect the military in a house in Sabzi

Mandi in early September, and holding a meeting in mid-December to discuss paying volunteers at K. P. Shankara's house in Daryaganj (Chopra 1976, 387). Gobind Saran Gupta even spoke of returning home from the bazaar and his wife handing him a chit from Asaf Ali informing him that she would be holding a secret meeting in his house that evening. At 8:30 p.m. Sushilla, Mrs. Radha Raman, Mrs. Atma Devi Suri, Mrs. Yudhvir Singh, and Gauri Devi arrived. Asaf Ali told them they had to do more to politically awaken the women of the city and they should go to the houses of factory owners and encourage the womenfolk there to induce their husbands to stop helping the war effort.[22] Dr. Sarup Singh described a similar incident when he was lecturing at Hindu College in 1942. Due to the cancellation of a venue, Asaf Ali held a meeting at his house in Jawal Nagar near Delhi University north of the old city, without him actually knowing. He returned to find her there talking to students. The police arrived just as she left, leaving Singh to convince the authorities he was conducting a private tuition.[23]

Many of the sites in New Delhi have been highlighted above, which included the homes of nationalist volunteers as well as the Delhi elite. Raj Narain's CID statement mentioned repeated meetings with Brij Kishan Chandiwala in Narendar Place near Connaught Circus in New Delhi and at quarters opposite Lady Hardinge Medical College, northwest of Connaught Place.[24] Before going on to picket the Legislative Assembly in September, he met M. M. Shah and others at Lakshmi restaurant in the capital and was later dispatched to a bulletin publisher who also worked for the *Hindustan Times* from his house on School Lane, off Connaught Place. Editor Devadas Gandhi's flat above the *Hindustan Times* office in Connaught Place was a key meeting site for the Delhi elite, as was the New Delhi bungalow of Desh Bandhu Gupta at 12 Keeling Road. The latter's son, Vishwa Badhu Gupta, suggested in an interview that, especially when his father went to jail, the house opened up to people like Asaf Ali, describing it as an open house but one that was, to them, also protected (Legg 2003, 18). The spacious compounds in New Delhi meant there were more escape routes and allowed the house to function as both a headquarters and a home. But such immobile and treasured possessions could also, of course, be a weakness. Kishore Khanna later suggested that Desh Bandhu Gupta had eventually offered himself up for arrest rather than go underground because, like the other Delhi leaders, he was declared an absconder under the Criminal Prosecution Code when the Quit India campaign began leaving his property open to confiscation.[25]

## INFRASTRUCTURE

The underground was threaded together and made logistically possible by large networks of volunteers. This subaltern infrastructure of workers is only just visible at the edge of documents and testimonies. Where they do figure they were often termed "peons." The term has special significance in Delhi, where a whole quarter of official residence in the capital city had originally been reserved for government peons, being messengers or low-ranking members of office staff (Legg 2007, 44, 79). Their role for the underground was similar, providing the mechanisms and messengers that allowed the organizers to survive in, and communicate from, their domestic shelters.[26] They provided local services but also connected local undergrounds to national networks. Manohar Lal Mansukh Lal Shah of the Delhi Cloth Mills stated to the CID after his arrest in January 1943: "I was amazed to see the network of perfect messenger service which even in the underground state of working, the AICC [All India Congress Committee] was able to maintain" (Chopra 1976, 288). The AICC was said to be getting regular reports from provinces while also sending out bulletins, programs, and, it was suggested, formulas for different types of bombs, fire bottles, incendiaries, and explosives. M. M. Shah confirmed that the AICC had been working from Bombay, especially from Dahyabhai Patel's house, and sending out messages through "trusted couriers," with Sucheta Kripalani acting as touring office secretary (Chopra 1976, 343).

At the local level the elite could draw on a large number of helpers who would circulate messages and procure the technology necessary to keep the underground going. Gobind Saran Gupta's CID statement was filled with details about the messengers who visited him and drew him further into the movement. Around 30 September 1942, for instance, he recalled being visited by a student from Hindu College named Girdhari who informed him that Asaf Ali and Kishore Khanna would be having a meeting at his house that night.[27] Girdhari was described as a messenger for the high command who communicated the place and time of meetings to workers. Around 13 October he contacted Saran Gupta and told him to go to Desh Bandhu Gupta's house that evening to meet Asaf Ali and Kishore Khanna. There he was given a complex series of messages to convey: one to Municipal Commissioner Shyam Nath, asking for help in organizing processions, and another to Vaid Girwar Narain telling him to see Basrurkar, manager of the New Garage in New Delhi, who had agreed to sell them two cars. Girdhari had heard via messenger Shanti, of Delhi Cloth Mills, that the vaid needed a car to help him with his "terroristic plans"; the other would be used by the high command to collect workers for secret meetings. Saran Gupta visited the car dealer and got one car issued in the vaid's nephew's name and the other in his name, which he then used to transport the high command around the city.

While these sources were being used to create the impression of an impressively organized and violent underground, later sources painted a very different picture, creating space for the agency and input of underground workers and the mass of Delhi's public. K. A. Desai recalled how Quit India was, as he put it, a "free for all movement all round."[28] The ethos was "go and fight anybody; do what you like and nobody is there to stop you," with there being no particular leader, and little control or discipline. While this may have been how the movement felt to the public once the main leaders had been arrested, there was a dedicated team trying to keep the underground active, although one rare source also gives a sense of the excitement, autonomy, and desperation that filled the life of the underground workers.

R. P. Puri was born in Hoshiarpur in 1920 and moved to Delhi in 1936 to found a news agency; this would allow him to become involved in the printing of propaganda for the underground movement in 1942. During the Individual Satyagraha phase a teacher at a local school put him in touch with the Delhi nationalist elite. He took part in the Quit India movement and was later arrested. In a 1971 interview he was startlingly honest about his lack of preparation for his police interrogation. He recalled how stunned he was that the police knew so much about what the underground had been doing, how he was tricked into making his initial statements, and how his resistance to the CID questioning had failed when it became apparent how much they knew.[29]

He recalled that his main job had been to organize meetings for Asaf Ali and Kishore Khanna. Unlike some of the higher-profile cases he had been involved in (such as the King George V statue case or the Jumna canal robbery, as described later), he admitted that he could not really remember what he was doing in his day-to-day contributions, describing it as more coordination and liaison work such as organizing the meeting of different groups, passing messages to the high command for approval and then coming back with their reactions, or distributing leaflets in the night. Ved (Vaid) Gian Chand Chopra suggested in his CID statement that this was a common means of communication, with those who had agreed to offer up satyagraha being ordered by Asaf Ali and Kishore Khanna to do so, "and that man gets the order through a poster at the dead of night at his place. That man cannot see as to who threw that poster and when was it thrown in his house."[30] While Chopra did not get such an order, he would sometimes find bulletins lying in his shop when he arrived in the morning, giving information on the broader movement.

Puri's recollection of the success of these measures, however, lacked the romantic nostalgia of other interviews. As the underground finally got more organized, he felt that public enthusiasm faded, and by the end it was more a matter of trying to keep their name at work. While the underground reveled in their successes, the public remained mostly unaware of them, having no idea about burned letter boxes and the like. The people had not been prepared or trained enough. His memory of the underground infrastructure was one of not knowing what was coming next: "I myself did not know what my role was going to be. We only had to guess, and try to get in touch with some people who could really direct us or tell us what we were supposed to do."[31] Mass sentiments were not, he suggested, lasting sentiments.

Puri's appeal to emotions was not uncommon, but the range of emotions he appealed to was relatively unique. Even his pessimistic recollection of the playing out of Quit India began with a much more familiar romanticism: "there was a sudden and a great stir; there was a sort of fire; there was a sort of spirit which let itself loose on Delhi; and I think many like me, more or less, got engulfed in that fire. We did not just know what to do, but we knew that we must do something."[32] This was, of course, followed by his disillusionment with the powers of police surveillance and the short-lived nature of mass sentiments. The range of emotional responses to the underground are difficult to unearth from the archive, but the occasional glimpse is given of the discipline needed to secure the movement.

In a CID statement Bhagwat Dayal Sharma suggested that Asaf Ali dismissed as impractical his suggestion that workers be placed in cantonments to distribute leaflets among the military (Chopra 1976, 388). Mool Raj, however, fared much worse. As described above, he had been drawn into the New Delhi underground and was trying to organize demonstrations in the capital, despite initially claiming that he did not know enough people and could not help.[33] He was requested by a colleague to get 1,000 rupees for this purpose, and although Kishore Khanna was surprised at the amount requested, Asaf Ali said that it would be provided (Phool Chand Jain later suggested that Asaf Ali distributed money very openly, giving 200–500 rupees to facilitate the burning of four shops).[34] Soon afterward M. M. Shah delivered 200 rupees, half of which was given to another worker and half Raj kept for himself. He paid thirty-three rupees of it to someone who said he would offer himself for arrest but then disappeared. Raj saw Asaf Ali that night and described her afterward as being very disappointed. She said that no program would be put before him again. He tried to explain the situation to her, "but she was very upset." Raj was stepped down to relatively minor duties from then on.

## Identities: Going Underground

As with the previous study of Shatrugan, the identities explored below will be threads through particular political spaces that have left relatively rich archival traces. Unlike Shatrugan, the work below is the result of not a single file but numerous reports, statements, and confessions. Like his life, the experiences below problematized Congress's commitment to nonviolence and the open declaration of one's nonviolent truth. But these lives, like those above, also attest to a courageous embodiment of a different, more revolutionary truth. The two lives explored here have their own overlapping geographies, namely, C. K. Nair's rural campaigns and Aruna Asaf Ali's urban underground. These two figures will provide roughly chronological narratives of the rural then urban turn in the Delhi underground.

These emphases should not, of course, overshadow the other key figures in the underground, many of whom featured in chapter 6. Devadas Gandhi, son of M. K. Gandhi and editor of the *Hindustan Times*, supported nationalists across the divide, controlled Congress funds, and successfully evaded arrest after being briefly held from 19 to 29 August 1942 (Chopra 1974, 109). As Jathu Bhai Vohra put it in a statement to the police: "He does not come into the open but pulls the wires from behind the scenes. On many occasion have met absconders of Delhi and outside at Devadas Gandhi's house" (281). Phool Chand Jain recalled him directing the finances of the Delhi movement, most of which went to Asuna Asaf Ali, and orchestrating contacts in key subpopulations of the city: Harprasad Agrawal among clothes traders, Hansraj Gupta and Samvadlal among iron traders.[35] Devadas Gandhi was also closely watched by the government; as the chief commissioner stated, "That a son of M. K. Gandhi should be actively furthering a campaign of violence, as seems to be the case, is significant."[36] Another worker who provided a comprehensively detailed, twenty-three-page typed police statement after his arrest, Raj Narain, also emerges as a key figure in the archive, if not in the movement, of Quit India.

But it was ultimately the arrest of Delhi's nationalist elite that allowed the more radical underground to flourish. While Satyavati had been increasingly influenced by the more violent factions of the left in the late 1930s, on 10 August her message as Congress dictator to a private meeting of organisers, as relayed again in Vohra's statement, had been to follow instructions from the AICC in Bombay (Chopra 1976, 279). She was arrested shortly afterward, leaving Aruna Asaf Ali and Jugal Kishore Khanna as Delhi's high command after their return on 13 August. They had decided before the Bombay declaration to go underground and worked closely together, though not always harmoniously. In a police statement M. M. (Manubhai) Shah, who had been in close contact with the pair until his arrest on 9 January 1943, suggested they did not always get on. Asaf Ali was depicted as the enthusiastic, inspiring, and liberal one, with Kishore Khanna as thrifty, pessimistic, and more of a true Gandhiist. The latter opposed acts of sabotage because they were expensive, and because of his "stingy nature" (Chopra 1976, 386). Kishore Khanna claimed in a later interview that he felt the use of grenades, arms, and pistols was futile, even though he was not necessarily nonviolent himself. He was sent to Rajasthan for the last half of December 1942 and was distressed when he returned to find the aftermath of Manubhai Shah's New Delhi campaign: "When I returned back, I was shocked to find that in Connaught Place, there was violent demonstrations, stone-throwing and something of that kind which unfortunately resulted in loss and damage to the shops. The Government did not suffer at all."[37] After this he claimed to have been slowly pushed out of the picture as Asaf Ali took control not only of the urban sphere but also of the rural sphere, whose organizer in Delhi she managed, eventually, to dissuade from his path of Gandhian ahimsa.

### C. K. NAIR AND RURAL SABOTAGE

C. Krishna Nair was born in Travancore in 1902 and was educated there, in Aligarh, and at Jamia Islamia College in Delhi in 1921 (Government of India [Secret] 1934, K-19). In 1935 the Delhi CID abstract of intelligence described him as looking younger than his thirty-three years of age, being five foot five, with a strong build, a large head usually adorned with a Gandhi cap, a dark complexion, a round face, thick black hair, good but protruding teeth, and large earlobes close to the head, and usually wearing kurta, dhoti, and chappals.[38] While working at the *Tribune* in Allahabad he was drawn to Gandhi's ashram, whence he was sent to Delhi to assist with the salt satyagraha in 1930 (Chopra 1974, 277).

He arrived in April 1930 and started an ashram in Daryaganj, training hundreds of satyagrahi in the city and participating in the march on the law courts in May that anticipated the gurdwara shootings.[39] Having noted the lack of participation from the villages and having stayed in a dharmsala in Narela, a village outside Delhi, in 1931, Gandhi gave him permission to establish an ashram there, in a donated house.[40] After the suspension of Civil Disobedience, Nair focused on local constructive work within the ashram and with peasants and Harijans in the surrounding villages. During this time he came to know a student worker whose later arrest would produce a remarkably rich account of Nair's role in the Delhi countryside (such that extracts of it were published in Chopra 1976, 271–72, 283–84) and his apparent acceptance of violence.

In the twenty-three-page statement he made to the CID after his arrest in October 1942, the twenty-year-old (former) student, Raj Narain, who lived in Churiwalan near Faiz Bazar, described how he had been kissed and blessed by Gandhi at age five when he had presented him with some money, and this had always stuck with him. He had been a member of the Sanatanist (orthodox Hindu) Arya Kumar Sabha in Chawri Bazar and learned techniques of political protest there, which he took with him to Hindu College before graduating in 1940. He had known Nair since 1933 and had spent a few days per year at his Narela ashram since then. He was committed to nonviolence and was inspired by Gandhi's speech at Bombay to join the Quit India movement. Reading the newspapers, he got the sense that the whole country "was going violent, and it was a psychological rage of the workers due to the arrest of Congress leaders which had burst in the form of violence."[41] His statement then describes how he joined the Delhi underground, giving rare insights into its working and the attempts to bring the countryside, and Nair, around to violence.

### The Turn to Violence

Nair had been arrested before Quit India, at the outbreak of the war, and was released from Rawalpindi on the morning of 9 August, just before orders for his further detention were received following the Bombay declaration. He made his way back to Delhi within a week but found all his previous workers had been arrested, leaving only Asaf Ali and Kishore Khanna as the two remaining "outstanding leaders."[42] He recalled that they persuaded him not to give himself up for arrest and to remain underground for three or four months, so as to focus on the rural communities with which he had such good relations. Knowing the population and all the paths connecting the villages, he managed to move between settlements on his cycle, evading the police.

On 15 August Raj Narain met Radha Raman, who told him he wanted to get students who knew the rural area to work with villagers, on the basis of what he had earlier seen in Allahabad. On 17 August Raman took Narain to Brij Kishan Chandiwala, to whom he had been introduced by Nair the previous summer, at Narendra Place and asked him if derailment and wire cutting were part of the Congress program. Chandiwala showed him the AICC "Do or Die" instructions, and Narain reported: "It seemed clear from those instructions that Congress had deserted its non-violent policy and resorted to violence."[43] He was told that followers of Gandhi had to adjust themselves to this violent policy and dislocate transport and communication.

Chandiwala had been awaiting Nair's return after his release from Rawalpindi. When he arrived, Nair stayed with Chandiwala at Narindra Place, and Narain met him there on 19 August. Nair expressed his commitment to nonviolence but agreed to let Narain do propaganda work in the villages. Satyavati also attended the meeting, shortly before her arrest on 20 August, and asked Narain to work among Delhi's students. The next day Narain and Nair set off for Ipu Sarai, Lado Sarai, Bijwasan, and two other villages by bicycle, followed by visits to Najafgarh, Jaffarpur, Nangloi, Kanjhawla, and Bawana villages the following day. Villagers were encouraged to withhold land revenues and "show lawlessness." On 22 August they arrived at the Harijan colony in North Delhi and heard of the arrest of Satyavati and Chandiwala. Narain visited Surrindar Nath Johar at his quarters on Lady Hardinge Road in New Delhi; Johar, along with Kishore Khanna, had left Chandiwala only five minutes before he and Satyavati were arrested in the police raid. Narain was taken by Kishore Khanna to meet the new deputies of the underground, including Desh Bandhu Gupta, Aruna Asaf Ali, and Nair.

Narain was excluded from their secret meetings but instructed by Asaf Ali to continue his student work. Over the next week he found it difficult to produce students who would do village work, though they would distribute illegal literature in the city, and Narain sourced forty students to join the picketing of the Legislative Assembly that Asaf Ali coordinated on 14 September. There were also some students who "belonged to the countryside" and "had left for their homes with the promise that they would organise their villagers for this movement. I believe that they must have done some work in organising the country-side."[44] Asaf Ali addressed the students once herself but said that Narain would henceforth be their contact point with the Delhi high command.

Narain's job remained, however, that of connecting the student and village work. In early September he had visited Nair in the village of Jatola, where according to Nair there were no more villagers left who could offer themselves up for arrest. Nair repeated this message a week later, saying "that he should better be left alone purely to work in the country-side" and gave Narain a letter for Asaf Ali detailing his rural work.[45] On 15 September Narain was told by Asaf Ali to bring Nair to her at Nath Johar's house at 52 Babar Road, which was when she impressed upon him Congress's turn to violence. Nair supposedly said that it would take time to bring the villagers around to the new creed of violence but he would try. They were then dropped at Devadas Gandhi's home in Connaught Place, where he apparently explained the new violent program to them for three hours, finishing at 2:00 in the morning.

On 19 September Keshav Dev Malaviya, nephew of Congress leader Madan Mohan Malaviya, had visited Devadas Gandhi. He brought a message from the AICC that Delhi needed to achieve something serious, in the shape of a train derailment or dislocation of communications (Chopra 1976, 284). Narain suggested that on 24 September Nair had insisted he would not encourage violent activities without further orders from Devadas Gandhi, orders that were allegedly issued in a meeting on 27 September (Chopra 1976, 238). In a later interview Nair stated that he always went to Devadas Gandhi's place in Connaught Circus to confirm his orders; Gandhi did not command violence directly but commented that "a lot of work remained to be done."[46] Jugal Kishore Khanna, however, suggested that "Shri Devdas himself was in the thick and thin of this [coordinating violent protests] with C. K. Nair."[47]

As Narain had come closer and closer into Asaf Ali's confidence, he was entrusted with greater responsibilities, having visited the Shankar Ayurvedic pharmacy in late September to confirm that dynamite was ready to be used. He met Asaf Ali that night at Desh Bandhu Gupta's house in New Delhi, and she asked him to let Nair know "so that he might make use of them." Narain stayed at the house of Dr. Yudhvir Singh that night, awaiting a message from Nair, but he was arrested the following day during a raid. While Narain's testimony ends here, the circulation of violence and its technologies did not, leading to attacks around Delhi, although they were not the first. At 2:45 a.m. on 22 August the Calcutta-Delhi-Kalka mail train had been derailed a mile north of the Delhi boundary and two miles from Narela village. At dawn the following day a combined force of army troops, mounted police, and armed constables raided the village, leading to several arrests. While a case of arson had been reported at Kishenganj railway station on 7 October, the rural sabotage program was most effective between 25 October and 12 November.[48]

*Rural Sabotage*

Just as Raj Narain's statement provides rare insight into Nair's apparent acceptance of the concept of political violence, so that of an even younger accomplice provides sensational accusations regarding Nair's turn to violence. This testimony came from Ajit Singh, a sixteen-year-old boy from Mahpalpur, a village in the Mehrauli district, to the southwest of New Delhi.[49] He was described as a Jat, a subcaste favored by the army, who was educated at a military school up to 1939 and then went to Ramjas High School in Delhi. Unlike the college city dwellers with village homes whom Raj Narain was trying to politicize, Ajit Singh claimed to have been motivated by previous Congress rural mobilization work. He opened his seventeen-page typed statement by describing how Congress members attended a fair, "near a pond" in the Mehrauli police station zone, where they were signing up members. He was told to come to the Congress office on Chandni Chowk, where he was given khaddar clothes. He clearly maintained his political connections while living in Delhi because, as he put it, "When I went home on some holiday, I fixed the [Congress] flag on a *Neem* tree in front of my house." He also attended a speech by Jawaharlal Nehru in Queen's Gardens but couldn't understand it because it was in English.

With the beginning of the Quit India movement Singh joined local Congress processions and protests, especially those that targeted local villages like Narela. During one of these walks Singh met Krishna Nair, who handed him a leaflet in Hindi titled "Instructions from Mahatma Gandhi" and asked him whether he could follow the "Do or Die" rules. Singh said he could, so he was told to go home and await instructions. In late September Nair and a colleague came to Mahpalpur and stayed in a local temple, where Singh provided them with food. In early October Nair returned and instructed Singh to meet him in Narela (Singh is imprecise on this date, though the resulting police case lists the date as 3 October, one week after Devadas Gandhi's second reported attempt to win Nair over to violence). Others had also gathered at an ashram and were taken from there to meet Nair; they were told they would commit an action that night. They had hoped to burn the patwar khana (local revenue office), but it was too close to the police station. So the assembled group met outside the temple after dark, placing their cycles in a hut by a well on the roadside, and went to the office of the Narela Notified Area Committee. The committee had been established in 1919 to administer the areas of Delhi Province outside the municipal limits; the building therefore symbolized the state in the countryside. Singh stood watch on one side and other students watched the perimeter, while Nair apparently carried out the arson with Ram Sarup (also known as Swami Sarupa Nand from his time with Nair in the Narela ashram).[50] Singh suggested that Sarup and Nair had jumped over the compound wall and entered the office by breaking the lock with an iron nail: "After a few minutes we saw the office of Notified Area Committee on fire, and Krishna

Nair and Ram Sarup running out of it."[51] The team ran to their bikes and cycled to the dwelling of a sadhu near village Sahibabad, where they passed the night.

Having passed this test Singh was entrusted with greater responsibility. On 21 October he was given a note in Urdu (reading "Masterji, please give to the bearer the thing about which I had told you") by Ramji Lal to deliver Hari Singh of Pathshala (village school) Shershah Janti and to take a gun from him to Madipur on the 23rd. On 4 November Lal took Singh to Madipur where he met Nair and Hari Singh in a house with one "kuchcha [kutcha or makeshift] room." There Nair received a delivery of two wire cutters, three torch cells tied together with iron bands, and one iron bomb fitted with wires. Nair apparently assembled the cells with wires and explained how to place them on a railway line. That evening they headed for Palam railway station and placed the bomb on the track between the station and the outer signal, sticking the switch on the rail such that the wheel would press the button and release the charge from the cells to the bomb. When a train reached the spot Singh saw a light and heard an explosion; the team ran away and spent the night at Singh's village. The bomb had indeed exploded under a train on the line from Palam, although no serious damage was reported.[52]

Singh was told to meet Nair the following day at Madipur where a new grouping of organizers, students, and villagers headed to Badli rail station with the intention of burning it down. They took with them a lathi, a gun, and two "country-made pistols." They made their way separately by bike and waited by a canal bridge until sundown, when they assembled in a garden about two furlongs (about 400m) from the station and had some food. At around 11:30 p.m. they went to the station, stowing their cycles in a ditch. As they approached the station with their pistols and guns armed, "Ratan Singh took out a spearhead from his pocket and fitted it on the lathi." Singh carried a kerosene tin, which he gave to Nair, and did some reconnaissance to see how well the station was guarded and to ask when the next train was. Singh roused one of the three rail employees who were sleeping on the veranda and ascertained that the next train was at 9:00 a.m. and that he and his friends could rest in the passenger shed. Hari Singh went into the office "but was rebuked and turned out by a coolie on duty. At about 1 a.m. Hari Singh at the point of pistol threatened the railway employees present there to sit together and not to move." They then entered the office, at which point Hari Singh fired a pistol and the sleeping clerk was taken outside. The records of the office were then collected on a table, and Nair sprinkled kerosene on it and set it alight, as happened in a neighboring room. Hari Singh removed cash from the booking office and then torched that room too. Ram Singh had been detaining the workers outside with a gun and ordered them to set some bales that had been lying outside the office on fire. From the station the party dissembled and spent the night in their respective villages. The attack certainly made an impact and was reported in the chief commissioner's fortnightly report as a raid by eight people using a "country made pistol gun" and spears.[53]

On 12 November Singh joined four others at Madipur, where Nair suggested they burn another station that evening. They set off on foot for Nangloi station, with Ram Singh carrying a gun, Ratan Singh a spear, Ajit Singh and Ramji Lal with pistols, and Nair with the kerosene. The station turned out to be too close to a police post, so they continued on to Gheora. Although Singh accidentally left his pistol at a place they had stopped on the way, they repeated the scenario from Badli, with Singh asking the guards when the next train was and taking rest in the passenger shed. He slipped out, fetched his pistol, and returned with the group. "We then went to the station, threatened the station staff, set fire to the record in [a] hurry, and went towards the Delhi-Rohtak road."[54]

Apart from various meetings and errands, the other major work was cutting telegraph wires. On 10 November Ramji Lal had suggested the wire cutters be used on the railway line between Bijwasan and Palam stations. Singh joined Lal after dark and tried to climb a telegraph post but failed, as did Lal, though Ratan Singh was successful on several posts. On 24 November further cutting took place on the line near Shahabad, Ratan Singh cutting the wires between ten spans, the wire being thrown into a well on the way home. Singh was left with the apparatus; he concealed some arms in the hay lying on the roof of his house and buried the cutters in a field near the hill.

The final act of the group took place on 29 November, although without Nair. The previous day Ramji Lal had called Singh to Madipur to take part in the burning of Patli rail station. He had been sent to assess the station and stayed in a nearby dharmsala. The next day they got the train to Patli station then changed in a nearby field and waited until midnight. Ratan Singh had a haversack of military pattern, a pistol, and a hammer. They entered the station office and asked the railway babu sleeping there to take his personal things and leave. Ajit Singh doused the records in oil while Ratan Singh broke articles with the hammer. Ajit Singh went outside to get the matches and then saw the station master running toward them, gun in hand. One of the group opened fire, and Singh was shot in the leg while fleeing. Although he made his escape, he was later arrested at Gadhi Harsaru station while waiting for a train. Singh concluded his statement by making it clear who the CID had been most interested in throughout: "Krishna Nair had great influence among the villagers. He was harboured every where. I always liked to live in his society. He was in charge of the movement in the rural area. He paid the workers. He gave me Rs. 5/- only once for my personal expenses.... He instigated us to do this sabotage work to paralyse the Government machinery and to hamper the war efforts and thus to force the Government to release Mahatma Gandhi and other Congress leaders."[55]

Ajit Singh's statement wavers in some of its detail, but the events described can generally be verified by Government reports and other testimonies. M. M. Shah, arrested on 9 January, claimed that Krishna Nair had been won over as more and more Congress workers came to approve of violent tactics. Shah claimed that Nair "had been able to burn a number of Patwar Khanas [dwellings][,] three or four Railway Stations like Badli, Gheora, Patli etc., and to cause a few derailments near about Delhi and cutting of wires of communications" (Chopra 1976, 386).

So what did Nair himself recollect of this period? In an interview in 1969 he remarked that rumors had spread that he had burned a station.[56] But in a later interview from 1974 he was more forthcoming. "In the course of his wanderings" between villages, he claimed, some people had organized sabotage work on rail lines and stations:

> Some young men, fired up with enthusiasm, organised such activities not under my guidance but, of course, keeping it within my knowledge, they did it. Some people think it was really a weakness on my part to have allowed them to do that sort of thing. Whatever one might think, I thought it was not wrong at that time and in the Quit India movement Gandhiji expected people to Do or Die. With this ideal before us we somehow conducted the movement in a way which, of course, was not in keeping with the real spirit of Gandhiji. But the sum total of our activities there kept the movement alive in the villages.[57]

Within his knowledge but not under his guidance is not, of course, compatible with dousing the railway account books with kerosene during a midnight raid. Pressed by the interviewer, Nair clarified that he had absolutely no hand in any of the attacks.

On 16 November 1942 Krisha Nair was arrested after having been spotted cycling near Narela by a new inspector who beat him off his cycle, searched him, and sent him to the city jail.[58] He was sentenced on 4 December under section 26(5b) of the Defence of India Act (failure to present himself to a magistrate). In a letter to the secretary of the Home Department on 2 January 1943, the chief commissioner stressed the importance of evidence linking Nair, a man who was so close to Gandhi, with violence.[59] The evidence was felt to be strong enough to secure a further prosecution on the basis of the police station attacks (resulting in eventual accumulative sentencing of six years, though he did not serve them out). This was despite the fact that Nair had been on hunger strike since 18 November. He later recalled that this was in solidarity with Gandhi who was on fast at the time. Gandhi had threatened a fast but did not actually start one until 10 February 1943.[60] After initial resistance he accepted artificial feeding, and the chief commissioner revealed the cynical biopolitical precision with which the political potential of the fast was assessed: Nair had been 8 stone 8 pounds when he entered jail, 8 stone 6 when he started the hunger strike, and 7 stone 12 on 31 December: "It does not appear that there will be any danger to the prisoner's life for some time to come, indeed, the medical officers in the jail estimate that for a fortnight or three weeks more he will be fit to appear in court if required."[61]

The home secretary agreed with the artificial feeding and recommended the use of the Defence of India Act to repress negative publicity should it start to circulate in the press. This could not, of course, affect the illegal Congress bulletins that were still being produced in the city. On 20 November the DPCC's bulletin no. 35 announced that "Nairji" had been captured after weeks of Deputy Commissioner L. F. G. Le Bailly gnashing his teeth and wringing his hands in frenzied rage at his police, who could not catch him. Deep anxiety in the city and the countryside was reported over his hunger strike. On 23 December in DPCC newsletter no. 41 the forced feeding was reported, in relation to the ethical core of the anticolonial campaign: "The example of impassioned sacrifice and self-immolation at the altar of Truth continues to inspire us."[62]

### ARUNA ASAF ALI AND URBAN SABOTAGE

A Central Intelligence Office (CIO) report on 24 November 1942 anticipated the planned activities of the fifteen people thought to be guiding the Delhi underground. The leaders of the Delhi Congress High Command were Kishore Khanna, M. M. Shah, and Devadas Gandhi, who supplied money from the nationalist industrialist G. Birla, but the chief organizer was Aruna Asaf Ali.[63] With Nair's rural campaign over, the twilight of Quit India in Delhi saw the invisible city manifest itself, under Asaf Ali's command, in a dazzling series of explosions in and around the new and old cities.

On 25 October a bomb had exploded near Sarai Rohilla under a passing train destined for New Delhi.[64] The form of the cylinders and screws used allowed the police to trace the manufacturers, leading to the eventual arrest of

Girwar Narain. Narain had been a devoted khadi wearer when he came to know Mohammad Asaf Ali. During 1942 he became acquainted with Aruna Asaf Ali, who got in contact on her return to Delhi from Bombay in August 1942. She apparently orchestrated this attack without Nair, marking one of her few independent rural campaigns. Roughly in line with Sarkar's chronologies, however, November saw the rural project founder after Nair's arrest and attention switch back to urban Delhi.

L. C. Jain (2010, 32–33) has explained how, as one of Aruna Asaf Ali's most trusted messengers, he would orchestrate the use of "bombs" in Delhi, most of which were made by chemistry students. These would be smaller devices, used for targeting cinemas, police stations, and government offices, though a good number were lost by the young carriers getting nervous and mislaying the devices or having to destroy them due to tip-offs of police raids.

Jathu Bhai Vohra, in a police statement, gave further details of six groups known to be engaged in sabotage activity in the winter of 1942 under the coordination of Devadas Gandhi (Chopra 1976, 280). One group, with members living in Daryaganj, Qarol Bagh, and New Delhi, had planted a powerful bomb containing dynamite and nitroglycerine outside the Odeon Cinema in New Delhi when the viceroy should have been attending on 31 October. The bomb was found in time, just as plans by a second group to either poison the viceroy when he dined at the Cecil Hotel or place a bomb in his car came to nought (Chopra 1976, 280). On 3 November an attempt was made to burn the post office on Chandni Chowk, although only the door was damaged.[65] A bomb explosion on 9 November at the Lakshmi ice factory at Mor Sarai near Old Delhi was caused by a container similar to that used in previous attacks, although an explosion on the 11th at Birla Mills was attributed to a different source.[66]

By 8 December the CIO reported that the Delhi scene was split between the violent activities of Asaf Ali and the apparent attempt to reorganize the movement on nonviolent lines by Devadas Gandhi.[67] The winter of 1942 and spring of 1943 would see a geographical shift to the violent attacks in New Delhi described above, followed by a crackdown in January that would bring to an end the intense period of Quit India activity. While this led to paralysis within the satyagraha campaigns, the networks that had been established for violent activities continued to function. In Old Delhi the most significant incidents were at Delhi Cloth Mills, a serious arson attack on 3 December, and a similar attack at the Hardinge Library in Queen's Gardens on 5 December.[68] The target in the latter attack, DPCC newsletter no. 38 announced, had been "the local microphone station," which had been "completely smashed when two brave guerrillas entered the station and set it on fire."[69] As a result, "All the street corner loud-speakers could not bleat out their lies throughout yesterday," ridding the city space of the "lying propaganda of the British bandits."

On 24 December 1942 a raid in Sabzi Mandi had unearthed fifty-four cylinders and bomb-making equipment.[70] Building on these discoveries, Shah was arrested while carrying important Congress documents on 9 January having been spotted in a procession to mark the five-month anniversary of the Quit India arrests.[71] During the first fortnight of January, twenty-six arrests were made, as well as the discovery on 14 January of 186 sticks of gelignite, 183 detonators, and 1,200 feet of safety fuse, while on 15 January thirty pounds of gunpowder, forty-six empty bombshells, and three bombs were discovered.[72] A further book was unearthed that included "recipes" for "Subhas Blasting Jelly," "Jawahar Grenades," and "Gandhi Blasting Sticks." Delhi's key organizers, however, eluded the superintendent of the CID, as he commented on 19 January that despite the seizures, "the underground organization although considerably weakened has not been finally smashed and Mrs. Asaf Ali and Jugal Kishore Khanna, both important absconders, continue to elude us."[73] This was despite their fairly constant appearances in CID files, including a note from the CIO in Lahore from 11 January noting that Asaf Ali moved around in public dressed in a burka while Jugal Kishore Khanna wore a false beard on the rare occasions he traveled.[74]

M. M. Shah later admitted to the police that between 28 December 1942 and 2 January 1943 the All India Coordinating Congress Directorate met in Mohammad Asaf Ali's flat at 12 Queensway Lane, New Delhi (Chopra 1976, 343). Those present included Jai Prakash Narayan, Ram Manohar Lohia, Devadas Gandhi, Mrs. Sucheta Kripalani, and Aruna Asaf Ali (28). The exclusive meeting agreed to launch another rural drive, using both orthodox and sabotage techniques, but also push for extensive observance of Independence Day on 26 January 1943. "Independence Day Instructions" were circulated from Delhi to Congress centers all over the country.[75] They were marked by a partial adherence to nonviolence but an increasingly open advocacy of sabotage and violence.

On Independence Day itself a small "bomb" was used in an attempt to start a fire at "Moti Talkies" cinema, but the magistrate deemed the item more a "cracker" than a bomb, as it had to be stamped on to start a fire.[76] The actual celebrations were the quietest in years.[77] On 30 January an unexploded bomb was found in the garden of Lieutenant W. Gilles in New Delhi, while on 1 February a small explosive device was used at the Wavell Canteen in Queen's Gardens, although no serious damage was caused.[78] In early February Asaf Ali left

Delhi and was mostly active elsewhere until her triumphal return on 2 February 1946, when the police finally lifted the orders for her arrest.[79] After her departure there were some sporadic outbursts of violence orchestrated by the underground. At 8:30 a.m. on 21 February a bomb exploded on platform 4 of Delhi railway station, seriously injuring two people and killing one, while on 25 February bomb-making material was discovered at a dwelling in Hauz Qazi.[80] Finally, on 1 March a peon from the Irrigation Department was robbed of 4,000 rupees.[81] R. P. Puri described the simplicity of this simple robbery, in which the money was snatched in broad daylight on Alipur Road, near the Jumna canal.[82]

### Quit India Suppressed, February–October 1943

Frustrated by his confinement and the failure of the Quit India movement to bring any advancement apart from that of the "Police Raj," Gandhi underwent a fast between 10 February and 3 March 1943 (Arnold 2001, 213). The chief commissioner of Delhi reported the widespread belief that the Mahatma would not survive, leading to hartals of between 50 and 75 percent of Hindu shops and, on 11 February, three small processions that toured the city area leading to fourteen arrests.[83] On 22 February the subordinate staff of the Secretariat in New Delhi launched a protest outside the viceregal lodge, demanding Gandhi's release and observing a three-minute silence.[84]

Following a series of small bomb explosions in New Delhi cinemas during March, the Government's reprisals were swift and effective. By the end of the month fifteen people had been arrested under the Defence of India rules, including government clerks and the sons of India officials believed to have been involved in the cinema bombings and the Alipore Road robbery.[85] On 24 March the registrar of the Chief Commission sent a warning to the superintendent of education advising that the grants for Delhi's colleges were conditional on the sufficient discipline of the students.[86] Radha Raman would later recall that with the arrests, "terror was caused in the minds of Delhi people" and it was hard to find volunteers who would face the police and the consequences that might follow, with rumors afloat of beatings, being put on a slab of ice, or being tied "to a running fan" (for other such accusations and the government's response, see Legg 2018).[87]

Jugal Kishore Khanna recalled that in July 1943 the remaining high command of Congress met in Calcutta to decide how the anniversary of the Bombay arrests would be celebrated. He admitted, however, as the chief commissioner's report confirms, that the processions and protests on 9 August were not a success. Attempts through August and September to get mill workers to strike, even with financial compensation, were unsuccessful. Following the further failure of the celebrations for Gandhi's birthday in early October, Kishore Khanna was arrested on 21 October 1943, marking the demise of Delhi's final high-profile underground agitator and the effective end of the Quit India movement in Delhi.[88]

While the Delhi Congress scene was undoubtedly decimated by the time of Kishore Khanna's arrest, success stories could still be told about the hard-fought campaign. One regarded those who were arrested, while one regarded those who were not. In terms of the arrested, the account above has drawn extensively on CID statements made by men (no women) who had been arrested. The detailing of places, people, movements, and violence was clearly being collated to provide evidence not only for individual convictions but to convict Congress itself of orchestrating a nationwide violent uprising. But despite the attempt, as Manubhai Shah would later put it, to assemble a conspiracy case against the underground, he felt that the evidence could not be assembled: "They could come to the outer, third or fourth, rings, but the first two rings around us were totally obscure for them: where the revolvers came from; where the deliveries were made; who was transferring the revolvers; who was giving the training to the volunteers in shooting on the ridge."[89] While the amount of information the CID had collected might have surprised Shah, as it did Puri, his spatial metaphor was telling. The tight control kept over the underground infrastructure, its locations, and its mobilities had made Delhi, for the central government in January 1943, the second most important center for the Quit India movement in the country (Chopra 1976, 339).

## CHAPTER 8

# Victory?

### Whose Victory?

On 21 October 1943 the arrest of Jugal Kishore Khanna symbolized the end of Delhi's Quit India agitation. On the same day, the Indian National Army (INA) was formed from twenty thousand Indian prisoners of war in Singapore, with the support of Germany and Japan. With its dramatic cry of "Delhi Chalo!" (March to Delhi!), the INA was one of the final anti-imperialistic flourishes of a period in which independence and partition painfully hove into view. The 1940s war economy had finally seen Indian trade boom, producing a net export surplus, which fortified the strength of the industrialist and middle classes. Yet the period also saw great poverty, the rationing of food, and the Bengal famine of 1943, widely attributed as much to mismanagement and Churchill's war strategy as to agricultural failure. Sarkar (1983, 414) identified two main forms of political activity between Quit India and independence. First, there were the sporadic, local mass anti-imperialistic protests that anticipated independence. Second, there were the elite discussions between the British, Congress, and the Muslim League, mostly in New Delhi, that accompanied the rise of communalism on the road to partition.

Local protests in Delhi, as elsewhere in India, were electrified by the British treatment of the Indian National Army. The INA had, under the command of Subhas Chandra Bose, begun their attempt to fight their way to Delhi in March 1944, but they were defeated at Imphal in June. While the military threat was small, their psychological impact on a subdued nation was immense. The government badly miscalculated in staging the public trials of a Sikh, Hindu, and Muslim INA representative in Old Delhi's Red Fort in November 1945. This resulted in a cross-communal outcry, which also rallied the population against the continued use of Indian troops to reinstall Dutch and French rule in Indonesia.

At the heart of New Delhi, by late 1943 a defeatist attitude had spread among elite Government of India officials (Stein 1998, 355). It was becoming clear that the repressive apparatus necessary to police India would not be supported by a war-devastated Britain. Meanwhile, the INC's reputation had grown during its period of imprisonment, while the Muslim League (ML) had gained in influence having cooperated with the British during Congress's imprisonment. In March 1944 Gandhi was released on grounds of ill health, while the rest of the INC Working Committee were released in June. Viceroy Wavell's attempts to get the INC and ML to cooperate in an expanded viceroy's council failed at Simla in July 1944. The ML later launched a day of "direct action" in August 1946 that led to communal riots across the country, including Delhi, which the government could do little to stem (Halperin 2022; Legg 2019a).

The British had also lost the support of the Communist Party of India (CPI) after the end of the "People's War." Since being legalized in 1942 the CPI had organized labor societies throughout the country, helping the All India Trade Union Conference to double its membership. In February 1946 the Royal Indian Navy at Bombay went on a strike that threatened to become an outright mutiny (Davies 2013), while in March a "Victory Day" of celebrations in Delhi that should have trumpeted the war victory over the Axis forces ended in a local uprising and a humiliating defeat for the Government. The events in Bombay increased the sense of the British having lost control, with strikes in Delhi taking place in the mills, the tram service, and even the police itself as the capital prepared for independence.

As with the period between Civil Disobedience and the Second World War, that between Quit India and independence saw continued forms of anticolonial parrhesia throughout the city. Colonialism was attacked in print, the city was mobilized, tensions between Congress and the left played out, and a final outbreak of urban violence raised questions again over the capacity or desire of Congress to discipline the violent strategies of a minor urban insurrection.

**Episteme: Colonial Violence, Tyrannicide, and the Subaltern**

On 20 March 1944 the CID recorded having tracked down someone distributing literature in villages around Delhi; he was "slapped" to the ground and his bag confiscated before he ran away.[1] The literature included charcoal sketches and short captions in English and Hindi. The pamphlet visually and textually reaffirmed the core truth of the anticolonial episteme: that of colonial vi-

Women shall not weep because barbarians adred to lay their unclean hands on them they shall avail the opportunity for revenge.

औरतें रोयेंगी नहीं, चूंकि अत्याचारियों के गन्दे हाथ इनके ऊपर पड़ते हैं; बल्कि मौके की ताक में रहेंगी जबकि वे अपने अपमान का बदला ले सकेंगी । और हम संतान, पति और भाई होकर कब तक इस अपमान को सहते रहेंगे ?

**FIGURE 8.1.** Women Shall Not Weep. Reproduced with permission, NMML/CID/VIII/3

olence. The images depicted men and women bearing the Indian flag being machine-gunned down (linking Quit India to the historical imagery of the 1919 Jallianwala Bagh shootings); women being abducted by colonial forces (figure 8.1); Indian prisoners being bound and lashed with the whip; and airplanes firing on and bombing a devastated Indian landscape. The machinery of war (the machine gun) was thus combined with the ancient technologies of violence (the lash and sexual abuse) to equate the British with the enemy they were facing in Europe and across the Bay of Bengal.

What the foregoing Quit India movement had made much more difficult, however, was an unequivocal commitment to nonviolence. The 1940s would see Delhi Congress leaders continue to grapple with the conundrum of Gandhi, the left, communalism, and freedom. Aruna Asaf Ali has left an articulate published archive of her attempts to grapple with these fundamental questions. These were from both the underground and, after her return in February 1946, the overground.

In an early piece Asaf Ali articulated the violence that the racism and capitalism of British imperialism was felt to do to the more liberal culture of India, and America. An undated printed poster "To the American People" by Asaf Ali was lodged by the CID in January 1943. It opened with a quotation from "your great poet" Walt Whitman: "Stranger, if you passing meet me and desire to talk to me, why should you not talk to me and why should I not talk to you."[2] The new (imagined, American) world of desire where every stranger would be a friend was compared to the hateful colonial world, where every stranger was a potential enemy. India and America were said to dream of the excitement of the friendship of strangers, but the class and race snobberies of Britain made this impossible. American soldiers were encouraged to oppose tyranny in India, which, like freedom, was indivisible and could not conscionably be supported in one place and not the other. Supporting Britain supported a world where strangers plotted against, but did not talk to, each other.

An underground Hindi magazine called *Hamara Sangram* (Our struggle) proclaiming itself "The Organ of the Delhi Provincial Congress Committee" had been established in December 1943, edited by Asaf Ali from the underground with the collaboration of Subhadra Datta (née Joshi; see below). Its fifth volume was issued on 9 July 1944 and showcased Asaf Ali's well-tested experimentation with the boundaries of nonviolence. A translation in the CID files noted the quotations with which the magazine opened, the first being from Gandhi himself: "Violence is bad but slavery is worse."[3] The magazine noted that the second anniversary of Quit India was approaching, the day when India had learned to live by dying and when thousands of children of India were targeted by the bullets of British fascists. The journal did, however, only recommend nonviolent means of celebrating the forthcoming anniversary.

After her return to public life and her reconciliation with Gandhi, Asaf Ali published a series of pieces in the journal *Janata* that grappled with fundamental questions facing the anticolonial movement in the dying days of Indian colonialism. They were collected and published as a book in 1947 with a foreword by Nehru himself, who acknowledged Asaf Ali's courageous parrhesia against both colonial and Congress orthodoxies, and the way this courageous embodiment of her truth ethically differentiated herself from other nationalists. Asaf Ali was a "difficult" subject, worthy of criticism but not deserving of it, being "a living, vibrant and challenging personality, who has shaken up many a sleeping person and become in many ways a symbol of these changing times. Symbols are often disturbing and challenges are disconcerting. And so Aruna is both a disturbing and disconcerting individual to many.... The real crusaders are always few in number and there is something of the crusader, to a cause to which she is passionately attached, about her" (Nehru 1947, iii).

In one piece from April 1946 Asaf Ali reflected on those who had chosen to face prison rather than the underground and had still not been released. Theirs was the philosophy of the overground: "Under a government which imprisons anyone unjustly, the true place for a just man is in prison" (Asaf Ali 1947, 5). She and others had, however, operated within the philosophy of the underground: "the 'tyrannicides' of society ought never to fall into the tyrant's hands" (tyrannicide being the killing of a tyrant, used by Hobbes in the sense of being both lawful and laudable). The former was the approach devised by Gandhi, who grafted on to the two loves born in 1857 (of freedom and of country) a religion of humanism. Asaf Ali barely disguised her ambivalence regarding this grafting: "Every fighter in the cause has attempted to better himself as an instrument under the influence of [Gandhi's] purificatory drives. The urge to act as one thinks, to elevate thought to the super-personal level and thereby link action with other than self-regarding ends, has been his message from struggle to struggle led by Gandhi. Indian manhood under his direction has withstood every challenge to it as well as it could" (Asaf Ali 1947, 5).

The sense of Indian manhood (Asaf Ali does not recognize women's contribution in these pieces) being purified, of the self being subjected to the superpersonal, was something attempted but only achieved partially. Only once were expectations matched, and that was in August 1942 (when Gandhi's truth was widely bypassed or taken to its limit). In this movement, for Asaf Ali, it was not Gandhian discipline of the mob that won out: "Crowds have never shown much respect for order anywhere and when the mood of elation is high it becomes unrestrained. The discipline of emotions is a tall order even for the elect" (Asaf Ali 1947, 7). The "elect" here are the elect of Calvinist Protestantism, the chosen few—that is, the bourgeois political elite. Unlike these centrist Gandhians, the people had celebrated the absconding leaders of the underground "with tumultuous affection." It was these everyday parrhesiasts who could make a utopia out of the forthcoming freedom: "In the storm centres where they worked they showed themselves not unworthy men. Fearlessness

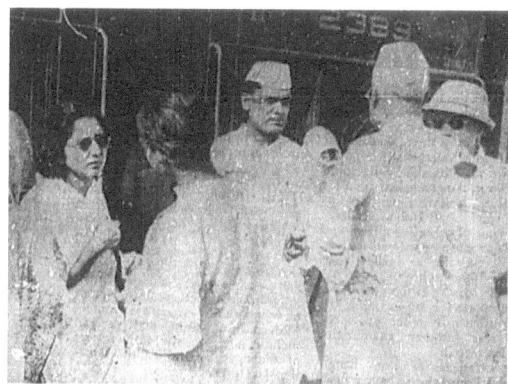

FIGURE 8.2. Aruna Asaf Ali, Narayan, and Chandiwala at Delhi railway station, *Janata*, 21/4/1946

and the abandon born of it are great qualities rare in a slave people" (Asaf Ali 1947, 8) (see figure 8.2, published alongside this article in *Janata*).[4]

In other pieces Asaf Ali was less ambiguous on Gandhi's legacy. The dynamic power of the masses had been used by "great men" to transcend themselves to "Godhood" (Asaf Ali 1947, 27). While Gandhi's methods had been successful in the past, they had outlived their efficacy, and the days of philosopher-kings and priest-kings were over. Asaf Ali, however, also shared with the Congress elites she criticized an ambivalence over the subaltern masses. While she acknowledged it was "little men" who build up "great men," the former were described as "our medieval masses" and a "slack-willed underfed, undeveloped body-mind" in need of "some external pressure" of organized action (27–29).

Asaf Ali vacillated between the subaltern being political and the solution to India's ills and being prepolitical and in need of mobilizing. Though she could lay claim as much as any Congress worker to have worked with the people during her time underground, her representation of the masses was frequently counterinsurgent. This was not colonial or bourgeois nationalist counterinsurgency but a socialist model of untapped revolutionary potential. Congress elite "oracle Leaders" (Asaf Ali 1947, 15) were criticized for not speaking to ordinary workers. Yet in the latter was found inhibitory backwardness and unformed, embodied political potential: "A pathetic faith in myths brings these countless unknowns together. Giving them mere slogan-formulas for vigilance-preparation and courage-building seemed ironic. All these qualities lay incipient in their eyes, voices and limbs, lean and athletic" (16). A natural subaltern awaiting civilizing and politicizing activation, whether by a leader or a worker, recurs in her writings: "Political thought and action even in their present day connotation do not usually attract the bulk of a people. Very largely people do not permit intelligent and coherent thinking in their mental sweep. The human bulk is influenced into reactions, both positive and negative. Its own initiative awaits a pressure. It is always the few who act as levers. It is the many who act in response" (32).

Inertia was not the only threat in the masses, however. At a meeting of the Delhi Congress Socialist Party on 11 November 1946 the CID reported Asaf Ali denouncing the communal violence breaking out across the country. She insisted the Muslim League's "Direct Action" Day in August 1946 was being engineered by the British, in collaboration with other "reactionary parties."[5] These included the Hindu Mahasabha, the Muslim League, and the Rashtriya Swayamsevak Sangh (RSS), which had been making inroads into local Congress support bases through voluntary organizations that were training and even militarizing communities to the extent that they were forming what the government called "private armies" (Raza and Roy 2015; Legg 2019a). For Asaf Ali the epistemic fortification of religious communities were the result of, but also resulted in, urban politics. British officers and the police were accused of provoking Muslim religious processions in order to spark riots, while according to the CID report of Asaf Ali's speech, "She deplored the fact that while a Muslim could not go into a Hindu locality and a Hindu could not go into a Muslim locality an Englishman could move freely in the city."[6] Asaf Ali concluded with a commitment to both anticolonialism and the violence she had advocated during her six years underground. Communal harmony was the only hope of an anticolonial revolution in the country, and if Englishmen rather than Hindus or Muslims had been murdered, freedom would have already been achieved.

Therefore, the underlying epistemic approach of Congress, especially before the local elite was released in June 1944, was riven by tensions. The party's published output and private discussions revealed it to be anticommunist but with strong socialist affinities; antifascist yet anti-war; critical of British imperial geopolitics yet anti-Japanese; attracted by American anti-imperialism but anticapitalist; supportive of the Quit India movement even into its dying days but with a resilient attachment to violence. These tensions played themselves out in the city as the release of Congress leaders saw a final flourishing of overground campaigning in the last years of colonial rule.

## Techne: Drilling the City

As the national capital and a city with a relatively autonomous history of protest in its own right, Delhi was the scene of much activity between 1943 and 1947. The imprisonment of local Congress leaders had disabled coordination across the city, but there were still campaigns and protests, though these were often responsive to national events such as the INA trials and Victory Day. From December 1946 extra national and international attention was focused on New Delhi as the 205 members of the Constituent Assembly gathered in the capital to frame a constitution for independent India (De and Shani, 2024). Beneath these large-scale events, however, was the ongoing rumble of local activism operating both within and beyond the realm of nonviolence.

First, ahead of the release of the Congress elite from prison, preparations were made to celebrate Independence Day on 26 January 1944. In anticipation the police arrested eight Congress members, and raids were carried out throughout the city.[7] The ban on processions and meetings was defied, leading to thirty-three arrests, seventeen being in front of the Imperial Secretariat, six in Connaught Place, and the other ten around the city area.[8]

Discontent across the new and old cities was noted through the spring. Labor agitation was recorded among government workers, with rumors of mass resignations over pay circulating among the lower-paid officials of the Supply Accounts and Railway Clearing Accounts Office. More worryingly, the local administration could not fill two hundred vacancies within the police force and was at a loss to explain why.[9] The private sector was also affected, with a hartal on 2 May 1944 among the shopkeepers protesting the government's wartime regulation of trade, whereas in Old Delhi there were protests against the government's failure to regulate evictions by "extortionate landlords" (Datta 2019a; see also Legg 2007, 78–80; Vanaik 2019, 58–90).[10]

Small-scale protests picked up over the next year, drawing on both local overground and underground traditions. Gandhi's release on 6 May 1944 was greeted with only a small procession, while four small fires in Delhi railway station prefigured a more serious fire started by a bomb on 9 June.[11] A strike within the Government offices finally broke out on 12 July when six hundred clerks absented themselves from work at the Railway Clearing Accounts Office, while two thousand employees at the Public Works Department refused to take their pay.[12]

Independence Day in January 1945, with the Congress elite released, was a success, drawing a crowd of two thousand to "Nehru Park" in Connaught Place, the largest since 1942 (see figure 8.3 for an undated photo of Nehru ad-

FIGURE 8.3. Nehru in Connaught Place. Photograph by Virendra Kumar/Prabhakar

dressing an audience in this park in the years before independence).[13] Grassroots work also continued, including a meeting on 2 February 1945 of the "All India Political Prisoners Relief Committee." This followed a meeting at the Gandhi ashram on Chandni Chowk to celebrate Mrs. Kasturba Gandhi Memorial Day, when a charkha symposium had been attended by a hundred people including released Congress affiliates such as Bahal Singh Jain, Muqeem-ud-Din Farooqi, Ram Chandra Sharma, and Shatrughan, as well as prominent female activists including Mirabehn (previously known as Miss Slade), Mrs. Y. D. Sharma (formerly Sarla Gupta), Mrs. Jugal Kishore Khanna, Memo Bai, and Chando Bibi.[14]

Local commemoration of Congress national days, and local Congress organizing, was overshadowed in the winter of 1945 by the trial in Delhi of the Indian National Army. On 3 November Jawaharlal Nehru addressed an estimated Delhi crowd of fifty thousand in anticipation of the INA trials, which would run until March 1946.[15] The court-martial began two days later in the Red Fort at the eastern terminus of Chandni Chowk, with Mohammad Asaf

Ali convening their defense (Raghavan 1994, 326). Crowds of students and agitators toured the central city and picketed the entrance to the fort area, proclaiming "Patriots not Traitors!" and shouting "Jai Hind" (Victory to India) at passing military entourages.[16] The protests continued during the following two-week adjournment while the student population erupted in protest on 26 November following firings on INA supporters in Bombay and Calcutta.[17]

The central government noted with concern how Congress was using the INA trials, as it had with that of Bhagat Singh, to bolster its own grassroots support in the city. On 5 December a Home Department note confirmed that a tea party had been held by Congress for INA men, followed by meetings in the cantonment and the city. A photo carried in the *Hindustan Times* on 10 December showed Nehru receiving a salute from what Cracknell in the Home Department described as "a most decrepit looking handful of individuals (alleged to be the ex. INA)."[18] While he believed the effect to be counterproductive, tolerating such quasi-military meetings and parades could encourage communal and congress voluntary organizations throughout the country. "Azad Hind" Congress voluntary corps had been reported as forming in Allahabad, adulating the INA, though the possibilities of the corps provoking outright violence in the street had tempered support from the Congress elite, and nothing had been found in Delhi.

However, on 15 December 1945 the *Hindustan Times* reported the DPCC as having relaunched the Congress Seva Dal under the oversight of Jugal Kishore Khanna, Dr. Yudhvir Singh, and Mir Mushtaq Ahmad. A later CID report listed Seva Dal aims as creating disciplined and healthy youths who undertook squad and lathi training (this was in the context of growing membership of the RSS and Muslim National Guard in the city; Legg 2019a), as opposed to standard Congress volunteers who maintained law and order at Congress meetings (the "people's policemen"; Guha 1997, 145).[19] Within weeks the DPCC and the commander of the INC Seva Dal had been warned that their drills were an offense under the Camps and Parades (Control) Order (1944), but the warning was ignored.[20] Because of this breach the commanders of the Seva Dal, along with Quit India stalwart Radha Raman, were arrested. The chief commissioner confirmed that this swift action had an effect on suppressing the activities of other groups such as the Muslim National Guard, who had been intensifying their efforts in the city. Efforts to suppress the Seva Dal continued into the new year (see figure 8.4 for the Qarol Bagh branch, two members of which had been arrested for military-style drilling).

Despite this the INA trials and the nationalist celebrities they brought to the city enlivened local Congress mobilization. On 27 January 1946 the Delhi Stu-

Members of the Karolbagh Congress Seva Dal, Delhi. Two among them, Raj Singh and Chiranji Lal (fourth and fifth from left, front row) were arrested by the Delhi Government. They are charged with having drilled in military style and are being tried in a Delhi court.

FIGURE 8.4. "Congress Seva Dal," *Janata*, 26/5/1946

dent Congress hosted Subhas Chandra Bose and P. K. Sehgal in Queen's Gardens.[21] Poems were read out by the students, one anticipating the imminent return of Aruna Asaf Ali. The CID reported forty khadi-clad male and female volunteers lining both sides of the entrance to the pandal where they saluted Bose and Sehgal "in Nazi fashion." After a portrait of Bose was unveiled, students entered carrying flags of Azad Hind Fauj (the INA), Russia, China, Indonesia, Iran, and Iraq, which were placed in line but below the Congress flag.

By 9 February 1946 the Intelligence Bureau could report that the Delhi Congress Leftist Group had hosted a meeting of the "Azad Hind Volunteer Corps," modeled on INA drills, following a smaller public meeting in Haveli Haider Quli in December 1946.[22] Badges were distributed to members, and the Delhi volunteers wore khaki dress but without badges of rank. Disconcerted by the rise of these Congress voluntary organizations, in early March orders were issued for the arrest of Seva Dal workers, the sub-inspector of Sabzi Mandi station insisting there was no difference between the Seva Dal and the RSS.[23]

The public, however, failed to respond to Congress's new military outfit. A survey in May 1947 estimated that 3,533 people in the city were members of voluntary organizations, but while the RSS attracted twenty-five hundred volunteers and the Muslim National Guard five hundred, Azad Hind was estimated to have only two hundred followers.[24]

In early January 1946 the results of the first INA trial had started to come through. The chief commissioner reported that, despite listing INC "atrocities," the trial had done nothing but increase their popularity and add greatly to Congress prestige.[25] The shock of heavier-than-anticipated sentences stirred up both the Muslim League and Congress in early February, meaning, as the chief commissioner put it, "we are now in the unhappy position of having both the Congress and the Muslim League ready to stir, and actually stirring, up riots and open defiance against civil administration and at the same time equally ready to fall at each others' throats."[26]

While the Azad Hind organization had failed to ignite much interest in Delhi, the Independence Day celebrations of 26 January 1946 had given Congress an opportunity to reestablish its networks of influence throughout the city. Jugal Kishore Khanna had regained the presidency of the DDCC and urged the Delhi people onto the streets for the celebrations, or to take the pledge from their home or place of work.[27] The traditional routine was reestablished and extended to New Delhi. The program included prabhat pheris from 6:30 a.m. in all the wards of New and Old Delhi, followed by flag salutations at 8:30 a.m. Over sixty meetings were reported throughout the cities during the day, with the Congress flag being hoisted over Indraprastha and St. Stephen's Colleges.[28] In addition, over nine thousand workers at Delhi Cloth Mills and three thousand at Birla Mills went on strike.[29] Spinning competitions were held in the afternoon, followed by a public meeting of an estimated hundred thousand people and flag unfurling at 5:00 p.m. in the Ramlila grounds between New and Old Delhi.

While this successful celebration harked back to the overground traditions of Civil Disobedience and Quit India, on 2 February 1946 Kishore Khanna was reunited with his old colleague when, after three and a half years underground, Aruna Asaf Ali returned to Delhi. Her warrant of arrest had been lifted on 29 January, and Delhi's nationalist elite, including the Bandhu Guptas, the Ansaris, Memo Bai, and Raghunandan Saran, greeted Asaf Ali. A telegram awaited her from Gandhi, stating: "So you had your way. Expect letter" (Gandhi 1999, 89:324). Asaf Ali gave speeches praising the Delhi people for their role in the nationalist movement, but she also used the platform for the socialist message she had been developing and publishing in her years underground. She insisted that "victory" would only come when the entire bureaucratic machine was smashed.[30] The chief commissioner reported a "stormy fortnight" at the beginning of February, with the further sentencing of INA troops, electioneering and provocative statements in the Legislative Assembly, and local talks by the Asaf Alis.[31] While a dazzling local celebrity, Aruna Asaf Ali represented a wider conjuncture between nonviolence and socialism. We can trace this defining, agonizing clash through another (then) subaltern life in the CID archives, whose identity emerged in response to the Delhi political landscape in general, and Asaf Ali's direct influence in particular.

### Identity: Subhadra Datta

Subhadra Joshi was a leading politician in postindependence India, serving in the Lok Sabha and campaigning against communal tension as well as serving as the president of the DPCC. She is less remembered as Subhadra Datta, her birth name, a "freedom fighter" who participated in the Lahore Quit India underground movement in her mid-twenties (Chopra 1974, 192). Rising to prominence in Delhi in the years before independence, she presents one way to track the difficult transition Congress was making from protest organization to an anticipatory government while addressing the rival popularity of communalism and communism. Her CID file, like that of Shatrugan, takes her life as a thread between a huge number of micro-events that present invaluable insights into the political minutiae of post–Quit India, pre-independence, and prepartition Delhi.

On 3 April 1943 W. D. Robinson of the Punjab CID forwarded a note on the "Duttas" to CID SSP Mellor in Delhi, describing them as "a thoroughly bad family."[32] Particular attention was drawn to the daughter, Subhadra, who lived with her father in Bharatpur State (a Hindu princely state between Jaipur and Agra) "and may at any time descend on Delhi and make a nuisance of herself to you. She is not really dangerous, but one of the fanatical neurotic nationalist type." Born in 1919, she had previously worked as a teacher in Lahore and had relatives in government service, one in jail for his role in the Quit India movement and one, her brother "Wishno Dutta," who taught at Senior Cambridge School in Delhi.

Subhadra Datta followed her brother into education in Delhi, being listed as principal at the University Tutorial College for Girls near Gol Market, to the west of Connaught Place, between New and Old Delhi, in December 1943. The following January a bulletin, coauthored by Aruna Asaf Ali, was intercepted in the post; the CID identified Datta as having received and distributed the literature, as well as having raised the Congress flag in the school compound. Her address had also been found in a house, raided in January 1944, that had been used to orchestrate Asaf Ali's Delhi underground. She had spoken during Congress National Week celebrations in Queen's Gardens in April 1944 and had expressed disappointment at the winding down of the Quit India movement. This took place on 13 April (between the release of Gandhi and the working committee) and was jointly organized by the Delhi branches of the Communist Party, the Majlis-i-Ahrar (a Congress-supporting Muslim party), the Jamiat-ul-Ulema, and the Textile Mazdoor Sabha (Labourer Society). It was presided over by "veteran" Congress worker Hanuwant Sahai, under a large Congress flag, with a dozen boys from the Harijan colony plying charkha throughout. Though rallying all the people of India to unite against the Japanese threat and to follow the example of Gandhi, he admitted that the Congress leadership (much of which was still imprisoned) had little following. Datta supported various resolutions but protested at the small size of the audience (around three hundred), suggesting that the Delhi people had no confidence in Gandhi. Sahai publicly rebuked Datta, suggesting that the people lacked the necessary leadership to display their sympathy for the Congress cause.

Over the following year Datta was mentioned by various CID sources as Congress attempted to reestablish its authority in the city. In July 1944 she was noted at a private Congress meeting discussing how to exploit shopkeepers' economic difficulties due to rations; observing Harijan and adult schools established by the "Azad Sewak Sabha"; and collaborating closely with Congress worker Mir Mushtaq Ahmad of New Delhi after his release from detention. In August she alone fell out with the local party after it decided to follow Gandhi's public statement and cease printing illegal literature. But she agreed to publicize Gandhi's constructive program for observing the 9 August Quit India second anniversary, prioritizing Hindu-Muslim unity and observing law and order. A secret meeting of Congress workers was held at Jhamuria Library in Kishanganj on 6 August to finalize the program for the 9th, at which Datta was listed as a prominent worker, and at which it was agreed that all underground and secret activities should be suspended.

On the anniversary itself, an edition of *Hamara Sangram* was published listing Datta as the editor and affirming its status as a Congress mouthpiece. In accordance with Gandhi's wishes it was openly available and expressed its ongoing opposition to fascism and imperialism in equal measure. Tribute was paid to the regular volunteers who had done door-to-door work, requesting individuals (not money) for "sacrifice at the altar of freedom." Even if these "oblations offered in a yagna [ritual sacrifice]" did not realize their efficacy themselves, "time sees it." The editorial concluded with common warnings that the British government would be burned to ashes and independence achieved.

During an interview in 2001 Subhadra Joshi recalled Gandhi telling her that if newspapers were banned then she should consider herself as a newspaper and spread information herself.[33] If her published output was short on the details of how independence would be achieved, Datta's political activities show her moving firmly in the direction of Aruna Asaf Ali's Congress-left. In August 1944 a joint meeting was held of fifty Congress, communist, and labor workers in Daryaganj. Datta was listed as a prominent Congress member, alongside leading communists such as Sarla Gupta, Ram Chander Tiagi, and Bahal Singh. The workers were willing to collaborate to establish representatives in every one of the city's sixteen wards, covering all communities, to collect money for the Kasturba Gandhi Fund before the looming deadline. This financial work would also be social work, instilling political beliefs in every house visited. A CID report on a further meeting, on 26 August, of "Congress workers" failed to identify any of the above as "Communists." A joint resolution was accepted wishing Gandhi and Jinnah luck in overcoming communal oppositions and condemning British refusal to grant independence. A further resolution recommended that Raghunandan Saran and Mir Mushtaq Ahmad lead Delhi's constructive program. Datta objected that no one should be allowed to lead who had not broken a restrictive order placed on them (like Ahmad). Leftists Farooqi, Bahal Singh, and Dr. Vijay Kumar denied that Gandhi had denounced working within restrictions, but several workers backed Datta's hard line on civil disobedience, though she lost a vote on her suggestion by thirty-five to twenty-two.

Datta spent the next three months in Madras but returned to Delhi in December, staying at the Gandhi ashram on Chandni Chowk while she looked for work in girls' schools. The CID did not rate her highly enough to place a censor on her mail (she wrote to them asking for her confiscated letters back, and they replied saying they had not confiscated any), but their "urban daily report" for 26 January 1945 described her as "notorious." She had been working hard to heal growing tensions within the DPCC on the run-up to Independence Day, which was to be celebrated peacefully. In front of the large crowd that had gathered in Connaught Place, about twenty people converged from different directions to hold a flag salutation ceremony. Ten were arrested, including the notorious Datta, for contravening the chief commissioner's orders under the Defence of India Rules. She was convicted on 28 February and sentenced to six months of rigorous imprisonment. A month later the *National Call* reported that appeals by eight of those arrested against their sentence were rejected but their sentences were reduced to three months. In line with her earlier sentiments about not contesting government restrictions, however, Datta refused to appeal her sentence. After her release, in July the CID logged an externment order, banning Datta from Delhi Province to prevent her acting in a manner prejudicial to public safety.

Datta, however, left Delhi when she was released, before the externment order had been passed, and it had lapsed by 6 February 1946, her next appearance in Delhi. She chaired a meeting in Qarol Bagh Park of 2,500–3,000 laborers at which Aruna Asaf Ali was being received, four days after her return to Delhi. In addition to Datta and Asaf Ali collaborating on the *Hamara Sangram* magazine, the CID had circumstantial evidence that Datta had assisted Asaf Ali in staying underground. But this was their first documented meeting, one of many over the next eighteen months as Datta moved farther to the left, though never abandoning Congress. At the meeting on the 6th, organized by the Delhi Textile Mazdoor Sewak Sangh (Labourer Union), poems were read and eulogies delivered to Asaf Ali, who praised the Delhi workers for their contribution to the Quit India movement but condemned communists as the government's "fifth column" within the nationalist movement. She also condemned the government for worsening communal feelings, by predicting Hindu Muslim violence as a result of 1942, whereas the imam of Sunehri Masjid (on Chandni Chowk) had sheltered Hindus during past disturbances. A revolution, she suggested, was in sight, for which every man and woman needed to prepare.

Asaf Ali became president of the six-thousand-strong Delhi Textile Sangh, and Datta attended various meetings with her where the workers were told to unite and overcome communal differences. The sangh rented a house for Datta in Qarol Bagh, but a report of 8 April 1946 noted that she still did Congress propaganda work among the families of mill workers. It was also anticipated that she would soon marry B. D. Joshi, who had offered resolutions at the February meeting with Asaf Ali and was influential in the textile sangh, and with whom Datta met Gandhi to explain the work done with the laborers in Delhi. On 25 April Asaf Ali held a meeting with laborers of the Textile Mazdoor Sangh at her home where she tried, again, to rally the members to think of themselves as workers more than members of religious communities. Even before her turn to socialism, Asaf Ali had criticized the "holiness" with which Indians approached and interpreted nationalism (Bakshi 1994, 7). By the spring of 1946 it was widely known that communities were collecting lathis and weapons for communal riots: "She advised that instead of Hindu Muslim riot they should try to bring about a conflict between the labourers and the capitalists. It was incumbent upon the Hindu labourers to kill Hindu capitalists and Muslim labourers to kill Muslim capitalists, she added." Were this to happen, Delhi would be under their control, so laborers were told to organize themselves in each mohalla and street. B. D. Joshi and Datta, along with Ram Singh, were charged with forming committees in each mohalla to increase unity and campaign against communal tension. This was anticipating the violence of 1947, but also in the shadow of Delhi's last violent problematization of Congress's weakening claim to be still leading a nonviolent form of anticolonialism.

### Problematization: Victory Day

In the spring of 1946 Delhi played host to one final self-consciously anticolonial and public rejection of the imperial state and its theatrics. It forcibly contested the imperial truth of war (a united empire against the Axis powers) and fitted the Congress narrative (a war at Indian expense without Indian consent). It also, however, marked another problematization of Congress's anticolonialism. A week ahead of the "V-Day" celebrations, DPCC leader Jugal Kishore Khanna announced that it would not give the event further publicity by forming a counterorganization. Others did not hold back, however, and showed little commitment to nonviolence.[34]

For 7 March 1946 temporary "Victory Arches" were erected throughout the city, through which it was envisaged that extensive military parades would pass, to the delight of local crowds (for summary pieces on the disturbances see Gupta 1998a, 1998b). As with the INA trials earlier in the year, the V-Day celebrations united disparate local groups in protest, with communists coordinating the counterprotests (despite having supported the war).[35] An army garrison was deployed to seal off and protect New Delhi.[36] So much attention was lavished on protecting the capital, however, that the police force in Old Delhi had only 70 percent of their strength to deal with what followed.[37]

The public holiday combined with what the police admitted was a complete hartal led to masses of people on the streets. Nirad Chaudhuri (1987, 795) recalled, "In New Delhi the military procession was jeered at, and had black flags waved at it. The soldiers, both British and Indian, were booed, and the procession into the old city was abandoned." Anand Gupta recalled the troops having to divert at Delhi Gate, skirting the outside of the Red Fort and entering "by the back door."[38] While the police cleared the main bazaars of the old city, sabotage and "incendiarism" spread throughout the city, leaving the victory gates, according to the *Hindustan*, "burnt to a crisp" and the decoration lights in Hauz Qazi and Chandni Chowk looted.[39] The Railway Clearing Accounts Office and the town hall were set on fire, despite Congress workers pleading with the crowd to desist; the town hall had just been reopened after refurbishment following the arson of August 1942. By 3:00 p.m. the fire had spread throughout the town hall, but due to the fire brigade station on Queen's Road being attacked, the fire was not extinguished until 5:30 p.m. On the following day the city was mostly calm by 5:00 p.m., but the tram drivers remained on strike and the local administration described the city to the Government as still nervous and in darkness, as workers had refused to fix damaged electricity supplies.

The *Hindustan Times* reported on 8 March that Delhi presented the sight "of a bomb-shattered city," that "the mobs followed the same tactics as they did in August 1942 and by sunset the city presented almost the same appearance as it did on August 11th 1942," a comparison also made by the *Hindustan* newspaper.[40] The chief commissioner reported three deaths from police gunfire and attributed the agitation to leftist Congress members with substantial help from local communists.[41] Muhammad Asaf Ali had a plea published on 8 March for the violence to desist, which argued that violence had been shown to lead to no good.[42]

As the cases against the demonstrators worked their way through courts over the following year, a picture of violence wrought against the landscape emerged. The chief commissioner later summarized the ongoing court cases for the Home Department.[43] All of them involved arson, with their targets being public buses, a post office on Library Road, the terminal tax post near the cloth mills and near Andha Mughal, the Railway Clearing Accounts Office, a timber godown, fire brigade engines, a small police van, an electricity substation near the town hall, an electric pole in Ballimaran, the town hall itself, and a nearby Victory Gate. In response to a question in the Legislative Assembly a year later, the chief commissioner listed the total number of accused in relation to the disturbances. The list ran to 101, though many had been acquitted.[44]

The *Janata* newspaper reported the picketing of the celebrations in the imperial capital, stating simply, "No one knew whose Victory it was" (see figure 8.5, displaying protestors at the Victory Day parade in Delhi, one of whom holds a sign declaring "This is not our victory"). Or, as Aruna Asaf Ali (1947, 20) put it, "The Imperialists have as yet not grasped the fact that they can force Indians into prisons, but they cannot order them to make merry."[45]

Within a fortnight the Delhi Administration faced a strike by its own police force. On 20 March the police went on strike over pay, food, and the treatment of staff. The following day over three hundred policemen refused to obey orders and had to be brought to order by British infantry.[46] On 22 March between eighty and a hundred men broke out from the police lines and headed toward the Legislative Assembly in New Delhi. The "mutinous officers" were stopped by troops in Daryaganj and surrounded in Faiz Bazar, during which six escaped onto a shop roof.[47] Tear gas had to be used to get the officers down from the roof, which led to considerable suffering because, the senior superintendent of police (SSP) reported, the officers wrapped cloth around their heads "to conceal their identities and stupid appearances."[48] Aruna Asaf Ali congratulated the police and demanded the dismantling of the disciplinary machinery that had been in place since 1942.[49] The SSP had summarized the causes of the despondent atmosphere among Delhi's three-thousand-strong police force, who had been demoralized by policing the INA trials, the navy "mutiny" started in Bombay, the strikes by government servants, low wages, corruption within the service, and fatigue.[50]

On 25 March Mohammad Asaf Ali countered this interpretation in moving that the Legislative Assembly adjourn. He argued that the strike was but

**FIGURE 8.5.** "This Is Not Our Victory," *Janata*, 17/3/1946

a symptom and that the quality of police food, the mishandling of their complaints, and their low pay were only partial explanations. What needed to be acknowledged was the demoralizing effect on the police of their use as corrupted tools of oppression, performing the disagreeable duties that betrayed their countryfolk: "Now we know where the disease is. The disease is not purely economic. It is something deeper. The seat of the disease is somewhere deeper in the—I shall not call it body politic—body secretariat, if you like, of the Government of India." The police were both disrespected and maladministered, as the organization for policing V-Day had shown, with thousands of men protecting the capital and hardly any policing Old Delhi. The police force was still being administered against the grain of nationalism, which was its disease. But if Mohammad Asaf Ali had one eye on the departing hegemon, his other was on the (subaltern) challenges that would face Congress hegemony. Echoing his concerns about the awakening masses from a quarter century earlier (Asaf Ali 1921), he insisted that unless the police administrators changed their attitude, "these troubles will multiply and I am perfectly certain that once these troubles multiply they will overwhelm the country and the chaos that will ensue will be uncontrollable."[51]

## Visualizing a New Delhi

The previous twenty years had seen anticolonial visions of Delhi brought into being, whether of an old city that was political and networked, or of a new city that was reenvisaged as a despotic symbol of oppression. With victory in sight, what vision of the future could the capital offer? For many, Delhi was as in thrall to the past as it had been when it attracted the British in 1911. From 1 July 1947 a DPCC political conference was held at Shahdara near Delhi, organized by J. P. Narayan and featuring Gandhi and other leading Congress figures (see figure 8.6, which shows Gandhi, Narayan, and Arun Asaf Ali on the dais with other members of the DPCC).[52] A review of the conference in *Janata* by "A. G." replicated many of the tropes that had featured in celebrations of the capital thirty-six years previously (Delhi as the graveyard of empires, a land of monuments, a city cowed in 1857).[53] But unlike imperial accounts, this review noted the impact of these successive empires on the local people. In the shadow of successive autocracies, most communities had not looked beyond village management. Now they could anticipate a people's government. But their condition had either remained the same or worsened under British Delhi, as Indians were excluded from the new city or forced to live in slums

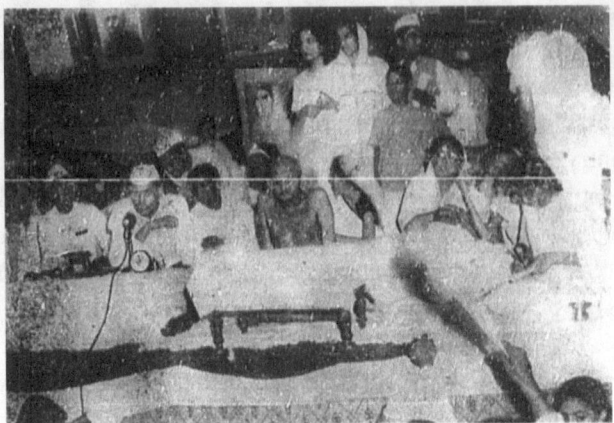

FIGURE 8.6. Gandhi, Narayan, and Aruna Asaf Ali at conference, *Janata*, 6/7/1947

in the old. Congress, however, had brought politics to the city in 1918 and had been working ever since to better the Delhi people.

Aruna Asaf Ali had taken the dais at the conference with Gandhi and others but had a very different take on the Delhi she had encountered since her return from the underground. She was keenly sensitive to the symbiosis of human geography, acutely aware of the impact that a British-constructed capital would have on the workings of an Indian government: "Environment and ecology shape minds, they invest one with material for fighting life's battles, or for accepting life as it comes.... On taking rigid measures to control the space-time, man-society parallelogram we live in, depends our ability to extract from every hour the hard grain of achievement" (Asaf Ali 1947, 9). While Asaf Ali defended Gandhi's space of the ashram from snooty critiques, her geography was that of scientific socialism and a focus on the actual lived conditions of rural and urban life. Her return to Delhi, joining Mohammad Asaf Ali in his government accommodation in New Delhi's 2 Windsor Place, exposed her to the "city-smug life of old" (2), which had not shed its trappings during the Quit India movement. On visiting Bombay she was reminded of a city where the "white men's bureaucracy does not inflict its presence on you" (16).

On the verge of political victory she found the capital unchanged. New prime ministers, viceroys, and new politics—"this is part of the *sutra* [ancient teaching] we must recite; *but New Delhi is New Delhi*" (Asaf Ali 1947, 45, emphasis in original). Would Delhi, the graveyard of ancient dynasties, become the burial ground of Anglo-Saxon imperialism? Not if the New Delhi rulers had their way and merely changed the managing agency when independence arrived. The capital was awash with constitution planning by people "living in the gentle-lawned houses and seeing the correct people. But there are others equally busy, men and women searching for Utopia" (50). For Asaf Ali it was Delhi's striking policemen that were feeders for a freedom that would be defined based on righteous resistance. Labour Party "British Imperio-Socialists" were not offering freedom, only seats under the old hegemony.[54] That, and a civil war "camouflaged as a communal war" (134), were the two prospects facing the constitutionalists anticipating victory in New Delhi.

## CHAPTER 9

# Conclusions

### Within and Beyond the City

The previous chapters have analyzed three coupled landscapes of anticolonial ordering that responded, directly or indirectly, to problematizations provoked by the capital transfer of 1911. The first pairing was one of Civil Disobedience and the Quit India movement, mass mobilizations a decade apart that desired disciplined and nonviolent parrhesia in the new and old cities. The second pairing was of problematizations of that nonviolence, in the shape of a shooting ordeal around a gurdwara and a murder across a railway line, but also in a shadow landscape on the fringe of the overground and of nonviolence. The final pairing contrasted Delhi beyond mass mobilization, as a city struggling with its capital status and with the insurgent popularity of leftist politics in both the mid-1930s and mid-1940s. After summarizing the book's broader contributions, this conclusion explores the political and analytical links between these periods and landscapes, before considering Delhi relationally in comparison and connection to other interwar cities and to the immediately postcolonial world.

*Spaces of Anticolonialism* has sought broader disciplinary, substantive, and conceptual contributions. In terms of disciplines, it has provided both a history and a geography of late anticolonial Delhi. As a history it has provided a loose chronology of anticolonial movements in the city from 1930 to 1947. Across these movements characters and places recurred, bringing alive the temporalities and spatialities of the longer and wider campaigns. The book has also attended to anticolonialism's multiple geographies in Delhi: its spaces, places, locations, landscapes, and braided scales. At its heart, this book makes the case for historical geographical approaches to anticolonialism.

In terms of its substantive contributions, the book has centered around

Congress as a mass organization but also as an association anticipating government. Congress did this through mediating figures between itself and the state, such as Mohammad Asaf Ali, the long-serving representative of Delhi in the central Legislative Assembly. But it also did this through its ongoing attempts to sway, discipline, and conduct the urban populations of Delhi into protest and self-formation. Exploring this process from the bottom up, a second substantive contribution has been to explore Congress's own account of its relationship to violence and the subaltern. Despite its professed nonviolence and mass appeal, Congress at times turned a blind eye to, or openly encouraged, violence and often lacked the control of subaltern populations it proclaimed itself to have.

A final substantive contribution, which I hope has emerged without being forced through the preceding chapters, is to make it clear how central women were to the movement in Delhi. From earlier roles as supportive wives and swadeshi campaigners, emerging for the first time in processions and pickets in 1930, Delhi's women went on to lead the movement in the city. While Satyavati and Aruna Asaf Ali were the most prominent women, the accounts above teem with the defiant parrhesia of women at diverse scales and spaces. This is not to say that they were not resisted, by British and Indian men, but that their contributions attest to the double refusal their anticolonialism embodied. Focusing on the spaces of this anticolonialism contributes to broader moves to speculatively engage histories of anticolonialism feminism not through its intellectual work but through its political work, located in action and in the streets (Sajed and Salem 2023).

Conceptually this book has made wider contributions to thinking about politics and the city through its analysis of anticolonial governmentalities. This was not done through a top-down approach to an aspirant bourgeois nationalist hegemony or a scattered and romantic study of resistant localities. Rather, this bottom-up approach has suggested that Foucault's last works, on parrhesia, allow us to explore courageous spaces where ethics (self on self) and politics (selves and others) intersected. Congress channeled parrhesia against the British but in so doing spawned it against itself. At the heart of these parrhesiastic governmentalities was the question of one's truth. Truth was a resource for institutions, but also for bodily routines, places, dreams, intimacies, and indeed the ordinary fruits and pleasures of human life (Banerjee 2021).

This has also been a postcolonial reading aware of colonial and anticolonial difference from European norms, governmentalities, and historiography. Despite its claims to be a liberal empire, the Government of India proved itself to be an autocratic and brutal state. This was whether operating through its military and CID during mass movements or through the more mundane and quotidian oppressions of everyday life beyond them. The anticolonial governmentalities that the British faced drew on European political traditions, but with a wholly different conception of spiritual and political sovereignty, ethics, and relations to more international (socialist) and national (communal) movements.

While separable in retrospect, *Spaces of Anticolonialism* has made the case that these contributions are best read together. The landscapes of Delhi were used to visualize and access the population, but the city was also used by the people to craft their own parrhesiastic politics. The cities of Delhi provided the space for symbolic protests and attacks, the stage for processions and outrages, the places in which to recoup, plot, and nurture, and the infrastructure that allowed the city to bifurcate into over- and undergrounds. These cities emerge in snatches and fragments from a voluminous archive, whether of the colonial state, nationalist repositories, or the memories and writings of participants and their families. All these records are biased. Colonial records tend to record violence more than its absence, while nationalist ones emphasize the successes of satyagraha. But reading across these records, the overwhelming sense is of the capital of Britain's largest and most prized colony in the grip of a world-historical experiment with violence and nonviolence. The challenge has been to represent the spaces of these experiments, acknowledging the power relations at play without occluding or overdetermining the contributions of the people that made these human landscapes—that is, to produce a non-counterinsurgent discourse or, put simply, to loop together three paired landscapes of insurgency.

## Interlinked Landscapes of Ordering

### PRACTICED CONNECTIONS

A political and ethical repertoire of truth relations can be seen to have built up in anticolonial Delhi from a base laid in 1919 and the 1920s but rapidly expanded, practically linking the mass movements of the 1930s and 1940s. Chief among these were Congress-sponsored forms of directed parrhesia, which drew on older traditions and took on lives of their own. Also increasingly prevalent, however, were modes of embodying truths that experimented with or openly embraced violence.

Courageous speech fills the archive, as slogans chanted, songs sung, or political speeches made, whether on the street or in the central Legislative Assembly in New Delhi. At its most controlled, the Individual Satyagraha campaign saw protesters selected and sent to break laws using proscribed seditious speech. The broader parrhesiastic quality of what was spoken related to forms of mobility. In motion this could include a song during a prabhat pheri procession in a hostile neighborhood, or an insult hurled while passing the kotwali. In situ it could be an attempt to dissuade a punter (hai hai'ing) from buying some grog from a liquor store. The written word was also used to express anticolonial truths, whether published, in letters, pamphlets, posters, or banners, or in graffiti stenciled onto the walls or streets of the capital in the dead of night. Courage of a different sort was required to change the way you lived your life and made your body via an affirmative biopolitics, changing what you wore, what you consumed, how you spent your money, and how you educated your family.

Many of these acts constituted tests that challenged volunteers to put themselves at risk for the cause. This might involve physical tests such as picketing a store, making salt illegally, carrying a message, or procuring components for making a bomb. There were also tests in which truth regimes clashed. This could see juridical claims based on state-generated facts and evidence contested with counterofficial reports and testimonials—words and bodies as standing testimony to colonial violence. Most proximate to violence were two extreme forms of test. One was the mortification of the fasts in Delhi, whether of Gandhi in 1924 or Krishna Nair in 1942. The other test was that of the ordeal, which those around the Gurdwara Sisganj faced in 1930 as did those targeted or caught in the crossfire around Chandni Chowk in August 1942.

The latter took place in a movement whose "Do or Die" slogan was taken by many as carte blanche to experiment with violence, against objects if not subjects. In this sense many of the acts did not stray too far from the Congress creed, cutting telegraph wires, burning post boxes or railway stations. But in their truth relations they were foreign to Gandhi's commitment to truth and openness. The underground produced revolutionary lives that embodied a different truth and produced an anti-Gandhian lie of the land.

### ANALYTICAL CONNECTIONS

While not unified into one rigid anticolonial regime, the analytical categories of the governmentality approach do allow comparisons to be drawn out across the landscapes and periods assessed. There was no one *episteme* informing each phase or geography, nor were explicit reflections on the more abstract methods for producing truth in the city always written or retained. But Civil

Disobedience was characterized by a relatively strict adherence to Gandhian nonviolence; the 1930s saw the growing authority of revolutionary appeals to violence within and without Congress, while the 1940s saw full-blown experimentation with violence and tyrannicide. Like Delhi's anticolonial episteme, its forms of *visibility* tended to be devised by Congress organizers. The Civil Disobedience movement saw the systematization of a way of visualizing the population of Old Delhi and envisioning New Delhi as a symbol of despotism, a picture that was painted of the whole Delhi Province in the 1930s. While these ways of seeing the city were resurrected during the Quit India campaign, its innovation was a form of *invisibility*, using material and mobile infrastructures across the two Delhis to create a third city underground. For those who emerged from this under-city, both the garden society of New Delhi and the new Delhi being planned for independent India left revolutionary hopes for a transformation, rather than a transfer, of power in tatters.

The *techne* of anticolonialism saw repertoires of intervention tailored to the landscapes of Delhi and developed alongside the means of conceptualizing and envisioning the broader political project. As a symbolic, institutional, and material space, New Delhi was more open to subversion than its defenses (against invasion) would suggest. The old city was a compact stage for the full dramaturgical performances of parrhesia, from public and temporary reclamations of the main bazaars, to the ritualistic and community-organized making of lanes, mohallas, and homes. Between disobedience and quitting, techniques of protest were trialed regarding constitutional, municipal, and labor disputes, focusing respectively on New Delhi, Old Delhi, and Sabzi Mandi. Quit India saw the disobedient city resurrected for a few days, but the underground operated for months longer, out of sight. Members of the underground tentatively supported the return to drills and the rituals of Congress commemoration as independence neared.

Students and women were new political *identities* for the disobedient city, Satyavati being an inspirational figure for men and women alike. Rather than focus on the ideal conduct of governed groups, the focus here has been on identities produced by anticolonialism in the city. These lives have guided us through subaltern spaces and politics, although their very recording suggests a degree of influence and status denied the broader non-elite. Shatrugan detailed the wavering between Gandhian and revolutionary politics in the 1930s; Krishna Nair and Aruna Asaf Ali embodied the turn to violence against objects but not subjects within the Congress fold, while Datta articulated the Congress left's stance against orthodox Congress, communal, and communist positions.

All governmentalities are driven by their *problematizations*, which provoke adaptation but also bring crisis and contradiction. The mass experimentation with nonviolence during Civil Disobedience, even after the training of the 1920s, made some failures likely. The shooting at the Gurdwara Sisganj problematized the local movement because of the attacks on the police (which were questioned but not wholly refuted) and because the later inquiry largely escaped Congress's control. The leftist problematization of the 1930s was partly resolved by the Congress Socialist Party, many of whose members supported the Quit India underground, which itself problematized Gandhi's project of satyagraha. A more fundamental challenge was posed by the murder at Pili Kothi by those participating in the Quit India disturbances.

The ongoing nature of these problematizations was inherent in an anticolonial movement that commanded people to disobey, but in certain ways. As such, this study of the spaces of an anticolonial governmentality has taken as its materiel diverse acts of *parrhesia*. All these acts required was a body, a place, and courage. Anticolonial parrhesia could be disciplined (picketing, salt making, speech giving), mobile (processions, note carrying, message giving, gun stowing), domestic (demanding the right to protest against a family's wishes), or violent (hitting, shooting, burning). What was shared across these parrhesiastic acts was the ethical differentiation the acts made. This was not between the true and the untrue, but between those who seized the moment and the place to courageously *be* anticolonial. Despite this, nationalist historiography has tended to ethically differentiate between an organizing elite and an awaiting mass.

Implicit within the foregoing chapters has been a concern with the anticolonial *ethos* that distributed tasks in line with presumed capacities. This is the question of the blurred distinction between elite and subaltern groups. But it is also a question of distinguishing counterinsurgent discourses on the subaltern from evidence of subaltern action within and beyond the mobilization and stimulation of Congress institutions. In terms of subaltern depictions, Mohammad Asaf Ali depicted the Indian people as slumbering and hypnotized while the police feared the awakening of the Delhi underworld. The crowds of 6 May 1930 were repeatedly described by officials as a mob out for mischief, although the Gurdwara Firing Committee rationalized their movements as those of concerned relatives and outraged citizens. The ability of figures like Satyavati to stoke support in the 1930s was put down by the police to her ability to command her "swarms" of followers. During the Quit Delhi protests the undisciplined crowds prompted the full gamut of subaltern stereotypes to run free in official reports—the scampering, wriggling, heaving mass causing mischief without leaders and bringing monstrous violence down on the head of Superintendent Sharif. After the war, Aruna Asaf Ali campaigned in the city for the common man and woman but, like her husband twenty-five years earlier, assumed a subaltern mass in need of stimulation (preferably by revolution).

Against these depictions, the archive is overflowing with evidence of the non-elite who were political, calculating, and mostly nonviolent, even if these acts tended to go unrecorded. From 1930 many mohallas self-organized; plans for symbolic attacks on New Delhi were drawn up against central Congress wishes; pickets were reinvented for the sterile capital landscape; government servants organized and attended political meetings; police attempts to break up salt production were resisted; furtive cloth traders were reported on by community networks; women refused their husbands by joining the movement; over seventy thousand people attended mass meetings; and during hartals and strikes tens of thousands of people withdrew their labor. The example of Mrs. Kohli's glance showed how expertly and delicately volunteers were experimenting with nonviolence. The Sisganj incident confirmed elite fears (both colonial and Congress) of subaltern violence, but the following investigation also saw subaltern forms of testimony, whether spoken, written, or presented through wounded bodies as transcripts of colonial violence. Shatrugan's rural campaigns in the 1930s evidenced villagers outraged and complaining against damage caused by military maneuvers. The Quit India movement saw plenty of evidence of a people without elite leadership resorting to violence, but the whole underground depended on ranks of supporters behind every arson attack, bombing, and village campaign.

The archive is heavily distorted toward anticolonial organizations and organizers. The colonial imperative was to find, surveil, and arrest when appropriate Congress organizers; the nationalist imperative was to prove Congress's effectiveness at stimulating the masses. Both sources depict political activity as a response. The sheer abundance of evidence collected here depicts a self-organizing and already political city that went with but also far beyond Congress organization. Aside from leading figures like the Asaf Alis or the Shraddhanand-Indra-Satyavati family network, Delhi's organizers were neither rich nor poor—a self-organizing subalternity of the elite (Chatterjee 1992).

Foucault was undoubtedly a Eurocentric thinker, but this book has worked with the generations of South Asian scholars who took up Foucault's concepts during his lifetime and repurposed them to help consider colonial and anticolonial difference (Legg and Heath 2018; Teo and Wynne-Hughes 2020). It has hopefully avoided being a Eurocentric work itself through being led by non-Western scholarship and by displacing Europe as the theoretical subject of this historical geographical investigation (Prakash 1994). It has also sought a nonabstract form of analysis that places the conditions and contexts of anticolonialism seriously, as a basis for conceptually reanimating postcolonial engagement with governmentality analytics (Getachew and Mantena 2021). It follows Foucault in seeking out alternative interrelationships of truth, subjectivity, and power.

What the book has traced is another attempt to create a revolution of political spirituality. Just as Foucault suggested that states and institutions were based on the micropolitics of circulatory techniques and norms, so the anticolonial governmentalities studied here emerged through directed but relatively autonomous spaces of ethical self-formation. The ultimate object of this analysis is Delhi, a city split in two, and then in three, which existed across its fragments (McFarlane 2021).

## Beyond Colonial Delhi

### SPACE

The approach to the spaces of anticolonialism here advocated has been inspired by research that sought to undo imperialist discourses regarding Indian politics and elitist, counterinsurgent discourses regarding subaltern politics by focusing on the lived experiences of Delhi. This aligns with a realist approach to Gandhian nonviolence, attentive to the violent potential of both constructive and disruptive programs (Mantena 2012, 2022). These programs were achieved through Congress organizations working themselves into the city, but also through people using these networks to embed their own repertoires of protest within the Congress apparatus (Pandey 2002). This interplay opened up spaces of relative autonomy for regional Congress politics (Chatterjee 2002). These might find their way into colonial spaces where civil society and formal politics intersected, such as municipal committees or legislative assemblies (Ray 1979; Kidambi 2012). But the majority spaces of anticolonial politics existed beyond the institutions of the state or Congress. In domestic and community spaces the scales of anticolonialism could be collapsed into each other, bringing the nation into the bazaar, mohalla, and home (Legg 2003; Masselos 2007).

Beyond a comparative contextualization, Delhi must also be situated within the many networks by which it was connected to spaces within and beyond the subcontinent. As the capital city, New Delhi obviously functioned as a national and international showcase for Indian anticolonialism, while the Khilafat movement had connected Delhi to the broader pan-Islamic world. The revolutionary outrages in the Legislative Assembly or on the viceroy's train garnered international attention. As the capital, visits of national leaders to Delhi for conferences or meetings have attracted the most attention to date, and the object of this book has been to provide a granular study of Delhi in its own right, but still mindful of its connections and relations.

The mass movements were nationally orchestrated and saw Delhi looking outward for its cues. The Civil Disobedience movement began with the conclusion of Gandhi's salt march to Dandi, and the Sisganj shooting was sparked by his arrest a month later. The inquiry into the shooting was quickly taken over by committees based in Amritsar, and telegrams of protest soon flowed in from sites throughout the Punjab. The 1930s saw Congress marshal a response to the exclusion of Delhi from India's new constitutional freedoms by proposing a union with surrounding territories, to no avail. The Quit India movement was sparked in Bombay, by Delhi's own Aruna Asaf Ali, who moved to and from Delhi, coordinating it as part of a national underground movement. The Delhi underground, more than before, threaded the urban campaign together with the rural, until Krishna Nair's arrest. Running throughout this book has been a more general attentiveness to national politics but also to the vibrant internationalism of the interwar years. Dominion status, as an international solution to India's constitutional deadlock, was debated in Delhi into the 1930s. Socialist internationalism, especially as interpreted by the HSRA, was influential around the same time, which the Congress Socialist Party capitalized on, although the Comintern was disparaged after the "people's war" union between the USSR and the British Empire in 1942. The final years of the Raj saw Delhi rejecting celebrations of a world war and being inspired by the mutinous navy in Bombay, as the Congress party transitioned to a Congress state.

### TIME

On 15 August 1947 in New Delhi the institutions and ceremonies of the colonial state were combined with those of Congress as Jawaharlal Nehru accepted the mantle of power from the British (Masselos 1990). The following day, twenty-five thousand people swamped the central avenue of New Delhi to see the Indian tricolor flag being raised. A similar number flocked to hear Nehru make his speech from the Red Fort in the heart of Old Delhi that evening. Houses and mohallas were lit up brighter than for Diwali, shepherding in a new era of hope for India and colonies worldwide.¹ Gandhi, however, was not among those celebrating in Delhi. He was in Calcutta, where he had arrived a week earlier in the hope of stemming the genocidal violence that had broken out between Hindu and Muslim communities in the city. Though a territorial rupture, for him the partitioning of India into India and Pakistan represented a melancholy continuity with the cyclical violence and divisions between Hindus and Muslims that had intensified in the interwar years.

Alongside Congress-led anticolonial governmentalities in interwar Delhi, there had been a growing communalization of communities and politics. These processes clearly intersected, whether through the influence of Hindu-supporting Congress leaders like Deshbandhu Gupta and Professor Indra, through Mohammad Asaf Ali's election campaigns (where he successfully won the votes of Hindu-majority Congress voters), or through the mohalla-level competition between Congress's Seva Dal, the RSS, and the Muslim National Guard. But the geographies of communal Delhi remained as willfully external to colonial policing (Legg 2007, 119–48) as they did to Congress visualization, penetration, and neutralization (Legg 2019a), and merit much broader analysis on their own terms (see Datta 2019a; Halperin 2022; Parveen 2021).

This book concluded its study of anticolonial Delhi not in August 1947 but in March 1946. On the 23rd of that month, "Pakistan Day" triggered the start of seven weeks of communal riots and disturbances in the city that saw twenty-nine people killed and seventy injured (Legg 2019a). The arrival of Punjabi refugees stoked tensions in the capital, spilling over into violence repeatedly in the run-up to the mass outbreak of violence in the city following partition (Pandey 2001). On the cusp of finally attaining all-India sovereignty, Congress lost control in Delhi and myriad places across the country, especially those near the new borders in the Punjab and Bengal. The violence continued into the new year, causing Gandhi himself to visit the capital. Using a phrase that had last been applied to the city following the British retributions of 1857, Gandhi commented on 12 January: "Gay Delhi looked a city of the dead" (Gandhi 1999, 98:218). He selected Delhi as the place in which to launch his final fast to restore peace, insisting on 13 January: "Delhi is the capital of India. It has always been the capital of India. So long as things do not return to normal in Delhi they will not be normal either in India or Pakistan" (98:227).

From the perspective of colonial governmentality, the challenge in studying 1947 is to show that not everything changed with independence and partition. New Delhi did not shed its imperial impulses with the departure of the British. The urban development of Delhi retained its objectifying worldview (Legg 2006); women's place in the employment market remained problematic (Datta 2019b), while Muslims remained excluded from their own neighborhoods in Delhi's long partition (Zamindar 2007). From the perspective of anticolonial governmentality, the challenge in studying 1947 is to show that much did change with independence and partition. The objectifying worldview of urban development in the city was used to pursue urban masterplans that hybridized Soviet state planning with colonial town planning (Krishna Menon 1997). Despite Gandhi's pleas, and his fast in Delhi to bring communal rioting and attacks to an end, the spirit of nonviolence had been eclipsed long before his January 1948 assassination in New Delhi by Hindu extremist Nathuram Godse. Congress cracked down on the RSS more ferociously than the late colonial state had been able to (Andersen 1972).

For those on the left this was just further evidence that Congress sought a bourgeois hegemonic takeover of the powers of the colonial state, not a revolutionary attack on sovereignty that would produce a government by the people. For Aruna Asaf Ali the coming of independence to India and Delhi on 15 August 1947 changed neither the city nor the racial capitalist structure of class oppression that it had orchestrated. Grasping more than anyone the power of the underground, she diagnosed at its inception what Kwame Nkrumah would term, sixteen years later, neocolonialism (Getachew 2019). With her typical insight, Asaf Ali refused the idea of independence as an epochal rupture, a dividing line between slavery and freedom. For her it marked the transfer of power between elites alone without handing sovereignty to the Indian people:

> As the train came into New Delhi I thought of the change that had come over it since I left it a month back. Was it no longer Imperial? Was it really the seat of national Government, provisional but undoubtedly national? On the surface Delhi is no more or no less Imperial than it was before the 2nd September.... British power in India has gone underground. It will in devious ways seek to stave off utter destruction. To fight a subterranean enemy requires more skill and preparation than one whose actions are blatantly obvious. (Asaf Ali 1947, 57)

# NOTES

**CHAPTER 1. ANTI-IMPERIAL DELHI**

The epigraph is from NMML/CID/III/6.

1. NMML/CID/III/6.
2. For a counterreading of this arc as one of tragedy, see Scott (2004).
3. For an excellent exploration of elite working-class interactions during the Civil Disobedience campaign in Bombay based on a spatial analysis, see Raman (2019).
4. On Swaraj Party organization at the community scale of the "para," see Ghosh (2020).
5. See also Joshi (2003) on Kanpur.
6. The direct link to Foucault's work on care of self and self-fashioning is explicitly made by Pandian and Ali (2010, 5).
7. See also Leela Gandhi (1996, 119) for the return to Socrates in 1932.
8. On Gandhi's description of Socrates as a satyagrahi who used satyagraha against his own people, see Skaria (2016, 94).
9. On the centrality of fearlessness to satyagraha, see Skaria (2016, 91–117).
10. On both the power and limitations of subaltern territorial embeddedness and resistance, see Guha (1983a, 278–79).

**CHAPTER 2. DELHI'S ANTICOLONIAL ARCHIVE**

1. The preparation for the document is described in NMML/CID/VIII/16; NMML/CID/VIII/364.
2. DA/1913/Confidential(Home)/14B.
3. NMML/CID/VIII/85; NMML/CID/VIII/86.
4. NMML/Transcript/B. K. Chandiwala.
5. Personal interview/Sarla Sharma, 16/5/2001.
6. NMML/All India Congress Committee papers/G94 for Delhi 1930–32,P8 for Delhi 1942–46.
7. NMML/Oral History/B. K. Chandiwala.
8. CSAS/Transcript/D. R. Chaudhry and C. L. Paliwal.
9. NMML/Transcript/P. C. Jain.

10. NMML/Transcript/B. K. Chandiwala.

11. See also the comparable police recollections of J. F. McLintic, BL/IOR/Eur.Mss/F161.197.

12. NMML/Transcripts/B. K. Chandiwala and P. C. Jain. The Hindi transcripts were translated by Ragini Jha in the summer of 2016.

13. See chapter 6 on leaks emanating from the Home Department in New Delhi.

14. For popular reactions to Mughal authority in the city, see Kaicker (2020).

15. For local agitations between 1883 and 1908, see Gupta (1981, 125–56).

16. On a parallel influx of Hindu organizations into Delhi, see Jones (1986).

17. DA/Home/Confidential/1920/30 B.

18. I am indebted for this point to conversations with Anish Vanaik.

19. FR 21 April 1917.

20. DA/Home/Confidential/1920/30B.

21. NMML/Transcript 6/Shri Sobha Singh.

22. BL/IORL/L/R/5/202.

23. DA/DC/1926/67.

24. DA/Military/1927/16b.

25. DA/*Delhi Province Political "Who's Who"* (New Delhi: Government of India Press, 1934), J7.

26. "Delhi Day by Day," *Hindustan Times*, 6/2/1928.

27. NMML/Transcript/B. K. Chanidwala and Shri Krishan Das Kohli.

28. FR 21 September 1929.

29. NA/Home(Political)/1930/4/XIII.

## CHAPTER 3. A DISOBEDIENT CITY

1. FR/ 20/2/1929.

2. DA/Home/Confidential/1929/11.

3. FR/18/3/1930.

4. DA/Home/Confidential/1930/30B.

5. On the origins and working of the NBS in Delhi, see CSAS/Transcript/B. C. Lal.

6. FR 6/2/1930.

7. DA/Home/Confidential/1930/30b.

8. FR 19/3/1931.

9. NMML/Transcript/P. C. Jain.

10. FR 15/12/1931 and 30/11/1931.

11. NMML/CID/VIII/296.

12. NMML/Transcript/B. K. Chandiwala.

13. CSAS/Transcript/J. K. Khanna.

14. NMML/Transcript/P. C. Jain.

15. DA/Home/Confidential/1922/2B.

16. NA/Home(Political)/1930/432.

17. NMML/AICC/G94/1930/Part 1.

18. NMML/Transcript/P. C. Jain.

19. NMML/AICC/G94/1930/Part 1.

20. NMML/CID/VIII/296.
21. NMML/CID/X/49.
22. DA/Home/(Confidential)/1930/29b.
23. DA/Home/(Confidential)/1930/29b.
24. NMML/Transcript/S. Singh.
25. NMML/AICC/G94/1930/Part 1.
26. "Police Assault Delhi Volunteer," *Hindustan Times*, 24/4/1930.
27. FR 4/8/1930.
28. FR 4/10/1930.
29. FR 19/1/1931.
30. "New Assembly Speaker," *Hindustan Times*, 16/1/1931.
31. NMML/Transcript/J. K. Khanna.
32. DA/Confidential/(Education)/1930/5B.
33. da/Home(Confidential)/1930/34B.
34. NMML/CID/IX/371.
35. NMML/CID/IX/371.
36. " 'Go Back Lothian' on Council House," *Hindustan Times*, 1/2/1930.
37. NMML/CID/IX/371.
38. NMML/CID/VIII/296. Musammat is an honorific used for North Indian women.
39. Front-page editorial, *Hindustan Times*, 10/2/1932.
40. "Picketing in the Assembly," *Hindustan Times*, 20/2/1932.
41. NMML/CID/IX/371.
42. NMML/Transcript/P. C. Jain.
43. For example, see *Hindustan Times*, 20–23/2/1930.
44. FR 19/3/1930.
45. "The Eventful Day Has Come," *Hindustan Times*, 7/4/1930.
46. NMML/Transcript/P. C. Jain.
47. NMML/Oral History/Chandiwala.
48. DA/Confidential/1930/24C.
49. "Delhi Satyagrahis Triumph over Police Violence," *Hindustan Times*, 10/4/1930.
50. DA/Confidential/1930/24C.
51. A khatri is a social grouping descended from the Kshatriya caste and associated with trade and administration.
52. DA/Confidential/1930/24c, emphasis added.
53. "30 Leaders Arrested in Delhi," *Hindustan Times*, 11/4/1930.
54. "Delhi Decorated from End to End," *Hindustan Times*, 28/1/1931.
55. DA/Home/Confidential/1932/1(12)B; fr 15/5/1932.
56. NMML/CID/IX/371.
57. NMML/CID/VIII/296.
58. NMML/CID/IX/371.
59. NMML/CID/VIII/296.
60. Recounted in full detail in CSAS/Transcript/J. N. Sahni.
61. NMML/CID/VIII/296.
62. "Police Raids to Locate Meeting of Subjects Committee," *Hindustan Times*, 24/4/1932.

63. NA/Home/Political/1932/14/22.
64. NMML/CID/Transcript/K. D. Kohli.
65. "Over Eight Hundred Arrests Made in Delhi," *Hindustan Times*, 26/4/1932.
66. NMML/CID/IX/371.
67. NMML/ Transcript/ C. L. Paliwal.
68. DA/Confidential/1930/24C.
69. "Progress of Salt Satyagraha," *Hindustan Times*, 21/4/1930.
70. DA/Home/Political/1930/256/I KWA.
71. DA/Home/Political/1930/256/I KWA.
72. NMML/Transcript/H. Mehta.
73. "Progress of Picketing," *Hindustan Times*, 26/4/1930.
74. DA/Confidential/1930/24c.
75. NMML/Transcript/B. K. Chandiwala.
76. DA//Home/Political/1930/256/I KWA.
77. NMML/ Transcript/B. K. Chandiwala.
78. NMML/Transcript/P. C. Jain.
79. DA/Home/Political/1930/256/I KWA.
80. NMML/AICC/G94/1930/Part 1.
81. FR 20/6/1930.
82. FR 3/7/1930.
83. NMML/Transcript/P. C. Jain.
84. NMML/Transcript/M. Bai.
85. NMML/aicc/G94/1930/Part 1.
86. "Delhi Ladies Activities," *Hindustan Times*, 2/8/1930.
87. "Khaddar Propaganda," *Hindustan Times*, 15/8/1930.
88. NMML/Transcript/P. C. Jain.
89. NMML/Transcript/M. Bai.
90. NMML/ Transcript/J. K. Khanna.
91. FR 18/9/1930.
92. FR 4/2/1931.
93. FR 18/12/1930.
94. NMML/AICC/G94/1930/Part 1.
95. NMML/AICC/G94/1930/Part 1.
96. NMML/CID/VIII/296.
97. DA/Home/Confidential/1932/1(12)B.
98. NMML/CID/IX/371.
99. NMML/CID/IX/371.
100. NMML/CID/IX/371.
101. NMML/Transcript/P. C. Jain.
102. CSAS/Transcript/C. L. Paliwal.
103. DA/Confidential/Education/1930/5B.
104. FR5/4/1930.
105. NA/Home/Political/1930/256B.
106. DA/Confidential/Education/1930/5B.
107. DA/Home/Political/1930/256/I KW.

108. DA/Confidential/Education/1930/5B.
109. DA/Confidential/Education/1930/5B.
110. NMML/transcript/B. K. Chandiwala.
111. NMML/transcript/P. C. Jain.
112. *The Graphic*, 26/3/1932.
113. "Lady Picketers Arrested," *Hindustan Times*, 5/2/1932.
114. Cited in NMML/AICC/G94/1930/Part 1.
115. NMML/AICC/G94/1930/Part 1.
116. NA/Home(Political)/1924/284.
117. DA/Transcript/K. D. Kohli.
118. NMML/Transcript/C. N. Paliwal.
119. Personal interview with Roop Narain, 6/6/2001.
120. FR 6/6/1930.
121. NA/Home(Political)/1930/432.
122. NA/Home(Political)/1930/432.
123. NMML/AICC/G94/1930/Part 1.
124. NMML/AICC/G94/1930/Part 1.
125. NMML/Transcript/B. K. Chandiwala.
126. NMML/Transcript/P. C. Jain.
127. NMML/Transcript/B. K. Chandiwala.
128. NMML/Transcript/P. C. Jain.
129. FR 18/8/1930.
130. NMML/CID/IX/83; NMML/CID/V/58; NMML/CID/IX/41.
131. NA/Home(Political)/1930/432.
132. FR 18/8/1930.
133. NA/Home(Political)/1930/432.
134. NA/Home(Political)/1930/432.

**CHAPTER 4. THE GURDWARA SISGANJ**

1. NMML/Transcript/S. Singh.
2. Personal interview with Kushwant Singh, 30/4/2001.
3. FR 19/5/1930.
4. DA/Confidential/1930/24C.
5. NMML/AICC/G94/1930/Part 1.
6. DA/Confidential/1930/24C.
7. NMML/Transcript/G. Rai.
8. DA/Home/Confidential/1930/55B.
9. FR 19/5/1930.
10. NMML/AICC/G94/1930/Part 1.
11. NA/Home/Political/1930/256/I.
12. DA/Home/Confidential/1930/55B.
13. DA/Home/Confidential/1930/55B.
14. DA/Confidential/Home/1930/54B.
15. DA/Confidential/Home/1930/54B.

16. DA/Confidential/Home/1930/54B.
17. DA/Confidential/Home/1930/54B.
18. DA/Home/Confidential/1930/55B.
19. DA/Home/Confidential/1927/18B.
20. NA/Home/Public/1931/119/I.
21. DA/Home/Confidential/1930/55B.
22. DA/Home/Confidential/1930/55B
23. DA/Home/Confidential/1930/55B.
24. DA/Home/Confidential/1930/53B.
25. NA/Home/Public/1931/119/I.
26. DA/Home/Confidential/1930/53B.
27. DA/Home/Confidential/1930/53B.
28. DA/Home/Confidential/1930/53B.
29. DA/Confidential/Home/1930/54B.
30. DA/Confidential/Home/1930/54B.
31. NA/Home/Public/1931/119/I.
32. DA/Home/Confidential/1930/53B.
33. NA/Home/Public/1931/119/I.
34. DA/Home/Confidential/1930/53B.
35. DA/Confidential/Home/1930/54B.
36. DA/Confidential/1934/9B.
37. NA/Home/Political/1931/119/II.
38. NA/Home/Political/1931/119/II.
39. DA/Home(Political)/1931/119/II.
40. NA/Home/Political/1931/119/II.
41. NMML/CID/VIII/296.
42. NA/Home/Political/1932/5/78.
43. DA/CC/Home(Misc)Confidential/1932/1(26)B.
44. "Maulana Azad Arrested," *Hindustan Times*, 14/3/1932.
45. DA/CC/Home(Misc)Confidential/1932/1(26)B.
46. DA/CC/Home(Misc)Confidential/1932/1(26)B.
47. *Legislative Assembly Debates*, 14 March 1932, 1985–2008.
48. NMML/CID/III/12.
49. NMML/CID/IX/371.
50. DA/cc/Home(Misc)Confidential/1932/1(26)B.
51. FR 15/12/1931.
52. NMML/CID/IX/371.

**CHAPTER 5. URBAN CONFLICT AND COLLABORATION**

1. FR 15/6/1934, 30/6/1934, 16/7/1934.
2. NMML/Transcript/P. C. Jain.
3. NA/Home/Politics/1936/4/19/36.
4. NA/Home/Politics/1936/4/19/36.

5. NMML/CID/X/48.
6. NMML/Transcript/B. K. Chandiwala.
7. FR 15/12/1934.
8. FR 16/3/1934.
9. FR 15/10/1934.
10. FR 31/12/1935.
11. FR 3/4/1936.
12. NMML/Delhi CID/IX/98/1939.
13. FR 2/2 September 1938.
14. FRS January 1938–December 1939.
15. NA/Home/Political/1936/22/86/36.
16. DA/Confidential/1938/83C.
17. NMML/CID/IX/31.
18. FR 1/2 and 2/2 March 1938; NA/Home/Political/1938/45/3/38.
19. NA/Home/Political/1938/45/3/38.
20. NMML/CID/X/47.
21. NA/Reforms/1932/117/5/32-R.
22. NMML/CID/X/47.
23. NMML/CID/X/47. The Andaman Islands had been used as a penal colony by the British and had held many prosecuted nationalists.
24. NA/Home/Political/1938/45/3/38.
25. FR 2/2 June 1938.
26. DA/Confidential (Confidential)/1938/44C.
27. FRS January 1938–December 1939.
28. "Delhi Hartal leads to 69 Arrests," *Hindustan Times*, 23/7/1938.
29. NA/Home/Political/1938/5/11/38.
30. FR 1/2 and 2/2 August 1938; NA/Home/Political/1938/22/54/38.
31. "Satyagraha in Delhi," *Hindustan Times*, 10/8/1938
32. "Repression in Delhi," *Hindustan Times*, 26/8/1938. The trope of an autocratic New Delhi in an increasingly democratic world would be resurrected in the 1940s; see item "5," *Janata*, 18/8/1946.
33. DA/Confidential/Home(Misc)/1937/1(10)C.
34. NA/Home/Political/1937/24/13.
35. NA/Home/Political/1937/24/13.
36. FR 15 April 1937.
37. NA/Home/Political/1937/24/13.
38. Legislative Assembly Debates, 2 April 1937, 2565–73, 2605–27.
39. Clipping in NA/Home/Political/1937/24/13. "Pinchbeck" meant that something was false or cheap.
40. NA/Home/Political/1937/24/13.
41. NA/Home/Political/1937/24/13.
42. NA/Home/Political/1937/24/13.
43. FR 31/5/1936.
44. NMML/Delhi/CID/VIII/139.

45. FR 15/7/1936.
46. DA CC/LSG/1938/608.
47. NMML/CID/IX/18.
48. NMML/CID/1938/IX/152.
49. NMML/CID/IX/98.
50. FR 1/2 May 1938.
51. NMML/CID/IX/98.
52. FR 1/2 June 1938.
53. FR 2/2 December 1938, 1/2 January 1939.
54. FR 2/2 May 1939.
55. FR 1/2 July 1939.
56. For comparable studies, see Joshi (2003) on Kanpur and Nair (1998) on Princely Mysore.
57. FR 30/6/1934.
58. FR 30/4/1935.
59. DA/CC/Industrial/1934/68B.
60. NMML/Delhi CID/VIII/92/Vol. 2; FR 15/9/1935.
61. DA/DC/1922/24.
62. FR 31/12/1935.
63. NMML/Delhi/CID/III/81.
64. DA/DC/1922/24.
65. DA/DC/1922/24.
66. NMML/Delhi CID/IX/18.
67. FR 19/12/1937.
68. FR 1/2 December 1937.
69. NMML/Delhi CID/IX/18.
70. FR 1/2 January 1938.
71. NMML/Delhi CID/IX/18.
72. NMML/CID/VIII/424.
73. NMML/CID/IX/31.
74. On village politics around Delhi, see Dhanedhar (2011).
75. NMML/CID/IX/31.
76. Legislative Assembly Debates, 2 February 1938, 229–31.
77. NMML/CID/IX/31. The entire account in this paragraph and the next are from this file.
78. FR 1/2 July 1939.
79. NMML/CID/IX/18.
80. NMML/CID/IX/18.
81. FR 1/2 January 1940; NMML/CID/1939/IX/108.
82. NMML/Delhi CID/IX/18.
83. NA/Home/Political/1940/3/13/40.

## CHAPTER 6. QUIT DELHI

1. For the pledge individual satyagrahis had to sign, see Chandiwala (1954), 126–27.

2. NMML/CID/1939/IX/108.
3. NA/Home/Political(I)/1941/137/41.
4. NA/Home/Political(I)/1943/3/7/43.
5. NMML/CID/1942/III/8.
6. FR 1/2 and 2/2 March, 1/2 April 1940.
7. NMML/CID/1940/VIII/193.
8. NMML/Transcript/R. Raman.
9. FR 2/2 November 1940.
10. "Congress Leaders Arrested," *Hindustan Times*, 1/12/1940.
11. Interview conducted on 6/6/2001: Narain was a Delhi-based Gandhian congressman and was active in the 1940s.
12. DA/Home/Political(I)/1941/3/3/1941.
13. CSAS/Transcript/Y. Singh.
14. DA/DC/1941/338.
15. FR 1/2 June 1941.
16. FR 1/2 December 1941; FR 1/2 January 1942.
17. FR 2/2 January 1942.
18. NMML/AICC/1942–46/P8.
19. FR 1/2 February 1942.
20. FR 2/2 March 1942.
21. FR 2/2 March 1942.
22. FR 1/2 April 1942.
23. FR 1/2 May 1942.
24. FR 2/2 July 1942.
25. FR 2/2 November 1942.
26. CSAS/Transcript/J. K. Khanna.
27. NMML/Transcript/P. C. Jain.
28. NMML/Transcript/P. C. Jain.
29. FR August 1942.
30. "Delhi Leaders Arrested," *Hindustan Times*, 10/8/1942.
31. NA/Home/Political/1942/3/30/42.
32. FR August 1942.
33. NMML/CID/IX/574.
34. FR August 1942.
35. NMML/CID/VIII/141/Vol. II.
36. NMML/CID/IX/574.
37. FR August 1942.
38. NA/Home/Political/1942/3/30/42; FR August 1942.
39. *The Statesman*, 11/8/1942.
40. FR August 1942.
41. FR August 1942.
42. BL/IOR/Eur.Mss/F161/786.
43. FR August 1942.
44. DA/DC/1942/381.
45. Interviews conducted on 8/5/2001 with Dharmendra Nath, a Delhi historian

whose mother was arrested for political activity in the 1930s, and on 6/6/2001 with Roop Narain, a Delhi-based Gandhian congressman who was active in the 1940s.

46. Confirmed in NMML/Transcript/B. K. Chandiwala.
47. "Crowds Set Fire to Delhi Buildings," *Hindustan Times*, 12/8/1942.
48. BL/IOR/Eur.Mss/F161/786.
49. FR August 1942.
50. DA/DC/1942/381.
51. FR August 1942.
52. BL/IOR/Eur.Mss/F161/786; "Crowds Set Fire to Delhi Buildings," *Hindustan Times*, 12/8/1942.
53. NMML/Transcript/P. C. Jain.
54. FR August 1942.
55. FR August 1942.
56. "Crowds Set Fire to Delhi Buildings," *Hindustan Times*, 12/8/1942.
57. FR August 1942.
58. FR August 1942.
59. NA/Home(Political)/1942/3/30/42.
60. FR August 1942; DA/DC/1942/40.
61. "Fire Opened Five Times in Delhi," *Hindustan Times*, 13/8/1942.
62. "Improvement in Situation in Delhi," *Hindustan Times*, 14/8/1942.
63. NMML/Delhi CID/VIII/141/Vol. II.
64. DA/DC/1942/381.
65. NMML/Delhi CID/VIII/141/Vol. II.
66. FR August 1942.
67. NMML/Transcript/B. K. Chandiwala.
68. BL/IOR/L/P&J/12/484.
69. FR 1/2 September 1942.
70. DA/DC/1942/381.
71. FR 2/2 September 1942.
72. BL/IOR/L/P&J/12/484.
73. NMML/CID/VIII/141/Vol. II.
74. NMML/CID/1942/IX/279.
75. NA/Home(Political)/1942/3/30/42; *The Statesman*, 11/8/1942.
76. *Hindustan Times*, 11/8/1942.
77. NMML/CID/IX/13.
78. Interview with Vishwa Bandhu Gupta, 25/5/2001.
79. Interview with Rajmohan Gandhi, 2/6/2001.
80. FR 1/2 September 1942.
81. NMML/CID/1942/III/44.
82. NMML/CID/1942/VIII/141/Vol. II.
83. NMML/Transcript/M. Shah.
84. NMML/Transcript/R. P. Puri.
85. NMML/Transcript/M. Shah.
86. Translated by Ragini Jha.

87. NMML/Transcript/R. P. Puri.
88. NMML/Transcript/M. Shah.
89. DA/DC/1942/381.
90. NMML/Transcript/J. K. Khanna.
91. NMML/Transcript/P. C. Jain.
92. NMML Transcript/B. K. Chandiwala.
93. NMML/Transcript/P. C. Jain.
94. CSAS/Transcript/J. K. Khanna.
95. NMML/Transcript/P. C. Jain.
96. NMML/Transcript/M. Shah.
97. NMML/CID/1942/VIII/141/Vol. II.
98. NA/Home(Political)/1942/3/34/42.
99. CSAS/Transcript/S. C. Gupta.
100. NMML/CID/VIII/141/Vol. II.
101. "Koi Hai?," *Janata*, 17/2/1946.
102. NA/Home(Political)/1942/3/34/42.
103. FR 2/2 September 1942.
104. NMML/CID/1942/VIII/141/Vol. II.
105. NMML/CID/1942/III/8.
106. NMML/Transcript/P. C. Jain.
107. NMML/Transcript/M. Shah.
108. NMML/CID/1942/VIII/141/Vol. II.
109. NMML/CID/VIII/196.
110. FR 1/2 March 1943.
111. NMML/CID/IX/601.
112. DA/DC/1942/40.
113. Calculated using the National Archives currency convertor, accessed 1/3/2022: https://www.nationalarchives.gov.uk/currency-converter/.
114. For a comparable study of Quit India violence in Isoor and the representational challenges it posed to Congress, see Nair (2007).
115. DA/DC/1942/381.
116. NMML/CID/VIII/141/Vol. II.
117. "Crowds Set Fire to Delhi Buildings," *Hindustan Times*, 12/8/1942.
118. *The Statesman*, 13/8/1942.
119. NA/Delhi Court Papers/Serial 3/Crown vs Feroz Uddin and Jagat Singh.
120. NMML/Transcript/P. C. Jain.
121. CSAS/Transcript/J. N. Sahni.
122. NA/Delhi Court Papers/Serial 3/Crown vs Feroz Uddin and Jagat Singh.
123. BL/IOR/Eur.Mss/F161/786.
124. NA/Delhi Court Papers/Serial 3/Crown vs Feroz Uddin and Jagat Singh.
125. This was repeated in NMML/Transcripts/P. C. Jain.
126. "Crowds Set Fire to Delhi Buildings," *Hindustan Times*, 12/8/1942.
127. DA/Confidential/1942/128/42C.
128. DA/Confidential/1942/128/42C.

129. DA/Confidential/1942/128/42C.
130. DA/Confidential/1942/128/42C.
131. FR August 1942.

**CHAPTER 7. THE UNDERGROUND**

1. NMML/Transcript/P. C. Jain.
2. NMML/Transcript/P. C. Jain.
3. Interview conducted on 6/6/2001.
4. NMML/CID/1942/VIII/141/Vol. II.
5. NMML/Transcript/J. K. Khanna.
6. NMML/Transcript/J. K. Khanna.
7. NMML/Transcript/R. P. Puri.
8. Interview with Kushwant Singh, 30/4/2001. His younger brother had collaborated with Aruna Asaf Ali.
9. NMML/Transcript/G. Rai.
10. NMML/Transcript/M. Shah.
11. NMML/Delhi CID/1942/III/44.
12. NMML/Delhi CID/1942/III/44.
13. NMML/Transcript/M. L. Parashar.
14. NMML/CID/1942/III/44.
15. NMML/Transcript/P. C. Jain.
16. NMML/CID/1942/III/43.
17. NMML/Transcripts/P. C. Jain.
18. NMML/CID/1942/III/44.
19. DA/Transcripts/S.N. Banerjee.
20. Interview with Professor Azra, 14/6/2001.
21. NMML/CID/1942/III/44.
22. NMML/CID/1942/III/44; repeated in NMML/CID/1941/IX/66.
23. Interview with Dr. Sarup Singh on 2/5/2001.
24. NMML/CID/1942/III/44.
25. NMML/Transcript/J. K. Khanna.
26. On his activities as a secret messenger in Delhi, codename "Santosh," see Jain (2010, 31).
27. NMML/CID/1942/III/44.
28. NMML/Transcript/K. A. Desai.
29. NMML/Transcript/R. P. Puri.
30. NMML/CID/1942/III/44.
31. NMML/Transcript/R. P. Puri.
32. NMML/Transcript/R. P. Puri.
33. NMML/CID/1942/III/44.
34. NMML/Transcript/P. C. Jain.
35. NMML/Transcript/P. C. Jain.
36. FR 2/2 November 1942.
37. NMML/Transcript/C. K. Nair.

38. NMML/CID/1935/VIII/424.
39. NMML/Transcript/ J. K. Khanna.
40. CSAS/Transcript/C. K. Nair.
41. NMML/Delhi CID/1942/III/44.
42. CSAS /Transcript/C. K. Nair.
43. NMML/Delhi CID/1942/III/44.
44. NMML/Delhi CID/1942/III/44.
45. NMML/Delhi CID/1942/III/44.
46. NMML/Transcript/C. K. Nair.
47. NMML/Transcript/J. K. Khanna.
48. FR 1/2 October 1942.
49. NMML/Delhi CID/1942/III/44.
50. NMML/CID/1937/IX/31.
51. NMML/CID/1942/III/44.
52. NMML/Delhi CID/VIII/196; also see NMML/Transcript/P. C. Jain.
53. FR 1/2 November 1942.
54. NMML/CID/1942/III/44.
55. NMML/CID/1942/III/44.
56. NMML/Transcript/C. K. Nair.
57. CSAS/Transcript/C. K. Nair.
58. CSAS/Transcript/C. K. Nair.
59. NA/Home/Political(Internal)/1943/3/32/43.
60. CSAS/Transcript/C. K. Nair.
61. NA/Home/Political(Internal)/1943/3/32/43.
62. NMML/CID/1942/III/8.
63. NMML/Delhi CID/VIII/141/Vol. II.
64. NMML/CID/1942/III/43.
65. FR 1/2 November 1942.
66. NMML/Delhi CID/VIII/196.
67. NMML/CID/VIII/141/Vol. II.
68. FR 1/2 December 1942.
69. NMML/CID/III/8.
70. NMML/CID/VIII/141/Vol. II.
71. NMML/Transcript/M. Shah.
72. FR 1/2 January 1943.
73. NMML/CID/IX 28/CON/159.
74. NMML/CID/VIII/290.
75. NMML/CID/VIII/290.
76. NA/Home/Political/1943/3/58/43.
77. FR 2/2 January 1943.
78. NMML/Delhi CID/VIII/196.
79. "Mrs Aruna Asaf Ali Arrives in Delhi: Rousing Reception by Citizens," *Hindustan Times*, 3/2/1946.
80. NMML/Delhi CID/VIII/196.
81. FR 2/2 March 1943.

82. NMML/Transcript/R. P. Puri and M. K. Johry.
83. FR 1/2 February 1943.
84. "Immediate Release of Gandhiji: Secretariat Staff's Demand," *Hindustan Times*, 23/2/1943.
85. FR 2/2 March 1943.
86. DA/Confidential/1943/35/43C.
87. NMML/Transcript/R. Raman.
88. NMML/Transcript/J. K. Khanna.
89. NMML/Transcript/M. Shah.

**CHAPTER 8. VICTORY?**

1. NMML/CID/III/8.
2. NMML/CID/III/6. The quotation is from Whitman's 1860 poem "To You."
3. NMML/CID/III/6.
4. *Janata* 21/4/1946.
5. NMML/CID/III/19. On the Muslim League as reactionary, see Asaf Ali's "The Counter-Revolutionaries," *Janata*, 3/11/1946.
6. NMML/CID//III/19.
7. "Arrests and Searches in Several Towns," *Hindustan Times*, 26/1/1944.
8. FR 2/2 January 1944.
9. FR 2/2 March 1944.
10. FR 2/2 April 1944.
11. FR 1/2 May and 1/2 June 1944.
12. FR 1/2 July 1944.
13. FR 2/2 January 1945.
14. NMML/CID/IX/66.
15. "British Rule in India About to End," *Hindustan Times*, 4/11/1945.
16. "INA Snippets," *Hindustan Times*, 6/11/1945.
17. "Conflict with Police Inadvisable," *Hindustan Times*, 27/11/1945.
18. NA/Home/Poll(I)/1945/21/19/45.
19. NA/Home/Poll(I)/1947/28/5/47.
20. NA/Home/Poll(I)/1946/22/50/46.
21. NMML/CID/IX/14.
22. NMML/CID/IX/167.
23. "Orders for the Arrest of Congress Seva Dal Workers," *Hindustan* (translated), 2/3/1946.
24. NA/Home/Poll(I)/1947/28/5/47.
25. NMML/CID/VIII/285; FR 1/2 January 1946.
26. FR 1/2 February 1946.
27. "Delhi Congress Leader's Appeal," *Hindustan Times*, 25/1/1946.
28. *Hindustan Times Weekly*, 27/1/1946.
29. A/DC/1942/273.
30. "Mrs Aruna Asaf Ali Arrives in Delhi: Rousing Reception by Citizens," *Hindustan Times*, 3/2/1946.

31. FR 1/2 February 1946.
32. NMML/CID/IX/71.
33. Personal interview with Subhadra Joshi, June 2001.
34. "Congress Will Not Take Part in Victory Program," *Hindustan* (translated), 27/2/1946.
35. DA/Confidential/CID Office Special Branch/1946/6/13/46.
36. DA/Confidential/1946/39/46C.
37. DA/Confidential/1946/40/1/46.
38. Personal interview with Anand Gupta, 21/5/2001.
39. "Strikes, Demonstrations and Firing in Delhi on Victory Day," *Hindustan* (translation), 8/3/1946.
40. "5 Killed in Delhi's Victory Day Firings," *Hindustan Times*, 8/3/1946; "Strikes, Demonstrations and Firing in Delhi on Victory Day," *Hindustan* (translation), 8/3/1946.
41. FR 1/2 March 1942.
42. "Don't Go on Strike," *Hindustan* (translated), 8/3/1946.
43. DA/Confidential/1946/98/46C.
44. DA/Confidential/1947/33/47C.
45. *Janata*, 17/3/1946.
46. DA/Confidential/1946/48/46C.
47. "Political Hunger Strikers Tear Gassed," *Hindustan Times*, 23/3/1946; DA/Confidential 1946 40/1/46C.
48. DA/Confidential 1946 40/1/46C.
49. "2000 Delhi Policemen on Hunger Strike," *Hindustan Times*, 22/3/1946.
50. DA/Confidential/1946 48/46C. See Davies (2013) for the similarity to explanations given for the Bombay revolt.
51. Legislative Assembly Debates, 25/3/1946, 2878, 2880.
52. FR 1/2 July 1947.
53. "End of a Political Order," *Janata*, 6/7/1947. Asaf Ali was publishing under her name in this paper, but this piece chimes with her other writings; AG could represent Aruna Ganguli, her birth name.
54. Aruna Asaf Ali, "Village Communities," *Janata*, 23/6/1946.

**CHAPTER 9. CONCLUSIONS**

1. CSAS/Transcript/S. C. Gupta.

# SOURCES AND ARCHIVAL REFERENCING

#### ARCHIVES

BL/IOR: British Library, London, India Office Records
/Eur.Mss: European Manuscripts
DA: Delhi State Archives, New Delhi
/CC: Chief Commissioner's files
/DC: Deputy Commissioner's files
NA: National Archives of India, New Delhi
NMML: Nehru Memorial Museum and Library

#### FORTNIGHTLY REPORTS

These were issued by the chief commissioner based on police and CID reports. They varied in nature from earlier handwritten reports, from 1914, to systematized reports for the first and second fortnight of the month from 1917 onward. These are referenced as "FR" by date up to December 1937 and henceforth as either 1/2 (first fortnight) or 2/2 (second fortnight) by month (a joint report for the month of August 1942 was issued). The reports were consulted in the Delhi State Archives with supplementary reports consulted in the National Archives of India and the British Library India Office Records.

#### ORAL HISTORY TRANSCRIPTS

Nehru Memorial Museum and Library, New Delhi, Oral History Project Transcripts
NMML/Transcript:
/M. Bai
233 (Hindi): Smt Memo Bai, interviewed by Dr. Hari Dev Sharma, 30/1/1970
/B. K. Chandiwala
381 (Hindi): Braj Krishan Chandiwala, interviewed by Dr. Hari Dev Sharma, 15/2/1968
/K. A. Desai
249: Shri K. A. Desai, interviewed by Dr. Hari Dev Sharma, 1/1/1967
/P. C. Jain

479 (Hindi): Shri Phool Chand Jain, interviewed by Dr. Hari Dev Sharma, 9/6/1971
/M. K. Johry
244 (Hindi): Magan Kishore Johry, interviewed by Dr. Hari Dev Sharma, 19/8/1975
/J. K. Khanna
177: Shri Jugal Kishore Khanna, interviewed by Dr. Hari Dev Sharma, 8/2/1969
/K. D. Kohli
862: Shri Krishan Das Kohli, interviewed by Shri S. L. Manchanda, 29/8/1989
/H Mehta
41: Smt Hansa Mehta, 21/9/1972
/C. K. Nair
264: Shri C. K. Nair, interviewed by Dr. Hari Dev Sharma, 25/11/1969
/C. L. Paliwal
357: Shri C. L. Paliwai, interviewed by Shri S. L. Manchanda, 6/1/1978
/M. L. Parashah
202: Shri M. L. Parishah, interviewed by Dr. Hari Dev Sharma, 3/9/1971
/R. P. Puri
207: Shri R. P. Puri, interviewed by Dr. Hari Dev Sharma, 22/6/1971
/G Rai
330: Shri Ganpat Rai, interviewed by Shri S. L. Manchanda, 7/7/1974
/R Raman
80: Shri Radha Raman, recorded 18/8/1967
/S Singh
6: Shri Sobha Singh, recorded 25/11/1968
/M Shah
328: Shri Manubhai Shah, interviewed by Mrs. Aparna Basu, 19/6/1968

Delhi State Archives, New Delhi, Oral History Transcripts
DA/Transcript:
K. D. Kohli
38: Shri Krishan Das Kohli, interviewed by Mrs. D. Pakrashi, 23/10/1989
S. N. Banerjee
78: Shri S. N. Banerjee, interviewed by his son on 24/3/1995

Centre for South Asian Studies, University of Cambridge, Oral History Interviews
CSAS/Transcript:
S. C. Gupta
228: Shiv Charan Gupta, interviewed by Uma Shankar, 23/8/1991
J. K. Khanna
207: Jugal Kishore Khanna, interviewed by Uma Shankar, 10/5/1975
B. C. Lal
210: Bhikshu Chaman Lal, interviewed by Uma Shankar, 19/8/1975
C. K. Nair
200: C Krishna Nair, interviewed by Uma Shankar, 25/7/1974

C. L. Paliwal
   195: Chiranjilal Paliwal, interviewed by Uma Shankar, 11/4/1974
J. N. Sahni
   203: J. N. Sahni, interviewed by Uma Shankar, 26/8/1974
Y. Singh
   206: Dr Yudhvir Singh, interviewed by Uma Shankar, 5/4/1975

# REFERENCES

Afary, Janet, and Kevin B. Anderson. 2010. *Foucault and the Iranian Revolution*. Chicago: University of Chicago Press.
Agnew, John. 2004. "Nationalism." In *Companion to Cultural Geography*, edited by James Duncan, Nuala Johnson, and Rick Schein, 223–37. Oxford: Blackwell.
Amin, Shahid. (1995) 2006. *Event, Metaphor, Memory: Chauri Chaura, 1922–1992*. Berkeley: University of California Press.
Andersen, Walter. 1972. "The Rashtriya Swayamsevak Sangh: III: Participation in Politics." *Economic and Political Weekly* 7(13): 673–82.
Anderson, Benedict. (1983) 2006. *Imagined Communities: Reflections on the Origin and Spread of Nationalism*. London: Verso.
Anderson, Clare. 2012. *Subaltern Lives: Biographies of Colonialism in the Indian Ocean world, 1790–1920*. Cambridge: Cambridge University Press.
Andrews, Charles Freer. 1929. *Zaka Ullah of Delhi*. Cambridge: W. Heffer & Sons.
Arnold, David. 2001. *Gandhi*. Longman: Harlow.
Asaf Ali, Aruna. 1947. *Travel Talk: Being the Collection of Articles from "Janata" Delhi*. Aundh: Aundh Publishing Trust.
Asaf Ali, Aruna. 1977. "Remembering a Brave Fighter." In Vachaspati, *Delhi's Joan of Arc*, n.p.
Asaf Ali, Aruna. 2006. "Looking Back on August 1942." In *Aruna Asaf Ali*, edited by National Federation of Indian Women, 30–32. New Delhi: National Federation of Indian Women.
Asaf Ali, Mohammad. 1921. *Constructive Non-cooperation*. Madras: Ganesh.
Bakshi, S. R. 1994. *Struggle for Independence: Aruna Asaf Ali*. New Delhi: Anmol.
Banerjee, Prathama. 2021. *Elementary Aspects of the Political: Histories from the Global South*. Durham, N.C.: Duke University Press.
Barnett, Clive. 2015. "On Problematization: Elaborations on a Theme in 'Late Foucault.'" Nonsite.org, Articles 16 (June 22). https://nonsite.org/on-problematization/.
Barrett, Jenny. 2020. "Counter-conduct and Its Intra-modern Limits." *Global Society* 34(2): 260–84.
Baul, Deepasri. 2020. "The Improbability of a Temple: Hindu Mobilization and Urban Space in the Delhi Shiv Mandir Agitation of 1938." *Studies in History* 36(2): 230–50.

Beckingham, David, and Jake Hodder. 2022. "Historical Geographies: Geographical Antagonism and Archives." In *Handbook of Methodologies in Human Geography*, edited by Sarah A. Lovell, Stephanie E. Coen, and Mark W. Rosenberg, 173–82. London: Routledge.

Beverley, Eric Lewis. 2011. "Colonial Urbanism and South Asian Cities." *Social History* 36(4): 482–97.

Bhattacharyya, Debjani. 2021. "The Indian City and Its 'Restive Publics.'" *Modern Asian Studies* 55(2): 665–95.

Binkley, Sam, and Barbara Cruikshank. 2016. "Introduction: Counter-conduct." *Foucault Studies* 21: 3–6.

Blake, Stephen. 1991. *Shahjahanabad: The Sovereign City in Mughal India, 1639–1739*. Cambridge: Cambridge University Press.

Blaut, James M. 1987. *The National Question: Decolonising the Theory of Nationalism*. London: Zed.

Bobb, Dilip, and Narayani Gupta. 2007. *Delhi, Then and Now*. Delhi: Roli.

Bose, Sugata. 2003. "Post-colonial Histories of South Asia: Some Reflections." *Journal of Contemporary History* 38(1): 133–46.

Bose, Sugata, and Ayesha Jalal. 1998. *Modern South Asia: History, Culture, Political Economy*. London: Routledge.

Brigstocke, Julian. 2013. "Artistic Parrhesia and the Genealogy of Ethics in Foucault and Benjamin." *Theory, Culture and Society* 30(1): 57–78. doi: 10.1177/0263276412450467.

Busteed, M. A. 2009. "Nationalism, Historical Geography of." In Kitchin and Thrift, *International Encyclopedia of Human Geography*, 255–60.

Butler, Judith. 2009. *Giving an Account of Oneself*. New York: Fordham University Press.

Census of India, 1931. 1933a. *Volume XVI: Delhi*. Lahore: Civil and Military Gazette Press.

Census of India, 1931. 1933b. *Volume XVII: Punjab, Part II, Tables*. Lahore: Civil and Military Gazette Press.

Chakrabarty, Bidyut. 1992. "Political Mobilization in the Localities: The 1942 Quit India Movement in Midnapur." *Modern Asian Studies* 26(4): 791–814.

Chakrabarty, Dipesh. 2007. "'In the Name of Politics': Democracy and the Power of the Multitude in India." *Public Culture* 19(1): 35–57.

Chandavarkar, Rajnarayan. 1998. *Imperial Power and Popular Politics: Class, Resistance and the State in India, c. 1850–1950*. Cambridge: Cambridge University Press.

Chandiwala, Brijkrishna. 1954. *At the Feet of Bapu*. Ahmedabad: Navajivan.

Chari, Sharad, and Samera Esmeir. 2021. "Introduction: The Anticolonial Impulse." *Critical Times* 3: 353–58.

Chatterjee, Partha. 1986. *Nationalist Thought and the Colonial World: A Derivative Discourse?* London: Zed / United Nations University.

Chatterjee, Partha. (1991) 2010. "Whose Imagined Community?" In *Empire and Nation: Selected Essays*, 23–36. New York: Columbia University Press.

Chatterjee, Partha. 1992. "A Religion of Urban Domesticity: Sri Ramakrishna and the Calcutta Middle Class." In *Subaltern Studies: Writings on South Asian History and Society*, vol. 7, edited by Partha Chatterjee and Gyanendra Pandey, 40–68. Delhi: Oxford University Press.

Chatterjee, Partha. 1993. *The Nation and Its Fragments: Colonial and Postcolonial Histories*. Princeton, N.J.: Princeton University Press.

Chatterjee, Partha. 2004. *The Politics of the Governed: Reflections on Popular Politics in Most of the World*. New York: Columbia University Press.

Chatterjee, Srilata. 2002. *Congress Politics in Bengal, 1919–1939*. London: Anthem.

Chatterji, Joya. 2013. "Nationalisms in India, 1857–1947." In *The Oxford Handbook of the History of Nationalism*, edited by John Breuilly, 242–62. Oxford: Oxford University Press.

Chaudhuri, Nirad C. 1987. *Thy Hand, Great Anarch! India: 1921–1952*. Reading, Mass.: Addison-Wesley.

Chopra, P. N., ed. 1976. *Quit India Movement: British Secret Report*. Faridabad: Thomson.

Chopra, Prabha. 1974. *Who's Who of Delhi Freedom Fighters*. Delhi: Delhi Administration.

Closs Stephens, Angharad. 2013. *The Persistence of Nationalism: From Imagined Communities to Urban Encounters*. London: Routledge.

Cohen, Lara Langer. 2022. *Going Underground: Race, Space, and the Subterranean in the Nineteenth-Century United States*. Durham, N.C.: Duke University Press.

Coleman, Mathew. 2009. "Sovereignty." In Kitchin and Thrift, *International Encyclopedia of Human Geography*, 255–61.

Cornell, Drucilla, and Stephen D. Seely. 2016. *The Spirit of Revolution: Beyond the Dead Ends of Man*. Cambridge: Wiley.

Dalrymple, William. 2006. *The Last Mughal: The Fall of a Dynasty, Delhi, 1857*. London: Bloomsbury.

Dalton, Dennis. 2013. *Mahatma Gandhi: Nonviolent Power in Action*. New York: Columbia University Press.

Das, Veena. 1995. *Critical Events: An Anthropology of Perspective on Contemporary India*. Delhi: Oxford University Press.

Datta, Anjali Bhardwaj. 2019a. "Genealogy of a Partition City: War, Migration and Urban Space in Delhi." *South Asia: Journal of South Asian Studies* 42(1): 152–69.

Datta, Anjali Bhardwaj. 2019b. " 'Useful'and 'Earning' Citizens? Gender, State, and the Market in Post-colonial Delhi." *Modern Asian Studies* 53(6): 1924–55.

Davidson, Arnold I. 2011. "In Praise of Counter-conduct." *History of the Human Sciences* 24(4): 25–41.

Davies, Andrew. 2013. "From 'Landsman' to 'Seaman'? Colonial Discipline, Organisation and Resistance in the Royal Indian Navy, 1946." *Social and Cultural Geography* 14(8): 868–87.

Davies, Andrew. 2019. *Geographies of Anticolonialism: Political Networks across and beyond South India, c. 1900–1930*. London: John Wiley & Sons.

Dayal, Maheshwar. 1975. *Rediscovering Delhi: The Story of Shahjahanabad*. New Delhi: S. Chand.

De, Rohit, and Ornit Shani. 2024. "Assembling India's Constitution: Towards a New History." *Past and Present* 263(1): 205–48.

Dean, Mitchell, and Daniel Zamora. 2021. *The Last Man Takes LSD: Foucault and the End of Revolution*. London: Verso.

Delhi Administration. 1989. *Guide to the Records of the Delhi Administration*. Faridabad: Government of India Press.

Devji, Faisal. 2012. *The Impossible Indian: Gandhi and the Temptation of Violence*. London: Hurst.

Dhanedhar, Reva. 2011. *Struggle for Freedom: Role of Delhi, 1919–1934*. Dehra Dun: Natraj.

Dillon, Michael. 2017. "Political Spirituality: Parrhesia, Truth and Factual Finitude." In *Foucault and the Modern International*, edited by Philipp Bonditti, Didier Bigo, and Frédéric Gros, 79–96. New York: Palgrave Macmillan.

Disorders Inquiry Committee. 1920. *Evidence Taken before the Disorders Inquiry Committee*. Vol. I: *Delhi*. Calcutta: Superintendent Government Printing.

Duncan, James S. 1999. "Complicity and Resistance in the Colonial Archive: Some Issues of Method and Theory in Historical Geography." *Historical Geography* 27: 119–28.

Dyrberg, Torben. 2014. *Foucault on the Politics of Parrhesia*. Basingstoke: Palgrave Macmillan.

Elden, Stuart. 2016. *Foucault's Last Decade*. Cambridge: Polity.

Evans, Hubert. 1988. *Looking Back on India*. London: Frank Cass.

Farooqui, Mahmood. 2010. *Besieged: Voices from Delhi—1857*. New Delhi: Penguin.

Featherstone, David. 2012. *Solidarities: Hidden Histories and Geographies of Internationalism*. London: Zed.

Featherstone, David. 2019. "Reading Subaltern Studies Politically: Histories from Below, Spatial Relations, and Subalternity." In Jazeel and Legg, *Subaltern Geographies*, 94–119.

Ferrell, Donald W. 1971. "The Rowlatt Satyagraha in Delhi." In *Essays in Gandhian Politics: The Rowlatt Satyagraha of 1919*, edited by R. Kumar, 189–235. Oxford: Oxford University Press.

Ferretti, Federico. 2018. "Teaching Anarchist Geographies: Elisée Reclus in Brussels and 'the Art of Not Being Governed.'" *Annals of the American Association of Geographers* 108(1): 162–78.

Foucault, Michel. 1972. *The Archaeology of Knowledge and the Discourse on Language*. London: Tavistock.

Foucault, Michel. (1977–78) 2007. *Security, Territory, Population: Lectures at the Collège de France, 1977–78*. Translated by Graham Burchell. Basingstoke: Palgrave Macmillan.

Foucault, Michel. (1978–79) 2008. *The Birth of Biopolitics: Lectures at the Collège de France, 1978–79*. Translated by Graham Burchell. Edited by Michel Senelert. Basingstoke: Palgrave Macmillan.

Foucault, Michel. 1979. *The History of Sexuality*. Vol. 1: *The Will to Knowledge*. Translated by Robert Hurley. London: Allen Lane.

Foucault, Michel. (1979–80) 2014. *On the Government of the Living: Lectures at the Collège de France, 1979–1980*. Translated by Graham Burchell. Edited by Michel Sennelert. Basingstoke: Palgrave Macmillan.

Foucault, Michel. 1982. "The Subject and Power." In *Michel Foucault: Beyond Structur-

*alism and Hermeneutics*, edited by Herbert Dreyfus and Paul Rabinow, 208–26. Chicago: University of Chicago Press.

Foucault, Michel. (1982–83) 2010. *The Government of Self and Others: Lectures at the Collège de France, 1982–1983*. Basingstoke: Palgrave Macmillan.

Foucault, Michel. (1982–83) 2019. *"Discourse and Truth" and "Parresia."* Translated by Nancy Luxon. Edited by Daniele Lorenzini and Henri-Paul Fruchaud. Chicago: University of Chicago Press.

Foucault, Michel. (1983–84) 2011. *The Courage of Truth (the Government of Self and Others II): Lectures at the Collège de France, 1983–1984*. Basingstoke: Palgrave Macmillan.

Foucault, Michel. 1986a. *The History of Sexuality*. Vol. 2: *The Use of Pleasure*. London: Viking.

Foucault, Michel. 1986b. *The History of Sexuality*. Vol. 3: *Care of the Self*. London: Allen Lane.

Gandhi, Leela. 1996. "Concerning Violence: The Limits and Circulations of Gandhian 'Ahisma' or Passive Resistance." *Cultural Critique* 35: 105–47.

Gandhi, Mahatma. 1999. *The Collected Works of Mahatma Gandhi (Electronic Book)*. New Delhi: Publications Division, Government of India.

Gandhi, Mohandas Karamchand. (1909) 2009. "Hind Swaraj." In *"Hind Swaraj" and Other Writings*, edited by Antony J. Parel, 1–123. Cambridge: Cambridge University Press.

Gandhi, Mohandas Karamchand. (1927) 1948. *An Autobiography, or the Story of My Experiments with Truth*. Ahmedabad: Navajivan.

Getachew, Adom. 2019. *Worldmaking after Empire: The Rise and Fall of Self-Determination*. Princeton, N.J.: Princeton University Press.

Getachew, Adom, and Karuna Mantena. 2021. "Anticolonialism and the Decolonization of Political Theory." *Critical Times* 4: 359–88.

Ghosh, Nabaparna. 2020. *A Hygienic City-Nation: Space, Community, and Everyday Life in Colonial Calcutta*. Cambridge: Cambridge University Press.

Gidwani, Vinay. 2009. "Subalternity." In Kitchin and Thrift, *International Encyclopedia of Human Geography*, 65–71.

Gooptu, Nandini. 2001. *The Politics of the Urban Poor in Early Twentieth-Century India*. Cambridge: Cambridge University Press.

Gopinath, Ravindran, and Amar Farooqui. 2014. "The Political Restlessness of Aruna Asaf Ali." In *The Evolution of a Nation—Pre-colonial to Post-colonial: Essays in Memory of R. S. Sharma*, edited by D. N. Jha, 579–604. New Delhi: Manohar.

Goswami, Manu. 2005. "Autonomy and Comparability: Notes on the Anticolonial and the Postcolonial." *Boundary 2* 32(2): 201–25.

Gould, William. 2004. *Hindu Nationalism and the Language of Politics in Late Colonial India*. Cambridge: Cambridge University Press.

Gould, William. 2021. "Nationalisms and Their Discontents in Colonial India." In *Routledge Handbook of the History of Colonialism in South Asia*, edited by Harald Fischer-Tiné and Maria Framke, 48–61. London: Routledge.

Government of India (Secret). 1934. *Delhi Province Political "Who's Who."* New Delhi: Government of India Press.

Gros, Frédéric. 2019. "Introduction." In Foucault, *"Discourse and Truth" and "Parresia,"* edited by Daniele Lorenzini and Henri-Paul Fruchaud, xiii–xx.

Guha, Ranajit. 1982. "On Some Aspects of the Historiography of Colonial India." In *Subaltern Studies I*, edited by Ranajit Guha, 1–8. Delhi: Oxford University Press.

Guha, Ranajit. 1983a. *Elementary Aspects of Peasant Insurgency in Colonial India*. New Delhi: Oxford University Press.

Guha, Ranajit. 1983b. "The Prose of Counter-insurgency." In *Subaltern Studies II*, edited by Ranajit Guha, 1–42. Delhi: Oxford University Press.

Guha, Ranajit. 1997. *Dominance without Hegemony: History and Power in Colonial India*. Cambridge, Mass.: Harvard University Press.

Gupta, Anand. 1998a. "A Memorable Day in the Struggle against British Imperialism, Part I." *New Age Weekly* (August): 2–8.

Gupta, Anand. 1998b. "A Memorable Day in the Struggle against British Imperialism, Part II." *New Age Weekly* (August): 9–15.

Gupta, Narayani. 1981. *Delhi between Two Empires, 1803–1931: Society, Government and Urban Growth*. Delhi: Oxford University Press.

Gupta, Partha Sarathi. 1997. *Towards Freedom: Documents on the Movement for Independence in India, 1943–1944*. Oxford: Oxford University Press.

Gurdwara Sis-Ganj Firing Committee. 1930. *Report on the Firing into the Gurdwara Sisganj, Delhi on May 6th 1930*. Amritsar: Shiromani Gurdwara Parbandhak Committee.

Halperin, Rotem Geva. 2022. *Delhi Reborn: Partition and Nation Building in India's Capital*. Stanford, Calif.: Stanford University Press.

Harcourt, Bernard E. 2021. "Foucault's Keystone: Confessions of the Flesh." *Foucault Studies* 29: 48–70.

Hardiman, David. 2013. "Towards a History of Non-violent Resistance." *Economic and Political Weekly* 48: 41–48.

Hardiman, David. 2017. "Nonviolent Resistance in India, 1915–47." In *Non-violence in Modern Indian History*, edited by David Hardiman, 51–89. New Delhi: Orient Blackswan.

Hasan, Mushirul. 1995. *M. A. Ansari*. New Delhi: Publications Divison, Ministry of Information.

Haynes, Douglas. 1991. *Rhetoric and Ritual in Colonial India: The Shaping of a Public Culture in Surat City, 1852–1928*. Berkeley: University of California Press.

Haynes, Douglas E., and Nikhil Rao. 2013. "Beyond the Colonial City: Re-evaluating the Urban History of India, ca. 1920–1970." *South Asia: Journal of South Asian Studies* 36(3): 317–35.

Hobsbawm, E. (1973) 1994. *Revolutionaries*. London: Phoenix.

Howard, Veena Rani. 2013. *Gandhi's Ascetic Activism: Renunciation and Social Action*. New York: State University of New York Press.

Husain, Intizar. 2016. *Once There Was a City Named Dilli*. Translated by Ghazala Jamil and Faiz Ullah. New Delhi: Yoda Press.

Hussain, Nasser. 2003. *The Jurisprudence of Emergency: Colonialism and the Rule of Law*. Ann Arbor: University of Michigan Press.

INTACH Delhi Chapter. 1999. *Delhi, the Built Heritage: A Listing*. Vol. I. New Delhi: INTACH.

Jain, Lakshmi Chand. 2010. *Civil Disobedience: Two Freedom Struggles, One Life*. New Delhi: Book Review Literary Trust.
Jalal, Ayesha. 2000. *Self and Sovereignty: Individual and Community in South Asian Islam since 1850*. London: Routlege.
Jazeel, Tariq, and Stephen Legg, eds. 2019. *Subaltern Geographies*. Athens: University of Georgia Press.
Jones, Kenneth W. 1986. "Organised Hinduism in Delhi and New Delhi." In *Delhi through the Ages: Essays in Urban History, Culture, and Society*, edited by R. E. Frykenberg, 332–50. Delhi: Oxford University Press.
Joshi, Chitra. 2003. *Lost Worlds: Indian Labour and Its Forgotten Histories*. London: Anthem.
Kaicker, Abhishek. 2020. *The King and the People: Sovereignty and Popular Politics in Mughal Delhi*. Oxford: Oxford University Press.
Kapila, Shruti. 2021. *Violent Fraternity: Indian Political Thought in the Global Age*. Princeton, N.J.: Princeton University Press.
Kearns, Gerry. 2014. " 'Up to the Sun and Down to the Centre': The Utopian Moment in Anticolonial Nationalism." *Historical Geography* 42: 130–51.
Kelly, Mark G. E. 2009. *The Political Philosophy of Michel Foucault*. London: Routledge.
Khan, Yasmin. 2016. *The Raj at War: A People's History of India's Second World War*. London: Bodley Head.
Kidambi, Prashant. 2012. "Nationalism and the City in Colonial India: Bombay, c. 1890–1940." *Journal of Urban History* 38(5): 950–67.
Kishwar, Madhu. 1986. *Gandhi and Women*. New Delhi: Manushi Prakashan.
Kitchin, Rob, and Nigel Thrift, eds. 2009. *International Encyclopedia of Human Geography*. Oxford: Elsevier.
Koopman, Colin. 2013. "The Formation and Self-Transformation of the Subject in Foucault's Ethics." In *A Companion to Foucault*, edited by Christopher Falzon, Timothy O'Leary, and Jana Sawicki, 526–43. Chichester: Wiley-Blackwell.
Krishna Menon, A. G. 1997. "Imagining the Indian City." *Economic and Political Weekly* 32(46): 15–21.
Kuracina, William F. 2010. *The State and Governance in India: The Congress Ideal*. Abingdon: Routledge.
Lahiri, Nayanjot. 2003. "Commemorating and Remembering 1857: The Revolt in Delhi and Its Afterlife." *World Archaeology* 35(1): 35–60.
Lais, Dimitrios. 2019. "Foucault as an Ethical Philosopher: The Genealogical Discussion of Antiquity and the Present." *Foucault Studies* 27: 69–95.
Lal, Kishan. 1999. *Revolutionary Activities in Delhi*. Delhi: Agam Kala Prakashan.
Lal, Lakshm Narain. 1975. *Jayaprakash: Rebel Extraordinary*. New Delhi: Indian Book Company.
Laursen, Ole Birk. 2021. "Spaces of Indian Anti-colonialism in Early Twentieth-Century London and Paris." *South Asia: Journal of South Asian Studies* 44: 634–50.
Lee, Christopher J. 2018. "Anti-colonialism: Origins, Practices, and Historical Legacies." In *The Oxford Handbook of the Ends of Empire*, edited by Martin Thomas and Andrew S. Thompson, 436–52. Oxford: Oxford University Press.
Legg, Stephen. 2003. "Gendered Politics and Nationalised Homes: Women and the Anti-colonial Struggle in Delhi, 1930–47." *Gender, Place and Culture* 10(1): 7–27.

Legg, Stephen. 2006. "Postcolonial Developmentalities: From the Delhi Improvement Trust to the Delhi Development Authority." In *Colonial and Postcolonial Geographies of India*, edited by Stuart Corbridge, Satish Kumar, and Saraswati Raju, 182–204. London: SAGE.

Legg, Stephen. 2007. *Spaces of Colonialism: Delhi's Urban Governmentalities*. Oxford: Blackwell.

Legg, Stephen. 2014. *Prostitution and the Ends of Empire: Scale, Governmentalities and Interwar India*. Durham, N.C.: Duke University Press.

Legg, Stephen. 2016a. "Anti-vice Lives: Peopling the Archives of Prostitution in Interwar India." In *Global Anti-vice Activism, c. 1890–1950: Fighting Drink, Drugs, and "Immorality,"* edited by H. Fischer-Tiné, R. Kramm-Masaoka, and J. P. Pliley, 246–69. Cambridge: Cambridge University Press.

Legg, Stephen. 2016b. "Dyarchy: Democracy, Autocracy and the Scalar Sovereignty of Interwar India." *Comparative Studies in South Asia, Africa and the Middle East* 36(1): 44–65.

Legg, Stephen. 2016c. "Subject to Truth: Before and after Governmentality in Foucault's 1970s." *Environment and Planning D: Society and Space* 34(5): 858–76.

Legg, Stephen. 2017. "City as a Site of Movements." In *Urbanization in India: Colonial Cities—1*, edited by Janaki Nair, 73–86. New Delhi: Indira Gandhi National Open University.

Legg, Stephen. 2018. "Colonial and Nationalist Truth Regimes: Empire, Europe and the Latter Foucault." In Legg and Heath, *South Asian Governmentalities*, 106–33.

Legg, Stephen. 2019a. "A Pre-partitioned City? Anti-colonial and Communal Mohallas in Interwar Delhi." *South Asia: Journal of South Asian Studies* 42(1): 170–87.

Legg, Stephen. 2019b. "Subjects of Truth: Resisting Governmentality in Foucault's 1980s." *Environment and Planning D: Society and Space* 37(1): 27–45.

Legg, Stephen. 2023. *Round Table Conference Geographies: Constituting Colonial India in Interwar London*. Cambridge: Cambridge University Press.

Legg, Stephen, and Deana Heath, eds. 2018. *South Asian Governmentalities: Michel Foucault and the Question of Postcolonial Orderings*. Cambridge: Cambridge University Press.

Lorenzini, Daniele. 2016. "From Counter-conduct to Critical Attitude: Michel Foucault and the Art of Not Being Governed Quite So Much." *Foucault Studies* 21: 7–21.

Lorenzini, Daniele. 2023. *The Force of Truth: Critique, Genealogy, and Truth-Telling in Michel Foucault*. Chicago: University of Chicago Press.

Low, David A. (1977) 2004. "Introduction: The Climactic Years, 1917–47." In *Congress and the Raj: Facets of the Indian Struggle*, edited by D. A. Low, 1–45. New Delhi: Oxford University Press.

Luxon, Nancy. 2004. "Truthfulness, Risk, and Trust in the Late Lectures of Michel Foucault." *Inquiry* 47(5): 464–89.

Maclean, Kama. 2015. *A Revolutionary History of Interwar India: Violence, Image, Voice and Text*. London: Hurst.

Mahmood, Saba. 2012. "Preface to the 2012 Edition." In *Politics of Piety: The Islamic Revival and the Feminist Subject*, ix–xii. Princeton, N.J.: Princeton University Press.

Malhotra, S. L. 1979. *From Civil Disobedience to Quit India: Gandhi and the Freedom*

Movement in Punjab and Haryana, 1932–1942. Chandigarh: Publication Bureau, Panjab University.

Mann, Michael. 2005. "Turbulent Delhi: Religious Strife, Social Tension and Political Conflicts, 1803–1857." *South Asia: Journal of South Asian Studies* 28(1): 5–34.

Mantena, Karuna. 2012. "Another Realism: The Politics of Gandhian Nonviolence." *American Political Science Review* 106(2): 455–70.

Mantena, Karuna. 2016. "Popular Sovereignty and Anti-colonialism." In *Popular Sovereignty in Historical Perspective*, edited by Richard Bourke and Quentin Skinner, 297–319. Cambridge: Cambridge University Press.

Mantena, Karuna. 2022. "Mass Satyagraha and the Problem of Collective Power." In *Political Imaginaries in Twentieth-Century India*, edited by Mrinalini Sinha and Manu Goswami, 51–71. London: Bloomsbury.

Masselos, Jim. 1990. " 'The Magic Touch of Being Free': The Rituals of Independence on August 15." In *India: Creating a Modern Nation*, edited by Jim Masselos, 37–53. New Delhi: Stirling.

Masselos, Jim. 1998. "Bombay, August 1942: Re-readings in a Nationalist Text." In *Turbulent Times: India, 1940–44*, edited by B. Pati, 67–101. Mumbai: Popular Prakashan.

Masselos, Jim. 2007. *The City in Action: Bombay Struggles for Power*. New Delhi: Oxford University Press.

Mathur, Y. B. 1979. *Quit India Movement*. Delhi: Pragati.

Maxwell, Lida. 2019. "The Politics and Gender of Truth-Telling in Foucault's Lectures on Parrhesia." *Contemporary Political Theory* 18(1): 22–42.

McFarlane, Colin. 2019. "Urban Fragments: A Subaltern Studies Imagination." In Jazeel and Legg, *Subaltern Geographies*, 210–30.

McFarlane, Colin. 2021. *Fragments of the City: Making and Remaking Urban Worlds*. Oakland: University of California Press.

McGushin, Edward F. 2007. *Foucault's Askesis: An Introduction to the Philosophical Life*. Evanston, Ill.: Northwestern University Press.

Miéville, China. 2009. *The City and the City*. London: Macmillan.

Miller, Paul Allen. 2021. *Foucault's Seminars on Antiquity: Learning to Speak the Truth*. London: Bloomsbury.

Moore, Francesca. 2010. "Tales from the Archive: Methodological and Ethical Issues in Historical Geography Research." *Area* 42(3): 262–70.

Nair, Janaki. 1998. *Miners and Millhands: Work, Culture and Politics in Princely Mysore*. New Delhi: Sage.

Nair, Janaki. 2007. "The Unspeakable Violence of Isoor, 1942." In *Enculturing Law: New Agendas for Legal Pedagogy*, edited by Mathew John and Sitharamam Kakarala, 97–116. New Delhi: Tulika.

Nair, Janaki. 2009. "Beyond Nationalism: Modernity, Governance, and a New Urban History for India." *Urban History* 36: 327–41.

Nehru, Jawaharlal. 1947. "Foreword." In *Travel Talk: Being the Collection of Articles from "Janata" Delhi*, edited by Aruna Asaf Ali, iii–vi. Aundh: Aundh Publishing Trust.

Nichols, Robert. 2010. "Postcolonial Studies and the Discourse of Foucault: Survey of a Field of Problematization." *Foucault Studies* 9: 111–44.

Pandey, Gyanendra. 1977. "A Rural Base for Congress: The United Provinces, 1920–40."

In *Congress and the Raj: Facets of the Indian Struggle 1917–47*, edited by D. A. Low, 199–224. New Delhi: Oxford University Press.

Pandey, Gyanendra. 1978. *The Ascendancy of the Congress in Uttar Pradesh, 1926–34: A Study in Imperfect Mobilization*. Delhi: Oxford University Press.

Pandey, Gyanendra. 1988. "Introduction: The Indian Nation in 1942." In *The Indian Nation in 1942*, edited by Gyanendra Pandey, 1–17. Calcutta: K. P. Bagchi.

Pandey, Gyanendra. 2001. *Remembering Partition: Violence, Nationalism and History in India*. Cambridge: Cambridge University Press.

Pandey, Gyanendra. 2002. *The Ascendancy of the Congress in Uttar Pradesh: Class, Community and Nation in Northern India, 1920–1940*. London: Anthem.

Pandian, Anand, and Daud Ali. 2010. "Introduction." In *Ethical Life in South Asia*, edited by Anand Pandian and Daud Ali, 1–20. Bloomington: Indiana University Press.

Parel, Antony. 2011. "Gandhi and the State." In *Cambridge Companion to Gandhi*, edited by Judith Brown and Antony Parel, 154–72. Cambridge: Cambridge University Press.

Parveen, Nazima. 2021. *Contested Homelands: Politics of Space and Identity*. New Delhi: Bloomsbury India.

Pernau, Margrit. 2013. *Ashraf into Middle Classes: Muslims in Nineteenth-Century Delhi*. New Delhi: Oxford University Press.

Philo, Chris. 2005. "Sex, Life, Death, Geography: Fragmentary Remarks Inspired by Foucault's Population Geographies." *Population, Space and Place* 11(4): 325–33.

Pothen, N. 2012. *Glittering Decades: New Delhi in Love and War*. New Delhi: Penguin.

Prakash, Gyan. 1994. "Subaltern Studies as Postcolonial Criticism." *American Historical Review* 99(5): 1475–90.

Prakash, Gyan. 2007. "Inevitable Revolutions." *Nation* (April 30): 25–30.

Prashad, Vijay. 2000. *Untouchable Freedom: A Social History of a Dalit Community*. New Delhi: Oxford University Press.

Prashad, Vijay. 2001. "The Technology of Sanitation in Colonial Delhi." *Modern Asian Studies* 35: 113–55.

Prozorov, Sergei. 2017. "Foucault's Affirmative Biopolitics: Cynic Parrhesia and the Biopower of the Powerless." *Political Theory* 45(6): 801–23.

Raghavan, Geerpuram Nadadur Srinivasa. 1994. *M. Asaf Ali's Memoirs: The Emergence of Modern India*. Delhi: Ajanta.

Raghavan, Geerpuram Nadadur Srinivasa. 1999. *Aruna Asaf Ali: A Compassionate Radical*. New Delhi: National Book Trust, India.

Raman, Robert Rahman. 2019. "Civil Disobedience and the City: Congress and the Working Classes in Bombay, c. 1930–32." In *Bombay before Mumbai: Essays in Honour of Jim Masselos*, edited by Prashant Kidambi, Manjiri Kamt, and Rachel Dwyer, 263–84. London: Hurst.

Ray, Rajat. 1979. *Urban Roots of Indian Nationalism*. New Delhi: Vikas.

Raza, Ali, and Franziska Roy. 2015. "Paramilitary Organisations in Interwar India." *South Asia: Journal of South Asian Studies* 38(4): 671–89.

Robinson, Jennifer. 2005. *Ordinary Cities: Between Modernity and Development*. London: Routledge.

Ross, Alison. 2008. "Why Is 'Speaking the Truth' Fearless? 'Danger' and 'Truth' in Foucault's Discussion of Parrhesia." *Parrhesia* 4: 62–75.

Roy, Srila. 2018. "Changing the Subject: From Feminist Governmentality to Technologies of the (Feminist) Self." In Legg and Heath, *South Asian Governmentalities*, 200–223.
Sahni, J. N. 1971. *The Lid Off: Fifty Years of Indian Politics, 1921–72*. New Delhi: Allied Publishers.
Sahni, J. N. 1977. "Delhi's 'Joan of Arc': Satyavati." In Vachaspati, *Delhi's Joan of Arc*, n.p.
Said, Edward. 1978. *Orientalism: Western Conceptions of the Orient*. London: Routledge & Kegan Paul.
Said, Edward. 1993. *Culture and Imperialism*. London: Chatto & Windus.
Sajed, Alina, and Sara Salem. 2023. "Anticolonial Feminist Imaginaries: Past Struggles and Imagined Futures." *Kohl: A Journal for Body and Gender Research* 9: 1–8.
Sarkar, Sumit. 1983. *Modern India, 1885–1947*. Madras: Macmillan.
Scott, David. 2004. *Conscripts of Modernity: The Tragedy of Colonial Englightenment*. Durham, N.C.: Duke University Press.
Sharma, Sunaina, and Madhu Kishwar. 1998. "Toofani Satyawati: An Unsung Hero of Freedom Struggle." *Manushi* 107: 24–28.
Sharp, Gene. 1973. *The Politics of Nonviolent Action*. Boston: Porter Sargent.
Siddiqi, Abdur Rahman. 2011. *Smoke without Fire: Portraits of Pre-partition Delhi*. Delhi: Aakbar.
Siisiäinen, Lauri. 2018. *Foucault, Biopolitics and Resistance*. London: Routledge.
Singh, Sangat. 1972. *Freedom Movement in Delhi (1858–1919)*. New Delhi: Associated Publishing House.
Singh, Sangat. 1990. *Gandhi, Rowlatt Satyagraha and British Imperialism: Emergence of Mass Movements in Punjab and Delhi*. Delhi: Indian Bibliographies Bureau.
Skaria, Ajay. 2016. *Unconditional Equality: Gandhi's Religion of Resistance*. Minneapolis: University of Minnesota Press.
Smith, Anthony D. 1991. *National Identity*. London: Penguin.
Sorabji, Richard. 2012. *Gandhi and the Stoics: Modern Experiments on Ancient Values*. Chicago: University of Chicago Press.
Spivak, Gayatri Chakravorty. 2010. "In Response: Looking Back, Looking Forward." In *Can the Subaltern Speak: Reflections on the History of an Idea*, edited by Rosalind C. Morris, 227–36. New York: Columbia University Press.
Spodek, Howard. 2011. *Ahmedabad: Shock City of Twentieth-Century India*. Bloomington: Indiana University Press.
Stein, Burton. 1998. *A History of India*. Oxford: Blackwell.
Teo, Terri-Anne, and Elisa Wynne-Hughes, eds. 2020. *Postcolonial Governmentalities: Rationalities, Violences and Contestations*. Lanham, Md.: Rowman & Littlefield.
Thapar-Björkert, Suruchi. 2006. *Women in the Indian National Movement: Unseen Faces and Unheard Voices, 1930–42*. New Delhi: SAGE.
Thapliyal, U. P. 1985a. "Freedom Struggle in Delhi—a Survey." In Thapliyal, *Who's Who of Delhi Freedom Fighters*, 2:v–xxxv.
Thapliyal, Uma Prasad. 1985b. *Who's Who of Delhi Freedom Fighters*. Vol. 2. Delhi: Gazetteer Unit, Delhi Administration.
Thompson, Edward John. 1925. *The Other Side of the Medal*. London: Leonard.

Vachaspati, Jayant. 1977. *Delhi's Joan of Arc: Sister Satyavati*. New Delhi: privately published.

Vanaik, Anish. 2019. *Possessing the City: Property and Politics in Delhi, 1911–1947*. Oxford: Oxford University Press.

Vatsayan, Kapila, Kavita Sharma, Suroopa Mukhejee, Tapan Basu, and Sunil Dua. 2000. "Introduction." In *In Retrospect*, edited by Kapila Vatsayan, Kavita Sharma, Suroopa Mukhejee, Tapan Basu, and Sunil Dua, 9–25. New Delhi: Har-Anand.

Wagner, Kim A. 2016. "'Calculated to Strike Terror': The Amritsar Massacre and the Spectacle of Colonial Violence." *Past and Present* 233(1): 185–225.

Walker, Gavin. 2022. "Introduction: The Late Foucault and the Allegories of Theory." *South Atlantic Quarterly* 121(4): 645–53.

Walters, William, and Martina Tazzioli, eds. 2023. *Handbook on Governmentality*. London: Edward Elgar.

Yack, Bernard. 2001. "Popular Sovereignty and Nationalism." *Political Theory* 29(4): 517–36.

Yack, Bernard. 2012. *Nationalism and the Moral Psychology of Community*. Chicago: University of Chicago Press.

Young, Robert J. C. 2015. *Empire, Colony, Postcolony*. London: John Wiley & Sons.

Zamindar, Vazira Fazila-Yacoobali. 2007. *The Long Partition and the Making of Modern South Asia*. New York: Columbia University Press.

# INDEX

All India Congress Committee (AICC), 37, 62, 130, 140, 144, 145, 160–62; Quit India, 169, 178, 192, 215, 219, 222
All India Political Prisoners Relief Committee, 240
All India Trade Union Congress, 151, 153
All Parties Sikh Conference (1930), 126, 128
Allahabad, 58, 219, 220, 241
America, 188, 190–91, 235
Amritsar, 110, 121, 122–30 passim, 262. *See also* Jallianwala Bagh massacre
Andha Mughal, 249
Anti-Flush Union, 150
*Arjun*, 74, 122
arson, 171, 183, 195–96, 202, 210, 222–23, 228, 249
Asaf Ali, Aruna, 206–7; before Quit India, 62, 151; during Quit India, 174, 176, 178, 186, 188, 190, 206–7, 211, 227–29; after Quit India, 235, 236, 243–44, 245, 247, 250, 252, 264
Asaf Ali, Mohammad, 48–49; before Quit India, 50–51, 53, 59, 62–65, 87, 133–34, 136, 142–43, 145–48; during Quit India, 167, 174, 176, 178, 192, 206, 210–11, 228; after Quit India, 240, 250–52
askesis, 27, 83
Aurangzeb, Emperor, 103, 177
Azad Hind, 241, 242, 243. *See also* Indian National Army

Badli Railway Station, 224, 225, 226
Bar Association (Delhi), 83, 105, 113
Baradari, 98
bazars, 57, 82, 86, 91, 96, 177, 180, 249, 258
Bengal, 14, 83; famine of (1943), 232

Bharatpur State, 244
Bhola Ram, 98
biopower, 5
Birla Mills, 152, 153, 179, 243
bomb, 52–53, 96, 249; making, 211, 224, 229, 230; use of, 171, 187, 227, 228, 229, 239
Bombay, 16, 77, 233, 244, 250, 252; Quit India and, 170, 174, 177, 179, 186–87, 192, 207, 210, 215
Britain, 1, 168, 233, 235
British Empire, 44, 67, 177, 189, 262

Calcutta, 14–15, 39, 57, 152, 230, 241, 263
Camps and Parades (Control) Order (1944), 241
Central Provinces, 187
Chandni Chowk: before Quit India, 40, 45, 48, 76, 81, 84–86, 93, 94, 96–97, 103–9 passim, 141, 146, 157; during and after Quit India, 179–87 passim, 198, 211, 213, 223, 228, 240, 246, 249
Chauri Chaura incident, 10, 51, 168, 197
Chawri Bazar, 146, 220
Chhapparwala Kuan, 155, 157
Chief Commissioner of Delhi: before Quit India, 32, 39, 48, 50, 60, 62, 69–91 passim, 105, 122–33, 139, 142–47 passim, 158; during and after Quit India, 179, 218, 226–27, 241, 243–44, 249
CID. *See* Criminal Investigation Department
cinema attacks, 195, 228, 229, 230
Civic Centre, 106
Civil Disobedience Day, 75
Civil Lines, 69, 90, 184, 213

cloth, picketing of foreign, 13, 79, 82–89, 91–96, 98, 147
Commercial College, 90
communalism, 4, 58, 62, 136–37, 144, 157, 232–33, 238, 244–53 passim, 263
communism, 32, 41, 152–53, 159, 168, 172, 233, 244, 245
Communist Party of India (CPI), 168, 233
conduct and counter-conduct, 3, 11, 18, 21–22, 25, 30–35, 46, 57, 64, 255
conferences, All Parties Sikh (1930), 126, 128. *See also* Round Table Conference
Congress, Indian National (INC), 9, 12; Congress Ministries Day, 157; Congress Socialist Party (CSP), 136, 138, 141, 145–46, 151–52, 154, 238, 262; Congress Workers' Union, 156, 157; Congress Working Committee (CWC), 12, 58, 68, 169; Forward Bloc Party, 136, 160, 162, 172; Seva Dal, 60, 67, 89, 103, 241, 242, 243. *See also* Delhi Provincial Congress Committee
Connaught Circus, 150, 195, 210, 214, 222
Connaught Place, 42, 73, 144, 176–77, 189–95 passim, 209, 214, 219, 239–40, 247
Criminal Investigation Department (CID): before Quit India, 1, 40–42, 67, 71, 79–80, 90, 95–96, 109, 141, 155–57; during and after Quit India, 172, 174, 185–91 passim, 212–20 passim, 231, 233, 244–47
Cutcherry, 104, 108, 112
Cynics, 23, 28–30, 57; Diogenes, 22–23

Daryaganj, 50, 71, 83, 86, 90, 214, 219, 228, 246, 250
Datta, Subhadra, 45, 235, 244–48, 258
Defence of India Act (1939), 163, 226, 227, 247
Delhi Cloth Mills, 77, 144, 147, 151, 179, 180, 191, 215, 228, 243
Delhi District Congress Committee (DDCC): Civil Disobedience, 60, 62, 66, 79, 85–87, 94–95; 1930s mobilization, 105, 137, 142, 144, 151, 160; Quit India, 175–76, 179
Delhi Improvement Trust, 149, 159
Delhi Municipal Committee (DMC), 48, 49, 143, 149, 156, 161, 196
Delhi Provincial Congress Committee (DPCC), 1, 4, 138, 144, 160–61, 177, 227–28, 235, 241, 244, 247–48
Delhi Railway Station, 50, 52, 150, 230, 237, 239

Delhi Student Congress, 241–42
Delhi Textile Mazdoor Sewak Sangh, 247
Delhi Textile Unions, 153
Delhi Women's League, 207
Delhi Workers League, 152, 153
derailment. *See* train derailment
Diogenes, 22–23
Direct Action Day, 238
discipline: Foucault, 21–23; self, 18–20, 33, 65, 175, 217; subaltern, 10, 12, 16, 57, 81, 233, 235
Dufferin Bridge, 180, 184, 199
dyarchy, 12, 39, 143

Faiz Bazar, 213, 220, 250
fasting. *See* hunger strikes
Fatehpuri Masjid, 50
flags, 35, 52, 60, 73, 147, 148, 159, 162, 173, 185, 242, 249
Foucault, Michel, 4–5, 19–35, 37, 206, 260–61; biopower, 5; subjectivation, 21. *See also* conduct and counter-conduct; discipline
Fountain Square, 106, 108, 109, 113, 131, 146

Gandhi, Devadas, 77, 191, 208, 214, 218, 222–23, 227–29
Gandhi, Kasturba: Kasturba Gandhi Fund, 246; Kasturba Gandhi Memorial Day, 240
Gandhi, Mohandas Karamchand, 4–6, 10–11, 17–20, 33–34; Gandhi Ashram, 83, 98, 162, 240, 246; Gandhi Day, 14, 51, 79, 89; Gandhi-Irwin pact, 58, 129; Gracia Gardens, 90; march to Dandi, 58, 68, 75, 262
godown markets, 85, 87, 98, 184, 249
Government of India: Central Intelligence Office (CIO), 187, 193, 208, 227; Intelligence Bureau, 1, 68, 186, 187, 242. *See also* Secretariat Building
—Home Department: opinions of, 137, 241, 249; Quit India, 192, 196, 208; report from, 69, 147; reports to, 82, 91, 172; secretary, 39
Government of India Act (1935), 133, 135, 138, 139, 142
governmentality, 3–6, 11–20, 20–23, 23–36, 39, 53, 57, 64, 135, 206, 257–61
Greece, ancient, 22
Gupta, Deshbandhu, 59, 60, 77, 87, 142, 178, 263
Gurdwara Bangla Sahib, 177
Gurdwara Firing Day, 177

hartals, 50–52, 77–78, 103, 143–46, 156, 175–76, 239, 249
Hauz Qazi, 146, 176, 230, 249
Hauzwali Masjid, 130–33, 199
Haveli Haider Quli, 45, 242
Hindu College, 90, 178, 180, 213–15, 220
Hindu Mahasabha, 238
*Hindustan*, 42, 249
Hindustan Socialist Republican Association (HSRA), 52, 60, 135, 151, 262
*Hindustan Times*: before Quit India, 59, 70, 72, 74–87, 144; during and after Quit India, 179, 189, 191, 197, 202, 208, 214, 218
Home Rule League (HRL), 48, 142
homes, 60, 82, 86, 87, 95, 98, 214, 221, 223
hunger strikes, 52, 89, 173, 227

Improvement Trust Union, 150, 151
Independence Day, 53, 59, 71, 79, 90, 161, 172, 177, 229, 239, 243, 247
India Coffee House, 187
India Gate, 52, 72, 187, 192
Indian National Army (INA), 232, 239–44, 250
Indian National Congress (INC). *See* Congress, Indian National
Individual Satyagraha movement. *See under* satyagraha
Indra, Professor, 53, 59–62, 74, 95, 141, 151, 159–61, 187, 260, 263
Indraprastha College, 91, 243
Intelligence Bureau. *See* Government of India

Jail Day, 74
Jallianwala Bagh massacre (1919), 14, 51, 177
Jama Masjid, 50, 77, 131, 133, 146, 212, 213
Jamiat-ul-Ulema, 130, 245
*Janata*, 42, 235, 237, 250, 251
Japan, 168, 232
Joshi, Subhadra. *See* Datta, Subhadra
Jumna, River, 75–76, 80, 86, 96, 106, 157, 212

Karol Bagh. *See* Qarol Bagh
Kashmiri Gate, 82, 85, 90–91, 104, 107, 180, 183, 198, 203, 213
Khaddar Day, 86
khadi, 79, 83, 86, 176, 242
Khilafat, 48, 51, 66, 84, 142
Khilafat Committee, 133
Kingsway, 52, 71, 72, 189, 192

Kohli, Mrs., 97–101, 108, 130, 146, 187
Labour Union, 151, 153
Lahore: before Quit India, 52, 53, 57, 68, 110, 122–27; during and after Quit India, 208, 218, 229, 244
Lahore Gate, 82
leafleting, 1–2, 170, 178, 223
Legislative Assembly, building, 52, 70, 73, 174, 191, 206, 214, 221, 250
liquor, picketing of, 50, 67, 79, 83, 91, 97–101

Madras, 170, 246
Mahila Congress Committee, 99
Maliwara, 82
Martyrs Day, 145, 173
Meerut, 87, 137, 142
mohallas, 45, 65–67, 83, 86, 131, 153, 263
morchas, 125, 127, 128, 129, 130
Mori Gate, 85, 98
Mosque Day, 133
Municipal Reform Committee, 150
Muslim League (ML), 50, 144, 232, 233, 238, 243; Direct Action Day, 238
Muslim National Guard, 241, 243, 263
"Mutiny" of 1857, 2, 47–48, 95–96, 104, 163, 183, 236, 251, 263

Nair, Krishna, 82, 91, 139, 143, 158, 160–61, 213, 219–27
Najafgarh, 154–59 passim, 221
Nangloi, 157, 163, 221, 225
Narela, 157, 219, 220, 222, 223, 226
*National Call*, 142, 143, 247
National Week, 58, 75, 79, 81, 140, 175, 177, 245
Naujawan Bharat Sabha, 60, 103
Nehru, Jawaharlal: before Quit India, 52, 58, 59, 68, 78, 127, 145, 149; during and after Quit India, 177, 191, 223, 235–36, 239–41
Nehru, Motilal, 57, 59
New Delhi Municipal Committee (NDMC), 143, 196
non-cooperation movement, 10, 16, 51, 62, 63, 72
North-West Frontier Province, 124, 174

Paharganj, 85, 141, 185, 191
Pakistan, 4, 43, 263
Pakistan Day, 263
parrhesia, 22, 27–28; biopolitics, 25, 28, 29; Diogenes, 22–23; governmentality, 23–24;

parrhesia (*continued*)
30–31, 258–61; Greece, ancient, 22; political, 28, 146; revolutionary, 30, 174, 205–6, 235–36, 255–56; satyagraha, 19, 33, 35, 86, 168, 175; spatiality, 23, 33. *See also* Cynics; Plato; Socrates
partition, 3, 232, 263–64
picketing. *See* cloth, picketing of foreign; liquor, picketing of
Pili Kothi incident, 184, 196–204, 259
Plato, 22–23, 28, 31
poems, 75, 242, 247, 278n2
post office attacks, 185, 228, 249
posters, 73, 83, 137, 216, 235
prabhat pheri, 139, 177, 257
prison, 1, 59, 78, 89, 96, 141, 206–7, 236, 239
purdah, 87, 91, 92, 182, 213

Qarol Bagh, 154, 155–59, 184, 213, 228, 241–42, 247
Queen's Gardens: before Quit India, 52, 60, 75–79, 91–92, 103, 106, 124, 136, 144, 145, 149–53, 162; during and after Quit India, 176, 179, 185, 211–12, 223, 228–29, 242, 235

racism, 235
Railway Accounts Clearing Office, 198–99, 239, 249
Ramjas College, 90, 184, 196, 223
Rashtriya Swayamsevak Sangh (RSS), 238, 241, 243, 263
Red Fort, 210, 212, 232, 262
riots, 14, 51, 62, 122, 145, 196, 202, 233, 238, 242–43, 248, 263
Roshanara Gardens, 149, 152
Round Table Conference, London (1930–32), 53, 57, 68, 72, 128, 135–36, 142
Rowlatt Disturbances, 50–51, 58, 62, 75, 79, 95, 145, 177
Royal Indian Navy, 233

sabotage, 170–72, 196, 203–4, 219, 222, 226, 228, 249
Sabzi Mandi, 66, 86, 149, 152, 153, 229, 243, 258
Sadar Bazar, 85, 99, 119, 184, 185, 187
salt production, 75–76, 81–86, 260
satyagraha, 18–19, 50–51, 64, 68, 82, 162, 172, 187, 216, 219; Individual Satyagraha movement, 163, 168, 174, 175–77, 206–7

satyagrahis, 19, 58, 69, 76, 82, 85, 89, 176, 187, 205–6, 219, 265n8
Satyavati; before Quit India, 63, 73, 78, 91, 95–97, 104, 138–39, 141–60 passim; during Quit India, 176, 178, 180, 186–87, 198, 207, 221
Second World War, 160, 233
Secretariat Building, 72, 184, 189, 194, 195, 208, 239
Shatrugan, 154–63
Shiromani Akali Dal, 126, 128, 129
Shiromani Gurdwara Parbandhak Committee (SGPC), 103, 106
Shiv Mandir dispute, 159, 182
Sikh League, 126, 128
Simla, 77, 233
Singapore, 168, 232
Singh, Bhagat, 52, 60, 153, 241
socialism, 97, 138, 149, 155, 162, 244, 248, 252. *See also* Congress Indian National: Congress Socialist Party
Socrates, 18, 22, 23, 28, 31, 265n7
song. *See* prabhat pheri
St. Stephen's College, 48, 59, 90–91, 178, 243
*Statesman, The*, 189, 197
statues, 192, 209, 216
Student and Youth League, 59, 103
students, 41, 59, 71, 89–92, 118, 145, 171, 178–80, 188–96 passim, 213–15, 220–28
Student's Park, 91
subjectivation, 21
Sunehri Masjid, 187, 247
Swadeshi League, 74, 83
swaraj, 19, 20, 59, 91, 145, 149
Swaraj Day, 59, 71

Tegh Bahadur, Guru, 103, 111, 120
telephone and telegraph lines, cutting of, 96–97, 169, 183–84, 195, 225. *See also* sabotage
terrorism, 134
Textile Labour Union, 153
Textile Mazdoor Sabha, 245
Tilak Day, 177, 178
Tonga Owners Union, 149
Town Hall, Delhi, 50, 96, 106, 146, 151, 177, 182, 196–97, 249
train derailment, 220, 222, 226
*Tribune, The* (Lahore), 147, 219
Turkman Gate, 211

Union of Soviet Socialist Republics (USSR), 1, 168, 262
United Provinces, 13, 51, 107, 152

Viceregal Lodge, 68, 141, 230
Viceroy, 40, 52, 57–58, 70, 124–34 passim, 141, 168, 170, 174, 195, 228
Victory Arches, 248
Victory Day, 248–51

Whitman, Walt, 235, 278n2
wire cutting. *See* telephone and telegraph lines, cutting of
World War II, 160, 233

Young India, 52, 63, 67, 129
Youths Study Circle, 151–52

GEOGRAPHIES OF JUSTICE AND SOCIAL TRANSFORMATION

1. *Social Justice and the City*, rev. ed.
   BY DAVID HARVEY

2. *Begging as a Path to Progress: Indigenous Women and Children and the Struggle for Ecuador's Urban Spaces*
   BY KATE SWANSON

3. *Making the San Fernando Valley: Rural Landscapes, Urban Development, and White Privilege*
   BY LAURA R. BARRACLOUGH

4. *Company Towns in the Americas: Landscape, Power, and Working-Class Communities*
   EDITED BY OLIVER J. DINIUS AND ANGELA VERGARA

5. *Tremé: Race and Place in a New Orleans Neighborhood*
   BY MICHAEL E. CRUTCHER JR.

6. *Bloomberg's New York: Class and Governance in the Luxury City*
   BY JULIAN BRASH

7. *Roppongi Crossing: The Demise of a Tokyo Nightclub District and the Reshaping of a Global City*
   BY ROMAN ADRIAN CYBRIWSKY

8. *Fitzgerald: Geography of a Revolution*
   BY WILLIAM BUNGE

9. *Accumulating Insecurity: Violence and Dispossession in the Making of Everyday Life*
   EDITED BY SHELLEY FELDMAN, CHARLES GEISLER, AND GAYATRI A. MENON

10. *They Saved the Crops: Labor, Landscape, and the Struggle over Industrial Farming in Bracero-Era California*
    BY DON MITCHELL

11. *Faith Based: Religious Neoliberalism and the Politics of Welfare in the United States*
    BY JASON HACKWORTH

12. *Fields and Streams: Stream Restoration, Neoliberalism, and the Future of Environmental Science*
    BY REBECCA LAVE

13. *Black, White, and Green: Farmers Markets, Race, and the Green Economy*
    BY ALISON HOPE ALKON

14. *Beyond Walls and Cages: Prisons, Borders, and Global Crisis*
    EDITED BY JENNA M. LOYD, MATT MITCHELSON, AND ANDREW BURRIDGE

15. *Silent Violence: Food, Famine, and Peasantry in Northern Nigeria*
    BY MICHAEL J. WATTS

16. *Development, Security, and Aid: Geopolitics and Geoeconomics at the U.S. Agency for International Development*
    BY JAMEY ESSEX

17. *Properties of Violence: Law and Land-Grant Struggle in Northern New Mexico*
    BY DAVID CORREIA

18. *Geographical Diversions: Tibetan Trade, Global Transactions*
    BY TINA HARRIS

19. *The Politics of the Encounter: Urban Theory and Protest under Planetary Urbanization*
BY ANDY MERRIFIELD

20. *Rethinking the South African Crisis: Nationalism, Populism, Hegemony*
BY GILLIAN HART

21. *The Empires' Edge: Militarization, Resistance, and Transcending Hegemony in the Pacific*
BY SASHA DAVIS

22. *Pain, Pride, and Politics: Social Movement Activism and the Sri Lankan Tamil Diaspora in Canada*
BY AMARNATH AMARASINGAM

23. *Selling the Serengeti: The Cultural Politics of Safari Tourism*
BY BENJAMIN GARDNER

24. *Territories of Poverty: Rethinking North and South*
EDITED BY ANANYA ROY AND EMMA SHAW CRANE

25. *Precarious Worlds: Contested Geographies of Social Reproduction*
EDITED BY KATIE MEEHAN AND KENDRA STRAUSS

26. *Spaces of Danger: Culture and Power in the Everyday*
EDITED BY HEATHER MERRILL AND LISA M. HOFFMAN

27. *Shadows of a Sunbelt City: The Environment, Racism, and the Knowledge Economy in Austin*
BY ELIOT M. TRETTER

28. *Beyond the Kale: Urban Agriculture and Social Justice Activism in New York City*
BY KRISTIN REYNOLDS AND NEVIN COHEN

29. *Calculating Property Relations: Chicago's Wartime Industrial Mobilization, 1940–1950*
BY ROBERT LEWIS

30. *In the Public's Interest: Evictions, Citizenship, and Inequality in Contemporary Delhi*
BY GAUTAM BHAN

31. *The Carpetbaggers of Kabul and Other American-Afghan Entanglements: Intimate Development, Geopolitics, and the Currency of Gender and Grief*
BY JENNIFER L. FLURI AND RACHEL LEHR

32. *Masculinities and Markets: Raced and Gendered Urban Politics in Milwaukee*
BY BRENDA PARKER

33. *We Want Land to Live: Making Political Space for Food Sovereignty*
BY AMY TRAUGER

34. *The Long War: CENTCOM, Grand Strategy, and Global Security*
BY JOHN MORRISSEY

35. *Development Drowned and Reborn: The Blues and Bourbon Restorations in Post-Katrina New Orleans*
BY CLYDE WOODS
EDITED BY JORDAN T. CAMP AND LAURA PULIDO

36. *The Priority of Injustice: Locating Democracy in Critical Theory*
BY CLIVE BARNETT

37. *Spaces of Capital / Spaces of Resistance: Mexico and the Global Political Economy*
BY CHRIS HESKETH

38. *Revolting New York: How 400 Years of Riot, Rebellion, Uprising, and Revolution Shaped a City*
GENERAL EDITORS: NEIL SMITH AND DON MITCHELL
EDITORS: ERIN SIODMAK, JENJOY ROYBAL, MARNIE BRADY, AND BRENDAN O'MALLEY

39. *Relational Poverty Politics: Forms, Struggles, and Possibilities*
EDITED BY VICTORIA LAWSON AND SARAH ELWOOD

40. *Rights in Transit: Public Transportation and the Right to the City in California's East Bay*
BY KAFUI ABLODE ATTOH

41. *Open Borders: In Defense of Free Movement*
EDITED BY REECE JONES

42. *Subaltern Geographies*
EDITED BY TARIQ JAZEEL AND STEPHEN LEGG

**43.** *Detain and Deport: The Chaotic U.S. Immigration Enforcement Regime*
BY NANCY HIEMSTRA

**44.** *Global City Futures: Desire and Development in Singapore*
BY NATALIE OSWIN

**45.** *Public Los Angeles: A Private City's Activist Futures*
BY DON PARSON
EDITED BY ROGER KEIL AND JUDY BRANFMAN

**46.** *America's Johannesburg: Industrialization and Racial Transformation in Birmingham*
BY BOBBY M. WILSON

**47.** *Mean Streets: Homelessness, Public Space, and the Limits of Capital*
BY DON MITCHELL

**48.** *Islands and Oceans: Reimagining Sovereignty and Social Change*
BY SASHA DAVIS

**49.** *Social Reproduction and the City: Welfare Reform, Child Care, and Resistance in Neoliberal New York*
BY SIMON BLACK

**50.** *Freedom Is a Place: The Struggle for Sovereignty in Palestine*
BY RON J. SMITH

**51.** *Loisaida as Urban Laboratory: Puerto Rico Community Activism in New York*
BY TIMO SCHRADER

**52.** *Transecting Securityscapes: Dispatches from Cambodia, Iraq, and Mozambique*
BY TILL F. PAASCHE AND JAMES D. SIDAWAY

**53.** *Non-performing Loans, Non-performing People: Life and Struggle with Mortgage Debt in Spain*
BY MELISSA GARCÍA-LAMARCA

**54.** *Disturbing Development in the Jim Crow South*
BY MONA DOMOSH

**55.** *Famine in Cambodia: Geopolitics, Biopolitics, Necropolitics*
BY JAMES A. TYNER

**56.** *Well-Intentioned Whiteness: Green Urban Development and Black Resistance in Kansas City*
BY CHHAYA KOLAVALLI

**57.** *Urban Climate Justice: Theory, Praxis, Resistance*
EDITED BY JENNIFER L. RICE, JOSHUA LONG, AND ANTHONY LEVENDA

**58.** *Abolishing Poverty: Towards Pluriverse Futures and Politics*
BY VICTORIA LAWSON, SARAH ELWOOD, MICHELLE DAIGLE, YOLANDA GONZÁLEZ MENDOZA, ANA P. GUTIÉRREZ GARZA, JUAN HERRERA, ELLEN KOHL, JOVAN LEWIS, AARON MALLORY, PRISCILLA MCCUTCHEON, MARGARET MARIETTA RAMÍREZ, AND CHANDAN REDDY

**59.** *Outlaw Capital: Everyday Illegalities and the Making of Uneven Development*
BY JENNIFER LEE TUCKER

**60.** *High Stakes, High Hopes: Urban Theorizing in Partnership*
BY SOPHIE OLDFIELD

**61.** *The Coup and the Palm Trees: Agrarian Conflict and Political Power in Honduras*
BY ANDRÉS LEÓN ARAYA

**62.** *Cultivating Socialism: Venezuela, ALBA, and the Politics of Food Sovereignty*
BY ROWAN LUBBOCK

**63.** *Green City Rising: Contamination, Cleanup, and Collective Action*
BY ERIN GOODING

**64.** *New Destinations of Empire: Mobilities, Racial Geographies, and Citizenship in the Transpacific United States*
BY EMILY MITCHELL-EATON

**65.** *Spaces of Anticolonialism: Delhi's Urban Governmentalities*
BY STEPHEN LEGG

www.ingramcontent.com/pod-product-compliance
Lightning Source LLC
Chambersburg PA
CBHW020638230426
43665CB00008B/225